Realism after Modernism

OCTOBER Books

George Baker, Yve-Alain Bois, Benjamin H. D. Buchloh, Leah Dickerman, Devin Fore, Hal Foster, Denis Hollier, Rosalind Krauss, Annette Michelson, Mignon Nixon, and Malcolm Turvey, editors

Broodthaers, edited by Benjamin H. D. Buchloh

AIDS: Cultural Analysis/Cultural Activism, edited by Douglas Crimp

Aberrations: An Essay on the Legend of Forms, by Jurgis Baltrušaitis

Against Architecture: The Writings of Georges Bataille, by Denis Hollier

Painting as Model, by Yve-Alain Bois

The Destruction of Tilted Arc: Documents, edited by Clara Weyergraf-Serra and Martha Buskirk

The Woman in Question, edited by Parveen Adams and Elizabeth Cowie

Techniques of the Observer: On Vision and Modernity in the Nineteenth Century, by Jonathan Crary

The Subjectivity Effect in Western Literary Tradition: Essays toward the Release of Shakespeare's Will, by Joel Fineman

Looking Awry: An Introduction to Jacques Lacan through Popular Culture, by Slavoj Žižek

Cinema, Censorship, and the State: The Writings of Nagisa Oshima, by Nagisa Oshima

The Optical Unconscious, by Rosalind E. Krauss

Gesture and Speech, by André Leroi-Gourhan

Compulsive Beauty, by Hal Foster

Continuous Project Altered Daily: The Writings of Robert Morris, by Robert Morris

Read My Desire: Lacan against the Historicists, by Joan Copjec

Fast Cars, Clean Bodies: Decolonization and the Reordering of French Culture, by Kristin Ross

Kant after Duchamp, by Thierry de Duve

The Duchamp Effect, edited by Martha Buskirk and Mignon Nixon

The Return of the Real: The Avant-Garde at the End of the Century, by Hal Foster

October: The Second Decade, 1986–1996, edited by Rosalind Krauss, Annette Michelson, Yve-Alain Bois, Benjamin H. D. Buchloh, Hal Foster, Denis Hollier, and Silvia Kolbowski

Infinite Regress: Marcel Duchamp 1910–1941, by David Joselit

Caravaggio's Secrets, by Leo Bersani and Ulysse Dutoit

Scenes in a Library: Reading the Photograph in the Book, 1843–1875, by Carol Armstrong

Bachelors, by Rosalind Krauss

Neo-Avantgarde and Culture Industry: Essays on European and American Art from 1955 to 1975, by Benjamin H. D. Buchloh

Suspensions of Perception: Attention, Spectacle, and Modern Culture, by Jonathan Crary

Leave Any Information at the Signal: Writings, Interviews, Bits, Pages, by Ed Ruscha

Guy Debord and the Situationist International: Texts and Documents, edited by Tom McDonough

Random Order: Robert Rauschenberg and the Neo-Avant-Garde, by Branden W. Joseph

Decoys and Disruptions: Selected Writings, 1975–2001, by Martha Rosler

Prosthetic Gods, by Hal Foster

Fantastic Reality: Louise Bourgeois and a Story of Modern Art, by Mignon Nixon

Women Artists at the Millennium, edited by Carol Armstrong and Catherine de Zegher

"The Beautiful Language of My Century": Reinventing the Language of Contestation in Postwar France, 1945–1968, by Tom McDonough

The Artwork Caught by the Tail: Francis Picabia and Dada in Paris, by George Baker

Being Watched: Yvonne Rainer and the 1960s, by Carrie Lambert-Beatty

Robert Ryman: Used Paint, by Suzanne P. Hudson

Hall of Mirrors: Roy Lichtenstein and the Face of Painting in the 1960s, by Graham Bader

Perpetual Inventory, by Rosalind Krauss

The Absence of Work: Marcel Broodthaers 1964–1976, by Rachel Haidu

The Filming of Modern Life: European Avant-Garde Fim of the 1920s, by Malcolm Turvey

Lucio Fontana: Between Avant-Garde and Kitsch, by Anthony White

Looking for Bruce Conner, by Kevin Hatch

Realism after Modernism: The Rehumanization of Art and Literature, by Devin Fore

Realism after Modernism

The Rehumanization of Art and Literature

Devin Fore

An OCTOBER Book

The MIT Press
Cambridge, Massachusetts
London, England

This publication is made possible in part by a grant from the Barr Feree Foundation Fund for Publications, Princeton University.

MIT Press books may be purchased at special quantity discounts for business or sales promotional use. For information, please email special_sales@mitpress.mit.edu or write to Special Sales Department, The MIT Press, 55 Hayward Street, Cambridge, MA 02142.

This book was set in Bembo by Graphic Composiition, Inc. Printed and bound in the United States of America.

Library of Congress Cataloging-in-Publication Data

Fore, Devin, 1972–.
Realism after modernism : the rehumanization of art and literature / Devin Fore.
pages cm—(An October book)
Includes bibliographical references and index.
ISBN 978-0-262-01771-8 (hardcover : alk. paper)
1. Arts, German—20th century. 2. Realism in art—Germany. 3. Realism in literature. I. Title.
NX550.A1F67 2012
700.943'0904—dc23
2011049222

10 9 8 7 6 5 4 3 2 1

Contents

Acknowledgments

It is only fitting that a book about the appropriation and repetition of cultural forms should begin by crediting its many sources. First, I am indebted to Andreas Huyssen, whose inspiring work has provided a model of inductive criticism that is both theoretically robust and historically precise. Through challenging questions and uncompromising scholarly rigor, Benjamin Buchloh pushed the evolution of my stance on interwar art, resulting in a final text far more ambitious and systematic than anything I could have produced on my own. If Andreas provided a language and Benjamin a question, the subject matter of this book, in turn, borrows extensively from Helmut Lethen, whose decades of pioneering research on Weimar culture set an important and exacting standard, shaping my thinking about this historical moment in ways too numerous to count. Nor would this project have come into being without the contribution of Boris Gasparov, whose approach to understanding the relationship between realism and modernism has exerted a profound methodological influence on this book. Truly a collective enterprise, *Realism after Modernism* would have been for me literally unthinkable without the scholarly precedent, intellectual generosity, and challenging commentary of these four people.

In addition to these debts, I am grateful to the editors at *October*, and especially to Yve-Alain Bois and Hal Foster for support and critical feedback, both formal and informal. I also benefited immensely from conversations with Alexander Kluge, whose careful interrogations changed my thinking about technology, labor, and the human in crucial ways. Friends and colleagues who gave precious time to read and respond to portions of the manuscript include Benjamin Conisbee Baer, Ed Dimenberg, Rachel Haidu, Meredith Martin, Sarah Whiting, and Siona Wilson. Along with Rachel Yuval Boim, Chris Bollen, Zahid Chaudhary, Douglas Greenfield, Daniel Heller-Roazen, Juliet Koss, Kristin Romberg, Stephanie Schwartz, Amy Sillman, Sergei Ushakin, and Anthony Yankowski provided intervals of levity that kept me afloat while writing. I would also like to express my heartfelt thanks to Stefan Andriopoulos, Geoffrey Winthrop-Young, Robert Norton, Nicole Stahlmann, Susanne Strätling, Galin Tihanov, and Georg Witte for their encouragement and helpful advice. And if there is any life in my writing, the credit must be given to Leo Bersani, Douglas Crimp, and Molly Nesbit, whose work is a constant reminder that intellectual projects must always have stakes.

I would also like to acknowledge the audiences at various academic institutions where I have presented material from this project, often still in tentative and inchoate form: the University of British Columbia in Vancouver, Brown, Columbia, the Freie Universität (Berlin), Harvard, the Humboldt Universität (Berlin), the University of Michigan in Ann Arbor, New York University, Notre Dame, Rutgers, Vanderbilt, and the Wissenschaftskolleg (Berlin). In 2008–2009, a working group organized by Gertrud Koch in Berlin offered a demanding context in which to test, revise, and in some cases, reject certain of the book's theses; and later that year, the graduate students in my seminar on anthropology and the return to order prompted me to further consideration and refinement of these arguments. I am especially grateful to friends and colleagues at Cornell University, where my research on interwar realism first began to take shape during a Mellon Postdoctoral Fellowship in 2005–2006: at that moment, Leslie Adelson, David Bathrick, Peter Gilgen, Tracy McNulty, Diana Reese, and Geoff Waite helped me to channel a vague set of hunches and impulses into a cogent research project; and more recently, Anette Schwarz labored through the final draft of the book, offering invaluable expert feedback on how to improve the manuscript. Additional institutional support for this book was provided by the American Academy in Berlin, where I spent 2008–2009, and the Alexander von Humboldt Foundation, which made it possible for me to research at the Berlin Zentrum für Literatur- und Kulturforschung in 2010. At the latter I am particularly grateful to Sigrid Weigel for her support. Thanks to all of these institutions, fora, and organizations for their generosity, but the lion's share of my gratitude goes to my colleagues in the Princeton German Department, not just for granting the sabbatical time necessary to complete this project but, equally importantly, for fostering a demanding environment of critical engagement and exchange.

In the book's final stages, Eric Banks offered crucial editorial suggestions and Daniela Fabricius navigated the morass of image rights. The book's last chapter appeared in *Grey Room* (no. 33, fall 2008, pp. 26–55), and I am grateful to the editors of the journal for permission to republish the text here.

Introduction

Nearly every variety of interwar realism took the human figure as a given. Consider the painting and the prose of this era, for example, in which the human body staged a dramatic comeback in the wake of modernism's withdrawal internationally.[1] Thus, after the cultural delegitimation of nonobjective painting, the reformed Dadaist Christian Schad began producing verist portraiture in Germany around the same time that Kasimir Malevich was adapting the geometric idiom and color palette of suprematism for the depiction of Russian peasant idylls. Echoing its return on the canvases of the period, the human body started to reappear at this moment in diverse forms of narrative prose as well, where modernist authors renounced their previous experimental ephemera and, with all the zeal of the newly converted, now set about writing novels populated with vivid and individuated characters. These strategies would be codified, and eventually dogmatized, in the theories of the influential literary critic Georg Lukács, who championed narratives depicting the psychological development of "positive heroes" and "living figures."

Even more complex and intriguing than the realist works that took the human body as their explicit motif, however, were the forms of mimetic figuration that had nothing at all to do with subject matter per se but instead pursued realism's humanist agenda at the level of artistic technique itself. Indeed, even where it was not evident in the content of the artwork or text, the human figure organized the very codes and conventions of realist representation. And while perhaps less obvious at first glance than its thematic variant, this structural anthropomorphism was arguably all the more pervasive and authoritative a paradigm precisely because of its latency. As evidence we can again reference developments in the visual arts and prose. In the case of the former, the rehabilitation of easel painting as a culturally valorized form of artistic creation was animated ideologically by a figural metonymy: against the avant-garde paradigm of the readymade, which had deskilled aesthetic practices by outsourcing artistic production to the industrial machine, painting was now repatriated to the human body, as it were, becoming once again became a manual craft defined by what Thorstein Veblen called the "honorific marks of hand labor."[2] The rehumanization of painting through the use of the easel was, in turn, complemented by the return of linear one-point perspective, a grammar of visual representation that, as the art historian Erwin Panofsky argued in 1924, produces an experience of space commensurate with the stable and centered post-Renaissance subject: this perceptual device, he wrote, was thus both the instrument and expression of "modern 'anthropocracy'" on an optical register.[3] Like those developments in the visual arts, in prose the resurgence of great narrative forms such as the novel was buoyed by the latent figuration that is inherent to narrativity as such: even when absent of positive heroes and living figures, the contours of the plotline itself are "inevitably anthropomorphous," as Roland Barthes observed, since the causal sequences and notion of action that are fundamental to narrative always already presume human agency.[4]

In short, man was back, his return in the motifs and techniques of art underwritten by an ideology of humanism visible everywhere in interwar culture. This development inverted utterly the trajectory of aesthetic modernism, the preceding cultural project that had striven toward the "dehumanization of art," as José Ortega y Gasset argued in 1925. In his essay of that title, the philosopher asserted that nonobjective painting had realized its will to aesthetic "purification" and hermetic nihilism through the "progressive elimination of the human, all too human, elements" in art.[5] It is indeed difficult to refute the influential terms of Ortega y Gasset's analysis, the echo of which can still be heard, for example, in Lyotard's later analysis of modernism, which aligned non-objective painting with the death drive and an aesthetics of the sublime, contrasting this "inhuman" project to figurative realism, which the French philosopher in turn associated with the pleasure principle and an aesthetics of the beautiful.[6] Indeed, for all the stylistic diversity and distinctiveness of modernism's various factions, it seems that these schools shared a common commitment to the non-human in all of its guises. This project enjoyed a remarkable aesthetic range: Paul Cézanne's phenomenological vision, which, as Merleau-Ponty wrote, "reveals the base of inhuman nature";[7] the sound poetry of Hugo Ball, whose critique of European civilization took the form of a primordial Ur-language; Rainer Maria Rilke's attempt to reconstitute the child's precategorical mode of perception; or the works of the Italian futurists, which fused the artist with the industrial machine. Similarly, the creaturely growls of the *za'umnik* Aleksei Kruchenykh reduced the poet to the mere meat of the vocal apparatus, while his colleague Velimir Khlebnikov pushed artistic language in the diametrically opposite direction, toward a metaphysical code wholly removed from the material and temporal limitations of the body. Finally, the cosmist Kino-Eye of the filmmaker Dziga Vertov demonstrated, in Gilles Deleuze's words, "a pure vision of a non-human eye, of an eye which would be in things."[8] Thus, from the child, the savage, and the celestial to the thing, the automaton, and the animal, each of these models of subjectivity reflects the shared modernist aspiration to achieve conditions of perception and consciousness outside of what is customarily arrogated to the human. Guillaume Apollinaire's 1913 pronouncement, in a key essay on analytic cubism, that "above all, artists are men who wish to become inhuman" epitomizes this aspect of modernism.[9]

Interwar realism's emphatic campaign to rehumanize art thus announced a complete *volte-face* from its cultural predecessor. But, as *Realism after Modernism* argues, within this countermovement dwells a glaring paradox, for although the human body, as both subject matter and technical precondition, served as the guarantor of mimetic realism's validity, the reassertion of the human figure at this historical moment was a deeply conflicted proposal, since the seemingly natural body had by this time already become a thoroughly vexed construction. The lability of definitions of the human was reflected in a variety of contemporary fields: confronted by "the obsolescence of the Freudian concept of man," psychoanalysis enlisted sociology to understand the mechanisms of ego formation after industrial media technologies and urbanization had transformed the autonomous individual into the mass subject;[10] an emphasis on standardization and functionalism in architecture dismantled the boundaries between the human body and its surrounding inorganic environment ("dehumanization is the very thing that leads to humanization, to anthropomorphism," observed the Bauhaus architect Adolf Behne in 1923[11]); and medicine promised to an anatomy shattered in the Great War a prosthetic supplementation that, ambivalently enough, simultaneously restored and rendered obsolete the natural human form. Hardly a stable fundament for art, then, the ideology of holistic individualism and the integrity of the human body were at this historical moment more tenuous than ever.

Thus the improbability, indeed impossibility, of figurative realism's return after aesthetic modernism, social modernity, and technical modernization had destroyed the anthropomorphic foundations of its artistic program. In response to this unlikely event, *Realism after Modernism* poses a series of questions about the paradoxical structure of interwar realism: If mimetic representation presupposes the inviolability of the body, how then is this neoclassical aesthetic articulated in a society in which natural anatomy has become indistinguishable from mechanical organs? How can verisimilitude and likeness be reconstructed after modernism's relentless campaign to demotivate the aesthetic sign turned the artwork from a communicative medium into mute, intractable matter? What spaces of subjective interiority and psychological depth can be claimed for a realist novel that is written in a culture where all speech has already been prefabricated for and transmitted through mass media? In sum, what happens to realism once the human is no longer a perfect integer?

Given mimetic realism's inextricability from the historical fortunes of the human, the answers to these questions will necessarily have a twofold pertinence, both for aesthetics and for anthropology. Indeed, in the course of its analysis, this book uncovers a close correspondence between conceptions of the human found in interwar realist art and the definitions of *Homo sapiens* that were being worked out simultaneously in the field of anthropology. Borrowing from Walter Benjamin, this conception of the human could be aptly characterized as a form of "negative expressionism." In the 1921 fragment that bore this title, Benjamin described a curious mimetic faculty common to humans at all phases of cultural development, that revealed man's supremely plastic nature: "Clown and natural peoples: negation of inner impulses and the body's core. A new integration of clothing, tattoo and body. . . . Following this logic, the discovery of a potential for profound expressiveness: the man sitting in a chair remains seated after the chair is pulled away."[12] Unlike essentialist anthropologies that define man positively through a fixed inventory of anatomical components, cultural capacities, and psychic drives, Benjamin's negative expressionism instead described a creature that evolves through the introjection of conditions and events external to its body. Constituted through the "negation of inner impulses and the body's core," this human is distinguished through an ontological absence, his skin a record of the ornaments that once adorned it and his musculature shaped by the alien armatures it has encountered.[13] Benjamin's image of a body that continues to trace the contours of the chair after its removal reflects a strategy of mimetic comportment in which the individual becomes indistinguishable from the technical artifacts surrounding him.

As the phrase would suggest, "negative expressionism" identifies not just an evolutionary strategy but also an artistic program, specifically, the emergent ethos of New Objectivity art, which inverted preceding expressionist notions of artistic production as the outward projection of inner psychic states. And while the specific aesthetic strategies of representational realism are not directly addressed in the 1921 fragment, fifteen years later Benjamin made explicit the connection between artistic depiction and negative expressionism, this time in a note on cave painting, a cypher for pictorial representation *tout court*. "Perhaps stone-age man draws the deer so incomparably," he wrote, "because the hand that guides the pigment still recalls the bow used to shoot the animal" (*Schriften*, 6:127). The art of Neolithic man, Benjamin observes, presumes artificial prostheses such as the bow, which have been incorporated into the very architecture of his body.

Even in the seemingly most expressive and creative artistic act, in which the artist's hand applies pigment directly onto the cave wall as if without mediation, a subcutaneous technicity is already at work. There is an ineluctable artificiality to this manual gesture. Following Benjamin's observation, this book argues that, for all its claim to immediacy and artlessness, the realist figuration of the 1920s, like the cave-scene at the dawn of representation, presumes these technical frameworks even where they are not readily visible. Just as the seated figure preserves the shape of the chair and the hand's movements rhyme the arc of the bow, humanist realism is always already an ensemble of technical devices. Thus, although the explicitly mechanomorphic motifs and montage fragmentation of, say, Dada may disappear from visual art at this time, the succeeding works were no less mechanical since human physiology was itself already a technical assemblage. Likewise, prose and drama may begin once again during these years to cultivate spaces of emotional interiority, but the psychic life of this reconstructed subject was now pieced together from readymade clichés and secondhand reports. Thus, rejecting the heuristically useless distinction between "authentic" human nature and "inauthentic" technical construct, this book's account of interwar realism will proceed by reconstructing, as it were, the ghosted cultural orthopedics that are no longer in the picture but whose impression remains indelibly upon the realist body.

The model of mimesis found in interwar aesthetic paradigms such as New Objectivity reflected conceptions of the human that were taking shape in other knowledge systems of the period.[14] Mirroring the rehumanization of art, the 1920s and '30s witnessed a "human turn" in other discourses as well, which, returning man to the epistemic center of inquiry, enthroned anthropology as a master discipline among the cultural and natural sciences. And here too, as in the art of the period, the revenant human was a paradoxical construction. "There is a crisis in culture," one author declared on the front page of *Die literarische Welt* in 1931. "[D]eeper reflection on the meaning of this phenomenon," he continued, "will reveal that the crisis of culture is but the symptom of a far more fundamental one, namely, the crisis of man himself. After ten-thousand years of history, man for the first time has become a puzzle to himself; he no longer knows what he is, but at the same time he knows that he doesn't know it."[15] Certainly the most characteristic expression of this paradox during the Weimar era can be found in the developing field of philosophical anthropology, where currents of existentialism and anatomical biology merged to produce a model of the human as a unfinished, world-open (*weltoffen*) creature. The summa of this school was *Man: His Nature and Place in the World* (1940) by Arnold Gehlen, who defined the human animal as a "deficient being" (*Mängelwesen*) and a constitutional mimic. Unlike other animals, Gehlen wrote, man is born into the world ill equipped and featureless, possessing neither the instinctual drives nor the concrete matériel necessary for survival. Following Nietzsche's famous formula, he defined man as *das noch nicht festgestellte Tier*, the "not yet determined animal."[16] At once a source of both freedom and disorientation, this fundamental lack engenders a technical imperative in the human animal, a "vulnerable, needy, exposed being" that compensates for its ontological poverty by devising artificial constructions in language (symbolic systems), technology (instrumentation), and society (institutions).[17] These cultural artifacts become the organs, so to speak, that the infant lacks at birth. In this way, man fashions for himself the anatomy and instincts, the body and psyche, that he was denied by nature. Thus, like the negative mimesis described by Benjamin, philosophical anthropology defined the individual as an artificial creature whose essence is to adapt to and incorporate the technical forms around him. As a consequence, the open evolution of man follows a centrifugal course: the more he perfects himself, the more the center of his being migrates outward and is objectivated in technology and culture.

The paradigms of philosophical anthropology were tainted in the twentieth century by their association with reactionary political formations. Gehlen, for example, who joined the National Socialist party in 1933, deemed man a "creature of discipline" (*ein Zuchtwesen*) and concluded that the species' "world-openness" generated a need for control, order, and authority as relief from the existential pressures of indeterminacy. Given the conclusions drawn by many in this school of thought, which were conservative at best, proto-fascist at worst, philosophical anthropology was for decades publicly proscribed among the Left.

But there were exceptions. The great theorist of otherness, Mikhail Bakhtin, for example, identified "philosophical anthropology" as the master rubric for his entire moral system, which defined the human through the constitutive experiences of exotopy (*вненаходимость*) and alterity (*другость*).[18] And more recently, radical philosophers have rediscovered in this school elements that are serviceable for leftist or Marxist thinking about collective politics. As a "deficient being," the subject of existential anthropology is, after all, a figure of pure relationality, a social creature who presumes collective existence as a necessary context for species evolution and personal self-realization. So, for example, two of the leading voices of German critical theory today, Oskar Negt and Alexander Kluge, have built their materialist anthropology of labor on a definition of the human as a "deficient mutant" (*eine Mangelmutante*), a "life form which, according to its metabolism, is not autonomous, but enters into concrete associations with others. Which is to say: it is a being that requires society."[19] Similarly, Étienne Balibar has drawn upon the tradition of philosophical anthropology as a resource for reconceptualizing notions of citizenship and public existence within a nonessentializing and post-nationalist framework.[20] And Bernard Stiegler has grafted the Derridean dynamic of the trace onto an evolutionary ontology of exteriorization, arriving at a model of subjectivity that is virtually identical to the one proposed by the philosophical anthropology of the interwar years.[21] The presence in *Realism after Modernism* of a number of contemporary conceptual models borrowed from these and other figures testifies to the powerful consonance between today's critical theory and the negative anthropology of the interwar era. Refunctioned by the Left, these models can serve as the basis for contemporary critiques of hegemonic power structures as well as a stimulus to think imaginatively about new configurations of collectivity and the conditions of public existence.

Like the philosophical anthropology of the period, the art of interwar realism has also been vigorously censured by the Left for its apparent passivity and accommodationism. Lurking behind this "negation of inner impulses and the body's core," as Benjamin phrased it, critics have discerned an ethos of resignation and political quiescence that was instrumental to the rise of totalitarianism in the interwar years. In 1928 the film critic Béla Balázs, for example, published an essay on New Objectivity railing against "this masochistic intoxication with self-denial, this desire to sink into matter, into the mechanism of social and technical operation, this desire to be an object, this estrangement of the individual from himself."[22] Mirroring the psychic and physical submissiveness of Gehlen's "creature of discipline," the artists and authors of New Objectivity seem to long for the strict authority of rigorous aesthetic convention, style, and tradition. Thus, for Balázs, the widespread recourse during the interwar years to preexisting models of artistic production reflects a failure on the part of the artist to individuate himself sufficiently. Against this passive subject, which he marks as feminine, Balázs revives Romanticism's heroic cult of the genius, calling for the triumph of creativity over the aesthetic conventionalism that threatens to enslave the individual artist.

Here Balázs touches on the familiar narrative of realism as subordination to convention. Indeed, realist representation, irrespective of its historical epoch, is typically understood to privilege collective codes over personal style, intersubjective communication over individualistic mannerism—in sum, mimesis over poiesis. Some scholars have argued, for example, that the binding norms of mimetic depiction, which are the backbone of any realist aesthetic, have served in the modern era to stabilize and ratify specific political configurations, first the estate system of absolutist governments and later the class hierarchy of the nation-state.[23] In championing heroic invention and personal fantasy, Balázs's neo-Romantic attack on New Objectivity thus takes aim at the artistic conventionalism that is fundamental to all varieties of realist depiction, a conventionalism that he marks as passive and feminine. Needless to say, this is the least tenable element of his critique, based as it is on an ideologically dubious cult of the creative (read: masculine) genius. But a different aspect of these allegations of psychic passivity and obedience to external convention must still be taken seriously: as numerous critics after Balázs have opined, it is, alas, regrettable that interwar art prioritized aesthetic convention over personal expression, but in fact the real defect of this art was its reliance on particular artistic conventions that were taken from a bygone era and that were, therefore, manifestly inauthentic. Whereas, in the nineteenth century, the realist paintings of Courbet and novels of Balzac still served a revolutionary political project, after the radical experimentation of aesthetic modernism, such critics reason, the reappearance of the same artistic devices found in the work of the previous century must necessarily be reactionary. This influential construal of interwar art as a moment of cultural regression is reflected in one of the period's stock designations: the *retour à l'ordre*.[24]

Although it is true that interwar art mimicked and repeated the methods of figuration used in earlier eras, there is nothing perforce reactionary about strategies of mimicry and repetition in and of themselves. As the philosopher Ernst Bloch argued in his contributions to the interwar debates about the "cultural heritage" (*Kulturerbe*), the recycling of aesthetic forms is hardly the same thing as their ideological reinstatement. Released from the cultural contexts that once gave them an internal coherence, bygone artistic devices, he observed in the 1930s, could now be refunctioned for new purposes and invested with contemporary political contents.[25] Take the critical mimicry of John Heartfield's post-Dada work, which, despite being both antiexpressive and constitutionally derivative, and despite its great debt to nineteenth-century forebears such as Honoré Daumier, hardly amounts to psychic regression or artistic capitulation à la Balázs. To the contrary, Heartfield's militantly appropriationist and synthetic practice is a deeply political one. The critical dismissal of interwar realism as merely an aesthetic restauration underestimates the degree to which the reappearance of older artistic devices in this period was an active and deliberate strategy to expropriate the capital of the "cultural heritage." For this reason, *Realism after Modernism* insists that interwar realism did not reiterate previous paradigms naively, but rather invoked them self-consciously. Indeed, when elements from the representational language of nineteenth-century realism recur in the literature and art of this period, they often appear as citations that are framed by quotation marks, suggesting a strategy of mimicry closely akin to the second-order referential practices of pastiche that are associated with the aesthetic of postmodernism. So while the specific formal devices and contents of interwar realism may hearken back to the nineteenth century, the general operational logic that motivates them in fact looks forward to the postwar period.

For this reason, *Realism after Modernism* argues that the manifest resemblance between interwar art and the art of the previous century confirms nothing so much as the ineluctable fact of their historical nonequivalence. Nothing would be more false than to flatten the formal correspondences between these two moments into a relationship of sheer identity (which would be no relationship at all). Simply put: Realism after modernism cannot be the same phenomenon as realism before modernism. On this point it is helpful to recall the theorization of repetition developed by Gilles Deleuze, who demonstrated that the recurrence of a paradigm does not mark a return to a previous moment, but, to the contrary, underscores the temporal difference from this earlier moment. In positing a relation of resemblance between two events separated by an interval of time, the strategy of repetition contours the very movement of history that separates these two moments. By loosening the timeless fixity of representation in this way, Deleuze argued, the event of formal repetition thus opposes the violence of conceptual identity. This notion of repetition as a spur of noncorrespondence and as "difference without concept" is, I would argue, extremely productive for understanding interwar realism's intimate connection to historical materialist thought.[26] Hardly a return of the same, the strategies of paradigm repetition found in this art and literature trace the vector of time itself, subverting conceptual identity and stimulating an objective awareness of what the formalist critic Viktor Shklovskii once called "the dissimilarity of the similar" (*несходство сходного*).[27]

All the works considered in this book belong to the aesthetic Thermidor that followed upon modernism's apparent withdrawal. Although most of these realist "lapses" also entailed a return to explicitly figurative content, far more important for the narrative of *Realism after Modernism*, are the types of anthropomorphism found within the technical matrix of the artwork itself, since these latent forms of figuration often tell a different story from the one proposed by the work's iconography. If, as we saw earlier, the human body underwrote the new realist art not just as a motif but also as a device, this book emphasizes the latter aspect, interrogating the work at the level of artistic form. Because the formal conventions and authority of realism differ from genre to genre and medium to medium, a general account of interwar art can only be established inductively, by examining a number of these individual mimetic devices. For this reason, each chapter of this book focuses on the return of a specific technique or genre associated with traditional realism: linear perspective, the novel, naturalistic drama, autobiography, and portraiture. As systems for the production of self-knowledge and as frameworks for organizing subjective perception, these five aesthetic systems have also historically contributed to a particular configuration of thought and experience now associated with the modern humanist subject. Indeed, each one of these five techniques or genres also entails a corresponding anthropomorphist postulate, respectively: the spatially centered Cartesian ego; the telic narrative of *Bildung*; the theatrical experience of bodily presence; the mnemonic integrity of the self; and the physiognomic expression of individualism. Drafted into Western civilization's campaign of anthropotechnical enculturation, these aesthetic devices, which format and interpellate the human subject in subtle yet concrete ways, contribute to the ongoing project that Engels and Freud both called *Menschwerdung*, or "hominization."[28]

However, through close formal analysis of these techniques of hominization, *Realism after Modernism* also demonstrates that these devices did not function in the 1920s as they did in the nineteenth century, and that, consequently, the strategies of interwar art do not signal the return of an old subject but herald the advent of a new one. Realism after modernism, to repeat, is not the same phenomenon as realism before modernism. As a consequence, each chapter confronts the paradoxical status of realist technique after the historical disappearance of the humanist subject to which it once corresponded. With their cultural decommissioning, as it were, these five strategies of representation no longer possessed in the interwar period the privileged and spontaneous relationship to structures of human consciousness that they previously enjoyed. Having outlived the epistemic paradigm that gave birth to them, these orphaned devices persist in the cultural production of the interwar period, although they now exist in this afterlife as mere technique or device (to use Shklovskii's well-known term) rather than as a binding period style. But this is not yet the final historical terminus of these five devices, for, as we will see, the process of ideological deterritorialization also frees each of them to recombine with other cultural forms in the provisional creation of new subjects and social configurations. Indeed, the struggle to remotivate and resocialize strategies of representation after modernism's relentless semiotic demotivation of the realist sign is a recurrent theme in this book.

The emphasis this book places on the formal dimensions of interwar art, and its relative indifference to questions of content, will strike some readers as misguided, even objectionable, for two reasons. Formalist methodology seems out of place in a study of interwar realism, first, because this work so vehemently denies its formal aspect, claiming for itself instead a condition of semiotic transparency. Compared with modernism's technical experimentalism and sophisticated interrogation of the aesthetic sign, the realist art of the interwar period seems not just formally impoverished but utterly facile from the perspective of art's signifying structures. For precisely this reason, scholars have tended to focus on the thematic aspects of these works, a tendency encouraged by the artworks' remarkable capacity to provide their own interpretation spontaneously, as it were. Because this period "stands before us as the most self-aware epoch in history," as Peter Sloterdijk observed in his study of cynical consciousness in interwar Germany,[29] the Weimar commentator is tempted to read its cultural production as one would read emblems, as both image and concept in one. This tack is understandable, since, as we will see in chapters 4 and 5, the interwar period marks the historical moment when signifying structures became fundamentally tautegorical, when the hermeneutic paradigm of criticism yielded to that of commentary. And if everything the scholar could need to know about the Weimar text is already miraculously manifest on its surface, why should she bother going through the trouble of deciphering what was never illegible to begin with?

But, in credulously taking interwar art at its word, this approach concludes too hastily that the formal structures of this work perform no ideological labor. In an essay on realism from the late 1930s, Brecht shrewdly observed that critics had fallen for the glib equation of modernism with "formalism" and realism with a corollary "contentism" (*Inhaltismus*).[30] No matter how transparent and obvious the ideological content of a given artwork may appear, and no matter how "self-aware" its author may be, analysis of the work demands understanding not just what it says but how it functions. Hence Brecht's famous comment from 1931 about New Objectivity photography, the very apogee of semiotic transparency and realist verisimilitude: "reality as such has slipped into the domain of the functional" (*Werke*, 21:469). Understanding the functional aspects of the work obligates the critic to undertake formal and material analysis precisely where art's meanings seem most transparent and self-evident.

There is a second reason why a formalist approach to the cultural production of the 1920s and '30s may provoke discomfort. With the spread of totalitarianism in Europe and Russia, few other historical moments urge the critic so forcefully to prioritize the overtly political dimensions of art. And although this book does not attend in depth to either the propagandistic content of the artworks or the political orientation of the artists it considers, this silence should not be taken to mean that these aspects are insignificant ones. Narratives of commitment and coercion are in fact of primary importance in reconstructing the experiences of artists during this tumultuous and highly politicized period. But they don't tell us much about the art. *Realism after Modernism* does not address questions of political allegiance because, in the end, these frameworks simply do not provide viable critical categories for aesthetic analysis. Even in 1934, one year after the Nazi takeover in Germany, Benjamin began a talk at the Paris Institute for the Study of Fascism with the observation that "the concept of political tendency . . . is a perfectly useless instrument of political literary criticism."[31] Too often this insight goes unheeded by scholars working on interwar realism.

Because of the situation in fascist Germany and the Soviet Union, where the state authorized figuration as the only permissible artistic idiom, many have a natural or motivated connection between anthropomorphic realism and totalitarian politics. It is an association that, of course, became a cornerstone of the ideological defense of abstraction during the cold war. And yet there is abundant evidence contradicting realism's purported connection to reactionary political formations: on the one hand, there are numerous cases of leftist realism, such as the work of the antifascist artists of the Popular Front, several of whom will be considered closely in this book; and then there is the converse proposition, fascist modernism, such as it developed in Italy, where the formal language of the futurists thrived until Marinetti's death in 1944.[32] However, the claim that mimetic realism can be assigned a fixed value on the political spectrum is most clearly refuted by the legion examples of realism's resurgence in contexts that were utterly oblivious to concerns of political exigency. From the reportage literature of Germany and the figurative painting of former cubists in France to the Group f/64 photographers in the United States, the paradigm of realism in the art of these decades does not exhibit allegiance to any one political program. Nor can it be confined to any one national context, as much recent work on Soviet socialist realism has attempted to do. And so, while the arguments of this book coalesce around a group of German-speaking artists and authors, the chapters also draw heavily on realist paradigms that emerged at the same time in other political frameworks, particularly in the Soviet Union (in chapters 1, 3, and 5) and France (in chapters 4 and 5). Understanding the phenomenon of interwar realism demands an international and comparative framework, and must resist anchoring its analysis in any one political context.

* * *

Each of the five chapters in this book focuses on a single artistic device or genre central to the phenomenon of interwar realism. Beginning with two of the most venerable and authoritative categories of consciousness, space and time, the first chapters consider how these dimensions of subjective experience acquire anthropomorphic contours through the use of two artistic devices, perspective and narrative. Chapter 1, "The Myth Reversed," examines the work of Bauhaus polymath László Moholy-Nagy, an artist whose life project, as his colleague Walter Gropius suggested, was dedicated to "the conquest of space."[33] At the moment that the modern "anthropocracy" of perspectival rendering was being reinstated in the visual arts, Moholy-Nagy developed two strategies that interrogated this device for the humanization of space. First, in his photographic practice, both with and without the camera, Moholy-Nagy employed a range of dynamic urban technologies such as automobiles as machines for perception, expanding the definition of photography beyond the technical parameters of the optical camera obscura and thus, as we will see, beyond the stable phenomenological space of Renaissance perspective. This same mobilization of vision reappears in Moholy-Nagy's use of reverse perspective in his photomontage work. Unlike linear perspective, which projects a homogenous space of infinite extension at the center of which is a durable and centered subject, reverse perspective posits space as a series of topological and discontinuous volumes, a site of material encounter that is shaped by the objects and vectors of movement found within it.

The following chapter focuses on three examples of the industrial novel, one of Weimar Germany's defining narrative forms. Through readings of Erik Reger, Franz Jung, and Bertolt Brecht, chapter 2 discovers an aporia at the heart of this genre, namely, a disjuncture between two scales of time, one human and one technological, that is articulated and played out in the narrative architecture of these texts. In Reger's industrial novel *Union of the Strong Hand* (1931), the most celebrated example of this genre, the conflict between human and capital is reflected in the text's centrifugal structure, which increasingly widens the chasm between the dense time of organic existence and the technical time of capital's "development." As we will then see, Jung's *The Conquest of the Machines* (1923) casts this same conflict between living and dead labor as a confrontation between, on the one hand, the physiological tempo and generational cycles of the proletarian body and, on the other, capital's own rhythmic ordinance and reproductive cycles. Finally, Brecht's *Threepenny Novel* (1934) reframes the asynchronism between human and capital as an epistemological problem. Focusing on the issue of primitive accumulation, Brecht's industrial novel uncovers a temporal paradox at the heart of its subject: the fact that capital has no origin, no history, and thus, no narrative. In trying to tell the story of an industrial enterprise through a "genealogy" of capital, Brecht arrives at the limits of anthropomorphic categories for thinking about temporality.

After examining latent figuration in the visual arts and the novel, *Realism after Modernism* then turns to anthropomorphism in theater, focusing on Brecht's two so-called socialist realist plays, *Señora Carrar's Rifles* (1937) and *Fear and Misery of the Third Reich* (1938). In their emphasis on domestic scenes and the emotional lives of characters, these two plays appear quite conventional in both technical and dramaturgical terms. Even Brecht himself was unresolved about whether they should be considered realist or avant-gardist. But as chapter 3 explains, the strategies of figuration pursued in these plays redefine the distinction between the mechanomorphism of avant-garde theater and the anthropomorphism of realist drama entirely. While the extravagant technicism and aggressive montage of Brecht's earlier plays were no longer apparent in works such as *Fear and Misery*, this did not mean that the machine had disappeared, as his socialist realist opponents had hoped. Rather, in these plays, the apparatuses of the mass media are now incorporated into the very body of the actor as a "higher order" of mechanization, Brecht proposed. By tailoring the appearance of the actor to the camera and rendering her speech suitable for radio transmission, Brecht dismantled the auratic presence and singularity of the body on stage, a pillar of naturalistic drama.

Chapter 4 then takes up the genre of autobiography, which enjoyed a meteoric career in the interwar years as a "kind of fossilized anthropology," to borrow Leo Löwenthal's phrase.[34] Here the book focuses on Carl Einstein's unpublished memoire *Bebuquin II*, which Einstein began composing around 1925 as a rewrite of his modernist novella of 1912, *Bebuquin*. A key document in Einstein's renunciation of modernism and his newfound "defense of the real," *Bebuquin II* was supposed to recontain the previous experimental text within a securely referential autobiographical framework. And while this impulse to refashion an earlier modernist text as an autobiography would seem to make *Bebuquin II* a perfect exemplar of the *retour à l'ordre*, closer examination reveals that the textual economy of this work is quite unlike that of traditional realist autobiography. If conventional autobiography reinforces the psychic contours of selfhood, *Bebuquin II* instead carries out an act of deindividuation. Seeking to undo the effects of enculturation, Einstein overwrites the contents of memory again and again, and, in this process of rewriting, mobilizes the "ego document" against the ego, as it were. As this chapter also explains, the mechanism of repetition and augmentation that is fundamental to Einstein's autobiography can also be observed in the relationship of the new realist art to its modernist precedent: more than just a textual device, overwriting was a fundamental poetological tenet of interwar realism, which replaced modernism's negation of reference with a surplus of reference.

Continuing with this examination of strategies of repetition and augmentation in interwar art, chapter 5 turns to the post-Dada work of John Heartfield. Whereas, before 1924, Heartfield's photomontages interrogated the conventions of signification through a radical and relentless semantic reduction, in the latter half of the decade his works instead began to accrete and multiply meanings, culminating in the complex and overcoded image-text rebuses that he published in the *Worker's Illustrated News* (*AIZ*, or *Arbeiter Illustrierte Zeitung*). Connecting this poetics of semantic excess with newly emergent forms of socialist realist art, chapter 5 explains that Heartfield's photomontage work, which was based on second-order practices of mimicry, exemplifies that process of cultural recoding taking place during the interwar period, when artists and authors recapitulated some of the key moments and strategies in the previous history of world art. A central idiom that Heartfield took from this "cultural legacy" was that of physiognomy, a form of anthropomorphic figuration that verged on a cultural obsession of the Weimar era. Chapter 5 argues that this pervasive interest in the relationships of likeness and similitude contained in the face was more than just a symptom of the humanist ideology of the interwar years: rather, as Heartfield's work demonstrates, the turn to the physiognomic sign during these years represents an attempt to rethink the mechanisms of signification after the exhaustion of the structuralist model of meaning—a model that had reached the apogee of its influence under aesthetic modernism. At a historical moment when the sign was undergoing a global mutation precipitated by the modern mass media, Heartfield's work explored physiognomy as a signifying system commensurate with this new epistemic system, establishing the possibility of a politicized artistic practice within what is now commonly known as the society of the spectacle.

The fact that so many aspects of interwar realism find their continuation in current artistic practices precludes a definitive ending for *Realism after Modernism*.

Instead of a résumé, then, the final pages of this book offer a bridge to the present. This coda reprises a number of the theses on figuration developed in the previous chapters through an analysis of Ernst Jünger's 1957 science fiction novel *Glass Bees*. Specifically, it shows how Jünger's book explores the mutable forms of the human through the question of measurement. His novel reflects on the displacement of anthropometric standards of mensuration (feet, inches, fingers, ells) by metrics that do not take the human form as their referent. Whereas the machinery of the classic industrial age was modeled on our anatomy—hammers, for example, echo the actions of our fists, while cranes duplicate the motions of our outstretched arms—the technologies of the postindustrial era, by contrast, have no equivalent human prototypes. No longer the measure of all things, man must learn in Jünger's book—as in our own era—to comport with parameters of experience that are calibrated to scales alien to the human body.

1

The Myth Reversed: Perspectives of László Moholy-Nagy

Between Object and Medium

László Moholy-Nagy was long ago consigned to the ranks of that artistic formation Kracauer once jokingly called the derrière-garde. During an epoch of radical polarization, he belonged to none of the extreme currents on the cultural spectrum, but instead pursued an aesthetic syncretism that struck many commentators as naïve and politically compromised. Neither clearly modernist nor distinctly realist, his works circulate noncommittally among a variety of rubrics from biomorphic abstraction to New Vision. As a consequence of this ideological and formal promiscuity, Moholy-Nagy has been dismissed variously as a vulgar opportunist, a middle-man of the avant-garde, and a vendor of revolutionary "style." Already in 1924, his former collaborator Alfred Kemény, for example, denounced Moholy-Nagy's work as a pale imitation of Russia's more radical artistic currents,[1] and El Lissitzky soon followed suit with similar accusations of derivativeness. Even though the charge of imitation made by avowed champions of revolutionary art like Lissitzky perpetuates a romantic ideal of the individual artist that is conspicuously anticollectivist and that should itself be interrogated, readings of Moholy-Nagy's work continue overshadowed by allegations of plagiarism. But even worse than his reputation as a purveyor of others' ideas has been leftist criticism's accusation that Moholy-Nagy aestheticized and marketed the militant artistic currents of the day. Whereas, in the Soviet East, Moholy-Nagy was denounced for corrupting the socialist utopia of production with capitalism's pernicious cult of consumer desire[2] (as one otherwise supportive commentator conceded in 1936, his light projections seem to fulfill a "reactionary" desire "to see a piece of Friedrichstraße in Magnitogorsk"[3]), in the European West, he touted a "disarmed" variant of radical Constructivism's "armed vision."[4]

One of the central proofs cited in this narrative about Moholy-Nagy's dismantling of the avant-garde is his work with photomontage. Compare the Dadaistic pandemonium of Raoul Hausmann's *ABCD* (1924) to Moholy-Nagy's *Leda and the Swan (The Myth Reversed)* (figs. 1.1, 1.2). Just one year after Hausmann's radical act of optical nihilism, Moholy-Nagy reintroduces a lucid order into the visual field, reclaiming the white of the page as a stable ground of pictorial representation. Within this post-Dada practice, the grid of linear perspective clearly enjoys privileged status as a tool for cleaning up the disorder of the preceding avant-garde. To further secure the semantic dimensions of this work, Moholy-Nagy outfits it with a title that effectively limits the labor of interpretation, locking meaning into the prefabricated scheme of a timeless mythological allegory. In an effort to distinguish works such as *Leda and the Swan* from the *disjecta membra* of Dada photomontage, Moholy-Nagy designated these compositions as "photoplastics," a term that suggests a return to pictorial depth and coherent spatial volume. The Dadaists, he wrote in 1929, had "brutally demonstrated the process of creation, the cutting up of photographs, the rough slice of scissors. These 'photomontages' were the true brethren of the Futurist, brutalist music composed of scraps of noise." Emphasizing the distance between such work and his own, he claimed that his photoplastics "are like a kind of organized chaos. It has a clearly discernible center of meaning and vision which permits a clear view of the whole."[5] By securing the errant photo-fragments within the fixed spatial scheme of linear perspective, Moholy-Nagy here restores the mimetic codes of pictorial representation and renders the surface of the page once again transparent to vision.

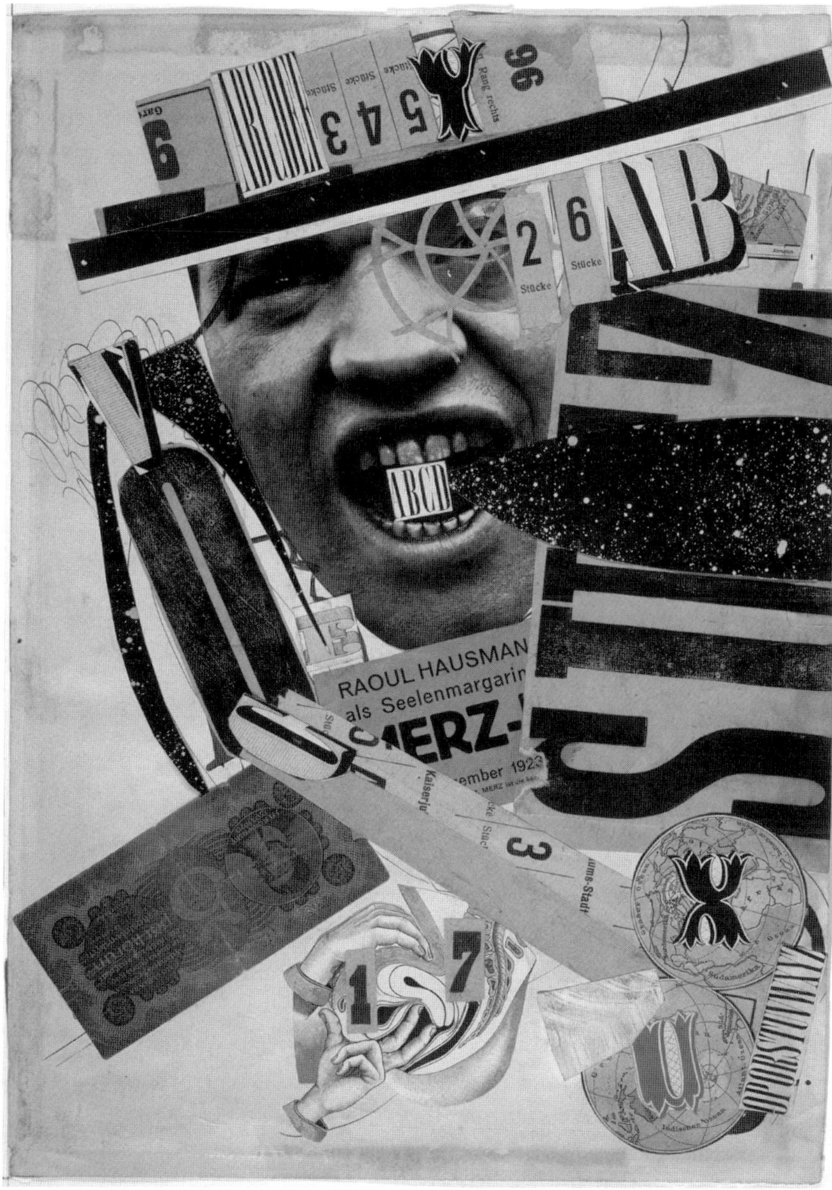

Figure 1.1 Raoul Hausmann, *ABCD* (1924). Image provided by CNAC/MNAM/Dist. Réunion des Musées Nationaux/Art Resource, New York. © 2012 Artists Rights Society (ARS), New York/ADAGP, Paris.

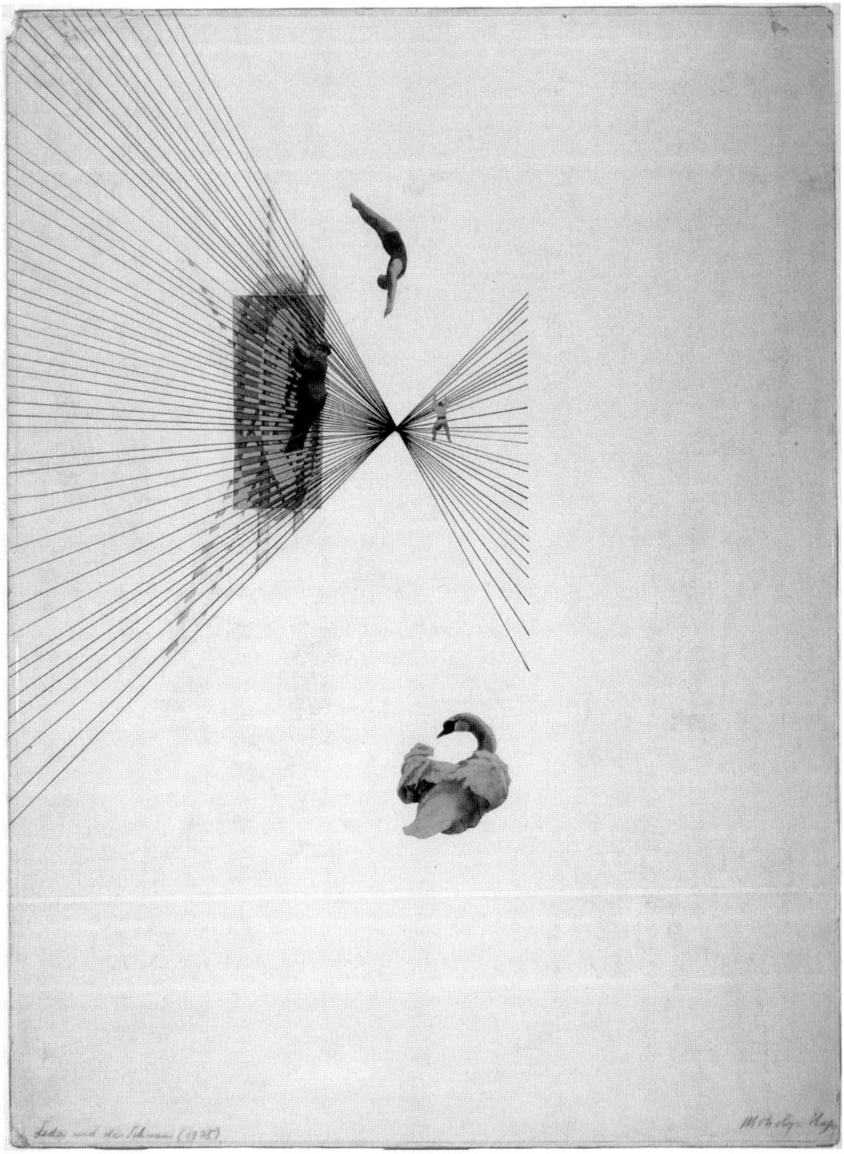

Figure 1.2 László Moholy-Nagy, *Leda and the Swan* (1925). Courtesy of George Eastman House, International Museum of Photography and Film. © 2012 Artists Rights Society (ARS), New York/VG Bild-Kunst, Bonn.

As Erwin Panofsky argued in his essay *Perspective as Symbolic Form*, written at the same time that Moholy-Nagy made *Leda and the Swan*, perspectival rendering is not merely a technique of visual reference. It is a rational and systematic architecture for thought itself. An invention of quattrocento painting, this device participated in an encompassing epistemological framework that emerged in the Renaissance and that included, as its corollaries, Newton's model of an isotropic and infinite universe and Descartes's notion of space as a positive entity that exists prior to the objects within it. Following Panofsky's analysis, Hubert Damisch thus designated perspective a *dispositif*, an ensemble of laws and a system of relations that makes the chaos of phenomenal perception available to ideation. It situates experience within a structured grammar of consciousness, Damisch observed: "*perspectiva artificialis* provided the painter with a formal apparatus like that of the sentence, with which it shares many features. Starting with its organization of point of view, vanishing point, and distance point, and the other corollary points designating *here*, *there*, and *over there*—which is sufficient to make it possible to speak, again nonmetaphorically, of a geometry of the sentence that would have its analogue in the figurative register."[6] Indeed, according to the neo-Kantian Panofsky and the structuralist Damisch, perspective has far more to do with intelligibility and ideology than it does with the physiology of vision and the perception of reference. Perspective not only shows us objects visually, it *demonstrates* them rhetorically, Damisch concluded. Ultimately, this pictorial technique is only one moment of a larger field of thought that emerged during the Renaissance—a field that Panofsky characterized as the paradigm of "modern 'anthropocracy.'"[7] As the Renaissance humanists were establishing man as the measure of all things, pictorial perspective humanized the surrounding environment by giving the modern spectator a privileged point of view within a homogeneous, stable, and infinite geometric space.

For good reason, then, one central strategy in the historical avant-garde's assault on humanist ideology was a critique of linear perspective, which had long served as the optical corollary to the stable and centered bourgeois ego. Emerging, in turn, through a negation of the negation, as it were, Moholy-Nagy's reconstitution and legitimation of perspective in the 1920s would thus seem to provide the perfect object lesson in that cultural paradigm known as the "return to order." And yet, as this chapter demonstrates, Moholy-Nagy's work from the 1920s in fact transforms the perspective paradigm at the very moment of its reconstruction in the visual arts. For Moholy-Nagy recognized that the outright abrogation of the perspectival order was not so simple a proposition as some members of the avant-garde hoped. If the avant-garde's negation of illusionistic depth was motivated by the impossible fantasy of achieving some kind of absence of perspective—a truly subjectless mode of perception—Moholy-Nagy's work, by contrast, never sought to leave behind the realm of symbolic forms *tout court*. After all, subsequent to the invention of perspective, Damisch writes, "artists faced a choice: they could either raise the stakes of the perspective rule, or they could take exception to it—but they couldn't pretend to be ignorant of it."[8] One can no more destroy perspective than one can destroy space or epistemology as such.

However, as we will see, linear one-point perspective is not the only resource for rendering space pictorially. At the margins of culture can be found grammars of vision that produce experiences of space and configurations of knowledge which differ significantly from those that emerged during the Renaissance. Recognizing the plurality of perspectival systems, Panofsky proposed, for example, that "it is essential to ask of artistic periods and regions not only whether they have perspective, *but also which perspective they have*."[9] This chapter responds to Panofsky's injunction by looking at Moholy-Nagy's idiosyncratic work of the 1920s, which seems neither to subscribe to the avant-garde's fantasy of a radical absence of perspective, nor to restore fully the centered subject of Euclidean space. In contrast to both the antihumanism of modernist abstraction and the old humanism of linear perspective, Moholy-Nagy prospects a new spatial logic using devices and visual codes that give expression to the epistemology that emerged with the retreat of the Renaissance subject.[10]

Moholy-Nagy's straight photography provides the perfect place to begin examining his relationship to linear perspective, since the device of the camera obscura is widely regarded as the technical hypostasis of the method of linear perspective. As Damisch remarks in *The Origin of Perspective*, the appearance of the camera did much to bolster the ideological authority of linear perspective, with the result that "our epoch is much more massively 'informed' by the perspective paradigm through photography . . . than was the fifteenth century."[11] During the mid-1920s, specifically, when the production of lightweight, small-format cameras such as the Ermanox and the Leica made photography available for the first time on a mass scale, artistic practices shifted away from the disjointed, composite spaces of Dada photomontage toward the contained, orderly space of straight (i.e., single-shot) photography—a development that would seem to corroborate Damisch's narrative about the camera as a machine that fueled the ideological prestige of linear perspective. Moholy-Nagy invoked this paradigm in a photographic scene that he staged several times in 1926, producing a series of pictures that together suggest a metapoetic statement by the artist about technologies of perspective (figs. 1.3–1.5). As if preparing to make a photogram, in each of these pictures Moholy-Nagy has placed a body on a plain white piece of fabric that captures, like photographic paper, the shadow projected onto its surface. The shadow of the fence reticulates the body of the supine subject, illustrating, with almost didactic clarity, how the perspectival grid maps out its visual field and makes it possible to translate volumetric space into the two-dimensional codes of the pictorial screen. The result is an unmistakable allegory of the process of photographic making.

Moholy-Nagy's staging contains one important and telling divergence from Dürer's famous pedagogical illustration of the correct technique for generating perspective (fig. 1.6): his displacement of Dürer's optical grid to the side. Shifted now to the left, the vertical latticework no longer serves as the orderly and transparent base of the visual pyramid, but instead underscores the incommensurability between corporeal volume and the two-dimensional screen of the representation. As it encounters the fitful topography of the human form, the regular grid surges and warps in Moholy-Nagy's photograph, exposing the inadequacy of perspective for depicting so irrational and ungeometrical an object as the body.[12] These photographs, which contrive to look *at* perspective rather than look *through* it, foreground the distortions created by this spatial grid as it is cast across its object and registered on the flat white surface below. As a result of

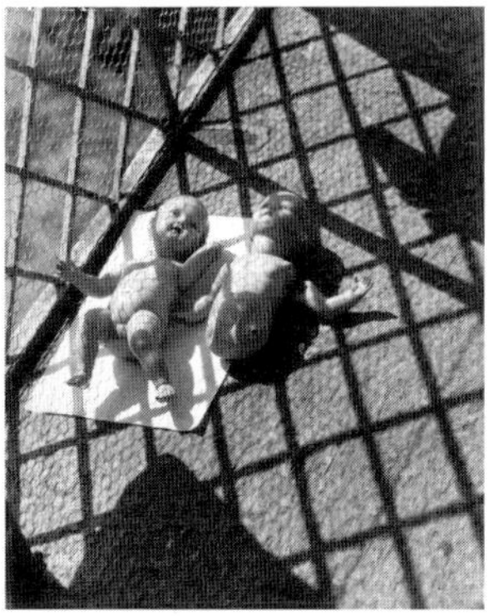

Figure 1.3 László Moholy-Nagy, *Dolls* (1926). Courtesy of George Eastman House, International Museum of Photography and Film. © 2012 Artists Rights Society (ARS), New York/VG Bild-Kunst, Bonn.

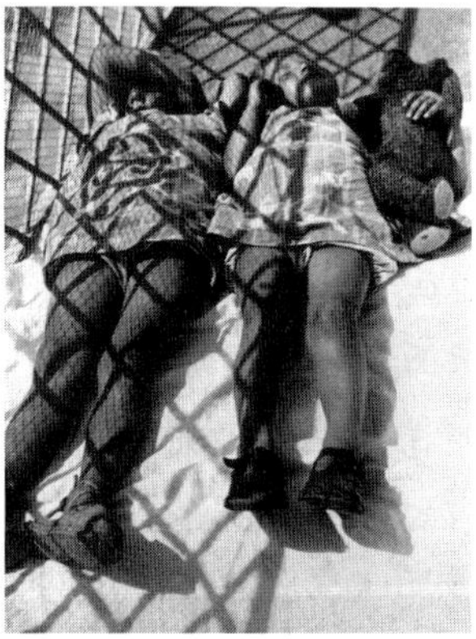

Figure 1.4 László Moholy-Nagy, *The Schlemmer Girls* (1926). © 2012 Artists Rights Society (ARS), New York/VG Bild-Kunst, Bonn.

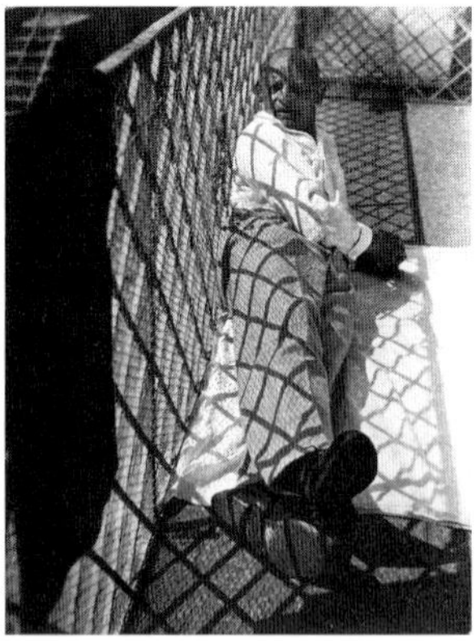

Figure 1.5 László Moholy-Nagy, *Oskar Schlemmer, Ascona* (1926). Julien Levy Collection, Gift of Jean and Julien Levy, 1978.1090, The Art Institute of Chicago. Photography © The Art Institute of Chicago. © 2012 Artists Rights Society (ARS), New York/VG Bild-Kunst, Bonn.

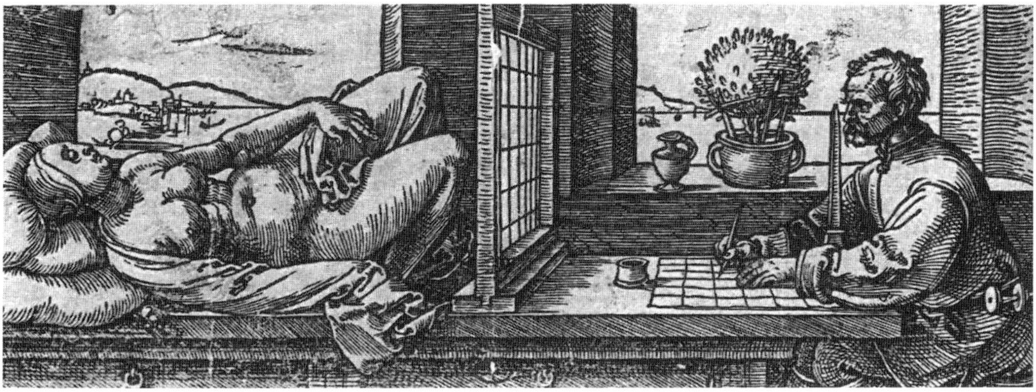

Figure 1.6 Albrecht Dürer, *Draftsman* (1525). From Dürer, *Unterweysung der Messung* (Nuremberg, 2nd ed. 1938); photo: Bibliothèque Nationale, Paris.

his oblique vantage, Moholy-Nagy sets up two disconnected, even competing, views within a single photograph. Here his strategy resembles Umbo's famous bird's-eye view of the *Mystery of the Street* (1928), which offers the spectator two distinct and noncoincidental sets of visual information: while the camera eye sees purely abstract forms, the raking light from below casts the profiles of these ambiguous shapes in silhouette, translating the compressed ciphers into a narrative scene about a sweeping worker and a woman walking hand-in-hand with a child (fig. 1.7). By establishing two divergent and competing spatial planes, Moholy-Nagy's photographs, like Umbo's *Mystery*, insist on the nonidentity of embodied vision and linear perspective.[13] In this regard they convey a contradiction central to New Vision photography: on the one hand, this practice sought to restore habits of looking to a condition of perceptual immediacy, helping the spectator once again to see the world in all of its phenomenal plenitude (rather than merely recognizing *signs* of this world); on the other hand, it proposed to achieve this state of unmediated experience through the device of *perspectiva artificialis* and its mechanical proxy, the optical camera. Paradoxically, it is only through technical mediation that it becomes possible to restore perception to its precategorical primacy.

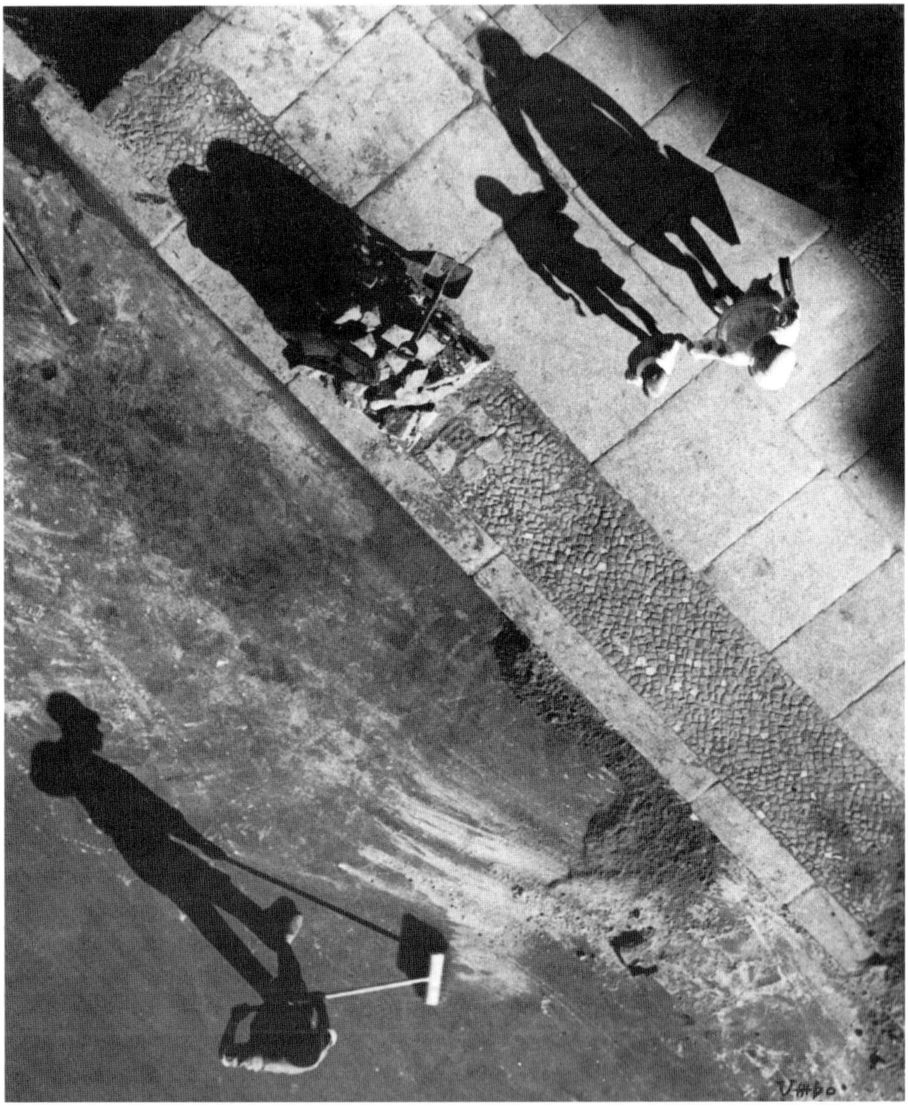

Figure 1.7 Umbo, *Mystery of the Street* (1928). Julien Levy Collection, Special Photography Acquisition Fund, 1979.114, The Art Institute of Chicago. Photography © The Art Institute of Chicago. © 2012 Gallery Kicken Berlin/Phyllis Umbehr/Artists Rights Society (ARS), New York/VG Bild-Kunst, Bonn.

Through the multiplication of vantages and the resulting relativization of the perspective paradigm, Moholy-Nagy's photographs illustrate Merleau-Ponty's famous distinction between *eye* and *mind*, between seeing and apprehending. The work of art that occasioned Merleau-Ponty's thoughts on this distinction, Rembrandt's *Nightwatch*, in fact resonates suggestively with the photographs by Moholy-Nagy. Taking note of the simultaneity of frontal and profile views in Rembrandt's painting, Merleau-Ponty writes: "We see that the hand pointing to us in *The Nightwatch* is truly there only when we see its shadow on the captain's body presents it simultaneously in profile. The spatiality of the captain lies at the meeting place of two lines of sight which are incompossible and yet together."[14] By contradicting the painting's dominant perspectival axis, Merleau-Ponty observed, the oblique vantage from the left makes it possible to grasp the figure as a real, material presence. This divergent axis suggests that the body may be more than just a representation—that it is "truly there," as Merleau-Ponty puts it. The incompatibility of these viewpoints challenges linear perspective, a device whose cultural prestige had been underwritten by the promise of a seamless correspondence between, on the one hand, a dynamic and ever-changing optical array and, on the other, a transcendental realm of abstract geometric forms. But, as we see here, this device in fact has no natural, motivated relationship to optical experience. The space of linear perspective is not coextensive with that of actual physiological vision, as Diderot already concluded in his famous *Letter on the Blind*, which demonstrated that even those without sight are capable of understanding the geometral spatial system of perspective.[15] In this series of photographs, Moholy-Nagy uses the camera obscura against itself, as it were, projecting visual planes that rival the axis that recedes into the deep space of the background and thus contradicting the sovereign unicity of one-point perspective. Presented with conflicting sensory data and multiple vantages, the sight-line of the spectator can no longer be contained by the monocular lens of the camera.

The collision between two perspectives in these photographs in effect cleaves the spectatorial subject, who, in order to make sense of the divergent projections, must establish herself in two places at once, at two bases of vision.

The effects of this splitting on the cultural legitimacy of the perspective paradigm are devastating, although in a way that is quite different from Dada's critique of perspective: if the Dadaists, fantasizing about a mode of perception devoid of human subjectivity, sought to eradicate the perspective paradigm utterly, New Vision photographers such as Moholy-Nagy sought instead to multiply, relativize, and denaturalize the device of perspective through, for example, the use of radically oblique angles. Whereas the Dadaists negated the device of realist representation, the artists that succeeded them multiplied it to the point of "incompossibility." Here it is telling that Moholy-Nagy compared the oblique perspectives of New Vision photography to anamorphic projections, which perform a comparable deconstruction of perspectival space. Grouping anamorphoses and oblique angles into a single category, he explained that these visual aberrations may at first glance appear to be "a 'distortion' if judged within the convention of the vanishing point of central perspective," but the "composite view" that they project is in fact nothing other than "vision in motion (rendered on the picture plane)."[16] The demand made by such pictures that the spectator occupy two distinct positions translates into the subjective sensation of movement, Moholy-Nagy observed. In a discussion of Hans Holbein's *The Ambassadors*, a central work in almost all discussions of anamorphosis, Jurgis Baltrusaitis, for example, demonstrated that anamorphic projection presumes the physical mobility of the viewer. To make sense of this painting, the spectator must view it from two positions, both frontally and laterally, Baltrusaitis explained. *The Ambassadors* even inscribes a symbolic narrative into the arc of the spectator's movement before the painting: while the viewer apprehends a display of the attributes of mundane power as he stands in front of the painting—globes, books, instruments of measure—when he exits through the door that stood to the right of the painting in its original installation, the skull, an emblem of the transitoriness of this life, comes into view, allegorizing the viewer's physical passage out of the room—and into the beyond.[17] Thus, while *The Ambassadors* on the one hand confirms the perspectival paradigm through a rigorous demonstration of its systematicity, its anamorphosis simultaneously "turn[s] the perspective order against itself," deconstructing it from the inside, Damisch explained, by presenting two fundamentally heterogeneous spaces of representation in an impossible state of coexistence and thereby "reducing the system of linearity to nonsense."[18] Applied to the raking angles of Moholy-Nagy's photography, this analysis of anamorphosis suggests that there is more at stake here than just the dynamization of the eye (a campaign promoted in the 1920s under the popular rubric of the *entfesselte Kamera*, or the "unleashed camera").[19] Here the unitary spectator is not just mobilized, but multiplied and refracted. Through this multiplication, the "composite view," as Moholy-Nagy called it, breaks apart the integral perspective of the Renaissance subject, freeing up the psychic apparatus of the spectator for investment in new sites of sensory embodiment.

A second series of photographs from the late 1920s proposed one such site of embodiment: a radio tower located just a few blocks from where Moholy-Nagy lived. Like the photographs of Schlemmer, his daughters, and their dolls, the obsessive consistency with which Moholy-Nagy took pictures from the Berlin radio tower, each time with a different set of variables, suggests a mind trying to work out a problem through a series of trial experiments. These photographs, we could thus conclude, seem to touch upon an issue that is pivotal to Moholy-Nagy's practice. The most famous one of this series recalls, again, Umbo's *Mystery of the Street* (also 1928), playing on the oscillation between the abstract flatness of the shapes seen from the bird's-eye view and the deep shadows cast by the low sun (fig. 1.8). But here, unlike in Umbo's image, Moholy-Nagy decides to include in the frame of the picture the openwork steel tower from which the photograph is taken. On the one hand, the intrusion of this construction into the picture exemplifies that modernist protocol of reflexivity which the Russian formalists famously dubbed "laying bare the device."[20] But the inclusion of the tower also performs a second function, that of reconfiguring the boundaries between the spectator and the technical media. As one reviewer explained in 1930, the tower in this photograph *conceals* at the same time that it is laid bare: "The steel beams are sinking into the depths in an unreal fashion and there is no way of knowing where they disappear above our heads. Their construction cannot be identified in any way. The daring foreshortening totally reverses the dimensions and denies us the perception of their very technological

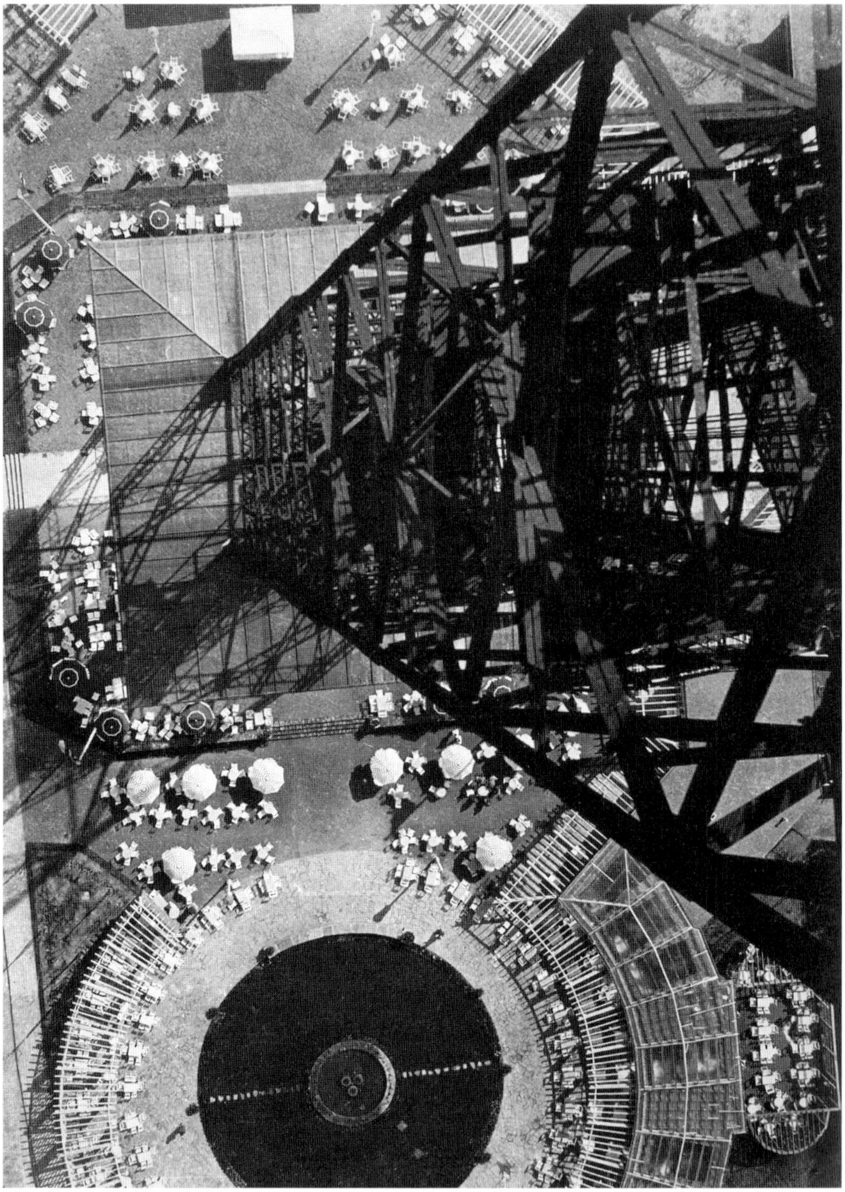

Figure 1.8 László Moholy-Nagy, *Berlin Radio Tower* (1928). Julien Levy Collection, Special Photography Acquisition Fund, 1979.84, The Art Institute of Chicago. Photography © The Art Institute of Chicago. © 2012 Artists Rights Society (ARS), New York/VG Bild-Kunst, Bonn.

structure."[21] Denied any synoptic view of the tower as a distinct and bounded object, the spectator is unable to establish its contours as a discrete figure within the visual field. To this reviewer, the radio tower seems to extend infinitely in both directions. The values of distance and proximity begin to blur. Confusing the "very technological structure" of the tower with the ground of vision itself, the spectator feels her vantage absorbed into the openwork construction. As a consequence, the tower ceases to be a distinct object standing apart from the spectator, but becomes itself transparent to vision. In this regard the pictures of the Berlin radio tower extend the proposition made in Moholy-Nagy's photographs of the Schlemmer family two years before: just as the Schlemmer photographs looked *at* the apparatus of linear perspective at the same time that they looked *through* it, Moholy-Nagy's radio tower series transforms the steel construction into a matrix of vision—a material object into a transparent medium of perception. In fact, again and again we find Moholy-Nagy photographing through various industrial structures (fig. 1.9). These photographs treat the open-work constructions themselves as perspectival systems (*per-spicere*: "to look through") that grant access to new realms of visual experience.

Looking at the Berlin radio tower series, we begin to grasp the full compass of Moholy-Nagy's expanded definition of photography, a definition quite unlike that of his contemporaries. In contrast to Albert Renger-Patzsch, for example, who ontologized straight photography as a natural and objective record of external reality, Moholy-Nagy never privileged the optical camera. For Moholy-Nagy, the camera obscura was but one component within a larger technical ensemble of devices for generating images, an ensemble that encompassed all variety of vision machines from towers and airplanes to artificial lighting and trains. Rejecting the metonymic reduction of photography to the optical camera, Moholy-Nagy argued that all sorts of technical constructions could serve as agents of perception, as potential sites for psychic investment and sensory embodiment. Already in his earliest theoretical texts on photography, Moholy-Nagy insisted that this medium had no natural, motivated relationship to the camera obscura, indeed, that it was not at all the calling of photography to make pictures or optical likenesses. The pictorial functions of the camera

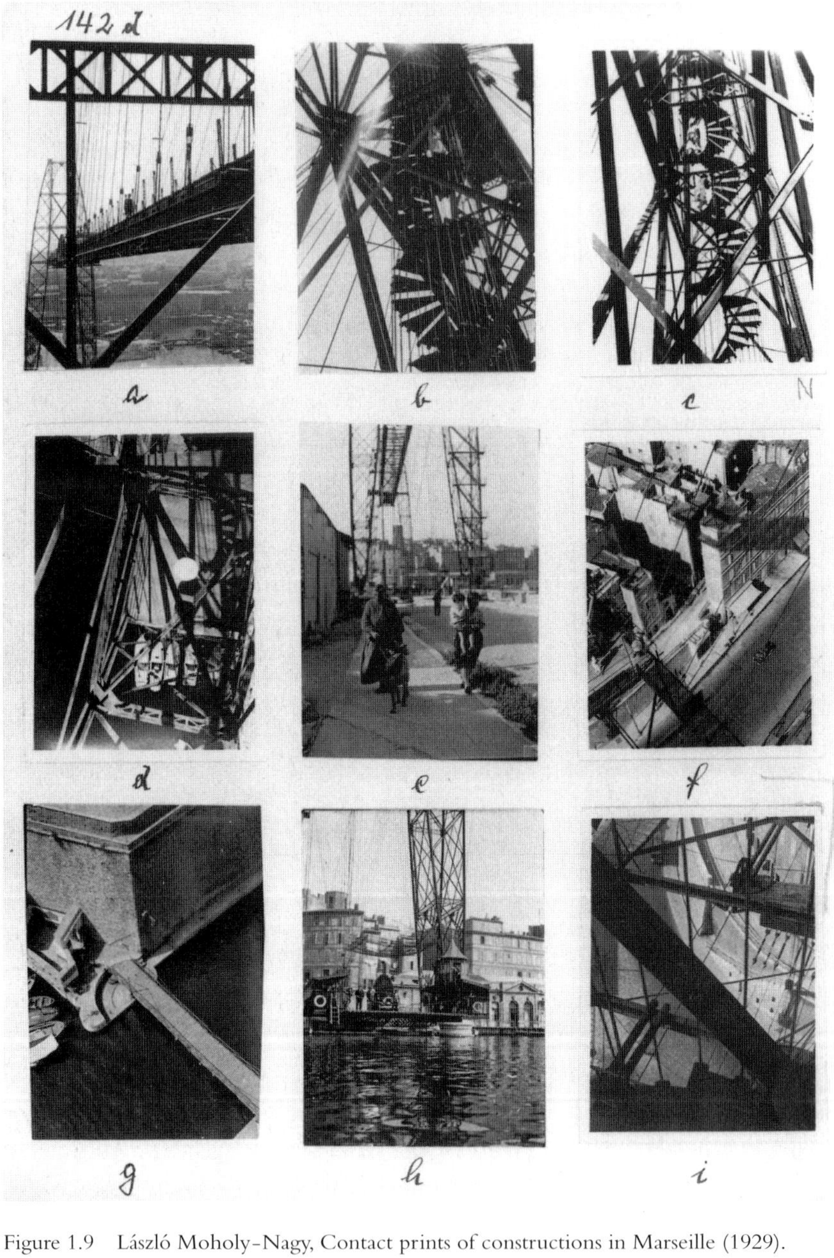

Figure 1.9 László Moholy-Nagy, Contact prints of constructions in Marseille (1929).

obscura were, for Moholy-Nagy, utterly secondary. It was precisely for this reason that one contemporary champion of photographic realism railed against Moholy-Nagy's "unleashed camera" (*entfesselte Kamera*), arguing in 1929 that these photographic experiments sought the "release of photography from the psycho-physiological laws of perspectival vision and of pictorial portrayal."[22]As this author recognized, Moholy-Nagy's photography posed a direct challenge to the conventions of realist mimeticism as codified in the perspective paradigm.

Moholy-Nagy's work, we could say, inaugurated the project of photography after linear perspective. His is a photographic practice liberated from the social context and pressures that had determined the medium's emergence in the nineteenth century. The parameters and prospects for such a practice—photography freed from the ideological baggage of the perspective paradigm—was the subject of much speculation in the 1920s, but was nowhere explored so brilliantly as in the essay "Photomechanics" by the theorist of production art Nikolai Tarabukin. Writing in 1925, Tarabukin observed that photography had arrived at a transitional phase in its history: although it was no longer subject to the regime of optical naturalism that had conditioned its appearance seventy years before, it was not yet possible to predict with absolute certainty what the coming postperspectival photographic practices would look like. "We cannot know how vision would be organized by the photographic apparatus [*установка зрения фотографического аппарата*] if it had been invented either before naturalism had already secured its dominance among the arts, or after our own time, when the currents of artistic naturalism will be much weaker."[23] Surveying the latest innovations in photographic technology, from the invention of anamorphic lenses to the use of oblique perspectives and multiple exposures, Tarabukin discerned the possibility of a fundamental "reorganization of the photographic apparatus itself" that would overturn the particular syntax of likeness, the "interpretation" of reality, which is proposed by optical naturalism.[24]

What Tarabukin explores here, in suitably tentative terms, is the paradoxical condition of photography after the historical disappearance of the perspective paradigm. With the historical passing of the bourgeois subject and the perspective *dispositif*, photography was, in effect, decommissioned as a symbolic form. But this does not mean that photography ceased to exist. Even though it had outlived the social context that birthed it in the nineteenth century, this orphaned technology nevertheless persists as a material apparatus; only henceforth the images that it produces convey no social "interpretation" of reality and establish no locus of community identity. Photography once again returned to its status as an experimental device, as it was in its early years before its technical development was commandeered by the agenda of mimetic realism. No longer a machine for producing likeness, after perspective the camera "enters the field opened by infinite research," Lyotard proposed. "It follows that the definition of what is a good photographic image, which was initially linked to the rules of artificial perspective, is subject to revision. . . . In this general movement, photography is released from the responsibilities of ideological identification it had inherited from the tradition of painting, and it henceforth gives rise to research."[25]

The notion of photography as "infinite research" proposed by Lyotard describes perfectly Moholy-Nagy's photograms, which reject photography's mimetic capacity and instead explore its potential as a productive industrial apparatus. These cameraless works, Moholy-Nagy believed, captured the essence of the medium far better than straight photography, which had diverted photography from its calling. In his various histories of photography, he accordingly give priority to the photogram over the camera obscura: "As a matter of fact, the main instrument of the photographic process is not the camera but the photosensitive layer."[26] Moholy-Nagy's procedures and instruments for making his photograms were extremely complex, and only rarely can be reconstructed by looking at the final abstract image. Unlike Man Ray's rayograms, for example, which arrange a set of recognizable objects in an evocative narrative scenario, Moholy-Nagy's photograms show little interest in the mimetic dimensions of representation. Moholy-Nagy had a panoply of techniques for manipulating light: using several, often oblique, light sources and multiple exposures, he refracted the rays through prisms, water, and acids, at times also magnifying and redirecting them with mirrors and crystals.[27] His photograms approach dense matter not as a substance, but as a lens, as a medium for sight. In these works Moholy-Nagy climbs into the dark interior of the camera itself and rearranges its component parts, proposing new configurations of the photographic apparatus from the inside.

Such works rearrange the conceptual territory that has long defined the debates between modernism and realism. From this perspective, the oft-invoked contrast between abstraction and figuration in all of its variants—montage versus organicism, facture versus illusionism, self-reflexivity versus reference and so on—turns out to be a mere surface matter diverting attention from the more fundamental question of the social matrix that underwrites these stylistic idioms. As Shklovskii observed in 1923 with his characteristic pithiness, "[t]here is no such thing as nonobjective art. There is only motivated art or unmotivated art."[28] For the Russian formalist, the distinction between realism and abstraction, which would soon come to occasion so much critical bluster, is just a red herring: the real issue is whether or not the bond between the sign and its referent appears nonarbitrary and natural; whether, as a result of this semiotic transparency, a given strategy of representation is endowed with the richness and depth of ideological meaning; whether, in short, an artistic device is motivated. For similar reasons Moholy-Nagy's own student György Kepes later argued that abstraction was not a stylistic designation, properly speaking, but a corollary to the condition of aesthetic demotivation, or what he called "the zero point of the meaning-organization."[29] Following this line of argumentation, we could surmise that the explosion of "abstract" photography in the 1920s, as exemplified in the work of Moholy-Nagy, was not first and foremost a visual or stylistic development, but instead reflected a transformation taking place at a deeper social level. Photographic practices become increasingly "nonobjective" at this historical moment because the perspective paradigm of the camera obscura, no longer in concert with the structure of consciousness, begins to lose its ideological motivation. In Moholy-Nagy's "infinite research," photographic technology continues to produce images, without, however, fully *understanding* them. With the epistemic waning of perspective during the interwar years, photography becomes increasingly abstract, opaque to vision, as is begins to approach what Kepes called "the zero point of the meaning-organization."

Stripped of the conceptual *dispositif* that had once determined its vocation, photography became, in Moholy-Nagy's work, radically asocial. It no longer presumed an ideological community. But this process of cultural deterritorialization also freed up photography to interface with other technical apparatuses and to participate provisionally in the creation of new social configurations. Outside the darkroom, Moholy-Nagy coupled photographic technologies with other mechanical devices, resulting in strikingly novel media ensembles. The close alliance in Moholy-Nagy's work of photography with other material forces of production—rather than with optical media such as painting—recalls Marx's position in *Das Kapital*, where photography is mentioned only once alongside a spectrum of industrial transportation and communication technologies that include telegraphy, gasworks, and the railway.[30] Within this expanded conceptualization of photography, the possibility for variation, Moholy-Nagy's experimental work shows us, is virtually limitless.

One recognizes the same materialist approach to the technical media in many of his nonphotographic works as well, which, oscillating between transparency and opacity, hover undecidedly between two callings, as a luminous medium and a dense object. The *Light-Space Modulator* of 1930, to give just one example of Moholy-Nagy's heterodox approach to questions of medium, is at once both a light projector and a kinetic sculpture (fig. 1.10). Significantly, in the short film that he made of the *Modulator* that same year, he never provides a single long-shot of the object itself. Like the radio tower, it is never presented to the viewer in its totality as a complete and closed form. The *Modulator* was not contained within the frame of the movie camera because, as Moholy-Nagy understood it, the construction was itself the frame of vision, the very condition of the perceptual field.

Moholy-Nagy's materialist redefinition of photography echoes that of the Soviet filmmaker Dziga Vertov, whose *Man with a Movie Camera* exerted an immense influence upon the artist. Introduced to the film when it was screened in Germany for the first time at the famous *Film und Foto* show in Stuttgart in 1929, Moholy-Nagy was captivated by one particular sequence, which he later recalled in *Vision in Motion* (1947):

> The scene showed a group of film men arriving at a railway station. They mount a troika harnessed with three racing horses and depart. They are photographed from a motorcar which runs beside the troika. This car is photographed from another which drives

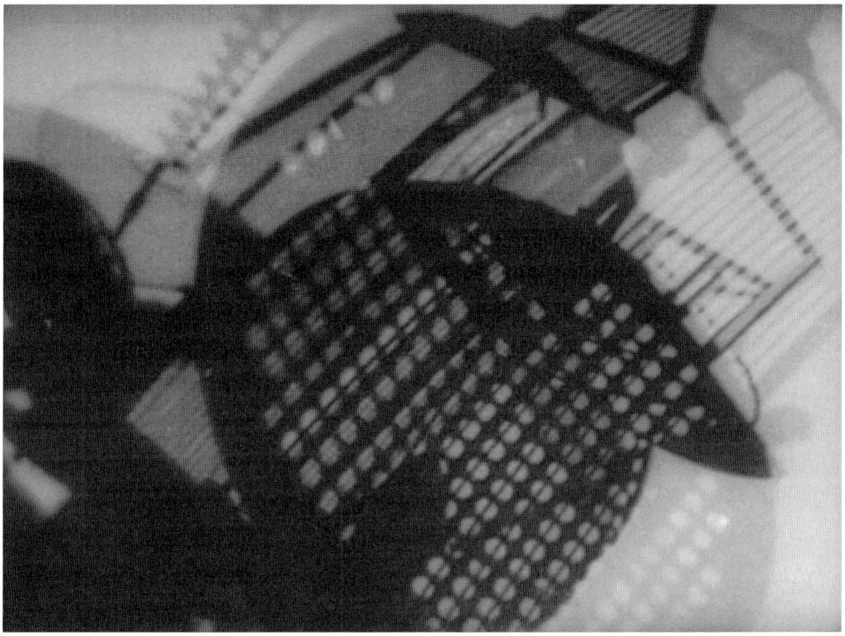

Figure 1.10 László Moholy-Nagy, still from *schwarz weiss grau* (1930). © 2012 Artists Rights Society (ARS), New York / VG Bild-Kunst, Bonn.

> parallel to the galloping horses. The auto is seen from the troika and again from the other auto. The negative of this film is then seen in a film printing laboratory where the positive print, made from the negative, runs through the fingers of the editor, and again through the editing machine. After this another scene shows a theater with the audience looking at a large screen on which the troika scene is projected. Among the spectators are the travelers themselves. (*Vision in Motion*, 280)[31]

This passage focuses on how, spiraling upwards to ever higher orders of observation, *Man with a Movie Camera* embeds each scene in a subsequent one that depicts the act of recording its predecessor (fig. 1.11). In this way, the condition,

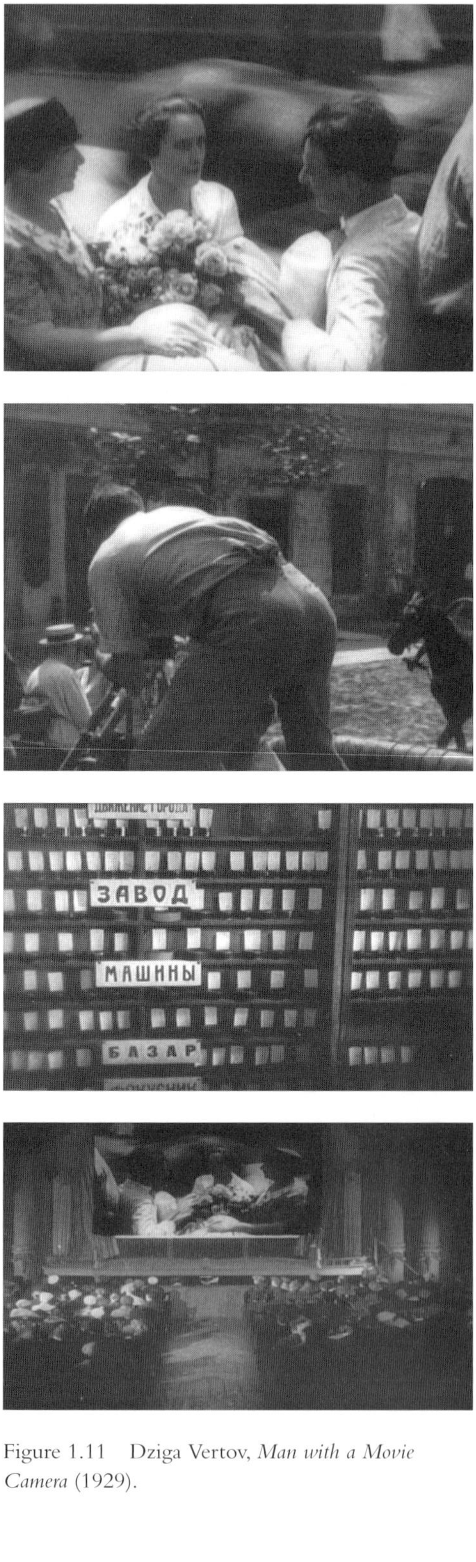

Figure 1.11 Dziga Vertov, *Man with a Movie Camera* (1929).

or frame, of vision in each scene becomes the subject matter of the scene that follows it. The ground of the apparatus shifts from troika to motorcar to laboratory to cutting bench to auditorium, at which point it loops back to the men at the train station. With each transposition, a previously transparent medium is rendered opaque, recontained. Each time that the medium of vision is itself made into an object, a different component of this ever-expanding media apparatus then becomes the new super-basis of perception. This relentless relativization destroys cinema's aspirations to medium specificity as well as its claim to ontological immediacy. The apparatus of cinema cannot be reduced to the mechanism of the camera obscura, since cinematic visualization, as Vertov shows, is conditioned equally by numerous other technical objects—lighting and tripods, but also motorized vehicles, industrial editing equipment, and so forth. Like Moholy-Nagy's photograms, Vertov's film uses all varieties of dense matter as luminous media for vision. Hence Deleuze's observation that Vertov's calling was "to carry perception into things."[32] With Vertov, as with Moholy-Nagy, "the eye is in things."[33]

Moholy-Nagy was especially interested in vehicles as machines that engendered a perspectival order and a logic of space different from one-point linear perspective. The latter presupposed what Carl Einstein decried as a "platonic monstrosity"—namely, "the immobile spectator."[34] This was a disdain that Moholy-Nagy shared. Renaissance paintings, he observed, "had to be viewed from one certain point whence the scene would appear undistorted. We find unbearable this fixed relationship of the spectator to the painting in which his observation is permanently bound."[35] Moholy-Nagy argued that the stasis of the Albertian grid had become particularly "unbearable" after the mechanical mobilization of vision with the automobile and the airplane. The latter had arrived to usurp the place of the camera obscura, and with these new technologies arrived novel logics of perspective. "The renaissance painter constructed the scene to be painted from an unchangeable, fixed point following the rules of the vanishing point perspective. But speeding on the roads and circling in the skies has given modern man the opportunity to see more than his renaissance predecessor. The man at the wheel sees persons and objects in quick succession, in permanent motion" (*Vision in Motion*, 113). As Moholy-Nagy explained in these lines, the automobile is not merely a machine for the conveyance of bodies, but also an instrument for generating perceptual states. "For the motorcar driver," he noted, "distant objects are brought into a relationship for which the pedestrian has yet no eye." Without the automobile, it follows, such relationships fall below the threshold of perception. As evidence for this claim, Moholy-Nagy cited an experiment by Jean Carlu, in which the French poster designer "mounted two posters on two conveyer belts which moved at different speeds. The one poster by Toulouse-Lautrec, from around 1900, moved at eight miles per hour, approximately the speed of a horse and buggy. The other, a contemporary poster, moved at fifty miles per hour, the speed of an automobile. Both posters could be read easily." "It is easy to realize the implications," Moholy-Nagy concluded: "A new viewpoint in the graphic arts is a natural consequence of this age of speed."[36] According to Moholy-Nagy, the urban landscape "reads" differently through the car window—through the lens of the automobile, as it were. Even though Moholy-Nagy only rarely made the automobile the explicit subject matter of his art, an "automotive" mode of perception can be found throughout his work, where it appears under ubiquitous rubric of "vision in motion." The automobile, to reprise an earlier point, may not be visible as an object within the field of representation, but it is nonetheless present in these works as the field of vision itself. For him, the car becomes a medium for visualization.

Moholy-Nagy's conception of the vehicle as a rival to the camera and as a site for the embodiment of perception anticipates what the media philosopher Paul Virilio has called the "metempsychosis of the passenger," that is, the projection of the phenomenological ground of experience from the body of the operator into the motorized machine. In a passage that recalls the positions of Marx and Moholy-Nagy, Virilio argues that, after the transportation revolution, "between the audiovisual media and the automobile (that is, dromovisual) there is no difference."[37] He points out that this new mode of perception emerges from the interface between the automobile and a network of roads. Just as Vertov's *Man with a Movie Camera* extends the photographic conditions of perception beyond the camera itself, Virilio extends the matrix of "automotive" perception beyond the car, mapping out an entire vehicular complex made of auto-road-signage-architecture:

> "A speed machine" and not solely a "transport machine," the production of the vector-vehicle gives rise to the projection of a sort of illumination, the pairing of motor-wheels engages the pairing of car-road. . . . "Automobile," the means of rapid transmission, appears therefore equally to be "audiovisual," since its passengers are the prey of a gnosis, both visual and auditory. For them and them alone, the car plugged into the network of roads produces an illuminating energy, a visionary experience distinct from that of the pedestrian.[38]

As Virilio explains in these lines, advances in motorized transportation have given rise to spaces of experience and a corpus of knowledge that are foreclosed to those without vehicles. One must climb inside the automobile, Virilio proposes, in order to "decipher an enigma."[39] This enigma is an urban hieroglyph that remains illegible at the speed of walking. Virilio's concern, then, is not that urban space cannot be *physically* traversed by the pedestrian, but that this space, rather, cannot be comprehended by slow foot traffic. As Carlu's experiment suggested to Moholy-Nagy, motorization establishes a semiotic landscape that is cognitively inaccessible to the pedestrian. Just as the horse-drawn buggy works as a key to decode the poster of Toulouse-Lautrec, the automobile is indispensable for decrypting the language of the modern city.

Similar principles were behind one of Moholy-Nagy's most important projects for the production of nonlinear perspective, the *Kinetic-Constructive System* (1928; fig. 1.12). Like the *Light-Space Modulator* that he built two years later, this work is part object, part medium. Although the massive helicoid frustum of the *System* has an obvious debt to Vladimir Tatlin's *Monument to the Third International* (1919), Moholy-Nagy's *System* departs from Tatlin's iconic tower by casting off the openwork metal cage and placing the entire structure on a rotating platform. By removing the stable frame of Tatlin's tower, Moholy-Nagy

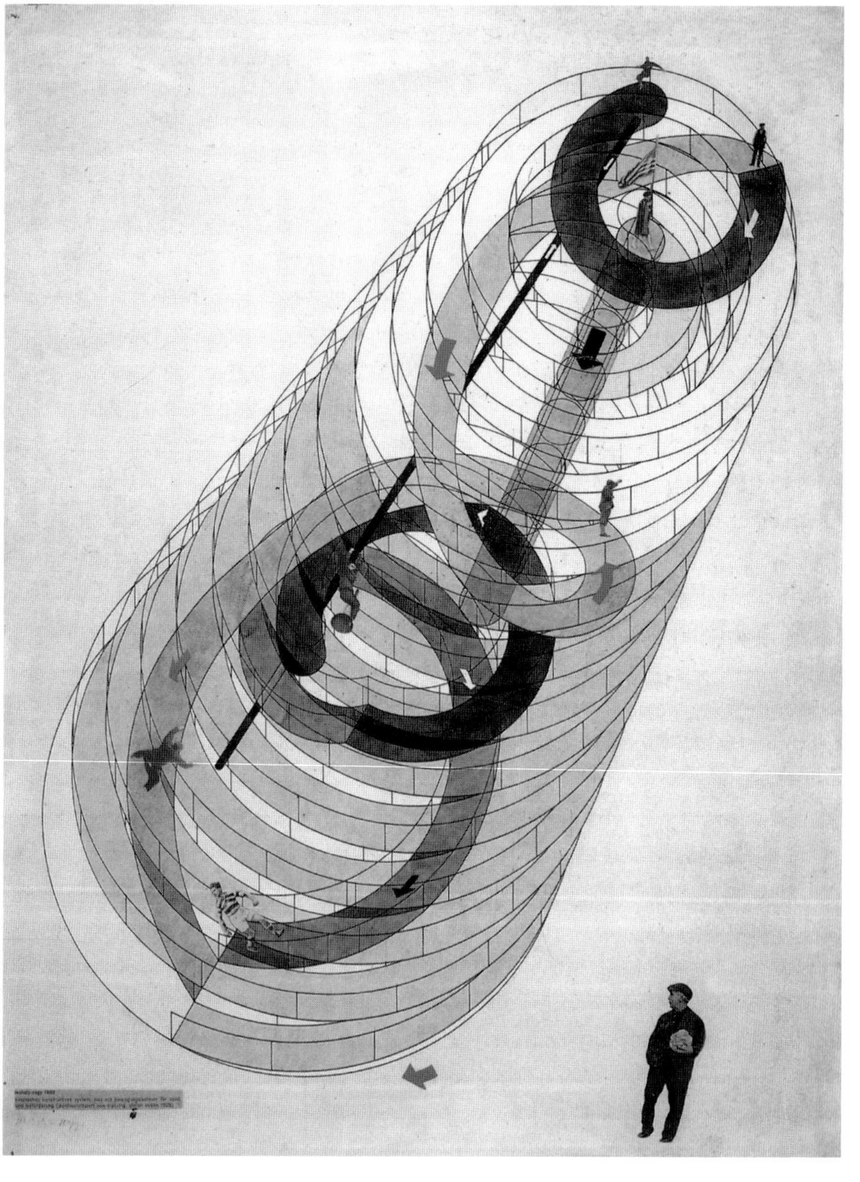

Figure 1.12 László Moholy-Nagy, *Kinetic-Constructive System* (1928). © 2012 Artists Rights Society (ARS), New York/VG Bild-Kunst, Bonn.

dynamizes the entire structure. A transitional form between the automobile and the building, the *System* represented the first step toward a mobile architecture of the future and, as he would later explain, belongs to the same class of constructions as mobile homes and sanitariums that turn with the sun. One of the most important shapes in Moholy-Nagy's vocabulary of forms, the rotating spiral is central to the visual logic of the *System*. Moving counter-clockwise, a primary ramp on the outside appears to drill into the sky, thrusting the ground upward, while an inner ramp produces the converse optical effect, driving downward into the earth. Reversing the rotation of the platform inverts the vectors of these movements. In either case, the revolving structure drives upward past the horizon at the same time that it bores downward into the earth, volatilizing the visual threshold between the ground and sky as it dissolves the horizon line, the stabilizer and guarantor of the perspectival order.

No less problematic than the distinction between ground and sky in the *System* is the distinction between the structure and its surroundings. Like Moholy-Nagy's photograph from that same year, which provides a view both *of* and *from* the Berlin radio tower, the *System* converts a discrete technical object into the ground of perception. According to Moholy-Nagy, with each rotation, the structure slackens the epistemological threshold between inside and outside. Its massive spiral, Moholy-Nagy observed, "revolves from the outside to the inside with constant ascent. Inside and outside are simultaneously seen" (*Vision in Motion*, 256). In an earlier statement on a related project, he explained that he wanted to design "open, eccentric (centrifugal) construction which indicated the tensions of forms and of space, without, however, resolving them."[40] This spatial tension challenged the "oversimplification of form limited to the horizontal, the vertical and the diagonal."[41] In this regard the spiral of the *System* undermined the basic structural principles of the modern skyscraper, which is built out of a series of vertically stacked volumes and which, Moholy-Nagy noted in the early 1920s, is an "unhealthy construction not to be emulated."[42] The oblique bearing of the *System* overturns the fundamental architectural opposition between the wall and the floor[43] at the same time that it challenges the isotopic elementarism of Moholy-Nagy's Bauhaus colleagues. Against the modularity of Bauhaus design, Moholy-Nagy's spiral is an open anti-Gestalt that oscillates inconclusively between figure and ground, between object and frame of vision.

The planimetric projection of the *System*, which Moholy-Nagy made with the help of the engineer Istvan Sebök, shows a structure that is exceedingly complex visually. Pointing to certain ambiguities in the overlapping spirals on the interior of the structure, some critics have suggested that Moholy-Nagy's design was illegible and, as depicted in these plans, impossible to build. Yet the design is in fact extremely precise. Significantly, however, the structure becomes intelligible only when time and movement are factored into the encounter. A recent four-dimensional animation of the model, for example, has demonstrated, against the critics, the utter transparency and feasibility of the *System*.[44] In contrast to the basic shapes used in Bauhaus architecture and object-design, whose elementarity perfectly illustrates the Gestalt principle of *Prägnanz* ("conciseness"), the *System* cannot be comprehended visually all at once from a single vantage. "In order to grasp the true nature of space the observer must project himself through it," explained Siegfried Giedeon, a close friend of Moholy-Nagy.[45] The *System* does not subscribe, then, to the epistemological distinction between subject and object, but instead observes the logic of what Virilio has called the "traject."[46] Here space is experienced not as a perspectival grid but as a topologically dynamic field that must be navigated physically—an aspect underscored by Moholy-Nagy's stipulation that the *System* be used as an athletic complex. Inaccessible to summary visual synopsis, the structure becomes intelligible only by moving through its space, only through an embodied physiological experience.

Reverse Perspective and the "Urge to Isolation"

By thus mobilizing the static spectator—the "platonic monstrosity" of linear perspective—the *System* choreographs an experience of space that is fundamentally at odds with the Euclidean model of space as an empty, infinite, homogeneous container. As his colleague Walter Gropius observed in a 1946 eulogy, Moholy-Nagy had spent his entire life prospecting this particular space: "The goal of his greatest artistic efforts was the conquest of space: he directed his genius into the realms of science and art in order to unravel [*lösen*] the phenomenon of space."[47] The word used by Gropius here, *lösen*, is telling, for it implies both "solving" the riddle of space as well as "releasing," "detaching," or "loosening" those static spatial coordinates that Moholy-Nagy had once described as "unbearable" in their fixity. As we already observed, however, this unbinding of space did not lead the artist to the radically aperspectival compositions of, say, the Dadaists. Moholy-Nagy, who insisted on the essentially constructive nature of his work, searched for new visual logics to depict the experience of non-Euclidean space, rejecting both linear perspective (camera obscura) as well as its determinate negation (Dada), and seeking instead a para-perspectival language that could serve as a symbolic form, or *dispositif*, adequate for this new model of space.

His work does in fact observe a spatial grammar that is not the logic of linear perspective and its Renaissance "anthropocracy." It is a visual system for rendering space that is evident in the glaring perspectival irregularity of the *Kinetic-Constructive System*. As the spectator looks down from the top of the frustum, the figures become larger toward the bottom of the building, violating the law of linear perspective, which stipulates that distant objects appear smaller than proximate ones. Here Moholy-Nagy provides a textbook example of the phenomenon known as *reverse perspective*. Although seldom discussed today as anything other than a pictorial curiosity, the phenomenon of reverse perspective was a central subject of critical discourse in the 1920s, especially in Russia, where the technique became an important strategy for the avant-garde in its quest, after abstraction, to reconstruct spatial systems in visual art without lapsing into the linear perspective long associated with realist painting. (Given Moholy-Nagy's close connections with leading artists in Russia, the appearance of reverse perspective in his work at the same time is unsurprising.[48]) Two years after publishing the above-mentioned essay on the optics of the camera obscura, Nikolai Tarabukin, for example, gave a talk on reverse perspective at the State Academy of Artistic Science's (GAKhN) Section for Spatial Art in 1927.[49]

Better known, however, is the appearance of reverse perspective in El Lissitzky's important essay "A. and Pangeometry" (1925), where the constructivist addressed an entire series of devices for depicting volumetric space on a flat plane, including the staggered overlay of figures, reverse perspective, linear perspective, and axonometry. His catalog of perspectival techniques recalls Panofsky's injunction "to ask of artistic periods and regions not only whether they have perspective, but also which perspective they have." Indeed, the sheer diversity of methods presented by Lissitzky suggests that linear perspective, while still recognized as one possibility for rendering space, had by this point lost its preeminence among these devices. The plurality of spatial devices discussed by Lissitzky reminds us, as well, that the term "*reverse* perspective" is in fact a misnomer, since the device is hardly the opposite of linear perspective: there are more than just two forms of perspective, and, as scholars working on reverse perspective have noted, these two systems do not even perforce exclude one another.[50] Indeed, both regularly appear alongside one another within a single work of art. Linear and reverse perspective emerged at the same time in antiquity and, depending on the model of space dominant within the cosmology of a given culture, each has subsequently enjoyed priority over the other at different moments in the history of art.

"A. and Pangeometry" provides a diagram illustrating the difference between linear and reverse perspectives (fig. 1.13). Lissitzky observes here that the "tip of the visual pyramid either lies in our eyes—therefore in front of the object—or we project is on to the horizon—behind the object. The former concept was chosen by the East, the latter by the West." In the case of reverse perspective on the left, the table with the vase projects out of the pictorial plane into the space of the spectator, while the receding lines of linear perspective, exemplified here by a thumbnail sketch of Leonardo's *Last Supper*, retreat backward to the horizon. Between the two tables, Lissitzky makes a reference to Malevich's great icon of Russian abstraction from 1915, the *Black Square*. This square, which Lissitzky reads as the base of a visual pyramid, oscillates ambiguously between projection and recession ("Where does the tip lie? In depth, or in front?" he asks[51]), echoing Russia's own geographical position between East

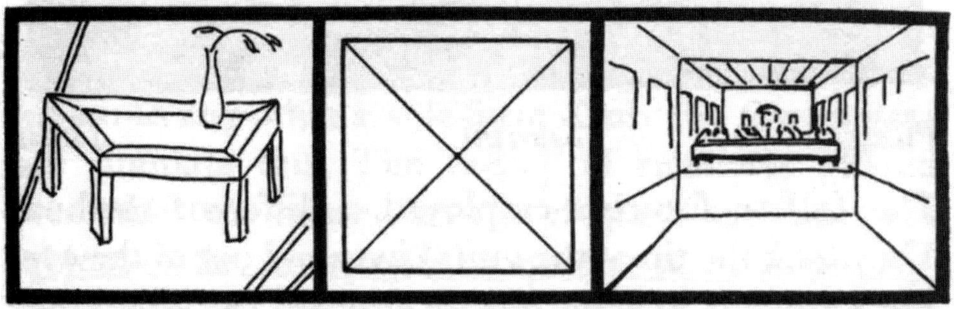

Figure 1.13 El Lissitzky, diagram from "A. and Pangeometry" (1925).

Asia, where reverse perspective dominated in art, and Western Europe, where linear perspective had been the rule since the Renaissance.[52] Lissitzky's identification here of linear perspective with the experience of spatial recession and, conversely, of reverse perspective with that of projection, was a key aspect of Russian analyses of perspective in the 1920s. Since an artwork that is constructed in reverse perspective thrusts outward to the viewer, the evolution of this device culminates with the transition into actual space. For Lissitzky, this development can be seen in the move from cubo-futurist painting to Tatlin's *Counter-Reliefs* (1914), which, he noted in "A. and Pangeometry," are "built from the perspective plane forward into space."[53]

This account of the phenomenology of reverse perspective is borrowed from the work of the philosopher and engineer Pavel Florenskii, with whom Lissitzky and Tarabukin taught in 1921 at the Moscow art school VKhUTEMAS (Higher Artistic-Technical Studios). In 1920 Florenskii had written "Reverse Perspective," an essay now recognized to be one of the most important statements about the device, and in the early 1920s he lectured regularly on the subject at RAKhN (Russian Academy of Artistic Sciences) and VKhUTEMAS, where he held a chair in the "Analysis of Spatiality in Works of Art."[54] In the seminal 1920 essay, he argued, like Panofsky several years later, that perspective has no natural, privileged relationship to sight and that it is, rather, one "method of symbolic expression" on par with other conventional languages.[55] It is but "one of several possible representational schemas," he remarked.[56] Also like Panofsky, Florenskii correspondingly regarded perspective as a cultural artifact rather than a purely physiological or optical phenomenon. He explained that, in contrast to Renaissance perspective, which draws the spectator into the visual expanse of the painting, reverse perspective produces the opposite effect, repelling the spectator "as a mercury sea [*ртутное море*] would repel our bodies."[57] As we just saw, this projectile quality was also noted by Lissitzky; and Tarabukin too observed in his 1927 talk on forms of "eccentric space" that reverse perspective "unfolds from within outwards in contradistinction to perspectival space which folds inwards."[58]

For Florenskii, a Russian Orthodox theologian, this experience of being repelled was integral to the psychology of Byzantine and Russian religious icons, which employed reverse perspective to return the gaze of the spectator in an almost dialogical manner. Presented in stark frontality, the icon depicted in reverse perspective invades the viewer's perceptual and psychic space. For this reason, when viewing a painting that uses reverse perspective, the spectator has the discomfiting sensation of being himself on view. By turning the tables on the viewer and transforming spectating subject into passive object, this device reverses the epistemological polarity of the "modern 'anthropocracy'" inaugurated by linear perspective. Florenskii, whose theological framework was, as one scholar proposes, "rather anti- (or perhaps better, 'otherly'?) humanist,"[59] describes an aesthetic event that displaces the spectator from the locus of perceptual agency, threatening the sovereign subject of Renaissance pictorial space and giving rise to a psychic state closely resembling paranoia.[60] Repulsed by the picture plane, the spectator loses confidence in the stability and security of his position in space. Instead of being the origin of vision, the spectator is now caught in its field.

Here Florenskii's challenge to Renaissance humanism evokes Jacques Lacan's model of vision, which, following Merleau-Ponty's distinction between eye and mind, insists on the difference between the *eye*, the physiological organ that receives optical data, and the *gaze*, defined by Lacan as the psychic field of symbolic intelligibility. The agent of physiological vision may imagine himself to be centered and sovereign, but the subject of the gaze, by contrast, is volatile and unstable. "I see only from one point," Lacan wrote, "but in my existence I am looked at from all sides."[61] What is more, Lacan and Florenskii each illustrated this paranoic condition with reference to two perspectival anomalies that, as we have already seen in this chapter, are closely interconnected in Moholy-Nagy's work: anamorphic projection and reverse perspective. Indeed, the similarities between Florenskii's and Lacan's accounts are striking. If we strip the theology from Florenskii's treatise on perspective, we arrive at a psychic structure that is almost identical to the one described by Lacan, who posits a self constituted as the object, or target, of a gaze originating from the outside. The only difference between Florenskii and Lacan is the name that each gives to the transcendental subject at the origin of this gaze, which Florenskii calls God and Lacan designates *le grand Autre*.

The epistemological inversion of subject and object enacted by reverse perspective was first noted in Oskar Wulff's "Reverse Perspective and the View from Above" ("Die umgekehrte Perspektive und die Niedersicht"), an essay from 1907 that, along with Florenskii's 1920 "Reverse Perspective," has become a cornerstone of research on the topic.[62] Like Florenskii, Wulff begins by observing that both linear and reverse perspectives can be found in antique painting, where they were considered equally legitimate devices for rendering space. This observation demonstrates again that neither system is perforce more accurate than the other; the fluctuating fortunes and authority of these two devices may have more to do with ideological and cultural variables than with physiologically objective depiction. For this reason, Wulff argued that the mechanism of reverse perspective must be understood not according to Renaissance criteria of optical verisimilitude, but through an aesthetic of empathy, or *Einfühlung*. Such art utilizes the faculty that Friedrich Theodor Vischer had famously defined as the "inscription of the human soul into something impersonal" ("die Eintragung der Menschenseele in Unpersönliches").[63] For Vischer, empathy is nothing other than the basic human capacity for *mediated* sensation: it is the psychic mechanism by which the subject projects consciousness into external bodies and comes to perceive the world through these objects.

For Wulff, the reverse perspective of Byzantine and medieval art exploits the human's innate capacity for *Einfühlung*, that is, for mediated experience. The premodern spectator, he writes, did not view the work of art with his own eyes, but instead identified, or empathized, with the dominant personage in the picture and perceived the other elements and figures in the image from this vantage. Thus, in the case of an ivory diptych leaf from 506 AD that shows the consul Areobindus viewing a hunt, Wulff argues that reverse perspective approximates the Roman official's vision as he looks down at the small figures in the Hippodrome below (fig. 1.14). Evaluated according to the criterion of linear perspective, the composition of the figures in the lower half of the relief appears highly idiosyncratic, but if viewed through the eyes of the consul, that is, from a viewpoint internal to the painting, the composition reveals itself to be utterly consistent and logical: from the latter perspective, the figures below do not appear layered on top of one another, as in a depiction of deep space, but each one instead occupies its own individual and separate area, as is proper for objects seen from above, where Areobindus sits enthroned. As with subsequent commentators, Wulff considered this earthward view, or *Niedersicht*, an essential aspect of reverse perspective.[64] The work of art made according to reverse perspective, he argued, was indifferent to the physical position of the spectator before the work, for "the point of departure was within the image itself."[65] Wulff and Florenskii thus concur that reverse perspective unmoors vision and projects the point of view into the artwork, giving rise to a mode of perception that is interior to the image itself. Through this device the ground of vision is installed in the object, which, as a site for empathic projection, becomes, in turn, a medium for sight.

Given the close association between reverse perspective and a mobilized, that is, mediatized, mode of perception, it is not surprising, then, that Moholy-Nagy, whose own optical experiments explored various means for this perceptual transfer from subject to object, would also employ the device of reverse perspective, although never to the exclusion of other systems for rendering space. As we saw earlier, after its decline as a symbolic form, linear perspective would continue to be used, even if it no longer enjoyed the cultural privilege

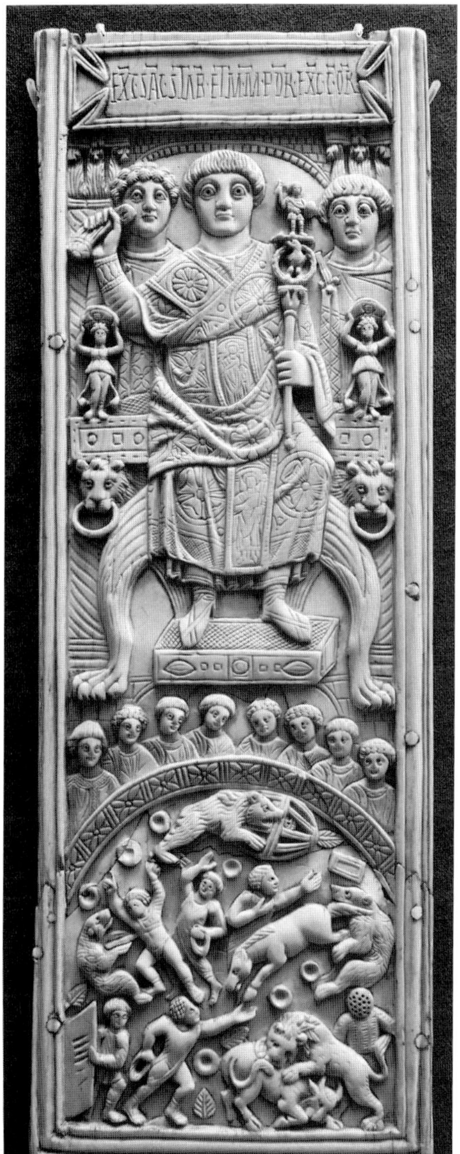

Figure 1.14 *Ivory Diptych of Areobindus* (506 AD). Musée National du Moyen Âge.

it once had. With characteristic syncretism, Moholy-Nagy often uses several of these perspectival techniques simultaneously. In addition to its utilization alongside axonometric projection in the *Kinetic-Constructive System*, he employs reverse perspective as well in his photoplastic from 1926, *City Lights*, also called *Unterseeboot*, or "Submarine" (fig. 1.15). At first glance the viewer assumes that Charlie Chaplin, depicted in his role as the tramp, is in the foreground looking up at the bathing-suit-clad women who are perched atop the translucent planar construction. But it soon becomes clear that the intersecting planes actually move forward from the base, opening toward the spectator and pushing the women in front of Chaplin. Moholy-Nagy's interest here in the physiological interplay of "receding and advancing values," as he put it, recalls Lissitzky's diagram of the optical pyramid oscillating between the linear perspective of the West and the reverse perspective of the East (*Vision in Motion*, 188–189). As is often the case in reverse perspective, objects that are closer to the viewer are here rendered smaller than ones in the distance. With this inversion in spatial polarity, rather than looking up at the women from Chaplin's vantage, the spectator suddenly finds himself looking down at Chaplin from where the women sit. Hence Moholy-Nagy's alternative title for the piece, "Unterseeboot," which puns on the homonym "Unter-*seh*-boot" ("under-*vision*-boat")—a corollary to the *Niedersicht*, or "view from above," that Wulff considered an essential component of reverse perspective.

One of Moholy-Nagy's photoplastics from the year before, *Leda and the Swan (The Myth Reversed)* (see fig. 1.2), presents an even more complex interplay between the "receding and advancing values" of linear and reverse perspective. Indeed, with its bundle of converging optical rays, *Leda and the Swan* invokes the formal conventions of Renaissance perspective almost too scrupulously, even flagrantly. But this system begins to buckle and warp. In this "reversal of the myth"—of perspective, perhaps—the two figures that scramble up the sides of the flickering rays are not drawn in by the receding orthogonals but are repelled by these lines. As in the 1926 photographs of the Schlemmers, the viewer is looking at perspective here rather than through it. Instead of rendering space transparent to reason, the converging lines become an obstacle that impairs the

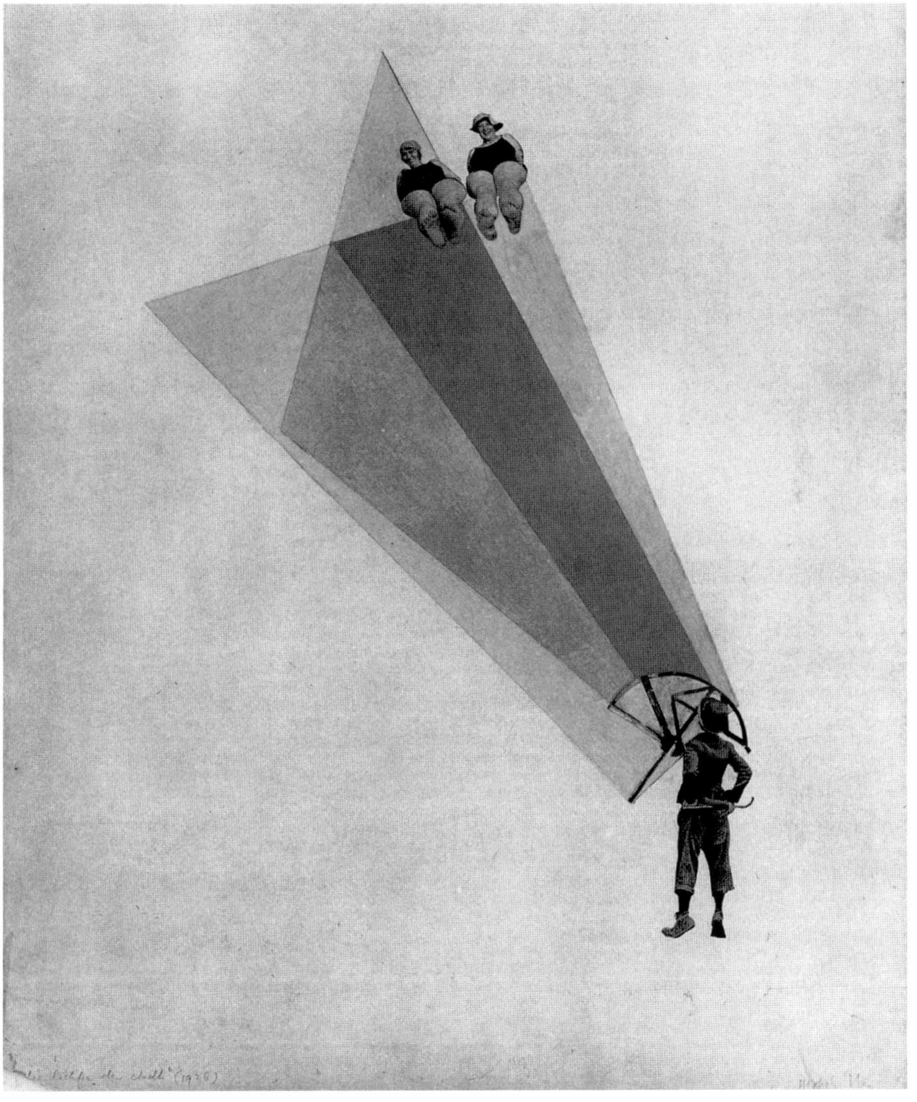

Figure 1.15 László Moholy-Nagy, *City Lights* (1926). © 2012 Artists Rights Society (ARS), New York/VG Bild-Kunst, Bonn.

intelligibility of the scene. What is the object that remains obscured to the left? Contrasted by the sweeping whiteness of the empty paper to the right, this congested mass illustrates what Rudolf Arnheim called the "visual calamity" of linear perspective, which piles objects one atop another so that "foreground hides background" and "front-side hides back-side."[66] In Moholy-Nagy's photoplastic, linear perspective grows opaque and becomes a dense object that, paradoxically, occludes the spectator's vision.

The space depicted in *Leda and the Swan (The Myth Reversed)* is not the homogeneous grid of Euclidean geometry but a fitful cluster of spatially unresolved elements. Moholy-Nagy emphasized the glaring nonintegrality of this space in a later commentary on this work, where he observed that "the best description of their effect would be perhaps to say that each element is pasted on vertical glass panes, which are set up in an endless series each behind the other."[67] His description recalls Marcel Duchamp's *Large Glass*, a work in which, as is well known, the French "anti-retinalist" called the laws of linear perspective into question.[68] Although the receding lines of *Leda and the Swan* would seem to suggest a unified spatial volume, Moholy-Nagy himself claimed, to the contrary, that the space actually reads like a set of stacked glass panes on which each object occupies its own pictorial plane. The bundle of linear rays fails to suture together these partial spaces. Thus, despite their proximity to one another, each element in the photoplastic is completely isolated and sealed off in its own spatial enclosure, a condition Moholy-Nagy compared to the contingent experience of urban life, where random objects and people encounter each other daily in a surrealist overlay of events:

> We travel by streetcar and look out of the window; a car is following us, its windows are also transparent, through which we see a shop with equally transparent windows; in the shop we see customers and salespeople; a person opens the door, people pass by the shop, a policeman holds up a cyclist. We take in all this within the moment, because the windows are transparent and everything happens within our field of vision.[69]

These words describe a field of vision that is constituted as a series of autonomous and local blocks of space that have been superimposed one upon the other. What transpires in the car has no motivated relationship to the customers perusing the shop or to the interaction between the policeman and the cyclist, even though, for a split-second, all of these unconnected events coincide within the visual field.

Here Moholy-Nagy touches upon a spatial disposition found throughout the pictorial practices of New Objectivity. In a 1928 essay, "On the Spatial Psychology of New Objectivity" ("Zur Raumpsychologie der Neuen Sachlichkeit"), the art historian Alfred Neumeyer, a student of Wölfflin and Warburg, argued that the organization of optical space as a set of discontinuous volumes was a feature common to much contemporary painting. He began this analysis of space in interwar art with the observation that, although the artists of the New Objectivity march under a single banner, their paintings in fact have no "structural affinity" (*Strukturverwandschaft*) to one another, and that "New Objectivity" is a "fictive stylistic designation" whose use is unwarranted and erroneous.[70] Like many art critics since, Neumeyer thus maintained that New Objectivity is not a recognizable or consistent pictorial style. What unites the work, rather, is a "shared sensibility" toward the "experience of space," a particular *Raumerlebnis* quite unlike that of Renaissance painting ("Raumpsychologie," 67). The latter understood space as a single homogeneous spatial container, which, encompassing and connecting all things, served as the universal basis for relations between distinct objects. It was for this reason that Panofsky argued in his essay on perspective that the modernist movement most faithful to the principles of quattrocento linear perspective was Impressionism, since the latter's absolutization of atmosphere as a homogeneous field "creates room for bodies to expand plastically and move gesturally, and yet at the same time . . . enables light to spread out into space and in a painterly way dissolve the bodies."[71] The spectator, Panofsky consequently observed, experiences space in Renaissance painting as a "homogenizing fluid."[72] Such an apotheosis of atmosphere results in the total "dematerialization [*Entdinglichung*] of the discrete object," Neumeyer added, following Panofsky ("Raumpsychologie," 68).

By contrast, the painting of the 1920s depicted an aggregate of discrete, local volumes that are established by the things themselves. No longer does a grid unite the contents of the universe; no more ether flows between the objects. Thus, if quattrocento painting dissolved all substance into atmosphere, New Objectivity art, in turn, depicted what the art historian Wieland Schmied characterized as an "airless, glassy space," echoing Moholy-Nagy's description of his photoplastics as a series of "vertical glass planes." New Objectivity painting "eliminates everything that is 'atmospheric'; it seems as if the air has been sucked out" of the work.[73] For this reason, Neumeyer similarly noted that, unlike its Renaissance predecessor, contemporary realist painting produces spatial effects "not through *measurable, stable* distances, but through *dynamic, sensory* condensations" ("Raumpsychologie," 67). The "urge to isolation" that drives New Objectivity painting results in the "strictest segregation of the object" ("Raumpsychologie," 69). As with Moholy-Nagy's stacked glass planes, these works present a series of absolutely relative, local volumes that are unconnected to one another. The New Objectivity artist paints each element with equal detail, ignoring the optical changes that distance creates in the values of color (e.g., the shift from red to blue) and luminosity (e.g., vivid to muted).

In this way, New Objectivity paintings achieve a physiologically impossible compound view in which, according to Neumeyer, "individual elements are recorded in microscopic close-up, and then assembled together in a manner that presents them at a normal optical distance" ("Raumpsychologie," 70). This strategy, he wrote, "evokes images that the eye obtains through a reversed opera glass and that have an unusual depth which reaches far beyond that of reality; but at the same time, the clarity of the optical image does not degenerate with the increasing depth of vision" ("Raumpsychologie," 71).[74] Neumeyer's language here, which gravitates to metaphors about optical prosthesis, suggests that, despite its proclaimed antitechnicism, the easel painting of the 1920s continues to summon the visual effects produced by technical media, even if this mediation was obscured and disavowed by the myth of unassisted and unmediated artistic creation. The resulting view, which "mixes together images made at a distance and images made up close" ("Raumpsychologie,"

70–71), posits a radically uncentered space that recalls the mobility of Moholy-Nagy's "unleashed camera." This restless gaze encircles every object, no matter how distant, as if it were within immediate reach. Thus Neumeyer observes, for example, that the painters of the *valori plastici*, an Italian cognate of New Objectivity, work with a notion of a physical space that is "reconstructed haptically" ("Raumpsychologie," 70).

Commentators on New Objectivity painting have argued that the rigorous isolation of individual things, as well as the absence of any unifying atmosphere, serves as a metaphor for psychological anomie. This may well be the case, but this "spatial psychology," as Neumeyer called it, is more than a mere metaphor; it also registers a structural change in the symbolic modeling of space in the 1920s that had far-reaching consequences for categories of subjectivity and experience. According to the philosopher Oswald Spengler, the modern epistemology of nonlinear space bore a surprising resemblance to that of Greek antiquity, which conceived of space as a series of local stereometric volumes rather than as an infinite geometral grid. This model of space, he wrote, "includes each separate thing as a well-defined, comprehensible and present entity. The sum of such things constitutes neither more nor less than the whole world, and the interspaces between them, which for us are filled with the impressive symbol of the Universe of Space are for them the nonent (*τὸ μὴ ὄν*)." In the transition from antiquity to modernity, Spengler continued, it is "the underlying form *a priori* of Classical cognition, bodiliness as such, which is replaced exactly in the Kantian world-picture by that Space out of which Kant maintained that all things could be 'thought forth.' . . . The whole Classical mathematic is at bottom *stereometry* (solid geometry)."[75] Antique culture had no concept for space as a stable a priori of experience, that is, for a Euclidean space that "absorbs into itself and begets out of itself the substantiality of all things." Such a culture, which "knows no word for, and therefore has no idea of, space," forecloses the "homogenizing liquid" (Panofsky) of Renaissance perspective as "the nonent, *τὸ μὴ ὄν*, that which *is not*."[76] This stereometric model of space was, in Spengler's analysis, the experience of space to which post-Renaissance culture was now returning.

Florenskii too asserted the contemporaneity of the non-Euclidean and topological model of space. In a series of lectures entitled "The Analysis of Spatiality and Time in the Visual Arts" delivered at VKhUTEMAS, he elaborated on this heterogeneous and plural notion of space. Similar to Spengler, whose opus he likely read, Florenskii characterized the interstices between things as the "nonent" (*τὸ μὴ ὄν*): here it is the object itself that makes possible the existence of space, while everything outside of these local matrices of encounter simply *is not*.[77] For Florenskii, entities existed only insofar as they were external to, isolated from, and noncoincident with one another. This quality he called *внеположность*, or "extra-positionality."[78] In contrast to the isotropic space of Euclidean geometry and Kantian philosophy, which is "indifferent" (*безразлично*) to the objects that it contains[79] and which thereby denies the objective particularity and polarity of telluric space,[80] contemporary space, he wrote, must be navigated as an aggregate of local volumes. According to Florenskii, the discoveries of Lobachevsky, Poincaré, and Einstein had demonstrated that the structure of modern space was conditioned by the material thing, which he characterized as a "force field" (*силовое поле*). "One could say that things themselves are nothing other than 'folds' [*складки*] or 'creases' [*морщины*] of space, particular sites of spatial curvature."[81] Space, according to Florenskii, does not preexist the thing, because it is the thing that itself defines space. Space, in other words, has no properties extrinsic to itself.

What is more, Florenskii argued that reverse perspective served as the symbolic expression of this dynamic and decentered non-Euclidean space. Whereas linear perspective presumes an immobilized spectator who contemplates the world as if "though a chink in a prison wall," the subject who is interpellated by reverse perspective, by contrast, encounters the world as if "through the window of an automobile."[82] This mobilized spectator experiences the world not as a uniform space, but as a series of individual sites, local gyres of space-time. Such a cosmos, Florenskii concluded, is constructed according to the principles of solid stereometry rather than abstract geometry.

In a 1923 essay entitled "Linear Perspective in Art and the Visual Perception of Real Space," the Russian art historian Anatolii Bakushinskii (1883–1939) sought to demonstrate empirically the connection between reverse perspective and stereometric space.[83] A specialist in the physiology of perception, Bakushinskii was also a member of the State Academy of Artistic Science (GAKhN), the institution where Florenskii and Tarabukin both spoke on reverse perspective. (Bakushinskii would make reference in his 1923 essay to Florenskii's lectures on reverse perspective, just as Tarabukin, in turn, mentioned Bakushinskii's text in his 1927 talk.) Bakushinskii began his 1923 essay with the observation that the recent boom in scholarly research on reverse perspective indicated a far-reaching cultural crisis in the organization and representation of space.[84] However, he continued, he was not satisfied with the preceding accounts provided by Wulff and Florenskii, finding the former's recourse to empathy far too psychologistic and the latter's theology far too unscientific. Bakushinskii, by contrast, proposed a purely physiological account of the phenomenon, which, he argued, could be explained by the stereometric configuration of our optical apparatus. One of the schemes in his essay illustrates his argument (fig. 1.16). When the square *ABCD* is viewed from the two points S_i and S_{ii}, which represent the individual eyes, the resulting image—a synthesis of S_i and S_{ii}—will be the trapezoid abc_id_i. Because we are binocular creatures, the far side of this figure, bc_i, appears longer than the side that is closer to the viewer, ad_i. The trapezoid opens outward toward the horizon. The square, in other words, is seen in reverse perspective. As the object comes closer to the viewing subject, the parallax differential between the two eyes will increase, the far side will grow even longer, and the impression of reverse perspective will become even more pronounced. Conversely, with increasing distance the discrepancy in the angle of vision diminishes between the two eyes and the two images become more or less identical. At the greatest distance, then, the two eyes would become, in effect, monocular.[85]

Bakushinskii thus concluded that the optical impression of reverse perspective is most pronounced when objects are closest to the viewer, where they are perceived volumetrically. Such vision is dynamic and embodied. That Wulff had intuitively associated reverse perspective in art with the *Niedersicht* made perfect sense, Bakushinskii explained, because reverse, that is, volumetric perspective applies to objects that are close to the viewer and that are often located

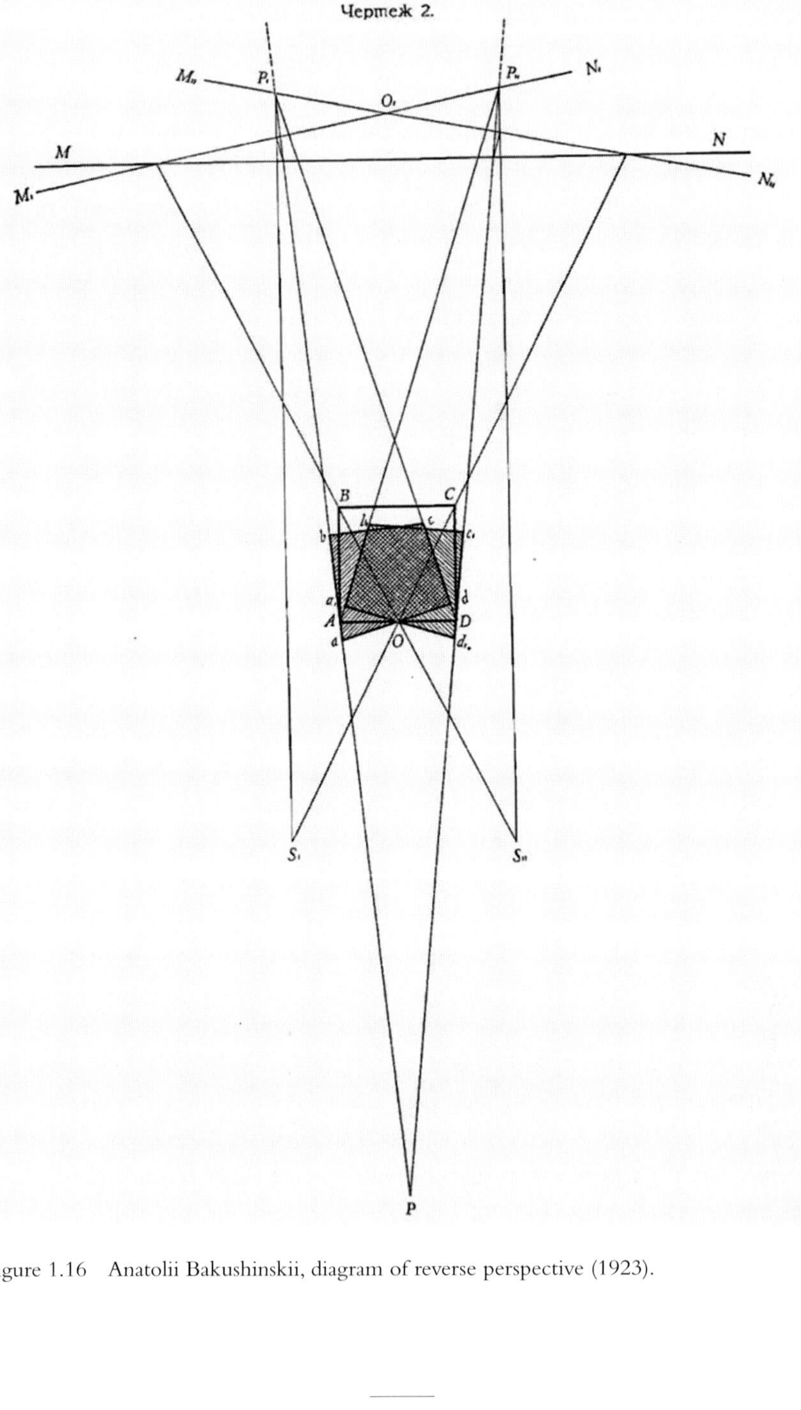

Figure 1.16 Anatolii Bakushinskii, diagram of reverse perspective (1923).

in the lower third of the painting, where the viewer looks down at the object as if it were in her very hands. This stratification of the artwork is clearly evident in the Areobindus triptych. In Bakushinskii's account, then, linear and reverse perspective are not mutually exclusive devices, for both are physiologically legitimate ways to depict space. For him, the difference lies, rather, in the qualities of the space that the artist chooses to emphasize: reverse perspective, which is binocular and stereometric, corresponds to objects that are proximate, tactile, and exist in curved space, while Renaissance perspective, which is monocular, better suits phenomena that are distant, purely optical, and arrayed within geometric space. Linear perspective pushes the field of vision away from the viewer, whereas reverse perspective thrusts it toward the viewer, into her hands. For this reason, the perceptual shift from linear to reverse perspective also entails an axial rotation, for linear perspective privileges the horizontal axis of the distant landscape, whereas reverse perspective privileges the vertical axis where the prehensile subject encounters the world of proximate and manipulable things. In turn, each mode of perception sets in motion an entire set of cultural and ideological valences that Bakushinskii, like Lissitzky, maps out geographically in the opposition between East Asia and Western Europe.[86] For example, Bakushinskii invokes the image of an Eastern man, a figure who, sitting on the floor and surrounded by objects that are in direct reach, makes his paintings in conformance with the *Niedersicht* of reverse perspective. In contrast to the intimacy and connectedness that Bakushinskii's Easterner experiences with the world around him—a world close at hand—the expansive, monocular vision of Renaissance man, he continues, presumes a haughty ego that posits itself at a distance from all things. Here Bakushinskii's account of the psychology of linear perspective and the vertical posture of easel-painting closely conforms to Heidegger's epistemology of modern man, who stands distinct and apart from the object (*Gegen-stand*) before him, and who maintains this degree of cognitive remoteness by interposing a membrane of representations between himself and the world.[87]

Bakushinskii's association of linear perspective with vast optical expanse and of reverse perspective with touch returns us once again to the work of Moholy-Nagy. For Moholy-Nagy, who regularly used the device of reverse perspective in his photoplastics, placed haptic values at the center of his artistic practice, exploring a condition that one media theorist recently dubbed "tactimediality."[88] His photograms, which were made provisionally, even gropingly, in the weak light of a darkroom, record events that transpire in a dim realm cut off from the pellucid field of the visual.[89] With Moholy-Nagy, the haptic and stereometric dimensions of aesthetic experience make inroads even into single-shot photography, a practice that previously had served as the technical apotheosis and ideological guarantor of linear perspective: as one of the artist's Hungarian compatriots observed in a 1930 essay on his work, even the straight photography of Moholy-Nagy demonstrates the fact that the camera's "vision is more tactile than man's with one eye, and in the case of a stereoscopic shot it reflects reality in a more tactile manner than man can do with both his eyes."[90]

This analysis, which complicates Damisch's claim that the modern epoch is "massively 'informed' by the perspective paradigm through photography," can be taken beyond the work of Moholy-Nagy and applied to New Vision photography in general. Thus, in an essay on German interwar photography, Rosalind Krauss observes, for example, that during the Weimar period the camera advances again and again toward the limits of the visual, and upon each encounter with the condition of its own possibility, lapses into the haptic. At these moments, the eye cedes its privilege to the hand, and New Vision comes perilously close to no vision. Krauss identifies "an image frequently repeated within the commercial photography of the '20s and '30s, in which the experience is of the photographer looking down at his or her own body." This "particular type of somatic setting," she explains, establishes a "prehensile relation to the world" that is constituted in the glance downward, to the hands.[91] In this pivot from the orthogonal projection down to the hands and to the objects within their immediate reach, photography enacts the *Niedersicht* of reverse perspective. Here, in the transfer from the optical to the tactile, the camera obscura attempts the impossible: to contradict the laws of linear perspective that are its very founding charter.

Thus we see why Moholy-Nagy chose to designate his photomontage work with the curious locution "photo*plastic*": following the perceptual structure of reverse perspective, the physiological experience of the spectator before these works is sculptural and stereometric before it is optical and geometric. It is not accidental that his comparison of the photoplastics to "glass panes . . . set up in an endless series each behind the other" evokes the impressions made by a stereoscope, the nineteenth-century binocular device that presents the spectator with a discontinuous succession of figures that appear like flat cutouts separated from one another by insuperable spatial intervals. The device anticipates the "spatial psychology" of New Objectivity, which Neumeyer diagnosed as an "urge to isolation." Against the unified ether of Renaissance perspective, the stereoscope depicts a congeries of discrete and incommensurable things, which are stacked one upon another like so many two-dimensional transparencies. The space that it posits is not gradual and continuous, but multiple and planar. For this reason, scholars have underscored the haptic dimension to the experience of viewing a stereoscopic image.[92] Despite their glossy finish, then, photoplastics such as *Leda and the Swan (The Myth Reversed)* turn out to be thoroughly tactile. Indeed, such works clearly demonstrate that even art with no emphatic material signature or discernible trace of its creator's hand can invoke the spectator's sensation of touch. Smoothness or polish in a work does not preclude a haptic dimension of aesthetic experience. Recognizing this, Moholy-Nagy, unlike many of his contemporaries, avoided identifying surface evidence of material workmanship with the sensation of touch. "I do not regard facture as being the equivalent of tactile values [*Tastwert*]," he declared in 1927.[93] A glossy photograph or advertisement can be experienced by the spectator haptically, he claimed, just as a coarsely textured canvas, conversely, can give the impression of pure opticality.

This preoccupation with stereometric space and *Tastwert* also explains the otherwise puzzlingly prominent place Moholy-Nagy gave to the painter Paul Cézanne in both of his major theoretical treatises, *Von Material zu Architektur* (translated as *The New Vision*) and *Vision in Motion*. The kinship that he felt with the French Post-Impressionist was sustained not by any stylistic filiations between their work, but was based instead on the "spatial psychology," to use Neumeyer's term, that they shared in common. Moholy-Nagy credited Cézanne with the discovery of "a new space-consciousness [that opposed] the cherished tradition of the renaissance painting" (*Vision in Motion*, 113). If, as the culmination of linear perspective, Impressionism irradiated and dissolved material bodies into a luminous atmosphere, Cézanne, by contrast, emphasized the tectonics of solid forms and a haptic mode of interacting with the world. Moholy-Nagy's debt to Cézanne was immediately recognized by his contemporaries. Kállai, for one, compared Moholy-Nagy to the French painter who had "tried to bring Impressionism to the same level of stability and monumentality as ancient art with the help of the architectonic laws of solid geometry,"[94] which is to say, the laws of stereometry.

Given the commonalities between the artistic projects of Moholy-Nagy and Cézanne, it is not surprising that scholarship on Cézanne long ago discerned the device of reverse perspective in his work, even if it was never identified as such. In the important 1938 study *Cézanne and the End of Scientific Perspective*, Fritz Novotny, for example, encountered spatial irregularities in Cézanne's painting that should by now be familiar to us:

> the spectator often cannot establish the size differentials between objects in the distance and those in the foreground with any certainty. . . . [I]n many cases actual changes in the relative magnitudes are introduced so that objects in the foreground, which are large in perspective, are depicted slightly smaller, or, conversely, that objects in the background appear magnified in the image.[95]

Seven years later, in his famous essay on Cézanne, Merleau-Ponty repeated Novotny's analysis, suggesting that this curious form of perspective generates a chiasmus between the optical and the proprioceptive that accesses the most creaturely and "inhuman" registers of embodied experience.[96] "By remaining faithful to the phenomena in his investigations of perspective," he observes, "Cézanne discovered what recent psychologists have come to formulate: the lived perspective, that which we actually perceive, is not a geometric or a photographic one. The objects we see close at hand appear smaller, those far away seem larger than they do in a photograph."[97] Thrusting forward into the spectator's space, this painting passes from the vertical to the horizontal, from the vista to the *Niedersicht*. To borrow the description of Yve-Alain Bois, Cézanne folds "the ground plane vertically over the elevation in the lower part of some of his paintings, as if, as the space between himself and the represented object narrowed, he were forced to lower his eyes to take in his feet."[98]

If Cézanne had discovered the value of reverse perspective and stereometric space for a critique of Renaissance humanism already at the close of the nineteenth century, wherein lies Moholy-Nagy's own contribution to this critique of linear perspective and its "anthropocracy" nearly three decades later?[99] It seems that the difference between their respective antihumanisms can be found in their contrasting orientations toward the human sensorium, the one phenomenological and the other radically historical. As Merleau-Ponty argued, Cézanne's work creates a deeply organic encounter with the world that seeks to turn back the evolutionary clock, as it were, by stripping consciousness of all trappings of industrial civilization and higher symbolic distinctions. Cézanne's haptic primitivism restores "primordial perception,"[100] as he put it. But Moholy-Nagy is blind to this aspect, viewing Cézanne not as a deserter from mechanical civilization but as its herald and engineer.[101] According to Moholy-Nagy, Cézanne "gave up the rigid classical viewpoint and tried to 'embrace' the object with both eyes . . . by shifting his position of observation in the same painting. This anticipated the visual situation of the driver at the wheel of the speeding car or plane" (*Vision in Motion*, 118). For Moholy-Nagy, the motorized machine did not preclude the perceptual chiasmus between sight and touch ("to 'embrace' the object with both eyes"), but, to the contrary, facilitates this synesthetic experience. Unlike Merleau-Ponty's version of Cézanne, which is underwritten by phenomenology's fantasy of primitive corporeal plenitude and which presumed an integral and timeless human body as the inalienable condition for consciousness, Moholy-Nagy did not presume the universality or uniformity of the body and its senses. For him the human sensorium is something to be actively created, not restored, as phenomenology would have it. And as we have seen, Moholy-Nagy drafted a diverse variety of technical apparatuses, from the camera obscura to the speeding car, into this project of configuring the senses. Whether audiovisual, dromological, or otherwise, each of the media works as a "grindstone for the senses" (*Vision in Motion*, 29), breaching new sensory channels and restructuring the foundations of aesthetic experience and artistic culture:

> The discovery of new artistic materials, the invention of photography and film, the existence of artificial lighting which can be controlled at will, the new possibilities in transport, the automobile and the aeroplane, the growth of new principles governing mechanical production and the conception of montage have not only contributed to produce a new architecture, but also brought about a new receptivity for the new fine arts which are just coming into being.[102]

As Moholy-Nagy observed in these lines, the task of these media is to incorporate new platforms of embodied experience, new forms of sensory "receptivity." They "establish far-reaching *new relationships* between familiar and as yet unfamiliar optical, acoustical, and other functional phenomena so that these are increasingly absorbed through the functional apparatuses [*Funktionsapparaten*]" of the senses.[103] If we bring these words into concert with the paradigms of negative anthropology discussed in this book's introduction, which charted an evolutionary path for man that proceeds through prosthetic exteriorization, it becomes clear why Moholy-Nagy considered the technical media as instruments in the ongoing project of man's hominization, or *Menschwerdung*. For a constitutionally "deficient being," the media represent models, or prototypes, of the human senses. To quote Friedrich Kittler: "There are media because man (according to Nietzsche) is the undetermined animal [*das nicht festgestellte Tier*]."[104]

Afterword: The New Geocentrism

If linear perspective's "evolution from aggregate space to systematic space" abandoned "the idea of a cosmos with the middle of the earth as its absolute center," as Panofsky noted,[105] it would be logical to infer, conversely, that the fortunes enjoyed by reverse perspective in the 1920s and the revival of a stereometric notion of space from antiquity entailed a return to a geocentric cosmology. And this was in fact the case. Two years after writing his famous treatise on reverse perspective, Florenskii published an essay that drew on his work in physics and electrodynamics to revive, in effect, the geocentric world-picture of antiquity.[106] This text argued that the topological space of Einstein's theory of relativity, at the foundation of which was Riemann's model of curved and nonhomogeneous space, refuted the Copernican cosmology and vindicated the Ptolemaic one. Here Florenskii was not alone. Following the lead of the physicist Ernst Mach, the progenitor of relativity theory who had asserted that "[b]oth the Ptolemaic and the Copernican modes are equally correct,"[107] during these years many artists and scientists moved away from the Newtonian idea of the universe as an endless, uniform, and static spatial container. After the overthrow of the Euclidean model of infinite space, the universe was now seen as an aggregate space made of local volumes.

The dismantling of the Copernican model continued through the century. Even in the 1970s, the Nobel Prize–winning astronomer Fred Hoyle would concur that "we cannot say that the Copernican theory is 'right' and the Ptolemaic theory is 'wrong' in any meaningful physical sense."[108] And while relativity theory's refutation of Copernicanism did not necessarily reestablish the earth as the absolute center of the universe, as Florenskii supposed, the stereometric model of space depicted by reverse perspective did nonetheless make the earth into the relative, or at least practical, nucleus of the cosmos. The earth becomes a privileged object among multiple possible centers. In the same way that linear and reverse perspective would coexist in Moholy-Nagy's work as two options for rendering pictorial space in its different qualities, the cosmological orders that inhere to each of these devices—the Copernican and Ptolemaic frameworks, respectively—would also henceforth both be considered legitimate and on equal par. On the eve of the twenty-first century, the cosmonaut Sergei Kriklaev would still defend geocentrism from a pragmatic point of view, explaining that the earth enjoys a psychological privilege over other celestial bodies. Even from space, "the Earth is given special consideration. And we end up differentiating one direction from the rest: the direction of the Earth. . . . So its direction can't be one among others."[109]

One of the most remarkable intellectual artifacts of the "geocentric turn" in the early twentieth century is a series of essays written by Edmund Husserl in the early 1930s that describe a phenomenology strikingly resonant with the reading of Moholy-Nagy presented in this chapter.[110] In these texts, which anticipate his important 1936 essay on the origin of geometry, Husserl concerns himself with issues of a decidedly pictorial nature, issues such as the system of optical perspective, methods for evaluating relative proximity and distance, the distinction between figure and ground, and relations of objects vis-à-vis the horizon line. Taking as a point of departure Einstein's theory of relativity and its topological model of space, Husserl arrived in these texts, much like Florenskii, at the conclusion that "the originary ark, the earth, does not move." The earth, Husserl explained, is beyond movement and rest since it is itself "the ark which makes possible in the first place the sense of all movement and all rest as a mode of movement."[111] Because it is the "primordial homeland" of humanity, he observed, the earth functions as the anchoring "ground" or "basis" (*Boden*) against which the movement of each objectual "body" (*Körper*) is measured.

One might expect that Husserl's recentering of the universe according to a Ptolemaic cosmology would reinforce the well-known phenomenological model of the subject as a stable, timeless, and static being—a mental configuration accurately characterized by Deleuzian David Rodowick as a set of "immobile poses."[112] But just the opposite is the case. In these late writings Husserl in fact revised this essentialist phenomenology, describing instead a consciousness constituted through movement and difference rather than stasis and identity. His topological model of space presents a "system of possible kinaesthetic sites as stations, as places where rest begins and where it ends for continuous kinaesthetic actions."[113] Borrowing from contemporary Gestalt psychology, Husserl continued to maintain the fundamental epistemological distinction between discrete objects (*Körper*) and the ground against which they move (*Boden*), and yet in these texts Husserl also noted that these two terms are constantly reversing their polarity in practical experience. Figure and background are continuously shifting back and forth into one another. As the site of transfer between stasis and movement, earth and figure, ground and body, Husserl identifies a third element, which he calls the "ground-body" (*Bodenkörper*). This is the name he gives to a moving object onto which have been transferred the properties of the ground, or phenomenological "basis."

In all of Husserl's examples, the "ground-body" is a motorized vehicle such as an automobile, a locomotive, or an airplane. For him, as for Moholy-Nagy, such machines possess an exceptional status within our perceptual system. As bodies into which the subject empathically projects sensation, these mechanical "arks," as he calls them, present new possibilities for somatization, new *Bodenkörper* for phenomenological embodiment. In this way, mechanical "arks" such as cars and trains resemble the *Ur*-"ark" of the earth itself, the primordial context for all human sensory perception. Each such vehicle functions, in effect, as a small earth, as a field of perception. Husserl observed, for example, that "I can be in a moving car which is then my ground-body; I can also be borne by a railway car, in which case my ground-body is first of all the body carrying me while moving, and in order for this to happen, the ground-body is again the railway car, etc." Although the "ground-body" of the car is itself a moving object, once the subject projects herself into it, making the vehicle into the basis of perception, "the car is experienced at rest. But when I look out the window I say that the railway car is moving even though I see that the countryside is in motion." Logically, the subject knows the car to be a body, or *Körper*, but empathically she experiences it as a ground, or *Boden*. As Husserl observed, each assimilation of a new mechanical apparatus to the perceptual framework of the subject necessarily reconfigures the values of figure and ground. "I encounter an auto-motive body. I can climb onto it, dismount or jump from it. The appearance of rest and motion of external bodies is reversed when I jump from an auto-motive body."[114]

Perhaps these mechanical "ground-bodies" are a means not just of conveyance but of sensation and knowledge, Husserl speculates in conclusion: "Does being moved in space, mechanically (for example: being driven, being carried etc.) accomplish nothing for the constitution, does it accomplish nothing essential for the possibility of empathy [*Einfühlung*]?"[115] Recalling Vischer's definition of empathy as the "inscription of the human soul into something impersonal," Husserl's discussion of motorized bodies begins to look strikingly like Moholy-Nagy's "vision in motion." Somewhere between an opaque object and a luminous medium, the automobile itself is a kind of symbolic form, a perceptual framework that, like linear perspective, can be looked through (*per-spicere*). Like photography, the motor vehicle offers a new site of incarnation, new flesh for the metempsychosis of the passenger.

2

The Time of Capital: Three Industrial Novels

Between Development and Natural History: *Union of the Strong Hand*

In October 1931, the Russian author Il'ia Ehrenburg wrote to Erik Reger requesting information about the sources of his documentary novel *Union of the Strong Hand* (*Union der festen Hand*), which had recently won the most prestigious literary award of its day, the Kleist-Preis. At the time, the prolific Bolshevik was himself at work on a massive reportage trilogy about revolution, industrialization, and modernity, entitled *Chronicle of Our Times* (*Khronika nashikh dnei*). In his letter, Ehrenburg explained that, although several of the characters in Reger's novel were obviously modeled on real-life figures such as the industrialist Gustav Krupp von Bohlen und Halbach and the far-right media mogul Alfred Hugenberg, it was more difficult to discern the identities of other figures in *Union of the Strong Hand*, which had been marketed as an exposé of Ruhr industry based on Reger's firsthand experiences working in the press and communications department at Krupp between 1920 and 1927.[1] Ehrenburg's request seemed reasonable enough: after all, what distinguished the documentary genre as such was its ironclad guarantee of referentiality.

But Reger refused to provide the key to his *roman à clef*. In fact, as a rule, he rejected all such inquiries about the sources of his book, prompting scholars to speculate that his reticence was calculated to protect the identities of those at Krupp.[2] Reger's written reply to Ehrenburg, however, suggests a different motivation for his refusal: "It is true that I worked in a documentary mode, but the names aren't just cover names for living people. Rather, they are distinct incarnations of industrial types that have been crystallized out of real-life models."[3] According to Reger, Ehrenburg's desire to know the real identities behind the characters misconstrued the purpose of *Union of the Strong Hand*, since it assumed that the novel documented individuals working in Weimar industry—when in fact the modern industrial enterprise was the last place one encounters individuals. The modern corporation produces not individuated personalities but abstract types. In asking for the names of actual people, Ehrenburg had thus committed a kind of category error. As Reger pointed out elsewhere, *Union of the Strong Hand* should not be mistaken for an *Erziehungsroman* (a "novel of education"),[4] a literature fettered by biographical conventions and thus unsuited to depict the highly abstract mechanisms of Ruhr industry. This kind of anthropomorphism was utterly out of place in the genre of industrial novel, which sought to depict the paradoxes of economic modernization. Today's rationalized industrial system had no use for individuals, Reger observed. "It is absurd enough that the character of the entrepreneur is put on display now more than ever before," he told an audience in 1933. "But this overcompensation can conceal only for a limited time the fact that, in reality, a dissolution has taken place."[5]

Weimar's most celebrated industrial novel, *Union of the Strong Hand*, depicts this dissolution through a tale of generational succession, in which the old Manchester-style industrial patriarch is replaced by a young management team. With this transformation in the power structure, leaders of industry such as the old Risch-Zander (whom Ehrenburg had assumed to be a veiled reference to Krupp) fade away, even though their apparitions are maintained by their corporate press departments to endow a diffuse industrial enterprise with an illusion of intentionality and a sense of human scale. After working for seven years in the publicity bureau at Krupp, Reger concluded that luminaries of industry such as Krupp "do not exist at all in reality; they have been made into slides that are put behind the lens of the press department and projected like gigantic shadows on a screen." Little more than a brand name, the old Krupp is no more real or substantial than Betty Crocker (also, incidentally, an invention of the 1920s). The integrated corporate enterprise of these years, which encompassed a vast economic system spanning banking, manufacturing, marketing, and distribution, represented a significant evolution beyond the earlier practices of capitalism, when the scale of the business enterprise was still modest enough to be overseen by a single individual. In the mid-nineteenth century, David Harvey explains,

> Industrial activity . . . was organized almost entirely on the lines of the family business enterprise, using methods of accounting and business practices which were extremely traditional in the sense that the entrepreneur of the 1840s would have felt quite at home in the business milieu of fourteenth-century Italian merchants. Ownership and management were one and the same, the size of the firm was such that the whole industrial structure could reasonably be characterized as highly decentralized.[6]

At this earlier moment, financial and marketing systems, for example, were not directly involved to any significant degree with actual production. But with the establishment of the first joint stock companies, a process of vertical integration ensued that eventually displaced the model of the family business completely. In an effort to overcome the managerial limitations of the family business, which was no longer capable of coping with the scale of the enterprise, ownership and management of the firm were henceforth increasingly separated. Industrial patriarchs such as Krupp were eventually phased out of the daily operations of the company.

Union of the Strong Hand recasts the transition from capitalism's so-called heroic phase to the era of modern monopoly capitalism as a literary-generic shift from the *Familienroman* to the *Industrieroman*. With this formal evolution the novel sheds its human countenance. In contrast to the nineteenth century, when management and ownership were still identical, and there was still a direct correspondence between the operations of the firm and the bourgeois entrepreneur, the company outgrows the contours of the individual's biography in the era of monopoly capitalism. Expanding corporate networks begin to integrate everything from the finance capital that backs the enterprise and the foreign colonies that supply the raw materials to the advertising firms that generate consumer desires for the product. Nothing remains of the quaint anthropomorphic contours of the company familiar from a century earlier. As the great industrialist Henry Ford himself observed in his 1923 memoire *My Life and Work*, a "big business is really too big to be human. It grows so large as to supplant the personality of the man."[7]

For Reger, then, industrial rationalization is just as fatal a process for the industrialist as it is for the assembly-line workers. It restructures all levels of the enterprise, from the factory floor and middle management to the press office and executive board. Over the course of the novel's 700 pages, the industrial Moloch swallows up every protagonist it encounters. The destruction of the identities of the characters is registered symbolically in the disappearance of their names, the very markers of selfhood. The two main characters in *Union of the Strong Hand*, for example, the revolutionary worker Adam and his sister Paula, both forfeit their family name, Griguszies. Adam Germanifies the name to become Grieghöfer, while Paula loses the same name through marriage. The effacement of names in the novel exemplifies for Reger the fate of identity and individuality within in an impersonal, decentered industrial complex. "Thus the trust devoured not only objects, but also names. Whatever it couldn't uproot from the soil it would at least erase from memory."[8]

Hence, tokens of selfhood were an anachronism at Krupp, a point that Ehrenburg missed in his request for Reger to name names. Two years after Ehrenburg contacted him, Reger repeated the same caveat to a Frankfurt audience: "I will have to disappoint those among you who expected . . . a kind of roman à clef, a pillory of some specific case. I don't know any specific cases"

(*Schriften*, 1:271). Systems, not individuals, were the subject of his novel, Reger insisted.[9] Because of his skepticism toward forms of biographical depiction, which he saw as particularly ill-equipped to deal with modern corporate entities, Reger had a predictably troubled relationship with traditional character-based narrative genres. He was in fact uncertain if he should even designate *Union of the Strong Hand* as a novel. So many of the devices that were specific to the realist novel, from its use of characters to the linear temporalities of narration, had no place in his analysis of Krupp. Modern industrial and commercial networks, Reger explained, had become so complex that it was no longer possible to locate individual actors within this infinitely elaborate system of trusts and filiations. He concluded that causal thinking was inadequate when trying to understand economic systems that do not operate according to the familiar models of agency and individual motivation. In the end, these abstract and impersonal networks do not conform to the Oedipal struggles and generational dramas that were the stock-in-trade of nineteenth-century literature. Factories that have been "rationalized and anonymized down to the last detail," he observed, "leave no room for father-son conflicts" (*Schriften*, 1:219).

Reger may have been ambivalent about which artistic form was best suited for representing the industrial enterprise, but he was certain that at least one was *not* adequate: theater. The stage was simply too mimetic. Although Reger started his writing career as a drama critic, as he began to turn his attention more and more to the corporate landscape of the Ruhr region, he outgrew his initial enthusiasm for theater, eventually dismissing the stage entirely for its lack of analytical precision. "The sociological problems of the day require explanation. A drama, however, cannot be written with footnotes" (*Schriften*, 1:224). No matter how critically penetrating a play may be, no matter how abstract its method, the very use of actors and concrete imagery on a stage perforce humanizes the processes that it depicts. Theater is too sensuous to represent contemporary reality. In the realm of modern business, Reger wrote, the "question of how to depict a banker, the owner of a department store, or the director of an enterprise requires an answer that is as complex and hypothetical as a query into the origin of the universe" (*Schriften*, 1:114).

Beyond its inherent figurativeness, a second aspect of theater further disqualified it from depicting the modern industrial enterprise: its fundamental need for temporal continuity. Even radically disjointed modernist pieces that have broken with the Aristotelian unities of action, place, and time must still conform to the linear format imposed by the theatrical performance itself, which commences at a given hour and concludes some hours later. The modern corporation, however, doesn't observe the same sequential laws of time and causality that structure the perceptual world of the individual:

> Today's issues cannot be pressed into three or five acts, into ten or twenty pictures. Never before have there been issues so vulnerable to imprecision and so adamant in their demand for exhaustive treatment. The laws of theater call for a so-called dramatic effect, they call for a plot, they call for a *sequence* [*Nacheinander*] that has been constructed with precision. But the reality today is that there is more *negotiation* than plot [*mehr* Verhandlung *als Handlung*]. At issue is a *juxtaposition* [*Nebeneinander*] that at times takes on extremely illogical forms. (*Schriften*, 1:225)

Analysis of the modern industrial concern, Reger explained, requires a structural approach (a *Nebeneinander*) rather than a genetic one (a *Nacheinander*). These relations are more accurately depicted using a technical diagram than a dramatic plot.

According to Reger, the written word possesses a much higher potential for abstraction than the theater. Because prose requires neither the concrete imagery of bodies on stage nor the temporal compactness of the dramatic performance, it becomes possible to shift the reader's attention away from the characters and figures in the foreground to those seemingly minor elements in the setting that are in fact decisive for the course of events. "The drama of the background, the depiction of the causal nexus, and the appeal of rigorous observation are reserved for the *epic*. It is for good reason that the *novel* has achieved the supremacy that it enjoys today" (*Schriften*, 1:226). In statements such as these, Reger clearly did not have in mind the traditional realist novel of the nineteenth century.[10] His analytic epic prose, which little resembled the highly plotted narrative forms from the previous century, prompted the writer Hermann Broch to coin a new generic designation for Reger's book: the "rational novel."[11] Reger's ideal was not organic "portrayal" (*Gestaltung*) but technical "reportage," to invoke the famous binary proposed by Lukács.[12] In this regard *Union of the Strong Hand* broke definitively with the structural anthropomorphism of plot that had long been a basic law of narrative form and that persisted in current definitions of the novel. In his analysis of the novel, Lukács, for example, drew upon Hegel's understanding of the teleology of plot as "the clearest revelation of the individual, in both his attitude [*Gesinnung*] and his goals [*Ziele*]."[13] Avoiding the temporal causality of narrative plot, which focalizes the story using an individual biography, Reger preferred instead a prose of "rigorous observation" that directed the attention of the reader toward the "drama of the background." Here causality is organized in a structural ensemble of components—a "juxtaposition" (*Nebeneinander*)—rather than a sequential plot. As one reviewer of *Union of the Strong Hand* noted, it seemed that time itself, as a dimension of experience, had been sucked out of Reger's novel. This "novel of an instant" (*Roman eines Augenblicks*) depicted a "reality without event."[14]

Despite containing massive amounts of technical information and numerous excursuses on the economics of the Ruhr region, Reger's book nonetheless remains committed to the novel as a literary form. *Union of the Strong Hand* may test the limits of the genre, pushing it toward scientific prose, but the questions that motivate the book are, in the end, those of an aesthetic nature. These questions concern the representability of modern economic processes: How can the artist represent the modern corporation as a sensuously perceptible entity? How is it possible to produce concrete representations of industry without lapsing into undue anthropomorphizing? Are the laws of development that govern the economic realm comparable to the causal sequences that the human mind projects onto the world around it? What, in short, are the contours of the corporate "body"? The very title of Reger's novel, *Union of the Strong Hand*, posits these questions within the field of tension between an abstract organizational principle (the "union") and a figural metonymy (the strong, or firm [*fest*] "hand").

The novel's aesthetic burden is somehow to mediate between these two seemingly incompatible scales, the decentered network of the industrial leviathan and the concrete bodies of its constituents.

Reger was hardly the first novelist to confront the formal problem of how to link together the "aggregate person" of the industrial enterprise with the empirical body of the individual.[15] But unlike most industrial novels that conceptualize the tension between the individual person and the abstract enterprise as a conflict in scales of physical magnitude, *Union of the Strong Hand* articulates this incommensurability as a disjuncture in scales of *time*. For Reger, the problem is not that the corporation is too gigantic, but that its temporality is fundamentally incompatible with the rhythms of human existence. Reger's theoretical writings designate these two irreconcilable temporal registers as *Entwicklung* ("development") and *Naturgeschichte* ("natural history"). The latter refers to the materially dense, quotidian time of creaturely existence, a temporal structure that Reger depicted in his early botanical miniatures. These short microcosmologies, brief allegories of organic existence that were a hallmark of his New Objectivity prose, were a literary form that Reger perfected at the beginning of his career in the early 1920s.[16] Initially sentimental and quietistic, these botanical sketches quickly assumed a more cynical, trenchant, and socio-critical stance.[17] A number of them were integrated as ecphrastic passages into longer texts, such as *Union of the Strong Hand*, which opens with a painstakingly detailed description of an epidemic of lice and caterpillars in the Ruhr region. The following 700 pages are punctuated with further zoological miniatures, accounts of gardening, village life in the workers' settlements, and myriad other biological processes taking place in the Ruhr. At the heart of Germany's most technically advanced region, where heavy industry has transformed the landscape completely, it is paradoxically nature that rules over historical time.[18] "Everywhere people seemed to be on the brink of a natural state; it seemed to be the dawn of a truly Rousseauvian era" (*Union*, 21). The very possibility of historical eventfulness is foreclosed in this state, where time exists only in its biologically most primitive condition, as an organic rhythm that pulses through the inhabitants of the region. "Time stood still, although there were just enough changes on the surface to prevent the people from noticing that time had stopped" (*Union*, 245). Here Reger's notion of "natural history" as a dense temporality out of sync with the metaphysics of teleological development anticipates Adorno's 1932 talk "The Idea of Natural History," which likewise understood *Naturgeschichte* as an unsublatable substratum of organic being and a reserve of nonidentity that arrests the Hegelian unfolding of absolute spirit.[19]

Reger contrasted "natural history" with the process that he called *Entwicklung*, or "development." If, for Reger, the former designated the primordial time of organic existence, the latter, by contrast, described the abstract, technical time of modernization. "Development" unfolds according to immanent mechanisms unconnected to the lived experience or agency of the individual. In a radio broadcast that coincided with the release of *Union of the Strong Hand*—a book that bears the designation "A Novel of Development" on its title page—Reger explained that "development" is a term that describes a process of industrial advancement that is precipitous and unbridled, but also without vision, direction, or explanation. It is time without a subject. "Development: it means a metropolis of millions, skyscrapers, Pullman cars, auto parks. Planless growth, overnight so to speak, expansion at any price, frantic expansion" (*Schriften*, 1:182). As he elsewhere explained, Reger chose to call *Union of the Strong Hand* a "Novel of a Development" to contrast the book explicitly with the traditional *Erziehungsroman*, which depicts the formation of an integral psychological subject through a series of encounters with the external world (Reger Archive, 182). As Hegel pointed out in the definition of plot quoted earlier, human time is suffused with intentionality. It arcs toward a goal. But "development" does not share in this telic structure, and has no psychic texture, unfolding instead without the slightest connection to interior mental life. Rather than striving toward an end, it unfolds and unwinds (*ent-wickelt*) entropically. "Development" thus designates a radically inhuman framework of time, as Lyotard proposed: "The striking thing about this metaphysics of development is that it needs no finality," he wrote. "Development is not attached to an Idea, like that of the emancipation of reason and of human freedoms.

It is reproduced by accelerating and extending itself according to its internal dynamic alone."[20]

The economic terms underlying Reger's distinction are not hard to discern: "natural history" describes the time of organic labor power and physical energetics, while "development" names the logic of capital, a *perpetuum mobile* that follows mechanical laws independent of qualitative psychological experience and influence. Reger valorizes neither term over the other, but, like Adorno, views them dialectically. For Reger, both of these temporalities, one creaturely and one mechanistic, are equally inhuman. The primitive barbarism of natural history is just as malevolent as the technical metaphysics of development. A properly human timescale would occupy a third temporality, somewhere between the microcosmic timescale of the zoological miniature and the macrocosmic scale of capital's development. The temporality of the human, in other words, would comprise a *meso*cosmic timescale capable of connecting these extremes.

But this mesocosmic, human time is precisely what is missing from *Union of the Strong Hand*. In the novel, the times of "development" and "natural history" never coincide completely, and capital is shown to be hopelessly out of sync with the time of labor power. The noncorrespondence between these two temporalities is registered in the very structure of *Union of the Strong Hand*, which falls into two distinct parts. The bulk of the novel is contained, on the one hand, in five sections that Reger calls *Stations* ("Ambush," "Confusion," "Adjustment," "Assemblage," "Entrenchment"), which describe in exceeding detail the phraseless continuum of everyday life in the Ruhr. Each of these five sections, save the final one, concludes in turn with a "Report of the *General Gazette*," which provides a parallel news account of the events that have just taken place over the period of time covered in the preceding "Station." Even though the two orders of the "Station" and the "Report" share the same calendrical time, their distinct realities never intersect. The insuperable chasm established in the novel by this differential structure relentlessly separates the *habitus* of everyday life from the time of capital's development. Although the coverage of the *General Gazette* may comprise the official historical archive, "the decisive moments within the individual stages are, however, the small or at least less conspicuous processes; these insignificant things are enormously revealing when arranged correctly" (Reger Archive, 182). The temporality of this micropolitical stratum is qualitatively different from that of "development." Whereas the time of the "Stations" is cyclical and biological in nature—Reger's term *Stationen* evokes the tradition of the medieval *Stationendrama*, geometrically constructed as circular and eternal—the contrasting temporality of the news reported in the *General Gazette* is linear, albeit without any psychological purposiveness or meaning. In the rare moments in the novel when the two temporal orders do in fact come into contact, the encounters tend to be utterly bewildering in their randomness. The episode in which a lesser character Otto proposes to Paula, for example, only underscores the incommensurability between finance capital and lived experience: "The dollar was quoted at 271 when Otto Wittkamp pressed Paula: he wanted to marry" (*Union*, 320). As this sentence shows, the absence of mediating terms between the two registers—a *Weltzeit* operating on a grand, telluric scale and a *Lebenszeit* embedded in the fabric of everyday life[21]—triggers a vertiginous plunge from the sublime to the bathetic.

A prevailing myth about industrialization is that factory automation and rationalization turn the worker into a robotic appendage of the machine, but, in Reger's novel, just the opposite occurs: as it strips away the scale of human time, mechanization transforms the worker into a purely biological creature, a heap of organs whose existence is determined by a "natural history" consisting of metabolic cycles. In the same way that motorization converted the horse into the value abstraction known as "horsepower," so too does factory rationalization reduce human beings to a set of primitive capacities that can be quantified according to a system of universal exchange. Hannah Arendt demonstrated this point forcefully in *The Human Condition*, where she observed how methods of industrial manufacture extract from the laboring body only that which can be calculated and put into circulation in the capitalist system of production. What remains after this process of extraction is the mute zoological residue that Arendt called "bare life." Far from becoming a machine, as New Objectivity bards such as Heinrich Hauser and Alfons Paquet had hoped, the industrial worker is instead "on the verge of developing into an animal species," Arendt portends.[22]

In a discussion of plot, Aristotle stipulated that good art is a matter of correct proportions. His *Poetics* argued that the artwork must have, among other qualities, an "appropriate size." This means that the story should, on the one hand, avoid being like an infinitely small animal "that would take almost no time to see"; conversely, the poet must also avoid creating a monstrously elaborate tale that, like a gigantic creature "a thousand miles long," "could not be taken in all at once." Thus, Aristotle reasons, "in the same way as living creatures and organisms compounded of many parts must be of a reasonable size, so that they can be easily taken in by the eye, so too plots must be of a reasonable length, so that they can be easily held in the memory."[23] Such proportionality, however, is completely absent from Reger's 700-page industrial novel, whose "natural history" and "development" occupy the extremes described by Aristotle: at one pole is the worm's-eye view of organic existence in the housing projects, which includes microscopically detailed miniatures describing, for example, an epidemic of lice (at the beginning of book one) or a mass die-off of fish (at the beginning of book four); at the other pole is the massive industrial concern that unfolds—*ent-wickelt*—on a plane of time untouched by human intentionality. What is missing is the time that falls between these two registers, the time that corresponds to the proportions of a mid-sized creature that is neither insect nor leviathan. When Aristotle characterized the good plot in his *Poetics* as a structure that is "one and whole like a living being," the living being that he had in mind was, of course, man. Barthes thus observed, with reference to the *Poetics*, that a narrative of proper scale will inevitably be anthropomorphic.[24] And this scale is absent from *Union of the Strong Hand*, which scatters this mesocosmic time frame centrifugally into creaturely rhythms, on the one hand, and the techno-metaphysics of capital, on the other.

As we will see, *Union of the Strong Hand* is by no means the only Weimar novel riven by this temporal conflict, which surfaces repeatedly in many industrial narratives of the period. That we find multiple novels encountering this conflict is perhaps not surprising, since the genre of the novel, as a cultural form, has always been a privileged instrument for adapting universal time to that of human existence. Indeed, as Paul Ricoeur observed in his phenomenological analyses of the novel, time "becomes human to the extent that it is articulated through a narrative mode." Narration, Ricoeur suggested, is eminent among those artistic forms that give abstract time a human countenance, rendering time compatible with our categories of experience and fashioning it to our needs.[25] In the same way that the calendar "cosmologizes lived time" and "humanizes cosmic time . . . by making a noteworthy present coincide with an anonymous instant," the novel similarly brings together two distinct registers of time.[26] Like space, the experience of which, as we saw in the previous chapter, must be "humanized" by cultural techniques such as linear perspective, time is not a universal a priori, but a product of noetic artifacts such as novels and calendars. In parallel with our analysis of the devices used by Moholy-Nagy to render post-Renaissance space visually, the present chapter will examine changes in the narrative structure of the novel as the genre attempted during the interwar period to cope with capital's unraveling or unwinding (*Ent-wicklung*) of time. As the art form most sensitive to the cultural architecture of time, the novel, we will see, was also the art form most violently affected by the breakdown in timescales in the first half of the twentieth century. In the Weimar industrial novel, narrative finds itself pushed beyond the limits of its capacity to render time in a human dimension.

Capital's Counter-Rhythm: *The Conquest of the Machines* (Part I)

The conflict between the time of organic experience and that of the anonymous economic system is also at the heart of *The Conquest of the Machines*, one of six industrial novels that Franz Jung wrote in quick succession in the 1920s. Written while the proletarian author was in prison for his role in the failed March 1921 uprisings in central Germany, this book was published in 1923 by Wieland Herzfelde's Malik Press. Like Reger's text, *Conquest* was partially based on firsthand experiences. And yet the tone of the text could not be less intimate. Even in its lengthy description of the 1921 uprisings—historical events in which Jung himself participated as a professional agitator—the book systematically avoids the interior voice of a memoire and flourishes of personal commentary. Nor do the novel's highly schematic characters possess any of the weight and concreteness that one would expect to find in a documentary text. Here *Conquest* avoids anthropomorphism even more radically and unrelentingly than does Reger's novel. Tellingly, the narrative opens with an empty landscape whose only contents are distant acoustic events: the thunder of cannons, the warbling of larks, the signal of a bell—but "nowhere were there any people" (*Werke*, 4:11). And when people do eventually enter the story, they appear largely undifferentiated and in mass constellations such as troop phalanxes, trade unions, and technocratic bureaucracies. There are no individuated human actors, only collective bodies.[27] In fact, dispensing entirely with the convention of narrative character, *The Conquest of the Machines* does not contain even a single proper name.

After forty pages describing the 1921 revolt, Jung turns his attention in the remainder of the novel to the mechanisms behind the event. A chapter entitled "The Hand on the Switch" examines the role of the Electricity Trust, or Electrotrust, in this political crisis. Like Reger's novel, the title of this chapter may invoke the concrete image of the hand, but the account presented is highly abstract and disembodied. Having "grown beyond its intrinsic contours" through vertical corporate integration, the Electrotrust has left behind its "modest origins" as a family company and metastasized into a shapeless and unsurveyable network of filiations (*Werke*, 4:45). Now "ripe for the museum" (*Werke*, 4:75), the great bourgeois dynasty that once controlled the corporation has given way to a decentralized and nameless "apparatus of clerks" (*Werke*, 4:73). As in *Union of the Strong Hand*, there are "no men behind the scenes, only those who have been pushed into the foreground" and who are easily replaced if necessary (*Werke*, 4:74). Although neither of the book's two sections, "The Uprising" and "The Hand on the Switch," contains any individuated characters, Jung's treatment of the Electrotrust in the latter section is still more abstract than the preceding account of the 1921 rebellion. The relative vividness of his narration of the uprising can be attributed in part to the fact that Jung is describing events that play out in historical time, whereas the analysis of the Electrotrust that follows, by contrast, diagrams an abstract schema of structural relations among a complex of industries, ranging from electricity producers to the manufacturers of cement and paper.

The political events of "The Uprising" may unfold in time, but the economic "development" of "The Hand on the Switch" does not.

Writing these latter sections came easily to Jung, who was educated as an economist in the early 1900s and who continued throughout his life to enjoy great success working in the finance sector as a trade journalist. Before moving to Berlin and becoming the "Rimbaud figure" of the revolutionary avant-garde, as Georg Grosz once called him, Jung had in fact pursued a doctoral degree in economics in Munich.[28] (He broke off his study of *Nationalökonomie* and relocated to Berlin in 1911 only because he was offered a prestigious position as editor of a leading stock market journal there.[29]) Because of its lengthy technical analyses, several reviewers in fact likened *Conquest* to a primer on economics. For example, Gertrud Alexander, who edited the feuilleton section of the Communist Party organ *Die rote Fahne*, noted in an enthusiastic review that large parts of Jung's book read like "economic report[s]" and "treatises on political economy."[30] The book so resembled a textbook that another reviewer proposed using excerpts from it as the basis for proletarian "discussion evenings" where "tactical and organizational questions" would be covered.[31]

This resemblance to technical literature notwithstanding, when *The Conquest of the Machines* was published in 1923 with a cover designed by John Heartfield, its title page bore the designation "Novel." In fact Jung had specified in letters from prison that the book be called not a *Roman*, but a *Zeitroman* (*Werke*, 9.2:78), a term that more accurately characterizes the book for two reasons:[32] first, *The Conquest of the Machines* was, like Ernst Glaeser's *Jahrgang 1902* (1928), a "novel *of* the time," a documentary record of recent historical events such as the March uprisings; second, and more importantly, Jung's book was, like Thomas Mann's *Magic Mountain* (1924), also a "novel *about* time," a book that uses the genre of the novel itself as a platform for reflection on the complex architecture of causality and temporality. The heterogeneous structure of time in industrial society is first addressed in the three short prose sketches that open Jung's book—"Piblokto," "Summer," and "Electrotrust"—each of which presents what could be called, after Bakhtin, a distinct chronotope, a particular narrative fabric of space-time. Within this introductory triptych, the first panel depicts "natural" man's traumatic encounter with the accelerated temporality of modernity. The miniatures that follow then elaborate on the two disparate configurations of time found also in Reger's novel. Thus the pastoral idyll of "Summer" depicts work as an organic function fundamental to all living beings. Like Jung's other theosophic prose, this section is written in the grammatical second person, as an address to the reader. The sketch begins, importantly, when the reader depicted in the miniature stops moving: it is the pause, the rhythmic interval, which paradoxically sets everything in motion. Only after "you" freeze, Jung writes, "the spider next to you begins to spin its web again, and now you notice how it waited in breathless tension to see if you would stretch your hand out farther. And so unfurls a picture of tremendous vitality out of the surrounding peace. Everything continues, everything moves forward. Outside is the bustle of labor" (*Werke*, 4:8).

In contrast to the rhythmic systole and diastole of organic labor depicted in "Summer," the mechanical temporality of the following miniature, "Electrotrust," has no qualitative texture. Just as capital deterritorializes geopolitical space through its imperialist projections, so too its technologies of acceleration level the dimension of time. For Jung, this continuous flow, unpunctuated by the break and renewal of organic time, is analogous to the structure of electricity, a phenomenon that "accelerates life, it drives forward and carves out its course; it subjugates everything and sets everything in motion. The world begins to dance. . . . Coal is purchased and extracted, means of transportation are established, new pathways are opened up. Traffic surges through the countryside. And following it is labor. Labor: captured in order to be consumed, arranged in the quivering fingers of the experimental subjects who can no longer stop the force of wage-labor" (*Werke*, 4:9). The contrast in each miniature between the images of hands is especially telling. Whereas in "Summer," the hand approaching the spider web pauses and then resumes, creating a rhythmic inflection that is the hallmark of natural labor, in the miniature that follows an inexorable force surges through the worker's shaking hands, which cannot stop moving and vibrate as if from electrical stimulation. In its striving for limitless circulation, capital quickens time: it "accelerates life" and "subjugates everything and sets everything in motion." Thus, *Conquest* does not view capital so much as a concrete physical phenomenon to be found in material forms such factory machinery. Capital is not matter, Jung proposes, but an architecture of time. As he observes in elsewhere *Conquest*, capital "is itself a living force. It is a power that is independent of man, a power that drives and enslaves him, a power whose bearers and agents serve without any pleasure. Capital is experiential: it draws in humanity, it devours life, and, *through a process of accumulation, it is gradually establishing a tempo that, sooner or later, will shatter all men*" (*Werke*, 4:75).

This conceptualization of capital as a rhythmic irregularity is repeated in Jung's theoretical opus *The Technology of Happiness* (*Die Technik des Glücks*), which appeared in two parts in 1921 and 1923. The abundant resonances between *The Conquest of the Machines* and *The Technology of Happiness* are attributable to the fact that he composed the industrial novel and the first volume of *Technology* during the same prison term.[33] As in *The Conquest of the Machines*, Jung's theoretical text focuses on the activity of labor as the theater of conflict between man and capital. But, in contrast to his industrial novel, which seeks to map a technical-financial network using precise economic analysis, *The Technology of Happiness* avoids the specialized terminology of economics. As Jung puts it, he wanted in this work to "leave economy behind" (*Werke*, 6:70–71). Needless to say, orthodox Communists such as Gertrud Alexander, who had enthused about *Conquest*, had little patience for *The Technology of Happiness*, which, indeed, abandons the critical vocabulary of political economy in favor of an esoteric admixture of biology, phenomenology, and psychoanalysis.[34]

At first glance, Jung's emphatic eschewal of economistic frameworks seems to lead to the wildest speculations. But we should not attribute this abstruseness too hastily to Jung's ignorance: as we have seen, Jung was more than capable of lucid economic analysis. His objective here is otherwise. For all its seeming unsystematic conjecture and willful obscurantism, the psychophysical account of labor that Jung presents in *Technology* in fact represents an important correction to the tendency among Marxists to focus exclusively on capital's aspect as dead labor. At the time Jung wrote the book, the classical Marxist hermeneutic considered capital only in objectivated and readily quantifiable forms such as factory machinery, neglecting to bring into its analysis the entire other half of the capitalist system, namely, the living forces of production—capital's human side, so to speak. "No one has ever undertaken to write a history of human labor," Jung observed in *The Technology of Happiness* (*Werke*, 6:133). Indeed his efforts to understand the condition of flexible capital from an experiential perspective was far ahead of its time. With only a few exceptions, most of which can be found in early Soviet researches on everyday life (*быт*), a robust and systematic analysis of human capital would have to wait until the postwar period, when Marxism finally began to take seriously the productive dimensions of the cultural superstructure and its role in the maintenance of the capitalist system of relations.[35] While Marxist thought of the interwar years remained fixated on technology and heavy industry, exploring—and exploiting—the features and composition of flexible capital was left to enterprising bourgeois economists such as the German ordoliberals, who were transforming economics from a quantitative science into a science of human behavior already in the 1930s.[36] At a time when the Communist Party failed to consider the role of subjective and behavioral factors in the capitalist system, Jung sought to correct this bias by asking, "What role is played by man in the economy?" (*Werke*, 1.2:60). And rather than answer this question with an abstract diagram of political economy, he instead replied in *The Technology of Happiness* with a meditation on what it is to *be* capital, describing capitalism experientially from the psychic interior of the reified subject. "The opposition between capital and labor, between the capitalist and the anti-capitalist economic systems, between private ownership and state ownership, with all of their subtle nuances and their differing views on society—this opposition revolves around the position of man, of the individual and of human society itself, in economic intercourse" (*Werke*, 1.2:60).

In lieu of economistic analysis, then, *The Technology of Happiness* frames labor using the categories of phenomenological psychology and psychophysics. Work, Jung writes following Marx, is a basic "human capacity" experienced by the laboring body as a mode of primary encounter and sensation (*Werke*, 6:133). According to Jung, it is through labor that the human organism achieves existential presence and realizes its potential as a social being. Like a motor that is "adjusted to a specific number of revolutions," Jung suggested, the individual ego strives through labor to attune itself with its environment and with other egos (*Werke*, 6:22). The successful synchronization of these "oscillations" (*Mitschwingungen*) transmutes the arbitrary links between individuals into organic affective bonds (*Werke*, 6:21), converting the pseudo-collective of society into community, or *Gesellschaft* into *Gemeinschaft* (*Werke*, 6:38). Labor, in short, is the foundation for "relationality as such" (*Werke*, 6:71). "The element that unifies—the living intensity of collective existence that forms, organizes, and, if necessary, delimits the community—is determined by the experience of happiness, by rhythmic accord and integration, by a synchrony of tempo. This element is experienced ambiently through labor."[37]

But, Jung continues, the historical advent of capital changed the rhythm of this encounter with the world. "[C]aptured in order to be consumed," the energies that once circulated freely are fettered by capital and given an objective form, the commodity, which directs the flow of these forces into discrete, fixed currents. The previously uninhibited energies of the organism are now confined within a closed libidinal economy. By segmenting and binding the forces of the psyche, capital begins to accumulate vital energies in material forms outside the laboring organism, eventually amassing so much energy in external bodies such the commodity and fixed capital that the balance of power between living and dead labor shifts definitively in favor of the latter. Having gained the upper hand, capital now begins to restructure the metabolic exchange between human and object according to its own laws, destroying the natural condition of psychic homeostasis and forcing the ego to accommodate its own mechanical cycles. From this moment on the frequency of the ego's oscillations can no longer accord with that of the objects around it, leading to a destructive desynchronization with the world. For Jung "property," a term that he uses interchangeably with capital, is the stuff of this morbid psychic congestion. As the etymology of the word suggests, *Be-sitz* designates a state of immobility and arrest. "Technically speaking," property is "a problem of circulation" that constrains the spontaneous functioning of the living organism (*Werke*, 9.2:37). For this reason, Jung observed, revolutionary politics requires not the redistribution of property but its outright destruction: "only a class that has no property or value is capable of, ripe for, and victorious in revolution" (*Werke*, 6:36).[38]

Capital's process of binding, occluding, and restructuring vital energies is experienced as a rhythmic irregularity in the psychic apparatus, which is why, Jung proposes, we intuitively speak of a "rhythm of the 'rate of profit,' . . . even of a melody of capital" (*Werke*, 6:19). Interposing itself between the individual and the world around her, capital—a "third element" (*ein Drittes*), as Jung called it—establishes rhythms and melodies that the ego cannot accommodate and that inhibit the proper functioning of the organism.[39] Indeed, Jung concluded, so many varieties of psychopathology have their shared etiology in the ego's inability to conform to the tempo imposed on it by capital. "As the mediator of the organic drive, capital—the dominant, third element—is a counter-rhythm [*ein Gegenrhythmus*] and a source of suffering that mutates at random" (*Werke*, 6:20). Psychic desynchronization may create many different symptoms, but it has only a single cause. Jung defines hysteria, for example, as a rigidification (*Erstarrung*) of vital energies, which, like "rigid," "lifeless," and "dead" property, is "the opposite of movement" (*Werke*, 6:158). As an "independent movement" (*Eigenbewegung*) detached from the psyche, hysteria establishes an inhibiting "counter-rhythm against the living" that results in "suffering, unhappiness, and an awareness of death" in the subject (*Werke*, 6:157). Jung's notion that mental disorders originate in the desynchronization of internal and external time can be traced to his initiator into psychoanalysis, the renegade analyst and Dada muse Otto Gross, who researched the temporalities of different mental illnesses. In the same way that Jung defined hysteria as a temporal congestion of the psychic apparatus, Gross similarly argued that that mind afflicted by schizophrenia is always out of phase with the time of the world around it. Schizophrenics, Gross wrote, are unable to adapt to environmental changes naturally and spontaneously because, in contrast to the healthy individual who reacts in real time to surrounding stimuli, the schizophrenic is trapped in a time that is always either too belated or too prospective.[40]

Despite his claims to "leave economy behind" in *The Technology of Happiness*, here I would argue that the thinking of Jung, an expert in *Nationalökonomie* and successful trade journalist, is indeed at its most economistic in this text. To wit: his construal of revolutionary struggle as a battle between biological time and the "counter-rhythm" of capital corresponds closely to some of the most advanced economic modeling of his day and exhibits an especial debt, it would seem, to the work of the Austrian economist Joseph Schumpeter, whose breakthrough text *The Theory of Economic Development* appeared in 1912 as Jung was reaching the end of his graduate studies in economics. This book, which characterized capital as an inorganic rhythm whose periods unfold independently of the living, provided the foundation for the famous theory of business cycles that Schumpeter developed and refined over the course of his life.[41] Like Jung, who conceived of capital as a "living force . . . independent of man," Schumpeter envisioned the evolution of the capitalist complex as a "distinct process generated by the economic system itself."[42] As he explained, he came to be convinced of capital's temporal autonomy by reading Marx, whose theory of economic crisis defined capitalism as a logic that unfolds according to its own inherent laws and teleologies.[43] Economic crises are not accidental, Marx observed, but are fundamental to the structural pattern of the capitalist system, which, alternating regularly between booms and busts, can never achieve a state of equilibrium. Building on Marx's insight, Schumpeter focused his research on calculating the periodicity of this crisis-cycle using the precise instruments of econometric analysis. According to Schumpeter, these economic patterns were so distinct that they could be discerned independently of political policies and historical events such as wars, fluctuations in industrial production, or mass migrations. Such external factors might inflect the course of the economic system's development, but they do not modify the basic pattern of its movement.[44] Like an organism, Schumpeter proposed, the body of capitalism can be afflicted by various lesions (social unrest, natural catastrophes, etc.), but the existence of such maladies does not change the fact that—again like an organism—the "lifespan" of the capitalist cycle will inevitably follow a distinct rhythm.[45] Capital, he concluded, always unfolds according to its own timeframe.

According to Schumpeter, the development of the capitalist system since its emergence in the era of the Napoleonic wars has followed three distinct cycles that vary in length but run simultaneously with one another. He named these three frequencies, or rates of oscillation, after the economists who first discovered them: the shortest is the Kitchin cycle, which lasts forty months; somewhat longer, the Juglar cycle has an average periodicity of nine to ten years; finally, with a lifespan of fifty-five years, Kondratiev cycles are the longest period in the capitalist system. Each of these periods can, in turn, be broken down into a four-phase cycle of prosperity, recession, depression, and revival. The crisis of 1826–1830, for example, was the depression phase of the Kondratiev cycle that ran from 1780 to 1842, just as the crisis of 1873–1878 was the depression phase of the next Kondratiev cycle, which extended from 1842 to 1897; immediately after the crash of 1929–1932, Schumpeter added this latest economic convulsion to the same Kondratiev cycle (which one could subsequently project, much later, into the crisis of 1987). Because all three cycles are running simultaneously, each one enhances or inhibits the other two, giving rise, as Schumpeter observed, to considerable irregularities in the fitful course of capitalism's historical development. However, Schumpeter insisted that the resulting impression of inconsistency in no way disproved the existence of the fundamental underlying patterns he had discerned; it only explained why these cycles had evaded detection by economists, who hadn't yet established the econometric models necessary to decode these inexorable patterns. Schumpeter's *Theory of Economic Development* thus described an entity whose "development" takes place outside contexts of human endeavor such as society and polity. Representable only through abstract calculation, the cycles of capitalism are literally beyond the limits of human perception.[46] They were indeed so obscure that establishment economists often refused to accept Schumpeter's theories because, they argued, these periodic patterns could not be verified empirically. Kondratiev depressions, for example, occur so infrequently that no person will ever experience two of them in her lifetime. To recall Aristotle's words about narrative plot, they are not "easily held in memory." Capitalism's waves correspond to none of the various timescales that are innate to human experience, from the twenty-four-hour circadian rhythm to the twenty-five-year generational cycle.

This influential model of capital as a cyclical force whose periodicities unfold independently of lived time has appealed to thinkers across the political spectrum. In the concluding lines of *The Decline of the West* (1922), the conservative Oswald Spengler, for example, sketched out the world-historical conflict between, on the one hand, "money" and "technology," and, on the other, the "irresistible rhythm of the generation sequence."[47] Closer in spirit to Jung's work, however, recent Marxist scholarship has investigated the irreconcilability between human reproductive cycles and the rhythms of capital. Focusing on the phenomenon of "turbo-capitalism," these researches have foregrounded the deleterious effects of accelerated development and the distortion of temporal scales.[48] The feminist scholar Teresa Brennan, for example, has argued that the capitalist order can in fact survive only by subordinating the life cycles of variable capital, that is, human labor power and natural resources, to the mechanical time of constant capital. Surveying a variety of the latest technical interventions into the sphere of production by capitalist R&D laboratories, Brennan discerns a prevailing drive to conquer organic time: in an attempt to accelerate the reproductive cycles of animals and food crops, genetic engineers have designed tractable strains of livestock and plants whose rapid development better corresponds to that of capital; conversely, the use of human fertility drugs postpones biological reproduction, allowing skilled human capital, which demands extensive investment and training, to extend its productive phase before it begins to direct its energies and resources into raising the next generation. Although these two strategies of acceleration and deferral seem on the surface to be opposed, they are both designed to maximize productivity by overcoming the organic reproductive clocks of variable capital. Capital, writes Brennan, "garners its energy by violent conversions, and these conversions follow rhythms that bear only an attenuated relation to the rhythms of natural reproduction, whose temporal restraints they ignore. In reproducing or producing its babies, capital has its own cycles and 'laws of motion.' Its parody of nature is almost complete."[49] The fundamental irreconcilability that she discerns between the reproductive time-cycles of the organism and capital's abstract rate of production[50] was in fact already anticipated by Schumpeter, who conceded that the rhythms of natural reproduction represented one of the only exceptions to his law of business cycles. In contrast with waves of technological invention and industrial revolutions, "special cycles" such as agriculture were, according to Schumpeter, "separate phenomena that do not necessarily fall within the field of expectation from the general theory."[51] In other words, cycles of organic reproduction are naturally in conflict with those of capital.

Capitalism's arrhythmia is embodied in the commodity form. Indeed, the commodity is nothing other than a temporal condensation, a segment of organic time that has been spatialized and bound. Commodities, to recall Marx's definition, are "definite masses of congealed labor-time." No doubt Jung had these famous words in mind when he observed, as we saw above, that labor must be "captured in order to be consumed." As an accumulation of time, the commodity is itself a delay that, paradoxically, instates a condition of simultaneity. Through this temporal involution, the commodity form erases the distinction between speed and stasis, all-too-human parameters for understanding the relation of time to space.[52] When the economist John Bates Clark reviewed Schumpeter's 1911 *Theory of Economic Development*, he expressed this temporal paradox eloquently. Praising the Austrian economist for being one of the first to grasp "the full part played, on the one hand, by time as an element in production and, on the other, by capital and organization as, in a sense, the antitheses of time and the synchronizers of labor and production,"[53] Clark explained that capital's bound time collapses the categories of causal thinking. The result is a phenomenon at once both bewildering and miraculous:

> goods require time in the making, and yet the producer does not have to wait for them. Laborers are able to eat as the work and the eating is the immediate consequence of the working. This synchronizing of labor and its fruits, as well as the multiplication of the fruits, requires capital; and it may be said, therefore, that capital is a condition of that kind of production which is organized, fruitful, and able to pay as it goes in fully "ripened" goods. Standing around the banks of a seething pool the laborers toss their products into

> it and at once draw out of it, in finished form, what they need for daily use.[54]

The accumulated time found in ensembles of factory machinery inaugurates a paradoxical condition of simultaneity that defies the laws of linear sequence that structure human consciousness. Like witches gathering around a cauldron, workers assemble around the "seething pool" of accumulated labor-power that instantaneously transforms raw material into "ripened" goods. Clark's scene recalls Goethe's Faust, whom Marshall Berman once famously styled the incarnation of modernity's desire for economic development.[55] Indeed, Faust longs to abrogate the laws of natural reproduction and achieve the very condition of simultaneity that is described by Clark and deplored by Jung: "Show me the fruit that rots before it's plucked / and trees that grow their greenery anew each day," he demands of the devil.[56] It is no accident, then, that Jung references *Faust II* in working notes made while he was in prison writing *The Conquest of the Machines* and *The Technology of Happiness*, for Faust represents the consummate capitalist entrepreneur who yearns to subjugate the intractable temporality of organic being.[57]

Because the rhythm of capital determines so many aspects of modern existence, from mental life to forms of sociality, revolutionary political strategy must focus, Jung concluded, on overthrowing this temporal regime. "The struggle for power is a conflict over the issue of tempo," he announced (*Werke*, 6:123). This definition of revolutionary struggle as a struggle for time led Jung to celebrate unrationalized patterns of time that were resistant to assimilation by capital. Forms of reproductive labor were particularly valuable resources in this struggle. This front of revolutionary activity was particularly important during the 1920s and '30s, when, as we already saw above, capitalism began aggressively to annex, incorporate, and manage activities that were located beyond the workplace but were nonetheless essential to sustaining the labor force. Jung wrote his industrial novels during the moment of historical transition when capitalism, facilitated by mass cultural formations, moved beyond the purely economic sphere into the administration of "lifestyle." With the assistance of sociological, subject-oriented approaches for modeling and managing the human organism as living capital, quantitative bourgeois economics was being transformed into a science of human behavior. Having recognized early on this "biopolitical" mutation in capitalist strategy, as Foucault called it in an analysis of interwar governmentality, Jung turned his attention to a spectrum of (monetarily) uncompensated activities that occurred outside of the workplace but that contributed to the ensemble of productive relations that maintains the capitalist status quo.[58] With capitalism's expansion beyond the valorized sites of labor and production, the zone of political-economic struggle had to be diversified to include activities that were social (forms of relationality and intimacy), cultural (education and ideological modeling), and domestic (childbirth and the provision of nourishment) in nature. "There is not a single person who believes in his core that labor, human labor, can be measured only according the value standards of the commodity," Jung wrote (*Werke*, 1.1:206–207). Although here, again, Jung ran afoul of the orthodox economistic thinking that dominated in the German Communist Party (KPD), which dismissed these superstructural activities as secondary elements and rallied its forces instead around sites of factory labor.[59] The KPD's blindness to new social strata such as white-collar workers (*Angestellten*), who did not fit into the Party's limited definition of industrial labor, led to catastrophic results, for these were precisely the disenfranchised demographics that made possible the National Socialist electoral victory in 1933.

Jung was justifiably skeptical of fixed definitions of the proletariat and questioned the portrayal of the working class as necessarily urban, industrial, or male. In fact he rarely wrote of *the* proletariat, preferring instead to refer, less monolithically, to *proletarians* in the plural. For example, his novel *Proletarians* (*Proletarier*, 1921) depicts a number of scenes from the everyday lives of women and men who perform a variety of forms of "productive" labor. This book transforms the meaning and iconography of the proletariat, expanding this rubric to embrace, among others, mothers, clerks, and prisoners. The numerous domestic scenes in this novel place a particular focus on states of intimacy and the habituated syntax of human relations, that is, on the forms of affective labor that sustain the capitalist system. Against the tendency to turn class pedigree into a quasi-biological category and hypostatize heavy factory laborers as the exclusive vanguard of revolutionary struggle, Jung expanded the KPD's restricted definition of the proletariat. In this regard, Jung revealed himself to be a sophisticated reader of Marx, who himself had avoided the temptation to substantivize the proletariat as such. As Brecht pointed out in 1934, "Marx addresses the workers with a new name: as *proletarians* (not as proletariat)" (Brecht, *Werke*, 22:48).[60]

It was for this reason that Jung placed women at the center of revolutionary struggle. As the custodians of a temporality that was still unassimilated to the rhythms of capital—namely, generational time—he considered women more subversive, in fact, than the urban industrial worker, whose labor time had long been rationalized and commodified. As the representatives of an intransigent, human time, women pave the way "to the first authentic revolution," he wrote: "Working class women quickly became more dangerous to [the state] than individual worker's parties, which could be manipulated and played against each other" (*Werke*, 4:94–95). At least until capitalism's biopolitical mutation, when it expanded beyond the productive sphere to embrace all aspects of "lifestyle," the forms of unregulated labor with which women were associated had not yet been subjugated to the counter-rhythm of capital. Thus women were, according to Jung, spontaneous enemies of the state who thwarted the rationalization and incorporation of dense temporalities of existence. Jung observed in a 1919 essay entitled "The Means and Ends of Class Struggle" that there is "an entire host of issues which undoubtedly bear the mark of class struggle, even though the standard methods for evaluation haven't designated them as class struggles. The most important of these struggles is the conflict between the sexes, the struggle that woman wages against man" (*Werke*, 1.1:229). Indeed, there is hardly a single book within Jung's oeuvre, either theoretical or literary, that lacks enthusiastic treatment of the maternal (*das Mütterliche*) or maternalism (*Mütterlichkeit*). *The Conquest of the Machines* is no exception, and features at its center a detailed chapter on "women's labor." The struggle for matriarchy, Jung explained, precedes the more recent conflicts of class warfare and is, in fact, politically more primary than the latter. For him, matriarchy provided a model for a utopian social order free of arrhythmia and psychic neurosis. Like Otto Gross, with whom he planned to publish a journal named *SIGYN* after the Old Norse goddess, Jung considered women, not urban industrial men, to be the bearers of modern political insurgency.

As a writer, Jung waged this struggle against capital's morbid counter-rhythm through the language of his literary prose, which foregrounded rhythmic arrangements that, he claimed, had the potential to collectivize its readers. Rhythm had always been a predominant feature of his writing since he first began to publish in the Expressionist journals *Der Sturm* and *Die Aktion*, although its importance became even more pronounced after his conversion to revolutionary politics.[61] In her review of *The Conquest of the Machines*, Party critic Gertrud Alexander claimed, for example, that Jung's highly rhythmic prose was far better suited than the traditional novel to "representing the tempo of great social struggles and the concrete destinies of the masses." If bourgeois subjectivity had found commensurate literary expression in narrative forms such as the novel, she observed, the most important structural device of proletarian literature, by contrast, was not plot, but rhythm. In the final lines of her review, Alexander lauded Jung for "the creation of a new proletarian epic, since the rhythm and movement of the mass correspond more to the pulse and structure of epic poetry than they do to the novel, a form which is difficult to parse and which is hardly suitable for expressing rhythm."[62] Because it establishes a "particular closeness between text and body," rhythmic language contains an exceptional phenomenological density that makes it a powerful technical-stylistic device for the creation of a "collective subject," as one critic has subsequently suggested.[63] Along similar lines, Jung enjoined the reader of one of his industrial novels from 1922 to pay close attention to the cadence of his prose, explaining that its rhythm is the "technical matter" linking his style as a writer to his political critique of capitalism:

> While reading, [the reader] should participate in the dissolution and creation [of the text], should control where the tempo begins to falter, and thus create an authentic connection between author and

> reader—the most important feature of this book's content. This is how content acquires a new rhythm. No longer is it just a matter of putting a plotline together; it is, rather, a matter of building a piece of the self, of making events in and with ourselves, our sensations, our collective existence as a living community. By integrating the action into our lives, we create a new form of rhythmicized existence. (*Werke*, 2:105)

It was in the rhythmic design of the text, then, that Jung discovered a concrete literary practice to fortify the subject's resistance to the baleful counter-rhythms of capital.

For Jung, rhythmic aspects of language operate not just at the level of verbal syntax, but can be found as well in larger units of text, as he demonstrated in another industrial novel from the 1920s, *The Red Week* (*Die rote Woche*, 1921). Composed of seven chapters beginning with "Monday," the structure of this book reflects the parsing of the workweek, where Jung again discerns a conflict between organic time and the divisions that capital imposes upon it. Significantly, Jung stipulated that the novel be published serially, since its segmented appearance in a newspaper or a journal would foreground the rhythms and periodicities of the story. Yet, as he further insisted in a letter from prison, the installments of the story do *not* correspond to the standard seven-day calendar week. In defiance of the work rhythms of the latter, *The Red Week* must "not be printed in 7 installments," as one would expect, but should appear "instead in a maximum of 3 installments, each consisting of 2 or 3 chapters." He continued: "That is how it fits together. Please send it to a daily newspaper. . . . *As long as one understands the rhythm* and doesn't disturb the rhythm of the totality . . . , it is possible to insert current events into the text improvisationally. Please maintain the exact rhythmic sequence of the images" (*Werke*, 11:55–57). Proposing in these lines that *The Red Week* appear in three rather than seven installments, Jung insisted that the narrative periods of the text cannot be mapped onto those the seven-day week. The "red week" transgresses against capitalism's ordinance of time.

Of all of the creative and sometimes wildly conjectural forms taken by Jung's experiments to restructure commodified labor rhythms, this one was perhaps the least fantastical, and in fact anticipated several Soviet campaigns to dismantle the traditional division of the calendar week into seven days, first by implementing a five-day week (*пятидневка*) from 1929 to 1931 and then a six-day week (*шестидневка*) from 1931 to 1940.

As was already noted, it would be decades after the publication of Jung's industrial novels before rhythm and generational cycles were at last recognized by Marxist thought as important aspects of revolutionary struggle. This perspective was at last systematized and integrated into the Marxist analytic by the postwar philosopher and sociologist Henri Lefebvre, whose method of "rhythmanalysis" resumed the project first outlined by Jung in the 1920s. Rhythm occupied a central position in both of Lefebvre's fields of inquiry, the theory of everyday life and the analysis of the social production of space.[64] It was, he observed, a key instrument in capitalism's "pedagogy of appropriation," a phrase he used to describe diverse spatial practices by which the complex and multicycle rhythms of the individual body are regimented and subjugated.[65] Lefebvre observed the conflict between biological and social temporalities on multiple levels of experience, from the most basic organic pulses of physiological existence to the higher psychosocial patterning that frames the development of sexuality and individual identity. Echoing Jung's observation that the "struggle for power is a conflict over the issue of tempo," Lefebvre observed that because rhythm was one of the means by which political orders structure quotidian existence, political transformation requires a regime change at the level of rhythm: "Objectively, for there to be *change*, a social group, a class or a caste must intervene by imprinting a rhythm on an era, be it through force or in an insinuating manner."[66]

Classical Marxist critique, Lefebvre explained, had completely failed to recognize the importance of the rhythmic dimension of a political system that "constructs and erects itself on a contempt for life and from this foundation: the body, the time of the living."[67] It had focused exclusively "on the two-term opposition *bourgeoisie—proletariat*, at the expense of the third term: the soil, agricultural property and production, peasants, predominantly agricultural colonies."[68] As with Jung, Lefebvre drew attention to the reproductive rhythms of this "third term," those "special cycles" that Schumpeter considered resistant to periodicities of capital. Indeed, according to Lefebvre, the historical rule of capital began not with technical accumulation and the commodity form, but with the first attempts to regulate these "special" generational cycles. The "domination-exploitation of human beings begins with animals, wild beasts and cattle; the humans associated with these inaugurated an experience that would turn back against them: killings, stockbreedings, slaughter, sacrifices and (in order better to submit) castration. . . . The castration of beasts, what power! And what a symbol of anti-nature!"[69] Having perfected these strategies of biopolitical management, the advent of capitalism proper ensues at the moment when the strategies for regulating generational cycles are transposed onto human society. In this conversion, overtly violent means of domination (slaughter, stockbreeding, castration) are "humanized" and traded in for more subtle and capillary, but no less effective, techniques of social control.

Capital's will to "anti-nature," as Lefebvre calls it, eventually culminates in the loss of generational distinction. As capital consolidates its hegemony, the gaps between generational groups become ever shorter until, at last, capital abrogates definitively the laws of linear causality and generational sequence. If once there were twenty-five years between generations, this period has been shortened to only five years or even fewer, he speculates. This contraction of the time span between generations is accompanied by a generalized state of amnesia that, by continuously wiping out the memory-traces on the individual psyche, prevents the accumulation of mnemonic stock and ensures that no differences emerge between the generations. Without memory, youth and maturity become indistinguishable,[70] leading to the fulfillment of Faust's wish to experience "the fruit that rots before it's plucked": "Today everything comes to an end virtually as soon as it begins, and vanishes almost as soon as it appears."[71] In the end, Lefebvre, like Jung, argues that one of the only resources left to challenge capital's will to development is the cache of unregulated, biological cycles. Although such animal rhythms are not social, or even (as Reger demonstrated) properly human, these organic pulses project a space of resistance outside capitalism's morbid accumulations. Humanity is a term found somewhere between these two states, between natural history and development. Thus, in search of this mediating term, Lefebvre presents a "task for theoretical thought: to confront the cumulative with the non-cumulative which remains external to it, that is to say, cyclical or discontinuous processes, the natural or 'private' side of man, the everyday, art, symbols, emotions. Symbolisms, sex, life cycles, hunger, thirst, sleep—these do not constitute an integral or integrating part of accumulation, which is based on memory and moves forward by 'snowballing.'"[72]

Fear of the Future: *The Conquest of the Machines* (Part II)

We can now return to the first miniature in the triptych of sketches that opens *The Conquest of the Machines*, which stages the collision between the biological rhythms of the second sketch ("Summer") and the counter-rhythms of the third ("Electrotrust"). This sketch is titled "Piblokto" after a nervous disorder that was discovered in Eskimo societies at the turn of the twentieth century by the polar explorer Robert E. Peary. In his book *The North Pole*, which appeared eleven years before Jung wrote *The Conquest of the Machines*, Peary described a typical attack of piblokto, or "arctic hysteria": "The patient, usually a woman, begins to scream and tear off and destroy her clothing. If on the ship, she will walk up and down the deck, screaming and gesticulating, and generally in a state of nudity, though the thermometer may be in the minus forties. As the intensity of the attack increases she will sometimes leap over the rail upon the ice, running perhaps half a mile." Pondering the "immediate cause of this affection," Peary speculated that "it seems to be the result of a brooding over absent or dead relatives, or a fear of the future."[73] Peary's description of this malady was quickly picked up in psychoanalytic, and later in ethnopsychiatric, circles, where scientists debated whether the causes of this disorder were primarily biological or cultural. The extensive bibliography of literature on the subject boasts a number of illustrious names. Abraham A. Brill, for example, who was the leading voice of psychoanalysis in the United States during its early years, wrote a study on piblokto in 1913 arguing that this "emotional outburst of the most primitive type" was doubtless a subcategory of hysteria—albeit not a conversion hysteria of the kind found in "persons of very complex psychic organizations" but one that more closely resembles the anxiety hysterias in children, who have not learned to repress their desires and wishes and whose hysterias are, therefore, "not as complicated and hidden as those of grownup and intelligent adults."[74]

At first glance it is unclear why Jung chose to open a book about the 1921 uprisings with a sketch about arctic hysteria. Specific details in Jung's sketch would indicate that his source was not Peary's original *North Pole* of 1910, but Brill's 1913 essay, which was likely made available to Jung through his friend, the anticapitalist analyst Gross.[75] That Jung's understanding of piblokto was mediated by Gross's psychoanalytic framework helps to clarify his interest in the subject. And here Jung's modifications to (or rather: misquotations of) Peary's and Brill's accounts are significant. In a loose approximation of Peary's observations, Jung writes that "for the most part [piblokto] seems to be caused by a *fear of the future*" (*Werke*, 4:7). Note here that the "dead relatives" are gone in Jung's paraphrase of Peary and "*fear of the future*," now in italics, has become the chief cause of "arctic hysteria." If, as we saw above, Jung considered European hysteria to be a violent reaction against the inorganic and life-binding temporality of the commodity, here we see that its arctic variant shares a similar psychogenesis: the Eskimo's natural response to the alien temporality of capitalism is a "fear of the future." Both European and arctic hysteria are thus related forms of psychic arrhythmia, afflictions of mental nonsynchronicity. For Jung, piblokto can be attributed neither to biological factors such as Eskimo nutrition nor to any innate cultural proclivity toward hysteroid behavior, as some researchers proposed. Rather, as he understood it, the outbreaks of hysteria that arctic explorers recorded in the Eskimo population were instead triggered by these very explorers themselves. In other words, the explorers were not mere observers of this malady, but its traumatic cause.[76] For Jung, piblokto represented a violent reaction to a psychic pathogen that the Western explorers brought with them: the future.

It is warrants recalling here that futurity, of course, is not a cultural universal, but a European invention of fairly recent vintage that emerged with the transition to bourgeois society in the seventeenth and eighteenth centuries.[77]

The privilege it enjoys within bourgeois culture can, moreover, be directly attributed to the capitalist mode of production. Linking together temporality and technology, the paleoanthropologist André Leroi-Gourhan, for example, has argued that the experience of time is neither the result of spontaneous perception nor a general a priori of human consciousness, but instead comes into being as a reflection of the technical forces of production in a given society. The shared methods and rhythms of labor used by members of a society to make things—what he calls "mechanical operational sequences"—establish the formal architecture that temporality will assume for an entire cultural group.[78] It is here, according to Leroi-Gourhan, in the most basic repertoires of collective work gestures, that the fundamental syntactical units in a given culture's grammar of time are first articulated. These practiced sequences, which surface in all varieties of activity from stoking a fire to receiving a guest, become the basis for social memory "through which human individuals receive the whole of their operating behavior."[79] Thus, Leroi-Gourhan explains, if the technical mode of production determines the physical countenance and design that artifacts will assume in a given culture, the syntax of making used by this culture also determines the shape and texture that time will assume "at a deep level of collective memory."[80] The mode of production generates physical things, but also time itself.

Jung placed the ethno-psychiatric malady of piblokto, or "fear of the future," at the beginning of his industrial novel because, I would argue, this phenomenon emblematizes the violent collision between two modes of production—the nomadic hunter-gatherer and the sedentary capitalist—and their corresponding architectures of time—presentist and futurist. To be sure, Jung's image of the Eskimaux as a revolutionary society without accumulation, without stored wealth or capital, without that morbid "knotting" (*Verknotung*) of psychic energy known as property (*Werke*, 6:18) is a European idealization of primitive communism. And yet, the connection that Jung posits between propertyless, nomadic cultures and presentist consciousness is not without some degree of historical insight. The historian Lewis Mumford, for example, explained that the ability to store alimentation (such as grain) and sources of energy (such as wood and coal) brings with it strategies of planning and deferral as its psychological corollary.[81] Methods of stockpiling and hoarding found in sedentary societies, Mumford observed, are essential technical preconditions for the social order of capitalism, with its consciousness toward investment and futurity. (These techniques of storage and the investment mentality are, however, only the necessary but not sufficient preconditions of capitalism, which, of course, also requires an additional element to function: the expropriation of the means of production, which, as Marx observes, drives the peasantry from the land and transforms them into proletarian workers who are henceforth "free and rightless," but also highly mobile [*vogelfrei*] nomads.)

In contrast to the capitalist system the mode of production found in hunter-gatherer societies does not rely so heavily on accumulation and a compound division of labor. As a result, the "operational sequences" here are different, as are the corresponding mental architectures of time. Techniques of storage are extremely limited for migratory arctic foragers such as the Eskimo, not only because there is no grain to store in a frozen environment devoid of phytogenic food sources, but also because their highly mobile existence precludes significant material accumulation. Since time is articulated in these societies not in vast cycles of investment and reward, but in short-term rhythms such as the circannual migrations of quarry, the future assumes a different countenance here than in capitalist societies.[82] Jung consequently imagined that psychic energies circulate freely among the Eskimeaux rather than being bound and delayed in the form of capitalist *Be-sitz*. Much like the celebrated nomads of Deleuze and Guattari, these mobile foragers struck Jung as natural enemies of a sedentary capitalist state that seeks to inscribe its subjects within a system of production based on fixity and accumulation. Their "fear of the future" was, for him, a strategy to elude capture within the temporal horizon that the European explorers brought with them.

In this regard Jung's nomadic and presentist Eskimo represents a countermodel to the capitalist entrepreneur, a hoarder who lives in a permanent state of expectation. Training his eye on the future yields of his investments, the entrepreneur is always ahead of himself, as Max Weber pointed out in his epochal *The Protestant Ethic and the Spirit of Capitalism* (1904–1905). The historical emergence of modern capitalism, Weber observed in this text, required more than just the convergence of an economic system (the rule of private property) with a technical mode of manufacture (factory production): a certain "mode of living" (*Lebensführung*) that originates in the Protestant worldview was necessary as well, a psychological component he described as a proclivity toward deferral and a fixation on the future. Having chosen to live in "deep spiritual isolation," the acetic Protestant sects that would eventually birth the "spirit of capitalism" dedicated their attention exclusively toward the afterlife, toward an eternal future to come.[83] Contemptuous of all this-worldliness and presence, their proto-capitalist doctrine displayed a fundamental "antagonism to sensuous culture of all kinds"[84] and encouraged its adherents instead to pursue a "systematic rational struggle to attain and retain certain knowledge of future (otherworldly) salvation."[85] This "exclusive preoccupation with the beyond," Weber observed, engenders a consciousness that is "entirely transcendental and utterly irrational" in its eschatological orientation. This consciousness becomes the psychological basis for the spirit and mind (*Geist*) of capitalism.[86]

As Weber's text forcibly demonstrates, capitalism emerges out of a treble scheme of determination: in addition to a legal order based on expropriation and a technical mode of production that promotes the accumulation of dead labor, it also requires anticipation, renunciation, and deferred gratification, that is, the psychological constellation commonly known as the profit motive. All three of these factors—legal, technical and psychological—converge for Jung in the system of *credit*, a phenomenon that he placed at the center of his narrative about capitalism's historical emergence in central Europe. In a short piece from 1919 entitled "The Proletarianization of Handicraft," Jung underscored the role that the introduction of credit played in the transition from artisanal modes of production to capitalist ones (*Werke*, 1.1:209–213). (The modernization of the old craft system was a subject he knew well, since his father was a member of the class of craftsmen and had himself published articles on the conditions of this class under industrialization.[87]) According to Jung, the introduction of credit was in fact more important to the progress of capitalism in Germany than industrialization and the restructuring of the mode of production. This is the case for two reasons: first, the use of credit increases the practical flexibility of capital, giving it more resiliency at historical moments of economic crisis; and second, by elongating the life cycles of money and investment, credit opens onto the horizon of futurity that is, according to Weber, essential to the experience of capitalist modernity. This latter aspect conjures up the famous line from Nietzsche's autobiography "I live on my own credit; it is perhaps a mere prejudice that I live" (*Ich lebe auf meinen eigenen Kredit hin, es ist vielleicht bloß ein Vorurteil, daß ich lebe*), in which credit establishes an existential debt that can be amortized only posthumously, in the afterlife.[88]

The modern European subject lives in and for the future, projecting himself into the temporal horizon established by a system of monetary credit that is, in effect, the secularized legacy of the Protestant afterlife. Within this framework, money operates as a "deposit against future settlements" that "introduces an omnitemporality," as Lyotard observed: it "*opens up* duration and the durable, permanence."[89] Niklas Luhmann similarly noted that bourgeois society's reliance on "time-using and time-binding mechanisms like money" has conditioned a subjective mentality that, being at home with a high degree of temporal complexity, can readily accommodate and navigate multiple *Temporalgestalten*, "forms" or "shapes" of time.[90] Because this worldview "operates on the premise of continuing its processes," Luhmann explained, it also requires "a present future for [its] present motivation." For capitalism to work it must guarantee a predictable course of accumulation and eventual reward. "Deferment of gratification is a main prerequisite for the economic system as a condition for capital investment." Without this promise of continuity, capitalism collapses. If the promise of "credit" were revoked and the temporal projection were to contract—if, in other words, the future were rescinded—capitalism's fate would be sealed: capital "would not survive a considerable shrinkage of time horizons," since this, Luhmann concluded, would "endanger trust in politics, political ideology, value schemes etc."[91]

Jung's revolutionary eudaemonics, his *Technology of Happiness*, thus proceeds by obliterating the line of credit and diminishing horizon of futurity. These strategies are foregrounded in the book's final chapter, which opposes "life" (*Leben*) to "destiny" (*Schicksal*) and demands that the reader choose between the two. With the former lie sensuous presence, pleasure, and collectivity;

with the latter futurity, deferral, and anomie. "Happiness devours the future, one could say" (*Werke*, 6:78). This unbinding of psychic energies is experienced by the individual as a simplification or flattening of time, an experience of *jouissance* in which "there is no more successiveness, no sequence, nothing that follows" (*Werke*, 6:78). Inaccessible to our logical parsing of time, the pleromatic condition described by Jung results in an "intensification" in the present (*Werke*, 6:69). Familiar units for quantifying time have no place here: "Fulfilled experience measures time differently from the way it is measured today. A year is not an eternally binding concept, but—a year of happiness?" he goads. "How long does such a thing last? Who could know?" (*Werke*, 6:99). Jung knows well that this notion of calculating happiness chronometrically is, of course, absurd. And yet it is a calculation that the bourgeois entrepreneur performs daily.

The psychological nexus of property and temporal complexity explored by Jung has a direct relevance to those questions of narrative form that have framed our analysis of the industrial novel. For if a culture's technical mode of production cultivates a particular way of perceiving time, this temporal architecture would naturally find expression in the narrative structures that the culture uses to map time symbolically. For Jung, the differences between the propertied bourgeoisie, with its ethos of deferred gratification, and the "*vogelfrei*" working class, which like the nomadic Eskimaux, lacks a sense of futurity, could also be observed at the level of literary genre. This explains, for example, Gertrud Alexander's claim in her review of Jung's *Conquest of the Machines* that novels are not the literature of the working class. As evidence for Alexander's thesis, we can cite the sociological studies conducted by Lawrence Leshan in the early 1950s, which, in an effort to understand the class factors determining the "deferred gratification pattern" and "future orientation" of individuals, included within their battery of tests one that compared the periods of time covered in stories told by children of different classes. Here Leshan discovered that "the middle-class group would produce stories covering a longer time-period from beginning (the starting of the action) to the end (final action) than would the lower-class group."[92] These findings suggest that the experience of temporal continuity over long cycles of investment and profit give children of the propertied classes a greater facility for understanding and manipulating the intricate causal schemes that are the basis for complex narrative structure. Simply put: the bourgeoisie cultivates better storytellers.

This collusion between capital, futurity, and narrative will come as no surprise to anyone familiar with the social history of the novel, an aesthetic form whose canonization in the eighteenth century mirrored the historical ascent of the bourgeois class. Indeed, the very defining feature of the novel's narrative structure was its open temporal horizon, Mikhail Bakhtin argued in his 1941 talk "The Novel as Literary Genre." In contrast to the traditional oral epic, which is an "utterly finished [*завершен*] thing" that is "absolutely completed," the modern novel is marked by "openendedness, indecision, indeterminacy."[93] Bakhtin explained that the novel, as a symbolic form, contributes to the emergence of historical consciousness as such, with its dynamic understanding of human existence and endeavor as unfinished processes. "For the first time in artistic-ideological consciousness, time and the world become historical: they unfold, albeit at first still unclearly and confusedly, as becoming, as an uninterrupted movement into a real future, as a unified, all-embracing and unconcluded process."[94] According to Bakhtin, this sense of dynamism and contingency constitutes the specific "'modernity' [*модернистичность*] of the novel."[95] However, Bakhtin continued, the novel's openendedness should not be misconstrued as plotlessness. To the contrary, the temporal concatenations and causal ligatures of plot are the very essence of the modern novel. It is in fact precisely because novels are philosophically open-ended and unresolved, Bakhtin reasons, that a compensatory demand emerges for *formal* completion and exhaustiveness, which is realized in the novel's punctual beginning, complex middle, and determinate end. A taut linear narrative propels the novel forward. Bakhtin thus observes that the novel's constitutional openness, its arc toward a contingent and ever-receding future, arouses in the reader a corresponding "impulse to continue," an "impulse to end." By its very nature the novel "demands continuation, it moves into the future, and the more actively and consciously it moves into the future the more tangible and indispensible its inconclusiveness [*незавершенность*] becomes."[96]

The system of "narrative desire"—the "desire *for* the end" that motivates the consumption of the novel—is thus nothing other than an ideological surplus value produced by the plotted narrative structure in order to sustain the complex temporal edifice of capitalism and its psychological pattern of libidinal capture and deferred gratification.[97] This particular aspect of the symbiosis between the novel and capitalism was proposed by Lukács, who observed in 1934 that the emergence of the novel coincided evolutionarily with the advent of the capitalist mode of production and its strategy of primitive accumulation.[98] In contrast to epic narration, which is "historically connected to a primitive phase in humanity's development,"[99] the novel, Lukács wrote, belongs to a civilization with a compound division of labor and a corresponding "need for genetic explanations."[100] With its protracted psychological cycles of tension and release, investment and reward, the capitalist mode of being requires a mode of temporal modeling whose complexity is alien to epic portrayal. Here the novel supplies a rich panoply of cognitive resources that help the subject to navigate the temporality of capitalist modernity: an extended causal network linking the most disparate and distant of events; a nuanced system of verbal tenses that map a vast territory between a fantasmatic past and a speculative future; and a notion of psychological identity that is constituted through continuity and mnemonic sedimentation.

It was in the great nineteenth-century novel that these devices reached the apogee of their refinement and influence. The historical mission of the novel at this time was to endow the abstract cycles of capital with a human face by synchronizing them with the generational sequence of the living. This structural homology between the business enterprise and the bourgeois individual was still possible in the early nineteenth century, when, as David Harvey observed, capitalist activity was still "organized almost entirely on the lines of the family business enterprise." At this historical moment, the *Familienroman* and the *Industrieroman* were still commensurable forms. But this structural correspondence is lost with the transition from capitalism's "heroic" phase to the phase of monopoly capital, when the business enterprise uncouples itself definitively from the generational cycle. With the liberation of capital's autarkic rhythm, the novel can no longer succeed at mediating between lived, experiential time and the tempo established by the mode of production. Having thus lost its human referent, the novel becomes so elaborate, its causalities so tenuous, that it can no longer be overseen or grasped by the mind. Here the horizon of futurity that was first disclosed by the novel's "openendedness, indecision, indeterminacy" (Bakhtin) expands uncontrollably.

If the nineteenth-century realist novel once satisfied the psychological "need for genetic explanations" that, according to Lukács, corresponded to the contemporaneous mode of production, with the transition to monopoly capital, this bond of adequacy was broken, and the novel began to cede its privilege as a narrative art. "The novel still exists," Shklovskii noted in 1929, "although it exists like the light of an extinguished star."[101] Just as photography lost its epistemic footing with the fragmentation of Euclidean space and the corollary decline of the perspective paradigm, the novel was similarly decommissioned as a symbolic form. With this loss of cultural motivation, the reality effects of the novel no longer work spontaneously, and the novel's resources for structuring time, once transparent, now became opaque and were formalized as devices. In Proust's epochal *In Search of Lost Time*, for example, the realist novel's techniques for navigating time have become subjectless: liberated but also autonomized, these devices begin to fold in on themselves and multiply, producing a mnemonic *mise en abyme* that eventually exceeds the conscious mind's capacity to regulate the flow of time. At this point, the orderly analepses of the nineteenth-century novel yield to *mémoire involuntaire*, a quasi-mechanical mode of recollection over which the individual has no control.

Judgment Day: *The Threepenny Novel*

Bertolt Brecht's *The Threepenny Novel* (1934) confronts the certain desuetude of the novel as a cultural form. Like *The Conquest of the Machines*, Brecht's novel articulates the nonsynchronicity between labor and capital as a distortion in the generational cycle, but whereas Jung addressed this conflict chiefly in terms of physiological tempo and biological rhythms, Brecht focuses instead on the issue of generation as an epistemological problem. Systems of lineage are a central concern for Brecht, whose *Threepenny Novel* frames an elaborate network of economic transactions within the causal-genetic scheme of the novel. Using the same *dramatis personae* as his enormously successful *Threepenny Opera* (1928), *The Threepenny Novel* relocates the original characters into turn-of-the-century London at the time of the imperialist Boer War. Paradoxically, the novel is both a recapitulation of the events depicted in *The Threepenny Opera* and a continuation of the earlier work. At once simultaneous with and posterior to the *Opera*, the very conception of the *Novel* raises questions about the serviceability of succession and lineage as analytic categories. As Benjamin observed in a review of the book, multiple distinct historical moments seem to coexist simultaneously in the *Novel*.[102] In chapter 4 we will analyze in more detail this curious logic of continuation-in-repetition, a central phenomenon of the poetics of realism after modernism, but for the moment it suffices to observe that Brecht's strategy to both resume and overwrite a previous work gives *The Threepenny Novel* a premise that is, from the perspective of narrative time, already quite complex.

Unlike the traditional industrial novel or its Soviet variant, the production novel, both of which foreground scenes of factory labor, Brecht's *Threepenny Novel* focuses exclusively on the maneuvers of finance capital, a form of enterprise unadulterated by the material stuff of productive capital. It depicts "development" in its purest metaphysical state. The plot of the novel is organized around three overlapping financial systems: Peachum's consortium of street beggars, Coax's ship venture, and Macheath's commercial syndicate. Having left behind his life as a street cutthroat long before the action begins, the Macheath of the *Novel* is an aspiring businessman and founder of a chain of discount retail stores called the B-Shops. In search of investment capital to finance his business, he begins, as in the *Opera*, to court young Polly, daughter of the wealthy Peachum. Through a complex series of machinations and plot turns, Macheath manages over the half-year depicted in the novel to restructure and expand his enterprise, absorbing the stores of his competitors and becoming, by the end of the novel, the esteemed director of a major bank.

Brecht borrowed Macheath's business strategies for the B-Shops from the latest corporate practices, modeling this system in part after the one pioneered by the Karstadt and Epa concerns in the late 1920s; an even more important source were the tactics developed by shoe manufacturer Tomáš Baťa, the legendary "Henry Ford of Eastern Europe" who combined factory production methods with a chain of retail outlets to create one of the first vertically integrated industrial concerns (*Werke*, 16:414).[103] Thus, the setting for the novel may recall London at the turn of the twentieth century, but the capitalist strategies depicted in the 1934 book were entirely state-of-the-art. Brecht describes these economic networks and transactions in exquisite detail. He writes, as one reviewer suggested, "with the utterly grueling meticulousness of a specialist," sparing the reader none of the technical minutiae of his protagonists' financial activities (quoted in *Werke*, 16:424). A sheet of calculations made by Brecht while writing *The Threepenny Novel* attests to his meticulous attention to such details (fig. 2.1). Here he drew inspiration from the novels of British author Samuel Butler, whose "pedantry in matters of money" he found to be "extremely productive literarily" (*Werke*, 21:361).

As the consummate modern capitalist, Macheath is passionless, motivated only by a purely rational calculus. Just as he feels no carnal passion for Polly but views her merely as an opportunity to capitalize his B-Shops, Peachum similarly sees in his daughter's marriage only a potential source of financial gain. None of the novel's conflicts originate in the drama of human passion, and few of its reversals of fortune offer emotional gratification to the reader. Certainly one feat of *The Threepenny Novel*, then, is that it manages to motivate narratively 400 pages of what are, in effect, financial transactions. Eschewing the "narrative desire" of the traditional dramatic novel, Brecht's book compels its reader without any recourse to emotional intensity and catharsis, binding the reader's attention instead with the more phlegmatic and sublimated pleasures of logical analysis, riddle solving, remainderless bookkeeping, and, of course, utmost verbal wit.

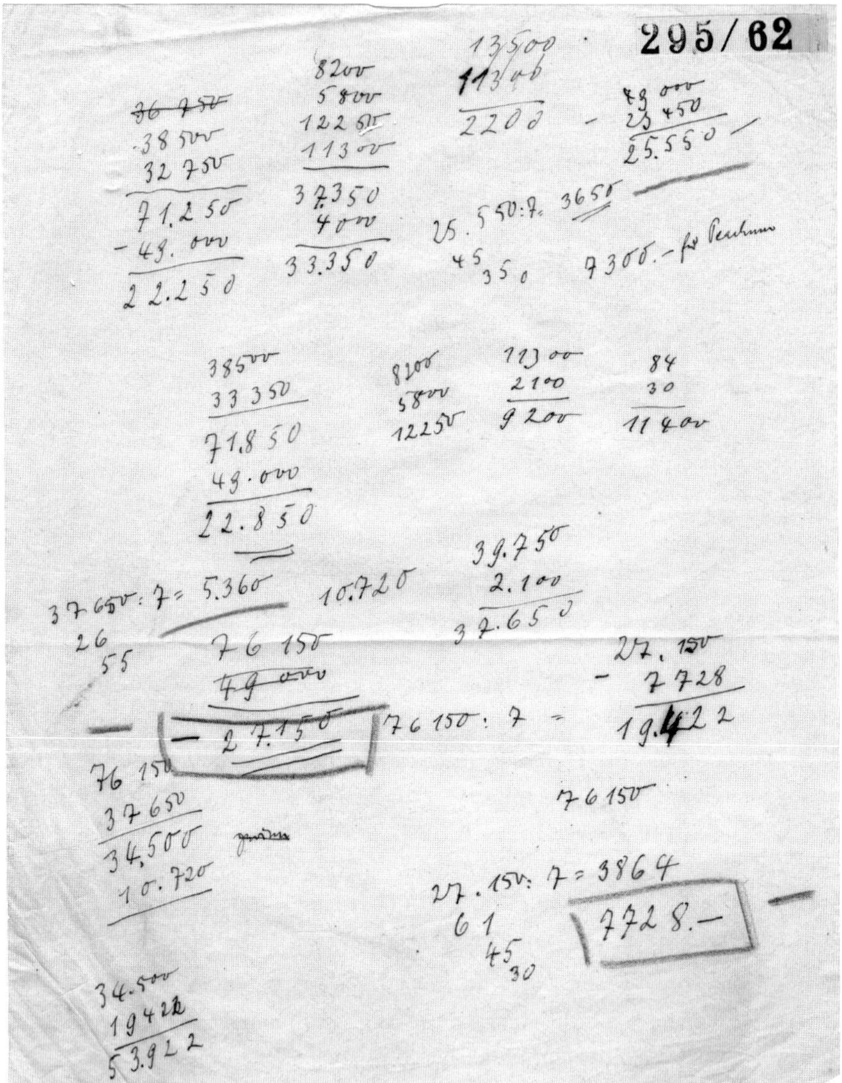

Figure 2.1 Bertolt Brecht's calculations for *The Threepenny Novel.* Akademie der Künste, Berlin, Bertolt Brecht Archive, 295/062.

As we have already noted, the version of capitalism depicted in *The Threepenny Novel* was one that, by this historical moment, no longer corresponded to any properly human scale. To recall again Henry Ford's observation from 1923: "big business is really too big to be human." Schumpeter similarly explained in 1928 that "the enterprise of the 'liberal' era was usually the enterprise *of one* man, i.e. of one family," while the contemporary corporation had exploded this anthropomorphism, substituting for it the abstract "entrepreneur function" (*Unternehmerfunktion*) that "is never purely embodied in concrete person; its essence [*ihr Wesen*: thus also 'its being'] must therefore always first be extrapolated analytically from a relatively complicated conglomerate."[104] As it incorporated ever more social functions into its integrated network of managed production and consumption, the corporation indeed began to merge with the state itself during the interwar years. Schumpeter thus explained that, from a sociological perspective, "the modern enterprise has outgrown the driving forces and human types of economic competition and, in its essence, structure and methods, has started to resemble a kind of public administrative body."[105] This was, of course, the decade in which the state began to assume control over the maintenance of human capital by introducing comprehensive social welfare systems, as Foucault observed in his late lectures on biopolitics; simultaneously, the state also began at this time to intervene in economic issues at the national level through policies of fiscal and monetary intervention that seem routine today but, as David Harvey points out, were unprecedented before the 1930s.[106]

Needless to say, capital's evolution from the assembly line to the multinational corporation and, eventually, to a quasi-state did not make for a great dramatic plot. As Brecht observed, the atrophy of the human dimension under monopoly capitalism was accompanied by a certain disfiguration of the novel's form. With a typically Brechtian reflexivity, the entrepreneur Macheath waxes nostalgic for the good old times as a street thug when everything was simpler, more straightforward, and more *human*:

> All of this haggling disgusts me, a former street gangster! Here I sit and quibble about percentages. Why don't I just take out my knife

> and stick it into them if they won't give me what I want? What an undignified way of doing business, smoking cigars and signing agreements! So I'm supposed to smuggle in little propositions and make subtle intimations! Why not just say straight out: Your money or your life! . . . All of this hiding behind judges and bailiffs is undignified! . . . Clearly one can't get anywhere today with the simple, straightforward and natural methods of street robbery. The latter have the same relationship to today's business practices as sailing ships do to steam ships. But the old days were more human [*die alten Zeiten waren menschlicher*]. (*Werke*, 16:358)

Sentimentalizing the simplicity, even humanity of his former gangster life in *The Threepenny Opera*, Macheath reminisces about an era before the endlessly mediated legal machinations of finance capital, the good old days when conflict was still chiefly dramatic, not bureaucratic. His words recall Kracauer's famous 1925 line about a celebrated Weimar murder case: "Only in a human world does a crime have a criminal."[107] Macheath, alas, is no longer a criminal because the world is no longer properly human.

But the distinction Macheath draws here between the old and the new is not solely one between two phases in the development of capitalism. The distinction also applies metatextually to the two phases of his life and exploits as a character in two different works, first in *The Threepenny Opera* (which takes place in 1837) and then in *The Threepenny Novel* (which takes place in the early 1900s). In other words, when he observes that "the old days were more human," the novel-character Macheath is speaking at once about an earlier historical moment of capitalism as well as his prior incarnation on the theatrical stage in *The Threepenny Opera*. Here Brecht provides a canny reflection on the status of figuration in the two *Threepenny* projects. Like the transition from "heroic" to monopoly capitalism, the transition from the 1928 play to the 1934 novel is accompanied by a loss in figural concretion and a dehumanization of the contents of the work. Indeed, because it always involves bodies on stage, theater is far more immediate and "human" than the written word. As Reger had argued, it was this ineluctable anthropomorphism that disqualified theater from representing the modern corporate enterprise. The dramatic arts were simply too mimetic, sensuous, and concrete to depict the abstract metaphysics of contemporary finance capital. Writing about the modern "petroleum complex," for example, Brecht once noted that "petroleum creates new relationships," although these relationships eluded representation in contemporary art and literature: "Petroleum resists depiction in five acts; today's catastrophes do not unfold in a linear fashion, but in cycles of crisis in which each fungible 'hero' changes with the individual phases, etc." (*Werke*, 21:303).

In a statement written between the *Opera* and the *Novel* and published in Reger's journal *Der Scheinwerfer* (*The Spotlight*) in 1930, Brecht's collaborator Elisabeth Hauptmann explained the difficulties that arose in attempting to depict modern economic processes on the stage. When Brecht recently attempted to write a play about the Chicago wheat futures market,

> We collected a lot of technical literature for this piece. I myself interviewed a series of specialists; and towards the end Brecht began reading texts on economics, since he found the financial practices to be extremely opaque and so he had to see how things stood with theories of money. But even before he began making discoveries about this material that were extremely important for him, he already knew that the (great) form of the drama as it was known then was just as unsuitable for representing modern processes such as the distribution of the world's wheat or the construction of railroads as it was for representing the lives of the individuals who control our era. The traditional form of the drama was not even suitable for depicting *actions with consequences* [*Handlungen mit Folgen*]. Such things, he said, are not dramatic in our sense, and if you "poeticize" them, then they are no longer true; furthermore, there is no such thing as drama any longer, and if you see that today's world no longer fits into the drama, well, then the drama no longer fits into today's world.[108]

Perhaps unsurprisingly, the project discussed here, *Joe Fleischhacker*, never made it to the stage, but instead shared the same fate as Sergei Eisenstein's unrealized project in the late 1920s for a film of Marx's *Das Kapital*. The resonances between the two projects are indeed noteworthy, as Eisenstein's film confronted problems very similar to those faced by Brecht. As Eisenstein explained in his working notes for the unrealized film, depicting the modern capitalist enterprise presented a unique challenge, since it required the thorough "de-anecdotalization" of the source material: the "detachment from a specific place," the division into "nonfigurative chapters," the leap "from representation of ordinary life to abstract and generalized imagery," and, thus, the "complete departure from the factual and anecdotal."[109] "De-anecdotalization" was effectively dedramatization. With the gradual movement away from "the factual and anecdotal," the artwork sheds its empirical referentiality and documentary specificity—a treatment of source material that, as we have seen, lay behind Reger's refusal to provide Ehrenburg with the names of the actual people after whom the characters in *Union of the Strong Hand* were modeled. (In an intriguing coincidence, Eisenstein planned to include in his film of *Das Kapital* a portrait of the industrialist Krupp, the central figure in Reger's industrial novel.)

For the same reasons, Brecht developed an art form that was far more abstract and analytic than the traditional theater. His epic technique—"drama with footnotes," as he called it—was already a step in this direction. More radical in its renunciation of the anecdotal and the mimetic, however, was the *Threepenny Novel*. For example, the book provides few vivid descriptions of the characters, giving the reader little idea of what Macheath or Coax looks like.[110] Equally antitheatrical is the almost complete absence of dialogue. Instead, the characters hold forth in lengthy, quasi-philosophical monologues, and at those rare moments when they do converse, their words are seldom rendered directly, in quotation marks, but are instead recounted and summarized by the narrator. Indeed, there is so little dialogue in the text that one is hard pressed to imagine that the author of *The Threepenny Novel* was one of the most important playwrights of the twentieth century.

Nevertheless, for all his novel's abstraction, Brecht insisted that sensuous perception could not be rejected entirely, that art must not be abandoned for the abstract analytic of science. What was needed, rather, was a strategy for depicting capital's mechanisms without spurious anthropomorphizing. "Here there was much to see, much to make visible," he wrote of his experiments in representing the capitalist system (*Werke*, 21:460). Ultimately what seemed to offer the ideal compromise between art and science was the detective novel, a genre that appealed to him because of its particularly close kinship to logical thought. In a 1938 essay "On the Popularity of the Crime Novel," he likened the detective story to a crossword puzzle, praising the structural rigor of a genre whose riddle is resolved through the meticulous and diligent application of the scientific method (*Werke*, 22:504–510). As if conducting an experiment, the literary detective proceeds by gathering data, eliminating hypotheses that are revealed as false, and positing causal schemes where probabilities run high. The affective corollary to this investigative method was a diffuse economy of attention, which Brecht praised as superior to the emotional intensity of dramatic catharsis. In contrast to classical dramatic forms such as the bourgeois tragedy, which hones the spectator's attention on the red thread of the plot, detective genres require an open mode of perception that proceeds inductively. To remain vigilant for possible clues, the reader cannot allow herself to be misled by the human drama of the plot. Since every trivial piece of information must be read forensically, as a potential clue to the text's riddle, the reader must pay equal attention to every bit of noisy detail and seemingly meaningless incident.

Of course, crime novels require murders and trials, and Brecht obligingly outfits *The Threepenny Novel* with two of each. But, significantly, in neither case is the actual culprit ever found. This is because in both cases the culpable party is a disembodied system, or collective agent. So, for example, an owner of one of the B-Shops, Mary Swayer, is driven to suicide as a result of the wolfish business practices of Macheath, who ruins his shopowners in order to gain advantage over a competing retail concern. In her case the accused is acquitted, because, under the laws of capitalism, murder through material privation is, of course, completely licit. Coax, too, is murdered, and seemingly more directly: attacked first by a member of Macheath's gang, he stumbles away only to be finished off minutes later by someone under the charge of Peachum. Yet like

Swayer's demise, the cause of Coax's death is *in*determinable precisely because it is *over*determined, the consequence of multiple batterings delivered by two parties working independently of each other. The agent responsible for delivering the death blow is not clear. Just as Swayer's death is not directly attributable to Macheath, who is only following good capitalist strategy when he pushes her to financial ruin, Coax's death cannot be blamed entirely on any one of his assailants, nor on the two men who commissioned the murder independently of one another. And when Coax's alleged killer is finally found, it is the wrong man who is tried and hanged. The book ends, then, with a third collective murder. In this last case, it is society itself that commits the crime, in an act of class justice.

The overdetermined deaths of Swayer and Coax raise complex questions about the attribution of guilt and agency in cases of collective crime. Such issues were of course highly relevant at the time that Brecht wrote *The Threepenny Novel* in 1933–1934, when the victories of European fascism prompted consideration of the relationship between collective violence and regressive social configurations. Novels about corporate crime, in particular, provide an important resource for thinking about the agency and behavior of such "aggregate persons" (*Verbandspersonen*), as Stefan Andriopoulos has demonstrated. Although on the surface *The Threepenny Novel* is a corporate crime story, the subtext of this narrative, with its focus on collective crime and guilt, is clearly that of European fascism. In strictly legal terms, corporate bodies, like the state, are not subject to the law because they lack the features of concrete personhood necessary to assume guilt for a crime.[111] And so despite the panoply of crimes in the capitalist jungle of *The Threepenny Novel*, from murder and theft to rape and extortion, in the end no responsible parties can be found for these acts. In a functionally differentiated and bureaucratized corporation that disperses agency across a number of individuals, these forms of violence are not attributable to any one person, but are, rather, shared by all. The guilty party cannot be established in Brecht's novel because the guilty party is the capitalist system itself. Thus, while *The Threepenny Novel* engages the conventions of the traditional detective novel, it simultaneously short-circuits the method of forensic inquiry that is intrinsic to this genre. Or to borrow Benjamin's words from his review of the book,

"Brecht's procedure consists in retaining the highly developed technique of the crime novel but neutralizing its rules" (*Schriften*, 3:447–448; *Writings*, 3:8).

In addition to the two trials that seek (and fail) to resolve Swayer's and Coax's murders, a third, still more significant trial takes place in *The Threepenny Novel*, which Brecht saves for the final pages. This event is nothing less than Judgment Day itself. Presiding over the trial is one of the characters in Peachum's outfit, an invalid veteran of the Boer War named Fewkoomby. The proceedings, which take place in a dream, promises to track down all those who have ever been responsible for economic exploitation and to repay all of those who have ever been expropriated. As the "greatest arraignment of all times," the trial promises, in other words, to discover the historical source of social inequality itself, the very foundational injustice of capitalism (*Werke*, 16:380). Needless to say, the task is not an easy one. Fewkoomby's conservative estimate is that the proceedings will last several hundred years. The investigation will be exhausting, but Fewkoomby reasons that the only way for capital to repay all its debts is to reconstruct the labors of all expropriated generations, both past and present.

So Fewkoomby begins by subpoenaing the dead. "Everyone who had ever set foot on this earth was allowed to voice his plaints" (*Werke*, 16:381). He questions not only physical laborers such as the suicide Mary Swayer but also those who performed the ideological work that perpetuated the injustices of capitalism. So, for example, the judge interrogates a priest who, earlier in the novel, promulgated religious parables that reinforce the political quiescence of the masses. As the inquiry proceeds, however, it becomes clear to the judge that he will never arrive at the definitive source of value. Each interrogation leads to still more interrogations. With mounting confusion, Fewkoomby begins to rave at the dead:

> There is the wall of the house—where is the bricklayer? Is he ever really paid in full? And this paper! Someone had to make it! Was he sufficiently compensated for it? And this table here! Is there really nothing owed to the man who planed the wood for it? The washing on the line! The line itself! And even the tree, which didn't plant

> itself here. This knife here! Is everything paid for? Fully? Of course not! We have to send around a circular asking everyone who isn't paid in full to register! The history books and biographies won't suffice! Where are the wage lists? (*Werke*, 16:391)

With the failure of this forensic inquiry, both the dream and the novel break off abruptly. Fewkoomby's noble but misguided attempt to reconstruct the genealogy of the commodity is doomed, since each particular instantiation of dead labor is always built on more labor. In the end, the trial may not arrive at the source of inequality, but this very failure succeeds in exposing the absurdity of the physiocratic conceit that there could be a foundational or natural "origin" of value.

Althusser once observed that Brecht's work displays two distinct "forms of temporality that do not achieve any mutual integration, which have no relation to one another, which coexist and interconnect, but never meet each other, so to speak."[112] In this noncoincidence, Brecht's industrial novel winds up demonstrating yet another aspect of the incongruous temporalities of capital and the human. The Judgment Day episode questions the very adequacy of a genetic framework for describing the "development" of capital. As we saw earlier, Lukács noted that the novel's historical emergence as an aesthetic form responded to capitalist society's "need for genetic explanations"; for a time at least, its genealogical narratives flourished from the structural resemblance between the evolution of the business enterprise and the generational sequence of the bourgeois family. But this homology was short lived. As Brecht's Judgment Day demonstrates, the mechanisms of monopoly capital had grown too complex by the 1930s and could no longer be modeled using the novel's genealogical framework. When the subjective temporality of *Bildung* yields to the abstract scheme of *Entwicklung*, when "formation" gives way to "development," the *Industrieroman* definitively parts ways with the *Familienroman*. The movement of capital, Fewkoomby discovers, does not observe the linear concatenations found in "history books" or the anthropomorphic time of "biographies." As his demand for "wage lists" suggests, mathematical languages are more adequate for depicting modern capital than narrative ones (fig. 2.1).[113] Fewkoomby's attempt to reconstruct the genealogy of capitalist production, to parse the commodity out in linear time, ends up trapped in a tautological circle, since the human mind cannot comprehend the paradoxical fact that capital seems always to presuppose itself.

It is worth pointing out here that *The Threepenny Novel* is not just a book about capital. It is also a book about *Kapital*. Brecht's commentators have amply documented *The Threepenny Novel*'s numerous borrowings from Marx's opus, such as the passage describing the death of Mary Ann Walkley, which Brecht quotes virtually verbatim from Marx.[114] But, beyond the content, correspondences between the two works can also be found at a structural level. Indeed, far more intriguing for our inquiry are certain parallels in the construction that raise questions about the aesthetic strategies Brecht borrowed from Marx to represent capital. It was likely Karl Korsch who can be credited for leading Brecht to the insight that the textual design of *Das Kapital* was integral to understanding capital's mechanisms. In his 1932 introduction to *Das Kapital*, Brecht's initiator into Marxism wrote, for example, of the "aesthetic attraction" of "the Marxian mode of presentation."[115] Marx's explication of capital's properties and logic is not purely theoretical or scientific, Korsch insisted, but relies on certain strategies of textual exposition. Because the mechanisms of capital can only be grasped within an "artistic whole," as Marx described his text, *Das Kapital* tries to develop a mode of presentation, or *Darstellung*, that is proper to its subject matter.[116] The challenge of presenting the system of modern capital adequately had in fact precipitated Brecht's turn to Marx in the late 1920s. As he confessed to a Moscow audience in May 1935, aesthetic concerns, not revolutionary sentiment or political conviction, led the playwright to Marx. While working on *Joe Fleischhacker*, the fragment discussed in the earlier quote by Hauptmann, Brecht ran aground on the problem of how to depict the mechanisms of the wheat futures market, which seemed to him to be "inexplicable" and "incomprehensible."[117] So he began to read Marx. He turned to *Das Kapital* because the structure of this "artistic whole" contained the solution to the aesthetic aporia that he had encountered in his attempt to bring the system of finance capital to the stage.

Nowhere is the structural rhyme between *The Threepenny Novel* and *Das Kapital* clearer than at the end of each book, where Fewkoomby's dream of

Judgment Day mirrors *Das Kapital*'s final section, "So-called Primitive Accumulation." Both chapters wrestle with a contradiction that is fundamental to the (il)logic of capital and thus a seemingly insuperable obstacle to its depiction: the impossibility of retracing the steps of accumulation back to a foundational moment of expropriation, back to an original crime. This task is impossible because capital has no historical genealogy system, but instead operates outside of linear time. "What Marx proved," Balibar noted, "is not the fact that capitalism has liberated the development of the productive forces once and for all, but the fact that capitalism has imposed on the productive forces a determinate type of development whose rhythm and pattern are peculiar to it, dictated by the form of the process of capitalist accumulation."[118] Confronted with these particular rhythms and patterns, Brecht frames Fewkoomby's investigation as the biblical Judgment Day, an event at the end of time that transcends the laws of historical sequence. Ultimately this investigation fails, breaking off abruptly, because Fewkoomby's forensic mode of inquiry has no purchase on the laws of capital's "development," which elude these causal schemes.

In his introduction to *Das Kapital*, Korsch described the contradiction encountered by Marx, who, even after hundreds of pages of detailed economic analysis, still faced "an unsolved problem to be elucidated, which proves in the last analysis to be non-economic in character. This problematic residue may be expressed in the following question: what was the origin, before all capitalist production began, of the first capital, and of the first relationship between the exploiting capitalist and the exploited wage-laborer?"[119] After explicating the structure and mechanisms of capital, Marx must still answer the impossible question of when and how the capitalist order first appeared in the world. This, of course, is precisely the question that motivates Fewkoomby's investigation. As Marx explains, however, this moment can never be located historically since capital has no genealogy. In the absence of any historical beginning, capitalism grounds itself in the legend of "so-called primitive accumulation," a mythical account that circulates as a justification for economic inequality. In authenticating the "naturalness" of capitalist governmentality, the myth of primitive accumulation "plays approximately the same role in political economy as original sin does in theology. . . . Its origin is supposed to be explained when it is told as an anecdote about the past. Long, long ago there were two sorts of people; one, the diligent, intelligent and above all frugal elite; the other, lay rascals, spending their substance, and more, in riotous living. . . . Such insipid childishness is every day preached to us in the defence of property."[120] This fairy tale—which Brecht, incidentally, lifts directly from *Das Kapital* and places in the mouth of a priest in *The Threepenny Novel*[121]—envisages an origin to a set of productive relations where, in reality, no such origin exists. The cosmological myth of primitive accumulation is an ideological strategy to conceal capital's tautological structure, Marx writes: "The whole movement, seems to turn around in a never-ending circle, which we can only get out of by assuming a primitive accumulation (the 'previous accumulation' of Adam Smith) which precedes capitalist accumulation; an accumulation which is not the result of the capitalist mode of production but its point of departure."[122] Fewkoomby's inquiry attempts to return to this point of departure, but, as Brecht shows, he cannot reconstruct the different phases of commodity production from the table back to the wood back to the tree. Capital is an underivable figure. By setting this figure within the narrative framework of a novel, Brecht exposes the limitations of the latter's intrinsically genealogical structure for an analysis of the modern capitalist enterprise.

In a letter sent to Brecht the same month that he wrote the conclusion to *The Threepenny Novel*, Korsch had in fact addressed this theological aspect of capital, noting the "profound consonance between [the] Bible and *Capital*."[123] Staging Fewkoomby's inquiry in a dream of Judgment Day, a state of absolute synchrony, posits a vantage beyond historical time from which it become possible to solve the metaphysical riddle of capital. It offers a view of the world as seen by the divine eye, a view foreclosed to human perception. As Frank Kermode argues in his famous study of narrative and apocalypse, *The Sense of an Ending*, the setting of the Judgment Day provides "what [the psychologists] call 'temporal integration'—our way of bundling together perception of the present, memory of the past and expectation of the future, in a common organization. Within this organization that which was conceived of as simply successive becomes charged with past and future: what was *chronos* becomes *kairos*."[124]

Because capital's development eludes linear modeling, because its mechanisms observe laws that are, by their nature, generic rather than genetic, understanding capital demands an ahistorical approach. Thus, on Judgment Day, Fewkoomby throws out the narratives of the "history books" and "biographies," calling instead for "wage lists," a precise diagram of what Marx called "the relations of capital" (*das Kapitalverhältnis*).

The impossibility of portraying capital's development through a series of successive moments, then, is the epistemological problem on which Brecht's industrial novel pivots. On the one hand, capital generates in its subjects a complex architecture of time: its psychology of credit and deferred gratification establishes a horizon of futurity not found in societies whose mode of production lacks private property and techniques for amassing resources. But at the same time capital exempts itself from the very temporal rule it has created, defying the basic laws of chronological sequence that are fundamental to the mechanisms of compound investment and accumulation. At least in the era of heroic capitalism, the development of the business enterprise could still be modeled on the generational sequence of human reproduction. By the time of the consolidation of the great industrial concerns at the turn of the twentieth century, however, capital had sloughed off this human face. Not surprisingly, interest in the concept of primitive accumulation has increased to the point where, today, in the era of global vertical integration, it has become utterly central to the Marxist analysis of capital. Recent accounts of primitive accumulation focus on the paradoxical temporality of this phenomenon, characterizing it variously as "something of an infinite regress," an "endlessly iterated event," or a "basic ontology of alienation."[125] As structuralist Marxism demonstrated decades ago, this aporia was central to the capitalist mode of production. Étienne Balibar's famous description of primitive accumulation as a case of "ahistorical historicism" captures the paradox succinctly: "Marx's critical recognition (against political economy) of the historicity of capitalism—the fact that capitalist relations are neither natural nor eternal but rather the product of conditions with a determined genesis—is balanced by an incapacity to think about and analyze the very history of capitalism."[126] The emergence of *das Kapitalverhältnis*—the capitalist relations of production—is not a historical event, but rather a "conjunction" or an "encounter" (*gegenübertreten*) between owners of the means of production and the workers who sell their labor-power. Once established, this relationship "reproduces itself on a constantly extending scale."[127] Thus, primitive accumulation is less an event that took place somewhere in the remote historical past than an ongoing process of continuous expropriation.[128]

The parallax construction of *The Threepenny Novel* attempts to capture the insoluble contradiction between the historical account of capital, which unfolds genealogically in the narrative about Macheath's enterprise, and the structural account, which is presented *sub speciae aeternitatis* in Fewkoomby's dream. Ultimately these two perspectives cannot be mapped onto one another, as the novel shows. In the body of the novel time moves inexorably forward, and yet when the end of the story is finally reached, the steps that led to the conclusion of the narrative, paradoxically, cannot be retraced. For Fewkoomby, the crimes cannot be reconstructed. This is the case, it would seem, because the temporality of capitalism, the time of "development," eludes mnemonic inscription. As Balibar observes, the "analysis of primitive accumulation thus brings us into the presence of the radical *absence of memory* which characterizes history (memory being only the reflection of history in certain predetermined sites—ideology or even law—and as such, anything but a faithful reflection)."[129] If, as we observed in the earlier discussion of operational sequences, the architecture of time and memory in any given culture is articulated by its specific mode of production, *The Threepenny Novel* demonstrates, further, that capitalism's violent expropriation of these means of production is also simultaneously an expropriation of time itself, the result of which is a generalized condition of amnesia in which history transpires without leaving a trace. Because human memory is inscribed and transmitted in symbolic languages and mechanical operational sequences that are exterior to the individual subject, every society, Leroi-Gourhan observes, will inevitably cultivate "false" memories in its subjects, memories that are by nature collective and transindividual.[130] But it seems that capitalist society alone generates the very incapacity to remember.

3

Gestus facit saltus: Bertolt Brecht's *Fear and Misery of the Third Reich*

To many contemporary observers, the Paris premiere of Bertolt Brecht's play *Fear and Misery of the Third Reich* on May 21, 1938, sounded the death knell of the avant-garde. It seemed clear that Brecht, until then one of the few remaining champions of formal experimentation and critical montage practices, had at last defected to the cause of socialist realism. To be sure, this volte-face was not entirely unprecedented: during a recent performance of Brecht's last play, *Señora Carrar's Rifles*, his lead actor Helene Weigel had even started to weep on stage in evident violation of Brecht's rationalist dramaturgical principles, which proscribed emotional catharsis and illusionistic flourish. Indeed, as tensions within the Popular Front grew between the realists and an embattled avant-garde, each of which struggled to define the strategy for a program of aesthetic resistance to fascist Germany, it was increasingly clear that the realist camp was gaining the upper hand. Under the banners of "humanism," "the individual," "culture," and "spirit," the campaign that had been launched at the August 1934 All-Union Soviet Writers Congress in Moscow and further developed at the July 1935 International Congress of Writers for the Defense of Culture in Paris seemed poised for victory. And then, with the apostasy of *Fear and Misery*, Brecht himself confirmed the defeat of the avant-garde from within its own ranks.

At the same moment that *Fear and Misery* debuted in Paris, one of the play's scenes, "The Informer," appeared in the leading forum for Popular Front strategy, *Das Wort*, where it caught the eye of Georg Lukács, the most discerning proponent of socialist realism in the German-speaking exile community. Lukács himself had an article in the same issue of the Moscow-based emigrant journal with the programmatic title "The Ideal of the Harmonious Man in Bourgeois Aesthetics." When he read "The Informer" Lukács exulted in Brecht's apparent conversion, even giving the scene a handsome endorsement in his canonical essay "Realism in the Balance": "In the third number of *Das Wort* Brecht published a one-act playlet (*The Informer*) in which he turns to what is for him a novel, highly-differentiated and subtle form of realism as a weapon in the struggle against the inhumanity of Fascism. By depicting *the fates of individuals*, he presents a living image of the horrors of the Fascist reign of terror in Germany."[1] For Lukács, Brecht's play confirmed many of the tenets in his own theory of realism, which called for naturalistic depictions of characters instead of self-reflexive technique and "living images" instead of abstract concepts. And he was not alone in seeing Brecht's latest work as a capitulation to the Lukáscian line. In a July 1938 letter to Willi Bredel, Fritz Erpenbeck, one of the editors of *Das Wort*, expressed a certain satisfaction that Brecht was at last following the program set by Lukács—even if the playwright still complained publicly about the rigid prescriptiveness of this program. Having moved beyond his experimental Learning Plays (*Lehrstücke*) such as *Round Heads and Pointed Heads* (1936), Brecht's most recent plays were now finally using realist techniques: "It is more important," Erpenbeck wrote, "to get a highly talented rogue like Brecht, despite his theoretical protests, to write *Señora Carrar's Rifles*, *The Informer* and *Judicial Process* [also a scene from *Fear and Misery*], and not *Round Heads and Pointedheads* and other 'Learning Plays.' He can get as worked up as he wants about the Lukácsian theories, so long as he still observes them in practice (despite his inner resistance)" (*Werke*, 22:1038–1039).[2]

Brecht himself could not have been less pleased to have the patronage of the "Moscow Clique," as he called them. Even more objectionable to him than their air of condescension was the fact that this endorsement was based on a profound critical misconstrual of his play, as he observed in a riled journal entry written after reading "Realism in the Balance":

> Lukács has already embraced "The Informer" as if I were a sinner coming to the bosom of the Salvation Army. At last, here is something taken from life! He has overlooked the montage of 27 scenes and the fact that it is actually nothing other than a table of gestures [*Gestentafel*], such as the gestures of falling silent, of peering behind one's back, of terror etc. Gesture under dictatorship. In this way *epic theater* demonstrates that it is possible to have "interiority" [*Interieur*] as well as elements that are almost naturalistic, without insisting on a distinction. (*Werke*, 26:318–319)

All too eager to incorporate "The Informer" into his humanist theory of realism, Lukács had failed to see that the 27 scenes did not constitute an organic totality but were instead composed using a discontinuous montage technique, and that, moreover, the mute exteriority of the "table of gestures" was often in direct conflict with the psychological motivations of the characters on stage. Although "The Informer" was both epic *and* naturalistic, as Brecht explained, Lukács had recognized only the latter.

Lukács's misprision suggests that the critical purchase and authority of the conceptual scheme opposing realism to avant-gardism, canonized in the Expressionism debates of the 1930s and still hegemonic in scholarly discourse to this day, was already analytically insufficient at the very moment of its emergence. Perhaps this distinction was stillborn from the very start. Indeed, as we will see in this chapter, Brecht's *Fear and Misery* cannot be easily accommodated under either rubric. For while the protests voiced in Brecht's journal entry clearly demonstrate that he was no follower of Lukács's program, he did not belong with the hardcore modernists in the opposing camp either, who, he observed, had devolved into a frozen parody of the movement's initial experimentalism ("the avant-garde has capitulated, but it has not died," Brecht wrote, in *Werke*, 21:447). Instead of capitulating to the Lukácsian program, *Fear and Misery* in fact attempted to move beyond the hackneyed opposition between the analytic techniques of avant-garde theater and the illusionism of traditional drama. Rejecting the prescriptive aesthetics of both sides, Brecht's *Fear and Misery* pursues instead a dramaturgy that is paradoxically both anthropomorphic and mechanical, both holistic and fragmented. As his journal entry suggests, we will find the key to understanding this novel reconfiguration of realism and modernism in the device that he called *gestus*.

Drowning in Reports

In both tone and technique, *Fear and Misery* is the work of an exile. Brecht had written the play while living in Denmark, where he was deprived of the German theatrical public sphere that he enjoyed during his Weimar years. "I sit here as someone who has been banished," he wrote in 1938, "and the greatest thing that has been taken from me are the readers and listeners in whose language I write. These are not just the people for whom I write, but the people with whom I share my deepest interests" (*Werke*, 22:356). But the distance that Brecht experienced when writing *Fear and Misery* was not just an emotional one, since writing a play about everyday life in fascist Germany also necessarily entailed describing a phenomenon about which he had no firsthand knowledge. Having fled the country at the end of February 1933, immediately after the National Socialists came to power, he had no actual experience of life under the Nazi terror himself, and, for this reason, was forced to base his play exclusively on articles found in the press and accounts from friends who left Germany after him. Since 1933 his collaborator Margarete Steffin had been accumulating as source material for the play a heap of newspaper clippings whose compass would eventually exceed more than ten folders.[3] Several years later, now "[d]rowning in reports about the extraordinary horrors in the Germany from which we fled" (*Werke*, 22:33), Brecht finally began to piece together *Fear and Misery* in 1937. For this reason the text of *Fear and Misery* exhibits the highest degree of technical mediation: forced by necessity to rely on newspaper articles and the reports of intermediaries, Brecht transformed compositional exigency into formal strategy, fashioning an entire work, in effect, out of secondhand speech. Even the play's most melodramatic displays of psychological intimacy—"Interieur," he calls it in his journal entry—presume the radical exteriority of Brecht's exilic vantage. The "private life of the master race," to recall the play's original English title, was assembled out of thoroughly public, indeed clichéd, parts of speech.

This disordering of the boundary between public and private speech is the theme of "The Informer," the episode that won accolades from Lukács. It is a scene about speech run awry, in which a couple tries desperately to maintain control over the circulation of language, both the propaganda that pours from the outside into their domestic *Interieur* as well as the dissidence that erupts spontaneously from their own mouths. In "The Informer" the Third Reich besieges its subjects with a panoply of media ranging from the telephone to the radio and the newspaper. Through these mass media, which Brecht prominently puts on display in nearly every scene of *Fear and Misery*, the language of the regime penetrates into even the most private recesses of domestic life. All too aware of the pivotal role that these media apparatuses play in the regime's ideological indoctrination, the couple in this scene develops a violent aversion not just to these media but to language itself. The father, for example, avoids the telephone, demands that the radio be turned off, and later snatches the newspaper out of his son's hands. Eventually the members of the family do not speak even to one another. The only remaining response is to withdraw from communication entirely, resulting, as Brecht put it, in the *gestus* of "falling silent."

In "The Informer" the bourgeois domestic sanctuary is doubly porous: propaganda streams in via the mass media at the same time that information threatens to hemorrhage outward through the young Nazi girl who works for the couple as well as through their own son, whom they also fear might be the eponymous informer. There is no utterance in *Fear and Misery* that is truly private or secure, no space of intimacy beyond the reach of the National Socialist apparatus of propaganda and surveillance. Under these conditions, all personal expression invariably assumes a public aspect, becoming a performative speech act with the gravest of consequences for its speaker. Totalitarian regimes know all too well how to do things with words. When the son disappears unnoticed from the living room, husband and wife quickly fall into a hysterical spiral of speculation about whether he understood their coded criticisms of the government and has left to report them. His eventual return at the end of "The Informer" then prompts a perverse take on the family portrait, a concluding tableau in which the parents are literally transformed into photographs, their horrified grimaces frozen on their faces like snapshots.

Brecht continues exploring the mass media's evacuation of the psychic *Interieur* in "The Jewish Wife," another repertorial favorite of the *Fear and Misery* cycle. This episode depicts a certain Mrs. Judith Keith as she prepares to flee Germany in order to avoid becoming a liability for her Aryan husband. Like "The Informer," "The Jewish Wife" takes place in the domestic space of a private apartment, where Mrs. Keith is alone until the arrival of her husband at the end of the scene. In between packing her bags, she telephones family acquaintances one by one to take leave, feigning in each conversation that she will be absent only for a short period of time. Even more than it was in "The Informer," the telephone is an integral component of the scene's dramaturgy. After making four phone calls, and giving in each a different reason for her departure, Keith begins to practice her departing words to her husband, which are alternatively melancholic, enraged, understanding, and accusatory. She plays through this scenario five times, offering in each iteration a different set of justifications and responses to her phantom interlocutor. Delivered in fits and starts, Mrs. Keith's monologue is broken off and resumed multiple times, effectively fragmenting "The Jewish Wife" into ten subscenes: four telephone calls, five practice runs, and a final confrontation with her husband. With each new start it becomes more and more clear that the figure on stage is engaged quite literally in an act of rehearsal. Indeed, to the audience at the Paris debut in May 1938, the scene of Mrs. Keith practicing her speeches must have looked strikingly similar to—indeed indistinguishable from—the actress Helene Weigel in the process of rehearsing for the role of Keith. Even the most intimate of relations, that between a wife and her husband, presume role-playing, rehearsal, and well-practiced adherence to scripts. In this regard, "The Jewish Wife," for all its celebrated naturalism and psychological interiority, is also blatantly metatheatrical in the manner of the classic epic system of Brecht. Unlike the conventional dramatic monologue, a device designed to provide an unobstructed glimpse into the temperament and intentions of the character on stage, Mrs. Keith's soliloquy reveals anything but a unified self; spoken by a multiplicity of characters, her broken monologue instead reflects a state of psychic disintegration. Although all five of Mrs. Keith's speeches are addressed to her husband, each one envisages a different interlocutor and each one offers a correspondingly different response. Like the four telephone calls, each one is delivered using a distinct mode of address, tone of voice, and affective comportment. "The Jewish Wife," we could say, is an ensemble scene with nine characters, but played by a cast of one.

There is little doubt that Brecht, who was known to compose roles for specific actors, had Helene Weigel in mind when he wrote "The Jewish Wife." In the original Paris production of 1938 as in the 150-odd showings of the play at the Berliner Ensemble after the war, Weigel established the standard for performances of Mrs. Keith, a role that was in fact likely modeled on one of her close friends.[4] That Brecht was thinking of Weigel personally when he wrote this scene explains certain aspects of its peculiar dramaturgy, which exploits her special talents as an actor—talents he later characterized as an unmatched "ability to fuse together stylized theater and realist theater" (*Werke*, 22:610). Weigel's bewildering mix of detachment and affect, *Verfremdung* and sentiment, seemed to render obsolete the distinctions upon which the Moscow Clique had staked their critical venture. Specifically, it was her capacity to reconcile spontaneous expression with secondhand reproduction that so intrigued Brecht at the moment when he was searching in his own work for a way to move beyond the stale opposition between realist and avant-garde theater. Take the example of her October 1937 performance of *Señora Carrar*, in which Weigel shocked the audience with her dramatic, teary turn. It is true that the actor wept on stage then, seemingly in violation of the epic theater's postulate of intellectual distance, and yet, as Brecht pointed out in his rejoinder to those who deemed this a return to naturalistic drama, Weigel "cried not as the peasant woman, but as an actor crying about the peasant woman" (*Werke*, 22:739). The tears, in other words, were Weigel's, not Señora Carrar's. For Brecht it was crucial that the cognitive distinction between the actor on stage and the character she depicted be maintained at all times—that representation, in other words, never devolve into expression. Despite her emotional display, Weigel had rigorously maintained this disjunction by presenting the words of her character as a scripted text. It was as if Weigel "had thought to herself 'To which the fisherwoman said' at the beginning of each sentence," Brecht observed. Although the words came out of her own mouth, Weigel "clearly spoke a sentence belonging to a different woman." Just as all her actions were "reenacted," all her words were effectively quotations (*Werke*, 22:354), reproductions of speeches that had already been uttered long before.

Weigel's ability as an actor to convert expression into representation, presence into absence, touches on a central aspect of *gestic* dramaturgy that Walter Benjamin designated as *Zitierbarkeit*, or "quotability" (*Schriften*, 2:519–531). Brecht had in fact first mentioned the concept of *gestus* in a review of Leopold Jessner's 1929 production of *Oedipus*, in which Weigel, cast in the role of Jocasta's maid, had delivered the news of Oedipus's death in the manner of a report.[5] The complex counterpoint between her voice and her face set her performance in quotation marks, Brecht noted (*Werke*, 21:278–279; 279–282). Benjamin would later designate this technique of epic theater as "the quotable gesture," explaining that the Brechtian actor "must be able to space [*sperren*] his gestures the way that a typesetter spaces type" (Benjamin, *Writings*, 4:305). Like the mechanically reproducible and clichéd diction of the newspaper, the highly standardized *gestus* possesses a "strict, framelike compactness," Benjamin observed (*Schriften*, 2:521). Such gestic idioms are not spontaneous or expressive but rigorously conventionalized and thus deeply social, which is why, Brecht insisted, the reflex of swatting a fly, for example, is not necessarily a social *gestus*, whereas movements made while working are. "The labor gesture is without a doubt a social *gestus*," Brecht explained, "since human activity that is focused on overcoming nature is a social matter, a matter that exists between people. On the other hand, as long as a gesture of pain remains so abstract and general that it never transcends the sphere of biology, it has not become a social *gestus*" (*Werke*, 22:33).

In addition to Weigel's performance as Jocasta, it seems that Brecht's thinking about *gestus* also had a second source from 1929: Sergei Tret'iakov's play *I Want a Baby* (1926–1927), the script for which landed in Brecht's hands that year and which then appeared in 1930 in a German translation attributed to Ernst Hube and Brecht.[6] Although scholarship has recognized the influence on Brecht of Tret'iakov, whom the German playwright once characterized as "my teacher," the details of this influence have remained largely biographical, leaving the formal and aesthetic dimensions of this exchange unexamined.[7] Close consideration of *I Want a Baby* shows that Brecht's encounter with Tret'iakov was indeed more than just an anecdotal matter, and in fact precipitated a host of new practices in the work of the German playwright, foremost among which was that paradoxical interweft of realist and avant-garde dramaturgy which he called *gestus*.

That *I Want a Baby* was so central for the development of *gestus* is perhaps not surprising, since Tret'iakov's play, written at a moment when the aesthetic of proletarian realism was gaining momentum in the Soviet Union, itself proposed a number of artistic strategies that pointed beyond the theoretical blind alley into which the debates between the realists and the avant-garde were headed. Just as *Carrar* and *Fear and Misery* "were the first works in which Brecht approached Socialist Realism," as one expert put it,[8] *I Want a Baby* constituted a "realist turn" in Tret'iakov's own practice. Indeed, this turn was all too obvious in Tret'iakov's case, since he in fact wrote the play twice, first as an eccentric avant-garde burlesque and then then as a cool, almost neoclassical display of human bodies. If ever there were a textbook case of the "return to order," certainly it is here, visible in the two radically dissimilar versions of a single play written one year apart. With reference to the agit-prop theater that Tret'iakov and Sergei Eisenstein had developed together in Meyerhold's Proletkul't theater during the early 1920s, Tret'iakov designated the first *I Want a Baby* a "montage of attractions." It was a kaleidoscopic series of "aggressive theatrical moment[s]" designed "to have a determinate emotional shock on the recipient."[9] Subsequently rewritten in 1927 under pressure from the censors, the second version of the play renounced the circus antics and energetic montage of the earlier play, now presenting to the audience instead a series of human prototypes to be considered and analyzed. Drawing an analogy with the display practices of the museum, Tret'iakov classified the second version not as a "montage of attractions" but as an "exhibition of standards" (*выставка стандартов*). The shift in Tret'iakov's formal strategies is, moreover, reflected in the temperament of the play's protagonist who, in the first, satirical version of the play, is employed as an agitator and cultural organizer of everyday life but becomes in the 1927 version a dispassionate and analytic genetic scientist. It was this second, "cooler" version of *I Want a Baby* that Brecht read and adapted in 1929.[10]

I Want a Baby is a play about the ideology of intimacy and its cultural locus, the domestic *Interieur*. It tells the story of Milda Grignau, an enthusiastic if rather homely agronomist who finds herself in the precarious position of wanting to get pregnant without a husband or boyfriend, without a nuclear family, indeed, without the entire apparatus of romantic love.[11] The Bolshevik has little patience for such bourgeois idiosyncrasies. Much to Milda's chagrin, however, the seemingly fundamental desire to reproduce is everywhere thwarted by the fact that, even in the enlightened context of postrevolutionary Russia, sex continues to be anything but a merely biological function. In the end, the androgyne Milda will have to deploy the full panoply of reactionary erotic ornament—perfume, powder, makeup, an alluring dress—in order to land Yakov, the proletarian sire of her choosing. As the "ardent feminist"[12] Tret'iakov explained, "*I Want a Baby* puts love on the operating table and examines its consequences for society."[13] The play's approach to sexuality is neither aesthetic nor erotic, but analytic and logical, in the manner of an "anatomical atlas."[14] Transposing the paradigm of rationalization from the productive to the reproductive sphere, this "problem piece," as Tret'iakov called the play, asks whether the Bolshevik program for restructuring Russia's industry could be realized in everyday life and interpersonal relations as well.

This demystification of romantic love proved too scandalous for the censors, who prevented the play from opening for three years despite excitement around the collaboration between Tret'iakov and two other stars of the Russian avant-garde, Vsevolod Meyerhold, who was chosen to direct the play, and El Lissitzky, who designed the play's costumes and an entirely new theater for

Meyerhold's production. The play would never be produced in Tret'iakov's lifetime. Denouncing *I Want a Baby* as a cynical and "loveless" play, Anatoly Lunacharsky numbered among the critics who failed to understand that the theme of the play was not the coercive expropriation of reproductive functions by the state, but Milda's own desire to reproduce. Tellingly, his review misidentifies the work's title as *Give Us a Baby* (*Daesh' rebenka*) rather than *I Want a Baby* (*Khochu rebenka*).[15] But Tret'iakov's play was hardly as prescriptive and dystopic as Lunacharsky and the censors seemed to think. Tret'iakov protested that it hardly endorsed any one approach to reproduction, either ultrarationalist or romantic: "It is not true that I am trying to force Milda upon the audience," he clarified in one of his statements: "I myself wrote into the play a series of moments that discredit her."[16] As one of the play's advocates explained, "this is a piece that provokes discussion, and this is a positive aspect. Milda is not a program, but a problem."[17]

The two directors in competition for the rights to produce *I Want a Baby*, Meyerhold and the Leningrad director Igor Terent'ev, both recognized that this play would require an entirely new approach to stage technology. Meyerhold's bid was backed by El Lissitzky's celebrated maquette from 1929, which, echoing the enlightenment agenda of this play, constructed a hygienic environment of transparency and illumination (figs. 3.1 and 3.2). The open, helicoid structure of Lissitzky's design transformed the illusionistic stage into a sober, podium-like platform that allowed the audience to view the actors from all sides. No shadows could appear here, since the figures were irradiated simultaneously from spotlights above and from lighting elements in the transparent floor below. Because the extreme clarity of the stage design and the absence of theatrical props allowed for unobstructed viewing of the actors on the bright dais, the success of the performance hinged entirely on the performance of the actors themselves. Eschewing all illusionistic scenery, this "exhibition of standards" took as its centerpiece the body of the "New Soviet Man," to use the well-known idiom of the day.[18] Lissitzky's maquette thus foregrounds the human figure, emphasizing the plastic, sculptural qualities of a body that can be contemplated and inspected from all sides. It was an apt vehicle for a play about

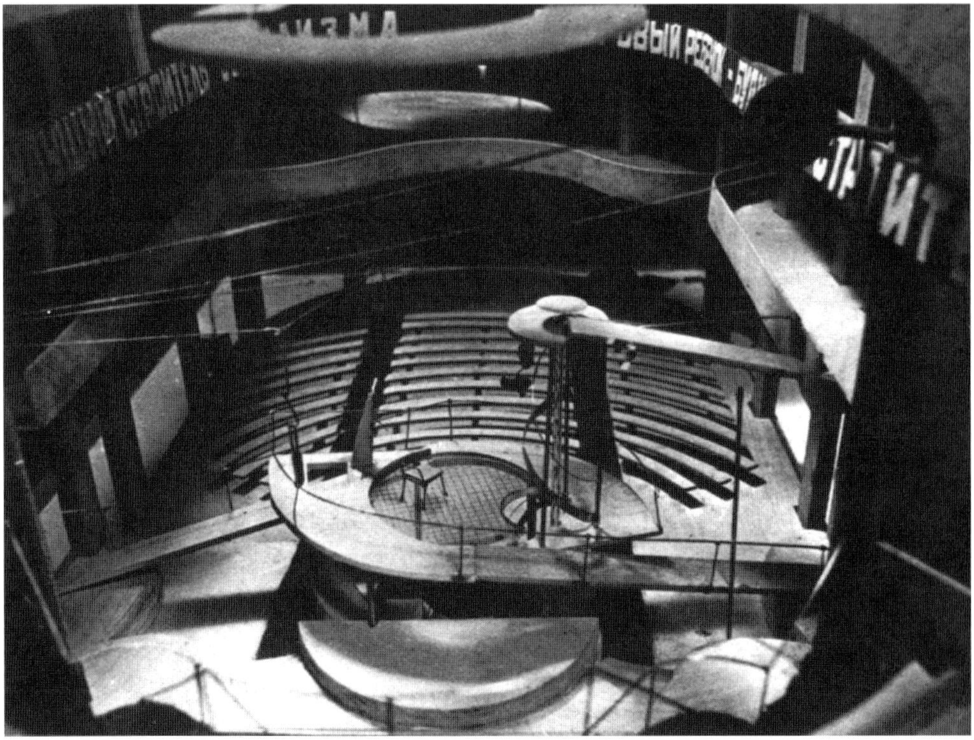

Figure 3.1 El Lissitzky, maquette for Sergei Tret'iakov's *I Want a Baby* (1929).

eugenics, which even concluded with an invitation to the audience to come on stage and examine an exhibition of actual children for their various genetic qualities.

Terent'ev proposed a slightly different context for exhibiting the human body. If Lissitzky's design suggests a neoclassical statuary, Terent'ev's, by contrast, recalls a surgical theater, a setting, he felt, that would provide the perfect theater of operations for Tret'iakov's "anatomical atlas." Introducing a third architectural element between the stage and the house, Terent'ev proposed suspending above

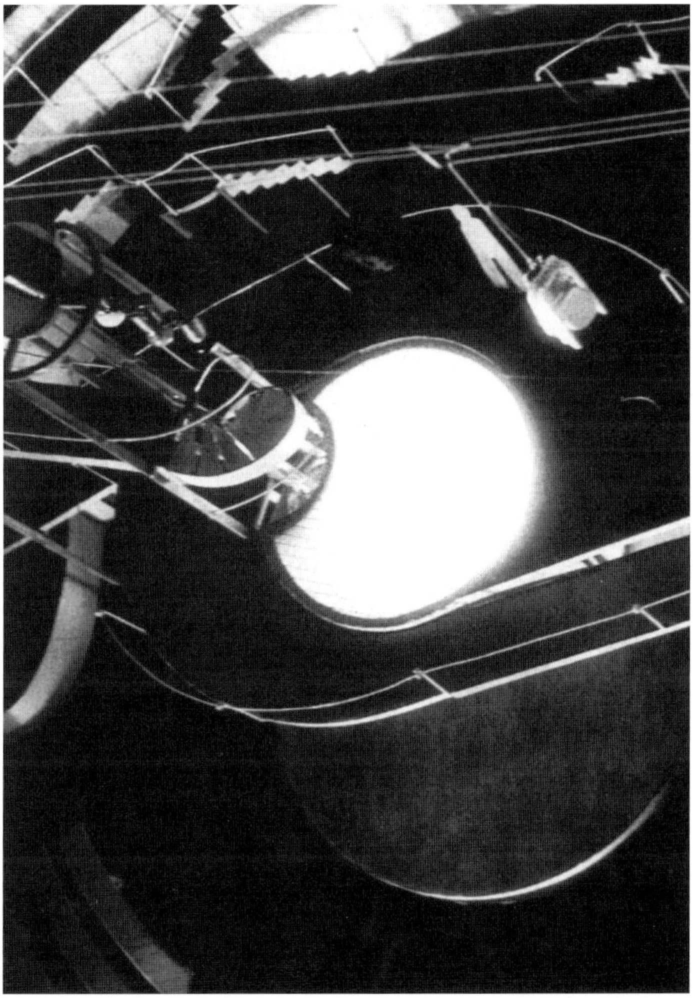

Figure 3.2 El Lissitzky, maquette for Sergei Tret'iakov's *I Want a Baby* (1929). © 2012 Artists Rights Society (ARS), New York/VG Bild-Kunst, Bonn.

the stage an "extended glass room" that contained the "staff of theatrical operations"—an engineer, a stenographer, and an announcer—"whose purpose is to take questions from the audience and to deliver answers by radio."[19] Terent'ev observed that this elaborate technical detour set up several possibilities for staging the play: "In the first version the 'staff' (of announcers) speaks for the actor [via radio], leaving the play of movements to the actor; in the second case the visual element exists in the form of a projected film—and in this case the actor will herself take on the spoken part of her role; in the third case (the unity of subject and emotions), the actor speaks and moves herself (without radio and without film)."[20] By separating the verbal text from the actor's movements, Terent'ev's analytic theater overturned a basic presupposition of naturalist drama, which, at least since Lessing, had privileged dialogue and speech as the exclusive vehicles of the plot. Such drama had dispossessed the actor's body of its gestural presence, reducing the physical figure on stage to a mere conduit for the voice.[21] But in Terent'ev's first two plans for staging the play, the body refuses to be sublimated into discourse in this manner. Here the body on stage insists on its awkward and apodictic facticity, not subordinated to, but set against, language and expression.

Terent'ev's ideas for *I Want a Baby* reflect the impact of sound cinema on theater. Proposed in 1928, one year after the arrival of the "talkie," Terent'ev's staging of *I Want a Baby* challenged the reality effects of the new medium by cleaving the body from the voice and thus destroying the illusion of integrality produced through the unity of sound and image. His analytic stage dismantles what Mary Ann Doane has called the "phantasmatic body," a body that is "reconstituted by the technology and practices of [sound] cinema . . . , which offers a support as well as a point of identification for the subject addressed by the film." As Doane observes, the "attributes of this phantasmatic body are first and foremost unity (through the emphasis on a coherence of the senses) and presence-to-itself."[22] But instead of unifying, Terent'ev dissects, recalling the dramaturgical strategy that Brecht famously characterized as a "division of the elements" (*Trennung der Elemente*). This "divided spectacle," as Barthes called the Brechtian system, operates "by the discontinuity of codes, by the caesura imposed in the different traits of the representation, so that the *copy* elaborated on the stage is not destroyed but shattered, scored, freed from the metonymical contagion of voice and gesture, soul and body, which entangles our actors."[23] By routing language first through a staff of ventriloquists who deliver the text over the radio, and then through the invisible actors who provide a voice-over to a filmed version of the play, Terent'ev pries apart body from psyche and destroys the "unity of subject and emotions" on which naturalistic drama had been based. His proposal was thus brilliantly suited for a play whose analytic approach to reproduction debunked the reified notion of sexuality as a natural, biological drive. *I Want a Baby* delivers a mute body resistant to society's script for romantic love.

And yet the body and the voice of the actor do in fact coincide in Terent'ev's third plan for staging the play. Importantly, however, the "actor speaks and moves herself" only after the radio broadcast has already spoken in her stead, and after she has recited speech as an offstage voice-over to a silent film. In the first two versions Terent'ev dismantles the unity of body and language, biology and ideology, foregrounding the incommensurability between the two in order then to put them back together in a third version that presupposes their previous mediation through technical devices. *I Want a Baby* severs thought and voice from body so that it can reintegrate and resynchronize them with the use of radio and cinema. The naturalistic "unity of subject and emotions" returns, in other words, only after the speech and movement of the actor have already been taken apart by the new media. What is on display in this "exhibition of standards," as Tret'iakov called the play, are quite literally *technical* standards: Milda's speech is clear and rhythmically inflected, delivered with the voice of a radio announcer, and her movements on the luminous stage have likewise been normed to accord with the technical parameters of film. Even without a microphone or a camera present, then, Milda is already a mechanical reproduction.

It is here that Tret'iakov's influence on Brecht's theory of *gestus* is most obvious. Although the 1927 version of *I Want a Baby* would seem at first glance to foreground the human figure in a neoclassical manner, the figure that it presents is neither holistic nor organic, but is already thoroughly mediated by technology.

This was in fact the definition of *gestic dramaturgy* proposed by Benjamin, who observed that the "discovery and construction of *gestus* is nothing other than a retranslation of the methods of montage—so crucial in radio and film—from a technological process back into a human one" (Benjamin, *Writings*, 2:584). With this in mind, Lukács's characterization of *Fear and Misery* as a "living image" (*ein lebendiges Bild*) appears to be both wrong and right: wrong, because the figure on stage is not quite *living*, its "presence-to-itself" undermined at every moment by Brecht's strategies of quotation; right, because these figures are unfailingly perceived by the audience as mediatized *images*. From the moment they walk on stage, they present themselves as mechanical reproductions. Brecht addressed this technique for incorporating technology into the organic body in a resumé about the development of German theater during the interwar period, in which he discussed his debt to his mentor, the avant-gardist director Erwin Piscator. There he acknowledged that his own minimalist productions would seem, at least on the surface, to be completely unlike Piscator's extravagant media phantasmagoria, famous in their time for using elaborate projections, hydraulics, lighting, and sound "so that the public finds itself in the middle of a surging sea, or so that masses of people charge towards them."[24] Compared with Piscator's state-of-the-art theatrical machine, Brecht's own dramaturgy appears downright low-tech, especially in the case of the *Lehrstücke*, plays so sparse that a contemporary reviewer once jokingly referred to one as a "*Leer*stück" (an "*empty* play").[25] Despite these superficial differences, however, Brecht had merely translated methods of montage and technical reproduction "back" into the human figure, as Benjamin put it. While Piscator had "revolutionized the stage" itself, Brecht wrote in his resume on German theater, "I was more preoccupied with individual people—or rather: with the relations between them—and I revolutionized the art of acting" (*Werke*, 22:123). Stylistic differences aside, the strategies of Piscator and Brecht were functional equivalents, he claimed: the same technification that Piscator realized in the architectural support structure of the theater, Brecht elaborated through exclusively dramaturgical means, by transforming "the art of acting."

Although not always obvious, media technologies saturate the Learning Plays that Brecht began to write immediately after his encounter with Tret'iakov's "exhibition of standards" in 1929. For example, the very first of these works, *The Flight of Lindbergh*, was a radio play cowritten with the composer Kurt Weill for a music festival whose theme was "Radio Art for the Masses in the Technical Age." Although photos of the Baden-Baden premiere show only a tiny radio perched between the speaker and the chorus, the modesty of this prop is belied by the fact that the radio determines all aspects of this play, from its narrative premise to its acoustic form (fig. 3.3). Every word uttered in *The Flight of Lindbergh*

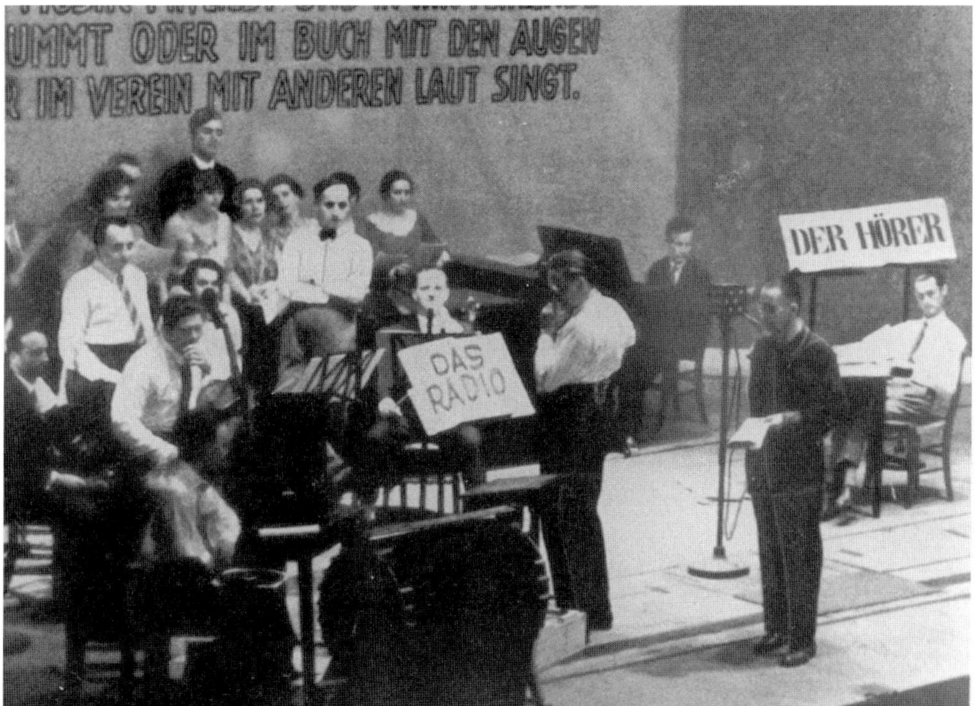

Figure 3.3 Baden-Baden premiere of Bertolt Brecht's *The Flight of Lindbergh* (1929). Akademie der Künste, Berlin, Bertolt Brecht Archive.

refers back to the radio as technical support and precondition. "The text should be spoken and sung mechanically, every line of verse at the conclusion should be made distinct, one should read along mechanically with the listening part," Brecht stipulated (*Werke*, 24:87). Stylistically, the text of *Lindbergh* repeats the laconic mechanicity of Brecht's 1927 collection of poetry *A Reader for City Dwellers* (*Aus dem Lesebuch für Städtebewohner*), a work that first bore the title *Texts for Phonograph Records* (*Texte für Schallplatten*) and was conceived for distribution not in the form of print but as an acoustic recording. Realizing that the technical norms of transmitting media determine the style of language used in a work, Brecht's Learning Plays developed a phonogenic diction that emphasized "precision" over "expression" (*Werke*, 24:87).[26] The precise calibration of the voice, Brecht wrote, must induce a "collaboration between the apparatus and the person rehearsing" (*Werke*, 24:87). Thus, even after the tiny radio had disappeared from the stage in those Learning Plays that were written after *Lindbergh*—works that were not even designated as radio plays—this apparatus nonetheless continues to persist in the phonogenic, distinctly articulated speech patterns that are typical of the Learning Plays as a whole. The most infamous of these plays, *The Measures Taken*, for example, nowhere mentions or displays the device, yet the work demands speech that is thoroughly radiophonic: as Hans Eisler, the play's composer, stipulated, its songs must be performed in a manner that is "strict, rhythmic, expressionless, cold, sharp, incisive, without feeling but with clarity."[27]

Ten years after his first Learning Play and one year after the Paris staging of *Fear and Misery*, Brecht published his most important statement on *gestic* language in the final issue of *Das Wort*, the same journal where Brecht had published "The Informer" and where Lukács, in turn, had recently saluted Brecht's conversion to realism. In this 1939 essay, "On Rhymeless Verse with Irregular Rhythms," Brecht observed that, as a result of new media technologies, "our acoustic environment has changed immensely" and proclaimed *gestic* speech as a language uniquely suited for this transformed soundscape (*Werke*, 22:363). Moreover, according to Brecht, *gestic* language was eminently suitable for Ally broadcasts into fascist Germany since it was "reasonably unaffected by interruptions (by jamming)." Indeed, it could tolerate high levels of interference because interruption was the very principle of its composition (*Werke*, 22:364). *Gestic* language had in effect already been broken apart, electrified, exteriorized, delayed, diverted, reassembled, and amplified, thus realizing the device of epic nonlinearity in the very syntax of the sentence. "On Rhymeless Verse" illustrated the *gestic* strategy of syntactic montage by contrasting two translations of the same biblical verse: "pluck out the eye that offends thee" versus "if thine eye offends thee, pluck it out." While semantically identical, the latter sentence, Brecht suggested, "is much richer and cleaner as far as *gestus* is concerned" (*Werke*, 22:360), its rhetorical impact heightened by the interval that is inserted at the midpoint of the sentence. As Brecht explained, this break enhances the meaning of the sentence because, unlike the linear syntax of the first sentence, the second one possesses an internal counterpoint. Although the injunction conveyed is the same, the second sentence, taken from Martin Luther, carries within it a dimension of judgment that is inscribed in its syntactic structure, a moral aspect that exceeds the utterance's mere informational content.

Fear and Misery is riddled with such syntactical caesura, which remap the semantic contents of the play's text around a series of *pointes* with pronounced social import. In "The Jewish Wife," for example, Mrs. Keith's irregular speech patterns move in fits and starts, illustrating Benjamin's claim that the "more frequently we interrupt a performer, the more *gesten* we obtain."[28] This discontinuous speech is given a naturalistic motivation by the telephone, which, like the radio in *Lindbergh*, symbolizes on stage the new "acoustic environments" that, as Brecht claimed, are restructuring the sound-shape of language. And yet, even after she has finished her telephone conversations, Mrs. Keith's *gestic* speech patterns persist as she rehearses the dialogues with her husband. She stops and starts a total of nine times in the scene, adding with each pause another *gestic* interval. Like Terent'ev's Milda, who is taken apart by film and radio but who continues to be subjected to their technical standards even after the devices have been removed from the stage, Mrs. Keith's speech remains telephonic long after she has put down the telephone handset.

In the same way that *gestic* speech presumed acoustic technologies such as the radio, the phonograph and the telephone, *gestic* countenance and movement were calibrated to standards established by photography, both still and cinematic. The same year in which Brecht encountered Tret'iakov's "exhibition of standards" and first began to write of *gestus*, he picked up a movie camera and filmed Weigel applying makeup, perhaps for the role of Jocasta's maid in Jessner's production of *Oedipus* that year (fig. 3.4). This brief sequence he then examined as a series of stills. "Every single frame," Brecht wrote, "showed a finished expression that was self-contained and possessing its own meaning. . . . 'Each of the gestures can be segmented into any number of further gestures, each of which is complete in and for itself'" (*Werke*, 21:811). It was only from looking at Weigel through the camera lens that Brecht realized what had been so captivating about her performance: she was staging a series of photographs. The camera revealed the *gestic* content of her expressions, each of which was complete and self-contained in the manner of a photographic still. When captured on filmic emulsion—that is, when repatriated to its native medium—the photographic and cinematic preconditions of Weigel's *gestic* performance became all too obvious to Brecht. In fact, he may have had the latent rhyme between *gestus* and cinema in mind when he later proposed that his socialist realist play *Carrar* be performed alongside "a documentary film showing the events in Spain": screening a film, he suggested, would mitigate the "technical disadvantages" of the play's realist aesthetic, perhaps by making explicit the technical medium that had been the very precondition for Weigel's performance all along (*Werke*, 24:225).

After 1929 the camera became an integral component of Brecht's stagecraft. During the 1931 staging of *Man Equals Man* (1926), now under his own direction, Brecht commissioned a silent 16mm recording of the new production by the filmmaker Carl Koch, and again the movie camera confirmed the *gestic* richness of his lead actor, this time Peter Lorre. "This very interesting experiment shows surprisingly well how perfectly Lorre manages, even in these long speeches, to reproduce through mime the basic meaning underlying every (silent) sentence" (*Werke*, 24:49). *Gestic* acting proved to be an especially valuable resource in the latter half of *Man Equals Man*, which had longer monologues

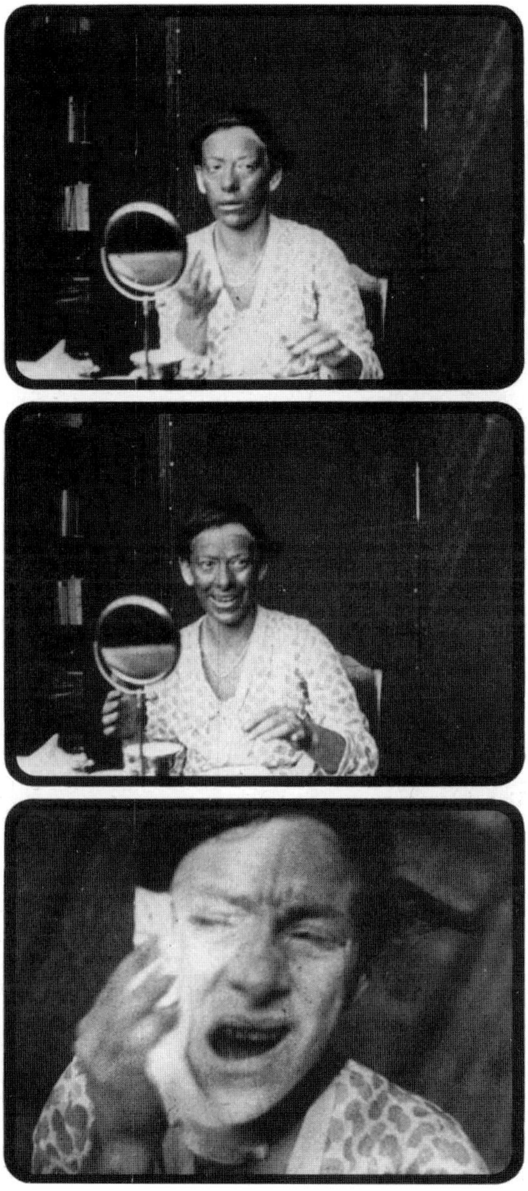

Figure 3.4 Frames from Bertolt Brecht's film of Helene Weigel applying makeup (1929). From *Bertolt Brecht: Sein Leben in Bildern und Texten*, ed. Werner Hecht (Frankfurt: Suhrkamp, 1978).

and, Brecht explained, was thus in great need of punctuation. Anticipating his later analysis of Luther's gestic language, Brecht claims that Lorre's montaged speech was, "as in a poem, split into separate lines by caesuras, so that it seemed like the different arguments followed one upon the other." In both movement and speech, Lorre's performance was "split up according to *Gesten*," revealing a "contradictory internal process." Like Weigel's Mrs. Keith, the mental *Interieur* of Lorre's character was conflicted and heteroglossic, cobbled together through "interruptions and jumps" (*Werke*, 24:49). In contrast to naturalistic drama, whose structure follows a linear plot and that Brecht thus described using Leibniz's phrase *natura non facit saltus* ("nature does not make jumps"), epic dramaturgy presents a series of discrete quanta, a systematic "table of gestures" that, as he put it, *facit saltus* (*Werke*, 22:109).

Brecht used the camera not just as a tool for understanding theatrical productions after the fact, but as an instrument to pattern and edit the future performances of his actors. His postwar deployment of photography to compose the tableaux on stage during blocking rehearsals at the Berliner Ensemble is well known, but he had already begun to follow technical standards for mass reproduction with the Learning Plays. "The Learning Play is based upon the expectation that the performer can be influenced socially by carrying out fixed types of action, by incorporating fixed attitudes, by the reproduction of fixed speeches etc. The imitation of highly proficient patterns plays a great role in this process" (*Werke*, 21:351). According to Brecht, it was not even necessary to have a troupe of performers to stage one of these productions, since the actor's goal in the Learning Play was to collaborate with the apparatus itself. The first of these works, after all, was a radio play in which children at home were provided a script and expected to speak and sing their parts in dialogue with the voices transmitted over the airwaves. This symbiosis between performer and apparatus could be learned as well through the use of the optical media: "In principle, the same learning effect will result if the partners of the performer appear in a film. The accompanying music can be provided by mechanical means" (*Werke*, 21:352). The dramaturgy Brecht described is almost identical to Terent'ev's staging of *I Want a Baby*, in which the live actor plays opposite a film reel or a radio broadcast. Here Brecht used the technical apparatus as both a partner for the performer, who would act opposite the camera or radio, and a feedback mechanism to assist the actor in achieving a gestically more charged performance.[29] So, for example, in the case of his 1929 film of Weigel applying makeup, the technical medium of film instructed the actor in the fine art of *reproducing* emotion without *expressing* it: "He also showed [the film] to Weigel, explaining to her how an awareness of her expressions would allow her to create atmospheric moods without experiencing them each time" (*Werke*, 22:811).

In Russia, this photo- and cinematographic dramaturgy was developed under the rubric of the "model-actor," or *натурщик*. It was a strategy that was enthusiastically endorsed by Tret'iakov at a roundtable discussion on cinema organized by the avant-garde group Lef in 1927, the same year that the playwright transformed his "montage of attractions" *I Want a Baby* into an "exhibition of standards." As Tret'iakov explained in his intervention at the roundtable, the model-actor suggested a way out of the endless debates about fiction versus nonfiction—the Eisensteinian "played" versus the Vertovian "nonplayed"—in which Soviet cinema currently found itself. This is because, unlike the traditional actor, the model-actor does not pretend to be something he is not: selected according to his natural features, capacities and technical skills, he is expected only to model and demonstrate these abilities, to perform as a prototype rather than play the role of a scripted character. As an example, Tret'iakov proposed the task of making an instructional film about proper woodcutting technique. In this case, he explained, the best person for the role would of course not be a dramatic actor, who knows nothing about woodcutting, but neither would it make sense to cast an actual woodcutter, who may be the most efficient worker in reality, but who does not necessarily know how to *represent* the act of chopping wood effectively. As Tret'iakov and Eisenstein had insisted in a coauthored essay written three years earlier, one must draw an essential distinction between actual labor gestures and their demonstration.[30] What was needed, Tret'iakov explained at the roundtable, was a third option that he identified as the model-actor, a performer whose physiognomy and movements are tailored to the technical parameters of the medium of transmission. This is the métier of the performer in the age of mechanical reproducibility: the model-actor, who knows how "to break down a movement and reproduce it,"[31] "is selected as material insofar as his concrete qualities, habits and the mechanicity of his movements correspond to the figure that we need to obtain on the screen."[32]

In effect, the model-actor provides a perfect symbiosis between the organic body and the media apparatus. This biomechanical convergence was, as we have already seen, the basic dramaturgical principle of Tret'iakov's "exhibition of standards": in *I Want a Baby* the lineaments of the "standardized" Milda give the impression of a photograph, just as her physical gestures emulate the movement of a film and her speech patterns are adjusted for radio transmission. The "New Soviet Man" put on display here may feign an integral and organic appearance, but this is a figure that has been cut apart in the surgical theater of the media, optimized according to the criteria of transmissibility, and then reassembled as a composite of natural body and mechanical reproduction. The model-actor, Eisenstein once remarked, was a "purely organic" paradigm of montage editing (*Works*, 1:56). Moreover, the dramaturgy of the model-actor interfaces seamlessly with Lissitzky's maquette for *I Want a Baby*, a vision machine in which the actors, irradiated from both above and below, are transformed into pure, lucent images. If the actors themselves appear like human photographs—indeed, one of Lissitzky's brilliant concepts for the play's costumes proposed that the actors carry "portrait photos" of their character pinned to their clothing[33]—the construction of the stage, in turn, resembles a gigantic film projector for illuminating these diapositives: fed into the central spool through the three connecting gangways, the model-actor moves like a celluloid frame toward the dais, where, flooded by light, she becomes, in effect, a picture, or representation, of the character in whose role she has been cast (fig. 3.2).

With good reason, then, Eisenstein once proposed that the model-actor exhibits the quality of *фотогеничность*, the Russian cognate of the French word *photogénie* (*Works*, 55–58).[34] Although the term was borrowed from Louis Delluc's influential book *Photogénie* of 1920, *фотогеничность* was somewhat less esoteric and spiritual than its French variant. By analogy with the native formalist concept *литературность*, or "literariness," the term *фотогеничность* was instead used by Russian critics such as Boris Eikhenbaum to designate the unique properties of film and photography that distinguished these media from all other modes of expression.[35] Following this definition, phenomena that were possessing of inherently cinematic traits and that thereby transmitted well on film would be deemed "photogenic."[36] Thus the Russian word *фотогеничность* had little to do with taste, aesthetic judgment, or prepossessing appearance. (If today the word "photogenic" is used in English as a synonym for "handsome," this reveals only the degree to which, following the French word *photogénie*, contemporary criteria of beauty presume the standards of the camera.) Played by a photogenic model-actor, the character Milda from *I Want a Baby*, for example, appears plain and homely, if slightly mannish; indeed, she is anything but a conventional beauty, since her highly artificial, machine-like appearance[37] is not beautiful, properly speaking, but "mediocre" and average—a "happy medium" (*le juste milieu*), to use Delluc's phrase.[38] In fact, Tret'iakov likely had the latter quality in mind when he called his lead character "Milda," a Latvian name that, as he well knew, also recalls the German word *milde*, meaning not just gentle but also bland and lacking distinctive features.

It is precisely because of her characterless photogeny that the mimic Milda can change her appearance so quickly and thoroughly in the course of the play. When it comes time for her to seduce Yakov, for example, she uses makeup and wardrobe to transform herself so completely that he can hardly believe that he is seeing the same person as before. Staring at Milda, he stammers: "She was one woman, and she became a different one."[39] Her transformation reminds us that one of the most important assets of the photogenic performer was her mutability in front of the camera. Here the most famous specimen of the model-actor school of Soviet cinema, Aleksandra Khokhlova, offers a case in point. Photographs of Khokhlova that appeared in a 1926 pamphlet by Eisenstein and Shklovskii show an uncanny shapeshifter who could perform any role for the camera (figs. 3.5, 3.6). Neither beautiful nor ugly by nature, she could become any type before the camera, as the pamphlet's diverse portfolio of photographs demonstrates. And so, when Eisenstein was working on his unrealized film of *Capital* and needed

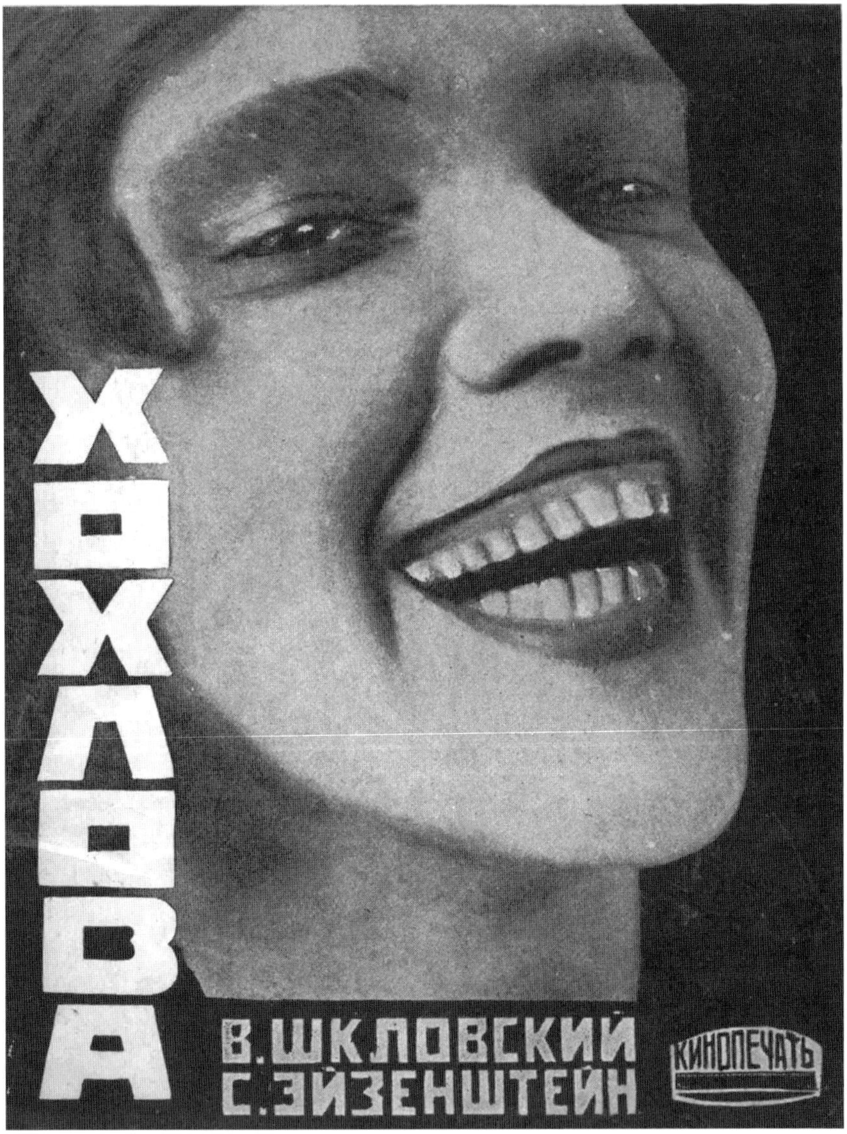

Figure 3.5 Aleksandra Khokhlova. From V. Shklovskii and S. Eisenstein, *Khokhlova* (Moscow: Kinopechat', 1926).

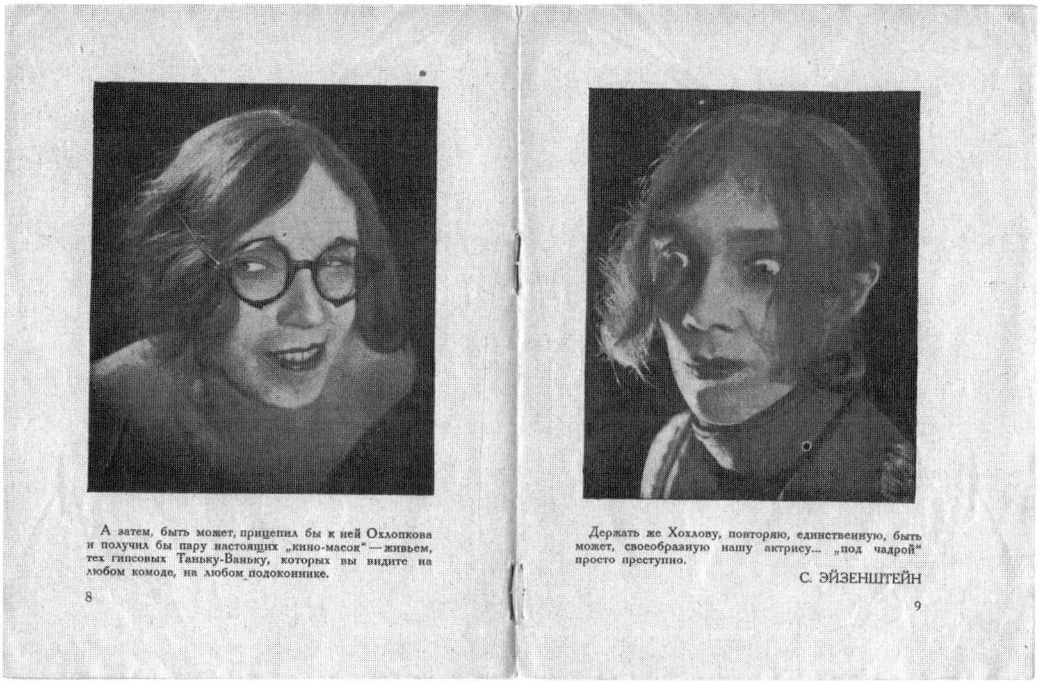

Figure 3.6 Aleksandra Khokhlova. From V. Shklovskii and S. Eisenstein, *Khokhlova* (Moscow: Kinopechat', 1926).

an actor to play "someone ugly becoming a beauty"—much like Tret'iakov's Milda—he immediately thought to cast Khokhlova.[40]

It was this same photogenic quality that Brecht discovered in Weigel when he filmed her applying her makeup in 1929. She was not "beautiful by nature," he remarked, "although she became beautiful through artifice, and through artifice she could also become ugly, both only through her performance" (*Werke*, 22:814). Endowed with a featureless face and a talent for virtually limitless transformation, Weigel, like Khokhlova, was a perfect mimic before the camera. Her performance was based not on natural qualities, but on convention and technique; her face was that of a human photograph, a blank screen primed for the reproduction of images. It was, moreover, precisely by transforming the face—the ideological locus of uniqueness and individuality—into a second-order representation, that *gestic* dramaturgy inverted the ontological privilege of original over copy. As a page from the 1933 photo-book *The Transformed World* proposes (fig. 3.7), the mass media have changed the human face into a mechanical "Abzug," an impression or copy taken from a photograph. Or, to quote the pithy formula offered in Kracauer's 1929 essay on photography, "the world itself has taken on a 'photographic face' [*ein Fotografiergesicht*]."[41]

Thus, when Brecht wrote, for example, that the actor "quotes a figure" and "supplies copies of the [figure's] behavior" (*Werke*, 22:560), under no circumstances should this act of copying be confused with the strategies of empathetic mimesis found in naturalistic drama. Trained in the art of technogenic dramaturgy, the *gestic* actor imitates not a person, as traditional actors do, but a mechanical reproduction. In this way, the "mimetic principle is dissolved, as it were, by the gestic principle," Brecht wrote in 1935 (*Werke*, 22:158). Borrowing an apt formulation from Derrida, this territory could be described as that of a "mimicry imitating nothing," "a double that doubles no simple."[42] With *gestus*, then, Brecht moves from the episteme of the representational sign to that of the simulacrum, challenging the metaphysics of mimetic representation by exploiting and maximizing the very condition of spectacularity. This dramaturgy of display, Brecht explained, was based on recent developments in industrialized media societies, in which mechanization had begun to infiltrate the body in increasingly subtle and capillary ways. With their increasing refinement, machinery and media became less and less distinct, eventually shedding the inorganic countenance they had during the era of Second Industrial Revolution. Merging with the body, they began to influence spontaneous social patterns and personal comportment. "As a result of industrial mechanization it would seem that *Gestik* disappears more and more," Brecht noted. "But in truth, it is transformed into a higher order. Transformed, of course, not by opposing *Gestik* to mechanization, but rather by making mechanization gestic. Thus, the mechanical should be emphasized, and should be advanced, into *Gestik*" (*Werke*, 21:357). If it seemed that the recent technological explosion had widened the

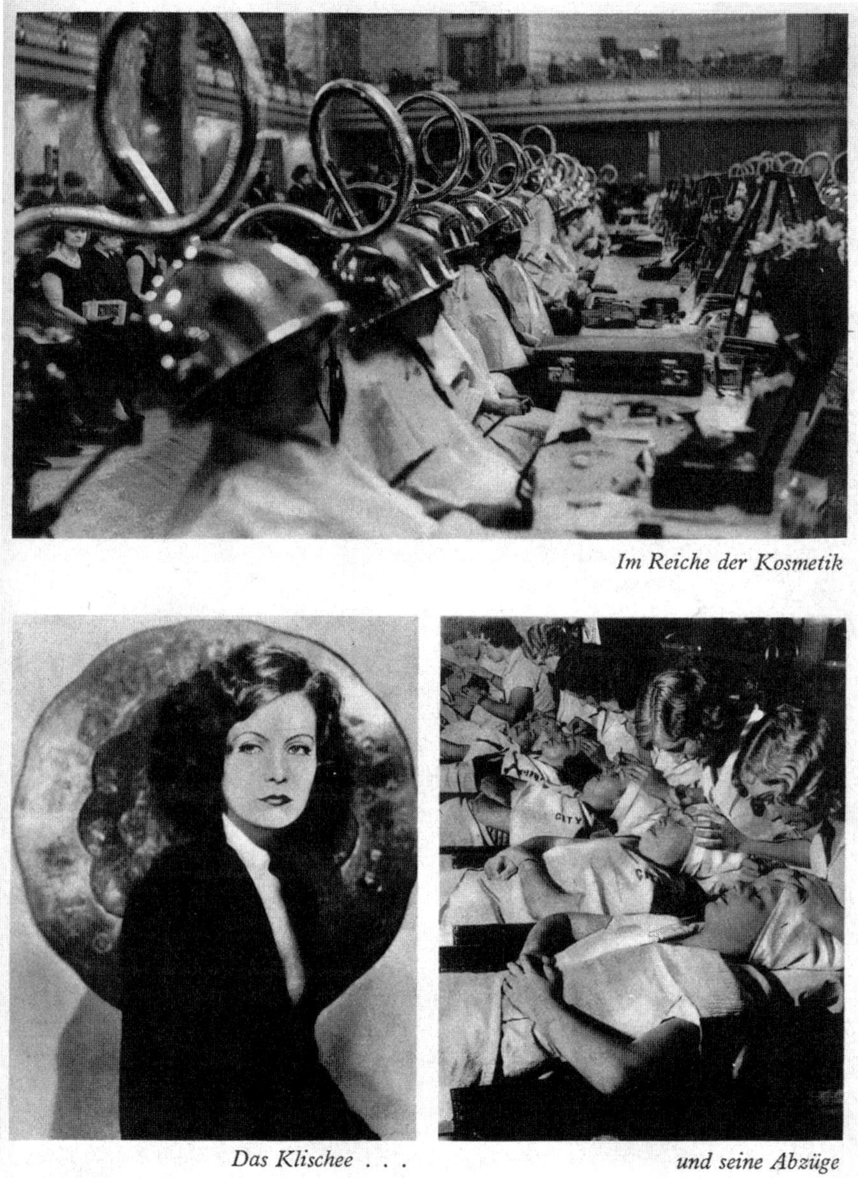

Figure 3.7 From Edmund Schultz, *Die veränderte Welt* (Breslau: Korn, 1933).

chasm between an organic humanity and the mechanical forces of production, setting each of these two terms in ever starker contrast against the other, do not be fooled by this specious opposition, Brecht cautioned, for technology had in fact migrated inward, into the interior of the human body.

The Speech of the Other

For all of its manifest reliance on the machinery of the mass media, it would be wrong to understand *gestus* as a solely technological development. The *gestic* shift from personal expression to collective quotation, Brecht insisted, also entails a process of socialization. A phenomenon could be considered *gestic* only if it could be "duplicated by anyone," he stipulated.[43] Brecht explored the social, and indeed ethical, dimensions of the *gestus* in another of the repertorial favorites from the *Fear and Misery* cycle, "The Chalk Cross." This scene, which takes place in 1933, depicts a conversation between a member of the Nazi paramilitary *Sturmabteilung* (SA), a maidservant, a cook, and her brother, a proletarian. "The Chalk Cross" builds its tension around the fraught interaction between the SA man and the worker, as the audience waits with anticipation to see whether the proletarian, who clearly loathes the fascist regime, will be caught voicing his seditious thoughts or whether, on the other hand, his criticisms of the government will elude the Nazi's apprehension. The worker masks his opinion under countless levels of prevarication that make it impossible to discern his actual position. Even his first words, as guided by the stage directions, are shrouded in ambivalence: "*the worker mumbles something that could be taken for 'Heil Hitler' if necessary*" (*Werke*, 4:347). Himself not without a certain guile, the SA man, in turn, demonstrates a trick taught to him by his squad for discreetly arresting those who are critical of the regime: after marking a cross in chalk on his hand, he gives the critic a friendly pat on the back, silently transferring the white cross to his shoulder; when the police afterward spot this marker, which identifies the person as a provocateur, they know to haul him in. Like this amicable pat, which condemns the provocateur to detention, and perhaps death, all of the *gesten* in "The Chalk Cross" hinge on saying one thing while doing another. There is in this scene a blatant discord between the outward sign and its actual meaning, a disconnect that reiterates the structural separation between words and deeds found in silent cinema, a medium that was a consistent point of reference in Brecht's writings on *gestus*. Like Terent'ev, Brecht insists on the separateness and noncommensurability of the two semiotic systems functioning at the same time, one gestural and one linguistic.

Whereas the couple in "The Informer" responded to the Nazi surveillance apparatus with the *gestus* of "falling silent," the worker in "The Chalk Cross" refuses to be silenced. The scene's high point is a tense round of play acting between the SA man and the proletarian, who recounts the words of a disgruntled woman whom he encountered on a welfare line. Unable to find any butter—which became famously scarce after the Nazis prioritized the armament industry over agriculture and consumer production—the woman launches into a rant against the regime. The worker's complex ventriloquy of the woman warrants quoting at length:

> I takes my sofa away from the Winter Aid People and goes to the second-hand dealer round the corner, I been meaning to buy half a pound of butter for some time. And at the dairy they tell me: no butter today, comrade, would you like some guns? I say, give me, says she. I say: come on what d'you want guns for, ma? On an empty stomach? No, says she, if I'm going to be hungry they should be shot, the whole lot of them starting with Hitler at the top . . . Come on, says I, come on exclaims I appalled . . . With Hitler at the top we'll conquer France, says she. Now we're getting our petrol from wool. And the wool? says I. The wool, says she: these days that's made from petrol. Wool's another thing we need. Any time a bit of good stuff from the old days reaches the Winter Aid the lot that run the place grab it for themselves, says she. If Hitler only knew, says they, but he knows nothing the poor lamb, never went to secondary school they say. I was shocked by so much subversiveness. (*Werke* 4:354)[44]

Here Brecht utilizes a mainstay of the modernist novel, indirect discourse, shifting at moments even into the more radical strategy of free indirect speech, in which the voices become completely indistinguishable from one another.[45] The result is a dizzying interplay of expression and quotation, theatrical presence and absence. Although much depends here on how the scene is staged, and whether it is performed with clear changes in vocal register and intonation, in the densest parts of this speech it becomes quite impossible to keep track of the alternations between speakers. Who, for example, pronounces the words "I say, give me, says she. I say . . ."? Enshrouded in a complex web of attribution, the worker's monologue poses as a polylogue, with an indeterminate number of voices. As we see here, it was with good reason that the philologist Theodor Kalepky characterized indirect discourse as *verschleierte Rede*, or "veiled speech," in one of the first essays on the subject.[46]

The most astonishing aspect of the worker's performance is just how much he manages to say without quite saying it. By using the rhetorical device of paralipsis, which draws attention to something under the pretense of dismissing or negating it, he is able to disseminate his seditious thoughts, uttering phrases such as "they should be shot, the whole lot of them starting with Hitler at the top" not just in public, but in conversation with an SA man no less. He is not expressing his own sentiments, the worker insists, only quoting those of others, which is perfectly licit. Although these ideas are presented under the pretense of their disavowal, this show of negation mitigates none of their force. As Freud explained, the deep recesses of the human psyche are ignorant of the forms of logical negation found in rationalist language. Indeed, a thought that is disavowed is, for that reason, all the more vigorously affirmed: just as the phrase "there is *no* rose" will, as Abelard pointed out, invariably call to mind a rose,[47] even inflammatory ideas that are repudiated in the act of their recounting will nonetheless continue to be inflammatory. And so the worker is able to stand before an SA man and call for the execution of Hitler, although he does so in the voice of an absent speaker whom he feigns to condemn.

"The Chalk Cross" builds on this game of cat-and-mouse, in which the worker ventriloquizes critics of the regime while the SA man tries to nail these words to their speaker. So long as the worker appears to quote the words of others, he can slander the regime all he likes, but as soon as he is perceived as expressing these thoughts himself, the game is up. "Did I play that one all right?" he asks the SA man nervously after rendering another scene (*Werke*, 4:355). The answer is a matter of life and death for the worker. At moments such as the passage above, when the quotation marks melt away and direct speech yields to free indirect discourse, the tension reaches a peak as the worker comes perilously close to erasing the distinction between himself and the voices that he channels. His deft disavowal recalls that skill which Brecht designated as "the cunning to spread the truth among many" in a 1934 essay (*Werke*, 22:81–89), which suggested as an example of such cunning that people make critical observations about Germany while pretending to be speaking about Austria—an Aesopism that was perfectly permissible, at least until the 1938 annexation of Austria.

The increasing emphasis that Brecht came to place on quotation and represented speech in the 1930s reflected a significant tactical reorientation within his practice as a playwright. Indeed, up until 1933, Brecht's work had been moving more and more toward the total unframing of the theatrical spectacle in the hope that, as he put it in an open letter to Fritz Sternberg from 1927, it would eventually be possible to "liquidate aesthetics" entirely (*Werke*, 21:202–205). These strategies of aesthetic deautonomization, which Brecht gathered under the rubric of the "Major Pedagogy" (*die Große Pädagogik*), called for abrogating the distinction between stage and house, incorporating the audience fully into the theatrical event, and in effect, eliminating spectatorship as such.[48] As he put it, the Major Pedagogy "sublates the system of actor and audience. It recognizes only actors who are at the same time students" (*Werke*, 21:396). In the manner of so many avant-garde projects, from Artaud's theater of cruelty to Kaprow's happenings, Brecht's dissolution of "art into life" strove to integrate the scene of performance into the space of everyday existence without remainder. The "innovative institute without spectators whose performers are at once both auditors and speakers" (*Werke*, 21:320), he wrote, achieved "a connection with *reality* of unprecedented intensity" (*Werke*, 21:443).

However, this phase of radical aesthetic abolitionism in Brecht's work was short-lived, quickly to be replaced by the Minor Pedagogy (*die Kleine Pädagogik*), which effectively reversed the trajectory of the avant-gardist project of "art into life" by reconstructing the proscenium between the observing audience and the images that unfold on stage. It is significant that Brecht created his last play in the Major Pedagogy at the end of 1932, and would write no more works using this method after Hitler assumed power on January 30 of the next year, when he began to reconsider the traditions of theater proper, with its panoply of aesthetic conventions and devices for depiction. The timing of this volte-face is hardly accidental. Indeed, the turn can be directly attributed to the disturbing successes of fascist spectacle culture, whose incorporation of the subject into mass scenarios of pseudo-participatory immersion had, in effect, outbid the avant-garde's project of aesthetic deautonomization. The distinction between the politicization of aesthetics and the aestheticization of politics was perhaps not quite as categorical as Benjamin claimed in his Artwork essay. Brecht could not help but notice the numerous resemblances between the artistic avant-garde and the fascists, whose aesthetic ambitious seemed all too manifest. In his journals and essays, for example, he often referred to Hitler as "the painter" (*der Anstreicher*[49]), calling the fascist leader "the greatest of all artists" (*Werke*, 22:469). As is well known, Hitler indeed excelled at Brecht's own art, taking acting lessons in Munich, where he was taught how to move and enunciate in the manner of a dramatic hero. Brecht avidly collected photographs of Hitler in these practiced theatrical poses. Having learned from theater numerous methods for choreographing spectacle, Hitler then redeployed the techniques, from the use of sensational lighting to the dramatic peripeteia, in the quotidian contexts of daily life. In his 1939 essay "On the Theatricality of Fascism," Brecht observed that the "oppressors of our age perform theater not in their theaters, but on the streets and in the gathering places as well as in their private apartments and their diplomatic chancelleries and assembly halls" (*Werke*, 22:536).

Because, as Brecht notes here, the National Socialists were performing everywhere *except* in the theater itself, then, he reasoned, the old, abandoned institution of theater has once again become available as a resource of critique, scrutiny, and analysis. Confronted with the fascist refeudalization of the public sphere and its false sublation of art and life[50]—the Nazi *Thingspiele*, for example, drew directly upon the practice of the Learning Plays—Brecht responded by reversing the trajectory of the Major Pedagogy, calling now for the reconstruction of the theater as a site of aesthetic distinction and distance, and reintroducing the apparatus of representation into his work. Such strategies of tactical enframing were the subject of *The Messingkauf Dialogues*, a project that he began immediately after completing *Fear and Misery*. The work depicts a conversation between theater personnel and a Marxist philosopher who wants to learn about the uses of art for revolution. Having discovered the artwork's value as an instrument for generating cognitive distinction and facilitating critique, the philosopher, a stand-in for Brecht, no longer wants to liquidate the theater, as he once did, but hopes instead now to steal from "the armory of aesthetics" (*Werke*, 23:65).[51] The four nights over which the *Messingkauf Dialogues* take place correspond roughly to the four phases of Brecht's own career: the technification of theater and its convergence with reality; the encounter with the "emotional racket" and "theatricality of fascism"; realist works such as *Fear and Misery*; and, in the "dialectical turn" of the fourth night, the "retranslation" of the avant-garde experiment back into theater. (Brecht's word for "retranslation," *Rückverwandlung*, is the same one that appears in Benjamin's definition of *gestus* as the "retranslation of the methods of montage . . . from a technological process back into a human one.") Not incidentally, the philosopher names Weigel, together with Chaplin, as the most important figures in this process of "retranslation" (*Werke*, 22:695–697).

The Moscow Clique may have celebrated Brecht's return to traditionalist theater in the mid-1930s, but the reconstructed strategies of representation found in Brecht's Minor Pedagogy should not be too hastily equated with the naturalistic drama of the nineteenth century. Pushing the conventions of theatrical representation to their absolute limits, Brecht's post-avant-garde theater replaced illusionism with showy, self-conscious presentation. In accord with Tret'iakov, he dubbed the latter strategy of display "demonstration," which he considered a third position that was neither the avant-garde's abrogation of mimeticism nor naturalism's slavish imitation of reality. Instead of eliminating representation entirely, Brecht compounded it by reproducing the reproduction, as it were, by quoting secondhand speech, by acting out the film. "Show that you are showing!" Brecht enjoined his actors, in anticipation of Derrida's "double that doubles no simple." An actor thus trained in the art of "double demonstration," as Brecht called it, will embody "no fewer than three persons simultaneously, one who demonstrates and two who are demonstrated" (*Werke*, 22.1:126).

Like the Chinese theater of Mei Lan-Fang, which made such a pronounced impression on Brecht during his 1935 trip to Moscow, the method of mimetic doubling "makes the actor simultaneously into his own spectator" (*Werke*, 22:560) and demands, as a corollary to this art of demonstration, a complementary "art of watching" (*Zuschaukunst*) (*Werke*, 22:124). While the practice of spectatorship returns in the reconstructed theater, it is no longer underwritten by acts of "remainderless identification" (*Werke*, 22:262)—be it the identification of the actor with her character or the identification of the audience with the actor—but instead cultivates non-cathartic strategies of observation and study. Indeed, the modality of aesthetic experience invoked by Brecht brings to mind an encounter with an artwork in a museum far more than any experience of watching naturalistic drama. It was perhaps for this reason that Tret'iakov, for his part, had designated *I Want a Baby* not a "play" but an "exhibition," or *выставка*, a word that recalls the museum as an institution of aesthetic distinction and autonomy. According to Tret'iakov, works such as *I Want a Baby* sought to "turn the stage into an exhibition, to operate by showing material and standards (of movement, speech, things, resolution of situations). Eisenstein and I were considering a type of play that would be an 'exhibition of the standard-human who is placed in circumstances that make activity difficult.'"[52] Like Brecht's own realist "turn," we should add, Tret'iakov's conversion of the theater into a place of display and demonstration had similarly been prompted by the failure of the avant-garde's attempt to sublate art and life, a program that, as Boris Groys has proposed, was commandeered and superseded by the great artist Stalin.[53] "The encounter between 'life' and 'art' has come to an end," Tret'iakov announced in 1927,[54] the same year that Stalin consolidated his power within the Central Committee and that the Futurist reconceived *I Want a Baby* as a museal "exhibition of standards."

A tactical response to the unframing of the aesthetic under totalitarian regimes, Brecht's efforts to recontain the field of representation also precipitated changes in the playwright's relationship to his language. As was brilliantly demonstrated by the philologist Viktor Klemperer, the transformation of the German vocabulary under the Nazis was an important ideological step for cultivating the authoritarian mentality, which demanded a populace imbued with a violent xenophobia, an étatist desire to submit to authority, and a preparedness for world-historical conflict.[55] But this transformation was not merely lexical. No less important was a transformation in the structure and nature of symbolic reference. Indeed, it would seem that authoritarianism always insists on a language in which all words are purely expressive, and therefore immune to complex interpretation. Within the jurisdiction of authoritarian language, Barthes observes, "there are no more words without values attached to them, so that finally the function of writing is to cut out one stage of a process: there is no more lapse of time between naming and judging."[56] Adapting Adorno's well-known phrase, we could say that authoritarian language requires not just a jargon of authenticity, but a semiotic of authenticity as well, which forecloses the lengthy hermeneutical processes that threaten to congest interpretation by opening up the sign to question and debate. Totalitarian regimes instead insist unconditionally on the univocality and semiotic transparency of language. And so, in order to halt the drift of the sign toward an uncontrollable state of exteriority, authoritarianism transforms every utterance into a performative speech act, every name into a judgment, resulting in a dystopic realization of the avant-garde dream of an Adamic language in which thing and sign, world and representation, exist in perfect correspondence with one another.

Responding to a linguistic regime that, in an effort to control the circulation of meaning, privileged the unmediated and expressive word, Brecht turned to strategies of reframing and citation. The worker in "The Chalk Cross" is a prime example: wrapping quotation within quotation, he insists that the criticisms coming out of his mouth be perceived as represented speech, as secondhand utterances, rather than as expressions of his own beliefs—even if, at moments of free indirect speech, he comes precariously close to the latter. Through the technique of quotation and displaced attribution Brecht sets about texturing the monologic surface of fascist language, introducing alien voices and countervailing perspectives that challenge the equation of naming with judging.

This duplicitous and inauthentic speech is related to the specialized linguistic strategy that Valentin Voloshinov identified as "speech interference" (*речевая интерференция*), a tactic that, as the Soviet linguist explained, undermines the "linearity" of authoritarian discourse by blurring the distinction between exteriorized, scripted speech and personal expression.[57] And indeed, the thoroughly mediated text of *Fear and Misery* would seem to illustrate perfectly not just the specific tactic of "speech interference," but also the more fundamental textual dynamic that Voloshinov identified as *чужая речь*, or "reported speech." This phenomenon, as Voloshinov observed in his 1929 opus *Marxism and the Philosophy of Language*, was a fairly recent linguistic innovation, which emerged at the turn of the twentieth century to become, just a few decades later, a cornerstone of language in contemporary society. Even if Voloshinov himself did not address what concrete historical factors may have precipitated this "entirely new interrelationship between authorial and reported speech,"[58] one is led to speculate that this structural mutation must have been caused at least in part by the explosion in the communication media, which dramatically expanded the channels available to language, but which also heightened the subject's awareness of the word's radical exteriority. This, to be sure, was the conclusion drawn by Roman Jakobson, who, preferring a more communication-theoretical idiom, rechristened Voloshinov's *чужая речь* as "displaced" or "relayed speech." As a result of technical media that allow us to connect with people across vast geographical expanse and at different moments in time, such spatially "displaced" or temporally "relayed" communication comes to play an increasingly important role in the syntax of intersubjectivity in the modern world, where social interaction no longer presumes the face-to-face encounter. To be sure, the exteriorization of language began long ago with the invention of writing, but this process achieves an unprecedented degree of alienation in the media age, when an extraneous "reported speech" began to infiltrate, restructure, and determine subjective consciousness. Jakobson confirms indeed that today transmitted language "may prevail in our discourse, since we are far from confining our speech to events sensed in the present by the speaker himself. We quote others and our own former utterances, and we are even prone to present some of our current experiences in the form of self-quotation, for instance by confronting them with statements by someone else."[59] Increasingly, Jakobson suggests, the architecture of the human mind is fashioned out of readymade "relayed" speech that has an origin external to us, giving rise to a generalized condition of heteroglossia in which the speaker begins even to represent her "current experiences in the form of self-quotation."

For Voloshinov, a member of Bakhtin's circle, *чужая речь* had an unmistakably ethical valence. The phrase literally means "the speech of the other." Even in the most private recesses of the self, the thoughts of the subject are penetrated by an inscrutable alterity, determined by anonymous voices that remain fundamentally alien to the individual psyche. The performance of Mrs. Keith, for example, who speaks telephonically while in the presence of her husband, reveals an *Interieur*, both psychic and domestic, that has been turned inside out. And actors are not the only ones who "Speak alien texts," Brecht also observed: "lovers / And salespeople too memorize alien texts, and how often / You quote expressions! In this way / Mask and verse and quotation have become commonplace" (*Werke*, 21:860). Just like the author of *Fear and Misery*, the decentered and diffuse psychological subject described here is "drowning in reports," fashioned out of mediated and secondhand speech. The ego, for Brecht, was not a resolved, unified structure, but a dynamic dialogue that is fashioned, as for Voloshinov, from a collective corpus of speech and symbols. As Brecht proposed in a note entitled "On Personhood," "'I' am not a person. I emerge in each moment and never endure past it. I emerge in the form of a reply" (*Werke*, 21:404).

From the perspective of this mediatized epistemology, Brecht's dramaturgy of the quotable *gestus* appears to be a close cognate of the method of "transitionless acting," or *беспереходная игра*, which appeared around the same time in the work of Sergei Eisenstein. Much like Brecht and Tret'iakov, Eisenstein had developed this technique in reconciliation with a realist aesthetic whose rising star had shifted the emphasis in art away from mechanical montage strategies and toward the depiction of the integral organic body. And if in Brecht's case the conversion to the realist cause resulted in *Fear and Misery*, while in Tret'iakov's case the same realist turn produced the second version of *I Want a Baby*, the analogous work in Eisenstein's oeuvre would be *The General Line* (1929), a film that, in contrast to *October* and *Battleship Potemkin*, is restrained, even classical, in its use of montage, and that places a distinct emphasis on the performance of the actor. At the time of its release, Eisenstein indeed played down the role of montage in his new film, boasting of the "extreme simplicity of the meter and scale" in *The General Line*.[60] Eisenstein's disregard for editing and his renewed concern for techniques of acting were wholly consonant with recent trends in Soviet cinema, which, in line with the rapid advances being made by the realist aesthetic in all the arts, had taken a new interest in the body and comportment of the figure on the screen. In a 1928 synopsis of the latest developments in film technique, Shklovskii, for example, observed that "[m]ontage, in which so much has already been done, has retreated to an auxiliary function or to hopeless parallelisms. This year the most important debate on principle has been the debate about the actor."[61]

Although it seemed to Shklovskii that the great montage experiment of Soviet cinema had come to an end by 1928, Eisenstein's work from this very moment shows that, even with the new emphasis on simplified structure and longer takes, film had hardly abandoned montage. The technique had just migrated into the figure of the actor itself, whose synthetic comportment and expressions would now operate as anthropomorphic, realist equivalents for such cinematic matters as editing, framing, and camera movement. Like the Brechtian *gestus*, "transitionless acting" did not revoke the methods of montage and mechanical assembly, but introjected these devices into the body of the actor, taking mechanization to a higher level. Recalling Eisenstein's description of the dramaturgy of the *naturshchik*, or model-actor, this technique could be described as a "purely organic" paradigm of montage, which segments and rearranges the performance of the actor without the intervention of the editor's scissors. Through the use of "transitionless acting," Eisenstein observed, it even becomes possible to achieve the effects of cinematography without cinema. In fact, the filmmaker claimed to have discovered this method by watching Japanese theater, a superlative art form that had emerged from a country that, he observed, lacked any significant cinematic tradition (*Montazh*, 492; *Works*, 138). "It is incorrect to assume that a construction is 'free of montage' just because the actor performs in a single unbroken strip of film and the director doesn't edit this strip on the cutting table! Hardly. In this case we only need to search for the montage elsewhere, namely . . . *in the very performance of the actor*."[62] Thus, Eisenstein cautioned, the critics of montage have celebrated their victory prematurely, for they have mistaken the invisibility of the technical apparatus for its absence. Like Lukács, who, according to Brecht, had "overlooked the montage" of *Fear and Misery*, these critics had perceived an organic and natural body where it did not in fact exist.[63]

Like the *gestus*, Eisenstein's montage dramaturgy works by producing collisions between discontinuous emotional states, resulting in a performance that is disjointed and full of counterpoints. Hence the designation "transitionless." Through this method, Shklovskii observed in a later essay about Eisenstein, "a condition—the stages of a condition—is depicted in fits and surges [*порожесто*], as if through small jolts—or we could say, imprecisely: through quanta."[64] With each jolt, with each transitionless interval, Eisenstein increasingly loosens the bond connecting a psychic state to a particular character, eventually uncoupling the two entirely from one another. Shklovskii cites as an example a sequence from *The General Line* that "depicted the state of one person, and then transitioned to another person, depicting the same emotion using different human material. He returned to the first person via the object that prompts the emotion—and this is the way that he produces a collision between states [*столкновение состояний*]. Each person was emotionally immobile, like a mask in antique theater."[65] Transitionless acting, Shklovskii explains here, parses and distributes an emotional state across multiple actors in an analytical fashion, incorporating into this psychological complex even inanimate objects. By means of this discontinuous performance, the director is thus able to diagram a set of social relations that exceeds the subjective boundaries of the individual, transcending the basic dramatic distinction between character and environment, and mapping instead a total scenography of relations that encompasses both actor and object within a single, integrated social schema. These fundamental social configurations constitute what one Eisenstein scholar has called a "structure of primary situations" (*структура основных ситуаций*).[66]

Brecht likewise designated these fundamental diagrams of encounter *Grundmodelle*, "primary models" in which the social relations depicted do not "belong" to any single character, but are instead rendered through the features of the surrounding space. As the importance of these *Grundmodelle* grew in Brecht's work, the playwright began increasingly to focus on strategies of stage design that made it possible to represent these abstract social schemes graphically. Thus, just several months before he began work on *Señora Carrar*—on the eve of his alleged conversion to socialist realism—Brecht wrote an entire series of studies exploring how to translate the principles of *gestic* dramaturgy into the architecture and contents of the stage. This system required above all overcoming the boundary that separated the actor from the objects and space around her, as he declared in a 1937 essay on stage design. Despite efforts to essentialize the boundary between people and things, this anthropomorphism, Brecht observed, was not as stable as the humanist realists had presumed: "Our representations of the human environment are formed by a knowledge of the 'metabolism between nature and man' as a social process that is historically variable" (*Werke*, 22:227). Depicting this open metabolism required a stage design that viewed space not as an indifferent container for dramatic action, but as a dynamic system that responds in dialogue with its human contents. Thus animated, the "environment acquires the qualities of a process," he noted (*Werke*, 22:238). By constructing an integrated but ever-shifting "field of play," Brecht's set unframed the figure on stage, as it were, dissolving the "character" into the architectural support around it and redistributing dramatic agency across a number of bodies, both organic and inorganic (*Werke*, 22:229). Like the *gestic* speech of the other, *gestic* dramaturgy frees the events depicted on stage from attribution to any particular individual, replacing the ontology of character with an abstract diagram of action. For Brecht, the actor was, at least qualitatively, no different from the objects whose space she shares, merely "the most important of all of the pieces of scenery" (*Werke*, 22:229).

By turning the performer into a conduit of her surroundings, Brecht's transhuman version of ensemble acting destabilizes a realist mode of figuration that required on principle the integrity and autonomy of the human body. If, as the Prague School structuralist Jiří Veltruský observed in an important essay from 1940, "Man and Object In the Theater," traditional realist drama arrests all "fluctuation between man and object" that could potentially impugn the ideology of heroic humanism,[67] Brecht's *gestic* stage, by contrast, liquefies these terms, restoring the dynamic metabolism between the individual and his environment. The corresponding effect of "action in the absence of the subject," Veltruský concluded in this essay, "is one of the most important social objectives of the theater" today.[68] The purpose of Brecht's *Grundmodell* was to depict such actions divorced from individual agents, ultimately demonstrating the fact that "humans have ceased to exist as autonomous beings who have things at their disposal; in particular the human *as such*, as a finished concept, has ceased to exist" (*Werke*, 21:320–321).

The same epistemological slackening of the boundary between self and other that is evident in Brecht's stagecraft permeates the very grammatical categories of his language as well. In his analysis of Brecht's poem from *The Measures Taken* "We Are They" ("Wir sind sie"), Jakobson, for example, noted a telling grammatical feature of his text: the astonishing prevalence of shifters such as pronouns and deictic words, which constitute over two-thirds of the lexical items in the poem.[69] In contrast to substantives, which convey a specific image-content, shifters, Jakobson reminded the reader, are purely "formal words" that denote nothing in themselves but instead sketch out a series of relative positions. "A formal word has no concrete, material characteristics whatsoever," he wrote. "It neither names nor describes any kind of phenomenon in itself. It merely indicates the relations that exist among the phenomena and that determine them."[70] Closely related to the contentless mathematical languages that, as we saw in the previous chapter, so fascinated Brecht in the early 1930s,[71] shifters are linguistic functionality in its purest state. For this reason, Jakobson concluded that these nonrepresentational words, which Greimas called *mots-outils*, were the very essence of Brechtian *gestus*. They provide nonmimetic diagrams of grammatical relations, *Grundmodelle* through which a mobilized subjectivity alternatively constitutes and dissolves itself as a sociolinguistic phenomenon. In the very title of the poem, for example, Brecht uses pronouns, the most common form of grammatical shifter, to sketch out one such psychic transition—in this case, a transition outward from the first to the third person, from "we" to "they." Through such grammatical transitions, his text provided a tentative and fleeting linguistic architecture for the ego of the speaking subject.

EPIC TRANSITIONS

The forms of psychic dedifferentiation that can be found simultaneously on the metatextual, physical, and linguistic registers of Brecht's work (in his use of quotation, non-anthropocentric stage design, and grammatical shifters, respectively) touch upon that famous late modernist project which Brecht and contemporaries such as Alfred Döblin designated an "epic" poetics. The modernist revival of this archaic paradigm entails more than just a set of aesthetic devices such as disjuncture, estrangement and montage, for these individual artistic strategies together comprise a comprehensive campaign to revise some of the most fundamental categories of consciousness and collective experience. For Brecht, the epic system presupposed an understanding of the ego as a mobile function that, as we have seen, circulates through the various *Grundmodelle* of social intercourse. Positioned within a "primary model," each character, he wrote, "is constructed out of relationships to other figures" (*Werke*, 22:747). Döblin, the other major "epic" modern, also explored these abstract and reversible social diagrams, which he likewise designated "elementary situations" (*Elementarsituationen*) and "elementary stances" (*Elementarhaltungen*).[72]

Central to the epic system, I would argue, was the phenomenon of mental transitivism, as defined in 1916 by the psychiatrist Eugen Bleuler as a condition in which "the patient's own experiences become detached from him and are ascribed to another person."[73] In Eisenstein's work, this mechanism fell under the rubric of "transitionless acting," which, as we have seen, projected a single emotional state across multiple actors and objects. For Brecht, such supraindividual schemes confirmed the differential law of the Hegelian dialectic, which, Brecht observed, stipulates that "the smallest social unit is not the individual, but two individuals," and that the "master is only a master insofar as the slave allows him to be." For this reason, he insisted, "the actor's learning must be conducted together with the learning of the other actors, the construction of his figure with the construction of the other figures" (*Werke*, 23:88). As a director, Brecht pursued a number of strategies for facilitating the experience of psychic transitivism in his actors. In rehearsals he regularly demanded, for example, that his actors assume all of the various roles, adopting a particular persona at one given moment and its dialogical counterpart at the next. By "seeing oneself in the third person and taking action as this third person," as he put it, the boundaries between self and other would begin to erode (*Werke*, 22.1:69). In certain works Brecht even took such exercises beyond rehearsal, building this practiced objectivation of the ego into the structure of the play itself. *The Measures Taken*, for example, requires each performer to assume a different role when she steps out of the chorus, forcing his actors to play opposite themselves, as it were.

At the level of linguistic construction, too, Brecht was constantly undermining the distinction between agent and patient, much to the chagrin of his Russian translator Tret'iakov, who once complained of Brecht's "special technique for hiding the grammatical objects" of his sentences.[74] Such ambiguous and reversible grammars capture the fundamentally dyadic logic that, according to Brecht, governs the psychological development of the individual. The subject emerges to consciousness, he observed, "By saying yes, by saying no/By beating and by being beaten/By joining the company of some and by joining the company of others/The human takes form by changing itself thus/And his image emerges within us/By resembling us and by not resembling us" (*Werke*, 22:812). There is a fundamental difference, Brecht observes in these lines, between the actual human being and the image that defines her, an image that is neither timeless nor universal, but which instead "emerges within us" through experiences of group compliance and trials of social conflict. We may pass beyond the mirror stage, to reference the famous concept introduced by Lacan in 1936, but the image of the human grafted onto us is fundamentally unstable and, as Brecht proposes, does not necessarily always "resemble" us. At some moments the individual subject corresponds to this collective image and is thus recognized as properly "human," while at other moments, in a kind of anthropic phase-shift, her contours no longer coincide with the given culture's prototype of the human.

This structure of psychic transitivism, which found a linguistic corollary in Brecht's willful equivocation around the distinction between subject and object, brings us to a central aspect of the modern return to the epic paradigm, which is the reanimation of the middle voice, a grammatical construction found in ancient Greek but absent in nearly all modern European languages (the exception being Icelandic). In contrast to active- and passive-voiced verbs, which focus respectively on the author and recipient of an action, the middle voice emphasizes the action itself over the people and things it involves. Like the grammatical shifter, it releases the event from the concrete image-content fixed in nouns. And while this verbal aspect no longer has formal grammatical markers in the major Western languages, there are grammatical constructions that at least elliptically still evoke the middle voice. In German and Russian, for example, its weak echo can be heard in certain intransitive uses of the reflexive verb. Although an even better modern equivalent is the English verb "to get" when used in combination with a past participle. To offer one example: *to kill* is an active construction, *to be killed* a passive one, while *to get killed* renders the action in a middle-voice, eliding the difference between agent and patient.

The Soviet philologist Viktor Vinogradov observed in 1938 that "the question about transitive and intransitive meanings . . . vastly exceeds the frameworks used to study purely grammatical relationships between the subject and object of an action."[75] And indeed, the use of intransitive, middle-voiced verbs is not merely a grammatical concern, for these constructions inflect the very categories through which consciousness understands the world. Unlike the modern ego that contemplates, wills, and acts from a vantage outside of historical events, the subjectivity that emerges through the middle voice remains immanent to the action of a verb and is, for this reason, a far more contingent being. In the *Messingkauf Dialogues*, Brecht proposed "to consider the individual an unfinished matter" that evolves "from utterance to utterance and from action to action" (*Werke*, 22:812). The middle voice evokes this fugitive consciousness, which is interior, rather than anterior, to the event. As Émile Benveniste explained: "In the active, the verbs denote a process that is accomplished outside the subject. In the middle . . . the verb indicates a process centering on the subject, the subject being inside the process."[76] Following the influential categories the early twentieth-century philosopher of language Fritz Mauthner, one could say, then, that the middle voice shifts the framework of subjective experience away from a substantival perspective, which locks consciousness into a set of fixed ontological relations, toward what he called a "verbal" *Weltbild*, which, suspending the logical distinction the subject and object of an action, instead expresses eventhood itself.[77]

Like Brecht's *gestus*, Eisenstein's "transitionless acting" rendered the epistemology of the middle-voice in dramaturgical terms. In fact, the label he chose for this practice, *безпереходная*, is entirely apposite in this regard, since this neologism would be translated as "nontransitive" in the vocabulary of linguistics. (A "transitive verb" in Russian is a *переходный глагол*.) In contrast to the unidirectional trajectory of the transitive verb, in which an action originates in a subject and passes over into an object, Eisenstein's "nontransitive acting" distributes a single emotional state across a series of actors and things, creating, as Shklovskii observed, an abstract and reversible image of a total social "condition" (*состояние*). In his address at the 1935 All-Union Congress for Creative Workers of Soviet Cinema, Eisenstein spoke at length about his nontransitive dramaturgy, which he described there as the "simultaneity of 'I' and 'not-I' in the creation and performance of a role."[78] Through modern forms of "metempsychosis" (*перевоплощение*) that he likened to the psychological mechanism of totemic identification found in tribal cultures, it becomes possible to burst open the epistemological "problem of 'I' versus 'he,'" he claimed,[79] liquefying the static dualism that, as Barthes put it in a later text on the middle voice, "sets person (*I* or *you*) in opposition to the non-person (*he* or *it*), sign of what is absent, or absence itself."[80] In place of this great opposition, Eisenstein proposed, nontransitive performance provides an image of pure action, what Mauthner would call a verbal *Weltbild*. As support for this eccentric and esoteric claim, Eisenstein turned at the 1935 Congress to the hard and fast bedrock of the Party classics, quoting a passage from Engels's *Socialism, Utopian and Scientific* (1880):

> When we consider and reflect upon nature at large, or the history of mankind, or our own intellectual activity, at first we see the picture of an endless entanglement of relations and reactions, permutations and combinations, in which nothing remains what, where, and as it was, but everything moves, changes, comes into being and passes away. We see, therefore, at first the picture as a whole, with its individual parts still more or less kept in the background; we observe the movements, transitions, connections, rather than the things that move, combine, and are connected.[81]

Commenting on this passage, Eisenstein pointed out how Engels emphasized not people or things, but the actions—"the movements, transitions, connections"—in which they participate. To illustrate his point, he contrasted two German sentences, one in the active voice and one in the middle voice: *Die Gänse flogen* (*The geese were flying*) and *Es flogen die Gänse* (*There were geese flying*). Through a "juxtaposition of words," in which "the description of movement and action (the verb) precedes the description of who is moving or acting (the noun)," the second image absorbs the geese into the action of flight itself, Eisenstein observed. *Es flogen die Gänse* thus describes "not . . . the object, but . . . the action and movement that have wholly replaced the [secondary] concept of '*what* it is that is moving.'"[82]

Of the various cultural artifacts through which modernists such as Eisenstein and Brecht encountered the archaic paradigm of the middle voice, none loomed as large as the tradition of Greek tragedy. Writing about the "nontransitive performance" of *The General Line*, Shklovskii, as we saw, observed that each actor performed "like a mask in antique theater," confirming the filiation between this dramaturgical technique and its Greek predecessor. In the case of Brecht's *gestus*, our referent is even more specific, considering the fact the playwright first used the term in a review of the 1929 production of *Oedipus Rex* in which Weigel had delivered such a stunning and bewildering Jocasta. Indeed, as the philosopher Charles Scott has noted in an essay on the middle voice, Sophocles's play depicts an "event that is filled with conflict, ambiguity, and transition and that shows the value of the middle voice in giving expression to the occurrence of events in their excess of activity and passivity." The result, Scott writes, conveys "something excessive regarding subject-object formations."[83] In sundry discussions of *Oedipus Rex* and other antique tragedies, Brecht similarly noted that these works presumed a system of interpersonal relations different from the one found in bourgeois society, whose ideology of heroic humanism vastly overprivileges the role and resources of the individual. Through its distinctive depictions of collective destiny, in particular, antique tragedy supplied a "representation of human coexistence" that conveys the profound interdependence between the person and the society in which he lives (*Werke*, 22:278). These plays depicted not the *in*dividual—an autonomous unit that, as the etymology of the word suggests, cannot be further divided into smaller units—but what Brecht instead proposed to call the "dividual," a social being whose existence is defined through the public life of the collective: if the individual subject is produced through a process that Brecht designated as *Teilung*, a procedure of mere abstract mechanical division, the dividual subject, by contrast, emerges through the operation of Ein*teilung*, a word also meaning "division," albeit division *into* an aggregate body (*Werke*, 21:359). It is only through *Einteilung*, Brecht wrote, that communal existence is transformed from something that is merely "tolerable"—a mass of isolated individuals—to something that is wholly "sensual" and properly collective ("vom Erträglichen zum Lustvollen"; *Werke*, 21:179).

Brecht's notion of the dividual recalls the negative anthropologies that were central to the Weimar image of man, which defined the human subject as a fundamentally medial creature, a "deficient being" and an esemplastic bundle of drives that requires social institutions, symbolic languages and material prostheses for its self-realization. The Greek word meaning "to be a human being" (*ἀνθρωπεύομαι*) is, significantly, a middle-voiced verb. As Aristotle explained in *The Nicomachean Ethics*, unlike other beings such as gods and animals, which are complete in themselves, humans require for their existence and development what he called "externals"—technologies, resources, as well as other humans. A creature destined to exist in the middle voice, the human is not defined at the moment of its birth, but instead evolves ontogenetically through acts of self-exteriorization that presume the context of human society and material artifacts for its realization.[84] For Brecht, this understanding of the human as a medial animal, which was essential to the epic paradigm, also had a concrete political value, insofar as it changed the terms in which revolutionary agency could be conceived. Emerging within the act itself, the middle-voiced subject is not a purely passive thing, but nor is she the sovereign master of her fate. The intransitive paradigm of agency found in Brecht's *gestus* thereby evades the errors of the two dominant models for conceptualizing mechanisms of political power: on the one hand, the structuralist model of scientific Marxism, which reduces the subject to a mere effect or symptom of objective world-historical events, and on the other, the model of bourgeois humanism, which, lapsing into the other extreme, monumentalizes the individual as the singular and heroic author of the historical process.

The mediality of Brecht's gestic dramaturgy should thus not be confused with passivity. To the contrary, as we saw earlier, the fundamental exteriority of the medial beings depicted in *Fear and Misery* was deeply inimical to the Nazi ideology of authenticity, with its injunction to speak using a language that was univocal, primordial and expressive, a language that collapses the act of naming into that of judging. Try as he does to nail language to its speaker, the SA officer in "The Chalk Cross," for example, can never hold the worker accountable for his seditious thoughts since they are conveyed in the quasi-direct discourse of *чужсая речь*. As "speech of the other," language never belongs completely to its speaker, and for this reason can become a resource of resistance in the hands of those who oppose the regime. Equally importantly for Brecht, however, is how this exteriorized language resists those who support the regime as well. For all their proclaimed immediacy, the language and gestuary of the Third Reich were artificial to an extreme: this "miraculous bacillus," as Brecht called it (*Werke*, 22:56–57), was a lab-engineered organism designed to thrive in the technical environment of the mass media, which dictated everything from the radiophonic inflections of Goebbels's speech patterns to the histrionic postures that the Führer took from photographs. Herein lies the vulnerability of fascist language, Brecht proposed: because it is so artificial, because it is in fact so inauthentic, this language is also fundamentally unruly, prone to all sorts of internal semantic interference. And so, while scenes such as "The Chalk Cross" demonstrate how the language of the regime can be actively subverted through crafty manipulation, other scenes depict the same subversion taking place spontaneously, causing the otherwise perfectly choreographed *langue de bois* of the regime to betray itself. In "The Worker's Hour," for example, the interviewee appearing on a radio program inadvertently fails to speak her line at the proper cue, and her ill-timed response unmasks the government's lies. At these moments, the "miraculous bacillus" that once faithfully served its master as an instrument of ideological hegemony turns suddenly against those who engineered it.

Taken individually, these failures of language and expression appear only to be so many idiosyncratic parapraxes. But when organized into a periodic table of gestures, or *Gestentafel*, these slips suddenly appear to be anything but accidental. Arranged alongside one another in *Fear and Misery*, these seemingly random incidents comprise a systematic pattern that cuts across political affiliations, mapping out unanticipated networks of solidarity and resistance among the individual speakers of language, revolutionary and Nazi alike. Out of the "quotable," and thus uncontrollable, *gestus* emerge the contours of a collective subject. For Brecht, a defining feature of the *gestus* was, therefore, its fundamental asynchrony: as in the silent cinema from which Brecht drew his inspiration, in *gestic* dramaturgy, language and action can never be made to coincide perfectly. The *gestus*, which so often contradicts the intentions of its speaker unexpectedly, inhabits a deep, collective temporality that defies the time-scale in which the individual experiences and wills. This is why it is chronically out of sync, why its appearance is always marked by a break or interruption: *gestus facit saltus*. As Brecht suggested in a short essay from 1935, "The Retention of Gestures across Different Generations" (*Werke*, 22:127), *gestus* has a lifespan much longer than that of the individual: "I often see, says the thinking man, that I have the stance [*Haltung*] of my father. But my deeds aren't those of my father. Why are my deeds different? Because what is necessary is different. But I see that the stance endures longer than the form of action: it resists what is necessary" (*Werke*, 28:34). Transmitted across generations, relayed across social strata, *gesten* constitute an alternative historical lineage that exceeds the individual lifespan which begins with birth and concludes with death.

This collective agent reveals itself in acts of what Oskar Negt and Alexander Kluge have called *Eigensinn*, a word meaning "obstinacy," but also "autonomy" or "self-will."[85] Such acts of spontaneous intransigence, they observe, reflect a dense evolutionary temporality that unfolds independently of civilization's linear history as parsed out and written by heroic authors.[86] As we have already seen, Brecht insisted that the alternate matrix of time embodied in the *gestus* comes into clearest view in the performance of labor activities, since work is the most collectivized of all of the movements in the gestural repertoire of the individual (an observation seemingly confirmed by Leroi-Gourhan's analysis of "operational sequences"). Understanding the patterns of these gestures provides a glimpse of a collective subject that inhabits a temporality different than that of the individual. When asked in an interview, "So you take it as a given that the individual faculties of labor have their own history?" Kluge responded:

> Yes, certain faculties of labor have been taken out of circulation. The division between private and public traverses all of history, not just that of capitalism, where this division of course is particularly exacerbated. Because they work in the manner of a mole, faculties of labor that have been taken out of circulation can once again be reactivated even after two- or three-hundred years.

To which Negt added:

> It is of no interest to us whether a trait that can be emancipated exists within an integral system or has been taken out of circulation.

Just because a working trait came into existence and was cultivated within a capitalist context or within the laboratories of the Third Reich such as the *Organisation Todt* doesn't mean this trait is more stable than any of the others. Just like all others, it can be reconstellated.[87]

4

A Necrologue of the Ego: Carl Einstein's Autobiography, *Bebuquin II*

Around 1925, the German author Carl Einstein began work on an autobiography that would remain unfinished at the time of his suicide in 1940. He called the project *Bebuquin II* after the earlier novella *Bebuquin oder die Dilettanten des Wunders* (*Bebuquin, or the Dilettantes of Miracle*), the acclaimed Expressionist novella whose serial publication beginning in 1907 had established his celebrity as a modernist writer. His choice of title for the autobiography seems to have been dually motivated. On the one hand, as personal correspondence about the project suggests, he was hoping to trade a bit on his previous publishing success in order to prepare the way for his great comeback to the literary scene from which he had first emerged. After all, since the publication of his *Negro Sculpture* in 1915, Einstein had focused almost exclusively on art criticism, and, now hoping to revive his reputation as a literary author, it didn't seem like such a bad idea to remind audiences of his earlier breakthrough work.

Yet there was also a second motivation behind Einstein's return to *Bebuquin* in the mid-1920s, one that had nothing to do with the pragmatics of marketing. This was the impulse to rewrite his earlier modernist monument. Like many of the texts and artworks produced during the 1920s and '30s, an interval of widespread and intense cultural retrospection, *Bebuquin II* presented its author with the opportunity to return to his roots, as it were, and revisit the legacy and devices of experimental modernism, this time under different historical conditions. During the interwar period, the purpose of this return was not to reinstate modernist paradigms but to revoke them, we are told, in accordance with what has been called an "aesthetics of stabilization." In Einstein's case the repeal of modernism took the form of a project that reframed the original experimental text within an autobiography, a genre that, in privileging the denotative function of language, disciplines stylized writing and the excesses of metaphor with an emphatic and incontrovertible notion of extratextual reference. In autobiography, reality trumps fiction. This strategy of recontaining a modernist novella within the secure referential framework of a memoir would seem to situate *Bebuquin II* as a work of the New Objectivity, a movement whose literary branch found its quintessential idiom in documentary genres such as reportage and autobiography. Trading in the wrought reflexivity and semiotic interrogations of modernism's literary experiments for the solid ground of objective reality and authentic experience, this positivist impulse found its highest expression in what Leo Löwenthal called, with reference to New Objectivity biography, a "kind of fossilized anthropology" (*eine Art versteinerter Anthropologie*).[1]

By and large, scholars of Einstein have accepted the place of *Bebuquin II* in this narrative of stabilization. Some have suggested, for example, that the turn to reality in this text reflected the author's need for psychological grounding and continuity under the emotionally difficult conditions of exile in France, especially after 1933, when this exile from his homeland became permanent.[2] Regardless of its motivation, *Bebuquin II* indeed shares little of the linguistic exuberance of its predecessor *Bebuquin*. Instead, its tone is sober, detached, and phlegmatic. If before the writing was open and unresolved, the hermeneutic puzzles of *Bebuquin* are now gone. Turning against modernism's self-referentiality, which Einstein now disavows as speculative and solipsistic, *Bebuquin II* seeks a language that is commensurate with reality, a language of consequence, accountability and direct political action. Together with its theoretical complement, the great antimodernist tirade *The Fabrication of Fictions: ~~A Defense of the Real~~*, *Bebuquin II* prepared the way for Einstein's final verdict on belletrism, delivered in 1936:

after joining the anarchist militia of Buenaventura Durruti in Spain that year, he would never publish another work of literature.

To be sure, the characterization of *Bebuquin II* as a realist work in the vein of the New Objectivity is certainly accurate at the level of the individual sentence, where Einstein drastically limits the explosive syntax and lexical ambiguities of the earlier text. But, I would argue, the realist conventions of representation break down at the larger scale of textual dynamics. Taken severally, the smaller units of the text make perfect sense, but, when brought together, a certain hermeneutic alchemy takes place. While the reader's immediate experience is of a work that is lucid and sober, a subterranean current pushes simultaneously against the intelligibility of these individual scenes, a current that gains cumulative force across the 1,300 unpublished pieces of text that are today housed in Einstein's Berlin archive. The issue is not so much that these textual units—some chapters, some just scraps of paper—do not add up, but that they instead add up to *too much*. Often Einstein will repeat an episode from his life, for example, each time recasting it with a different constellation of actors and a correspondingly variable outcome, giving the narrative architecture of *Bebuquin II* an uncannily circular quality. This temporal ambiguity is further compounded by the narrator's tendency to shift back and forth from the here and now of a diary to the departed preterite of fiction. The breaks between these two tenses, in turn, are announced in the text by a grammatical shift from the first to the third person, a shift that sets up an external perspective and ballasts the autobiography with a sense of objective historical reality. And yet at moments the exteriority and neutrality of the third person also gives an impression of extreme mental dissociation, as though Einstein were watching himself from the outside. Throwing off the delicate balance between objective record and psychological interiority that is proper to the genre of the memoir, *Bebuquin II* transgresses a fixed law of autobiographical writing: the document of the ego can sustain only so much objectivity, so much exteriority, before the certitude of its reality lapses into its very opposite, complete psychic derealization. At these moments, *Bebuquin II* sinks into a blurry paramnesia that undermines the reader's confidence in the existence of a hard and fast truth outside the text. Apparently this close feedback loop between *Bebuquin II* and its author's life began to undermine Einstein's ability to distinguish the two as well, for at one point he even began to sign his personal correspondence with the letter *B*, in reference to his protagonist.

Thus, although the individual episodes in *Bebuquin II* might give the impression of a straightforward and realist work, the view looks quite different on the metatextual register, where we find an autobiography that radicalizes certain precepts of the avant-garde rather than abrogating them. For one thing, the trajectory of *Bebuquin II* does not follow a path of *Bildung*, of self-fashioning through narrative development. Quite the opposite. Here the act of recollection instead serves to scatter the pieces of selfhood in a textual *auto-da-fé*. Announcing a "revolt against the ego," Einstein declared in his notes for the project that "I must disappear."[3] His self-described "necrologue of the ego" (Einstein Archive, 17) would take the form of a mnemonic obliteration, since the ego, he observed, was fundamentally "retrospective, an exhibition of memories" (*Werke*, 3:118) that defines and stabilizes itself through continuities with the past. A sclerosis of memory that blocks direct access to the world, the ego holds the individual psyche in the thrall of its past, foreclosing the possibility of new experiences in the present and of potential change in the future. Thus it was by razing the prison of the ego, a psychic structure that had become overbuilt during the age of bourgeois individualism, that Einstein hoped to clear the way for a more direct, less mnemonically congested encounter with the world. Destroying the ego was the first and most important step toward restoring the dynamic epistemological metabolism between subject and world.

But here an aporia within the operational logic of *Bebuquin II* immediately becomes apparent: if Einstein sought a technique to eradicate the self, why, of all instruments for this campaign, would he choose the genre of autobiography, which for centuries has served as the storehouse of memory and cultural sanctum sanctorum of selfhood? If the task was to shed the strictures of ego, surely it made more sense to flee the textual locus of individuality rather than to embrace it. Indeed, how could a project of self-prospecting ever be brought to work against the conditions of selfhood that it presumes as its very point of departure? Einstein's distinctly dialectical answer to this question is to force the autobiographical "hypertrophy of personhood" (Einstein Archive, 14) to its uttermost limit, where it lapses into its opposite, a "necrologue of the ego." In his hands, the memoir became a means to disperse the components of subjectivity rather than suture them together, an anamnesis that erased of the psychological core of selfhood through a superabundance of memory. He characterized this paradoxical convergence of recollection and forgetting in his autobiography as an "egoistic forgetting of the self" (Einstein Archive, 19).

The following chapter argues that the curious mnemonic economy revealed in Einstein's *Bebuquin II* also has far-reaching consequences for the issues of representation that are central to this book. Touching upon a number of compositional strategies that are characteristic of interwar art and literature, his project to dismantle the faculty of memory merges with a general critique of mimetic realism. This was the case, Einstein explained, because realism requires the well-ordered retrieval of mnemonic images in order to function: spanned in a delicate field of tension between oblivion and memory, mimetic representation is perturbed if the balance shifts too far towards either of these terms. The conventions of realist art, he thus reasoned, were vulnerable to disturbance from two directions, through the destruction and erasure of memory, but also through its excess and superabundance. As we will see, *Bebuquin II* opts for the latter strategy. Borrowing from the conventions and motifs of the traditional realist text, Einstein repeats these figures again and again until they begin to turn against the text's sense of veracity and to impugn the realist system itself. It was through the surplus of memory in *Bebuquin II*, through an "egoistic forgetting of the self," in other words, that Einstein intended to strike a blow against the foundations of resemblance and verisimilitude.

A Burial in Leaves

Einstein's critical writings on French cubism provide us with an initial sketch of the mechanism through which memory and representational realism collude. In an essay published in the journal *Documents* on analytic cubism (the phase of cubist production between 1909 and 1914), he argued that cubism's greatest innovation was not its shattering of the viewer's unified and coherent optic or the blow that this visual fragmentation leveled against the integrity of the spectatorial subject. These spatial effects were secondary to cubism's primary vocation, which was to subvert mimetic resemblance through a destruction of memory. Following the neo-associationist school of psychology prevalent in his day, Einstein explained in this essay that the legibility of an illusionistic painting hinges on the spectator's capacity to draw upon a mental stock of previous representations that can serve as a basis for comparison. "Descriptive art," as he called mimetic realism, works by cross-referencing the external phenomenon being perceived with an internal "deposit of a memory" (*Werke*, 4:163). As Sebastian Zeidler explains, for Einstein vision was "a process during which new stimuli are constantly compared to old ones stored in memory, such that their location and extension in space will be identified through an act of syllogistic generalization based on past experiences. This is a model of vision that assumes that a subject's experience of an object is temporally linear, epistemologically cumulative, and deeply backward-oriented, for the subject will always seek to interpret the new as but a variation of the old."[4] According to Einstein, the spectator does not perceive the realist artwork in its empirical particularity, but, turning inward, instead recalls a different object from her past, filtering out mentally the moments where the artwork before her diverges from this memory image. But the line between mental constancy and solipsistic tautology is a fine one. As Einstein explained, the realist system of representation tends toward a closed circle of autoreference in which its image-signs summon the identical memories over and over again. Comparing a realist painting with other memory "deposits" demands a shift from sensation to recollection, the final result of which is a closed loop of "slavish tautology" (*sklavische Tautologie*) that eternally conjures the mental forms from the storehouse of memory.

By severing this relay between optical perception and memory, the analytic cubists subverted mimetic realism's law of identity: "It was the cubists who interrogated the object that was forever identical with itself; which is to say: they interrogated memory, where concepts are brought into order one after the other. Their greatest achievement was to destroy memory's prefabricated images. . . . The mnemonic legacy of objects had to be destroyed, which is to say, forgotten; thus the image no longer served the fiction of a different reality, but became itself a reality with its own conditions" (*Werke*, 3:33). The program of analytic cubism annihilated resemblance through a campaign of practiced oblivion, Einstein notes here. One symptom of this forgetting, he adds, is the negation of pictorial depth, a perceptual shift toward the surface of the canvas and the material facture of the painting. "The precondition of cubist painting is the surface. One no longer works between two imaginary layers that supersede the canvas. The compass of the picture is achieved through its unverifiability and through the fact that the spectator does not leave the reality of the picture" (*Werke*, 3:34). As an illustration of Einstein's claim, consider one of Braque's analytic cubist works from 1910, which oscillates between the visual sign of a torso and the continuous plane of the canvas itself (fig. 4.1): as this painting shifts from semiotic absence to phenomenological presence, the aesthetic encounter is transformed from a retrospective act of imagining to an immediate event of perception. Here, Einstein notes admiringly, "painting no longer means mnemotechnics" (*Werke*, 3:263).

With its shift from illusionistic depth to painterly surface, Einstein's account of analytic cubism dovetails nicely with now-familiar scholarly narratives that define modernism as an aesthetic tendency that foregrounded the material presence of the artwork over the content it depicts. Realism, as we know from Jakobson, privileges semiotic transparency (the referential function), while modernism privileges the material facture of the sign (the poetic function). But this scheme grows more complicated when, five years after his *Documents* essay on analytic cubism, Einstein turned in a study of Braque's recent work to the subject of late-synthetic cubism. In this text from 1934, he again conceived of the cubist enterprise as a campaign against the mnemotechnics of "descriptive" realism, although now the terms and strategies have been significantly revised, even reversed. Unlike the paintings made during cubism's first phase, which tortuously attenuated the resemblance between the image and its referent, the postanalytic works no longer seek to challenge figuration and resemblance so directly, but instead invoke the tradition of figuration in order

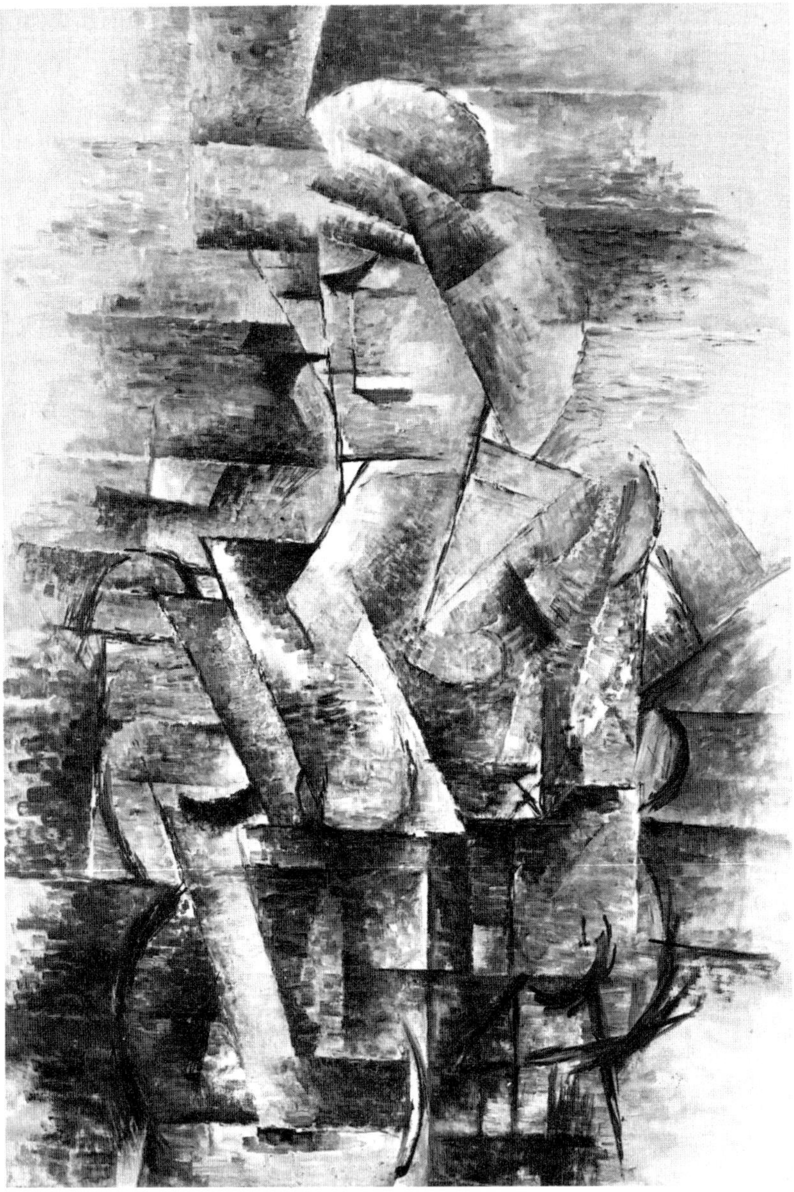

Figure 4.1 Georges Braque, *Torso* (1910). © 2012 Artists Rights Society (ARS), New York/ADAGP, Paris.

to imbue it with an enigmatic and hallucinatory depth. In *Themis and Hera* from 1934 (fig. 4.2), for example, figural contour has returned to Braque's work, although the forms in these images are hardly the integral gestalts familiar from traditional realist works. These "metamorphotic" figures, as Einstein called them, swell forth and interpenetrate one another. As Braque extends the line used to contour one body into the interior of its adjacent, he draws letters too into the arabesques, compromising the boundaries of each figure and exploding its profile into the surrounding textual space. The strategy of this "mythical realism" (*Werke*, 3:301), as Einstein called it, is to invoke the means of illusionistic representation but then outstrip it by retracing again and again the outlines of the individual forms, completely transforming the figural group with each additional loop of a single continuous gesture. Gazing into this unbroken web of lineation, it becomes impossible for the spectator to distinguish individual objects, or even to make the most basic perceptual differentiation between figures that are contained within the field of vision and the ground of vision itself.

It is extremely significant that Braque's method in *Themis and Hera*, as elsewhere in the late work, is one that is fundamentally additive. His choice here of the medium of etching reflects this tenet, since the technique of etching is notoriously unforgiving of mistakes: while drawings can be erased and canvases can be overpainted, it is far more difficult to expunge a line from an etching. Here Braque seeks a method that is more indelible, more irreversible than drawing or painting. Yet the lines of the etching do in fact remain open to revision and transformation, albeit only through the addition of still more lines. For Braque, this specific technical exigency of the medium expresses a general poetological principle that is fundamental to post-analytic cubism, a project that Einstein described as the "augmentation [*Vermehrung*], accretion of form [*Gestaltzuwachs*] and the enchantment of the real" (*Werke*, 3:324). In these works, Braque only adds. Subtraction is proscribed. Like a Freudian *Wunderblock*, the resulting "double style," as Einstein called it, presents several conflicting, mutually exclusive pictorial realities simultaneously. In this regard, the strategy of these works is completely different from that of analytic cubism. If, before, analytic cubism had demotivated the mimetic code of realist painting by

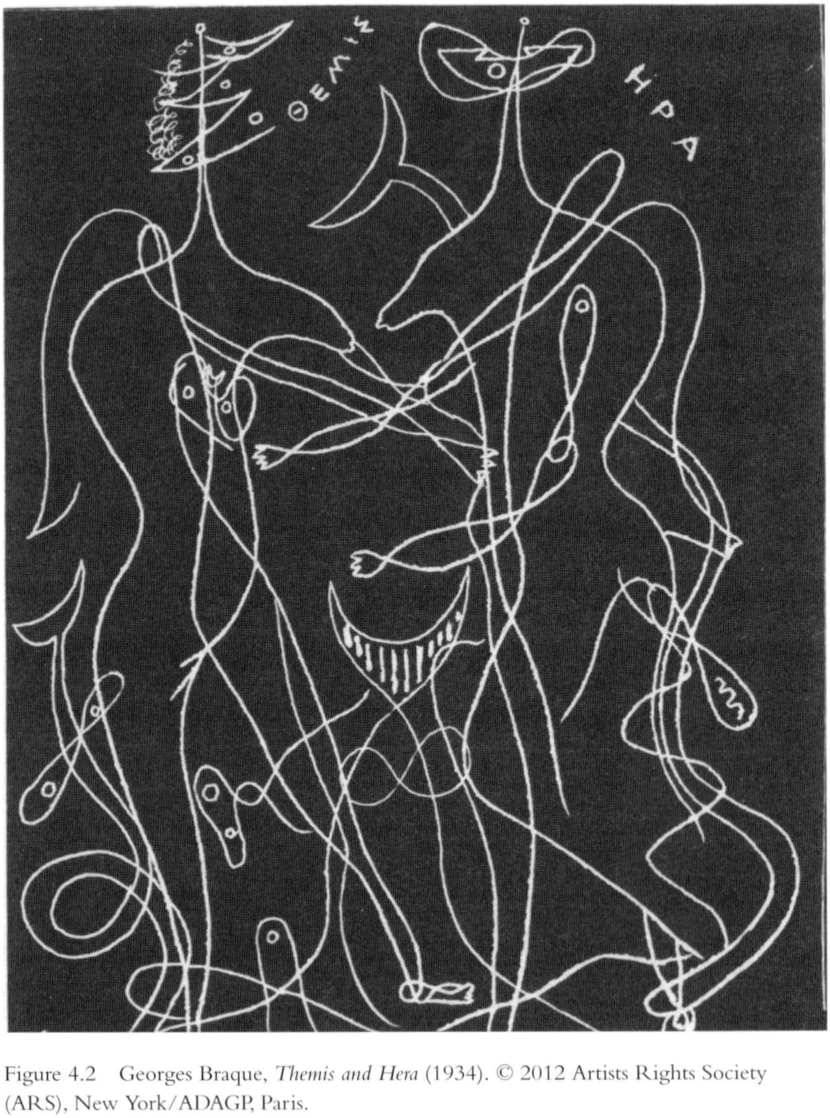

Figure 4.2 Georges Braque, *Themis and Hera* (1934). © 2012 Artists Rights Society (ARS), New York/ADAGP, Paris.

faceting the motif, pressing its image-signs toward the condition of opacity and flatness where they would converge with the plane of the canvas, the synthetic and postsynthetic work no longer tries to neutralize the signifying capacity of the image, but instead multiplies, recasts (*umdichten*), and metamorphoses the symbol (*Werke*, 3:324). These multivalent etchings do not negate the referential function of the sign outright, as was the case with the earlier works of Braque, but instead trigger, through a surplus of reference, a virtually endless string of visual analogies and forms that loop continuously back on themselves. Analytic demotivation is succeeded by synthetic overmotivation.

As Einstein's two essays suggest, each generation of cubist work challenged the conventions of mimetic realism, but they did so through opposed strategies. Analytic cubism is a subtractive art based on strategies of calculated impoverishment, whereas its late-synthetic variant is a hallucinatory art of supplementation and excess. Working centrifugally, analytic cubism dissects the object with formal rigor, splaying and unfurling its multiple facets across the canvas systematically (hence the conventional designation of "analytic" cubism). Synthetic cubism, by contrast, operates centripetally, crowding things together, piling object upon object seemingly without concern for their commensurability. Importantly, this shift from the negation of pictorial illusionism to the lysergic surplus of imagery also reflected a reversal in cubism's mechanism for subverting the collusion between memory and mimetic realism. Unlike analytic cubism, which "destroys" the visual memory-trace, as Einstein put it, synthetic and postsynthetic cubism supercharge this memory-trace through strategies of "augmentation" and "accretion of form." The eradication of the mnemonic image yields to its endless reinscription.

We have examined the reorientation of cubist strategies at some length because it provides us with a map of Einstein's own development as a writer. Indeed, the transition from an analytic to a synthetic method can be observed also in Einstein's literary work, exemplified in the shift from the modernist *Bebuquin* to the realist *Bebuquin II*. Certainly the historical overlap between the two phases of cubist painting and Einstein's *Bebuquin* projects proposes suggestive parallels: just as *Bebuquin*, which he began to write in 1906, reflected the analytic variety of cubism that was its contemporary, *Bebuquin II*, which Einstein began composing in the mid-1920s, likewise followed the artistic principles of late-synthetic cubism found in Braque's recent work. It is important to note, however, that the developmental parallels between painting and literature are based not upon any claim of morphological resemblance, which, of course, would always fall back on a dubious set of metaphors to connect the two arts. According to Einstein, the correspondence instead resides at deeper structural levels of enunciation. Thus, in his famous 1923 letter to the art dealer Daniel Henry Kahnweiler written shortly before he began work on *Bebuquin II*, Einstein insisted that cubism was a comprehensive cultural phenomenon whose ambit and repercussions could not be limited to the visual arts, since its general critique of mimesis embraced, on an epistemic register, all varieties of symbolic production, including literature.[5]

Like analytic cubism, *Bebuquin* directs the reader to the lateral play of signs on the surface of the language, where, for example, phonetic rhyme schemes dictate the sequence of words. By thus cancelling out the semantic dimension of the word, this technique undermines the mnemonic depth of representation: it destroys the mental image of the signified and, recovering language as pure acoustic value, induces in the subject the same condition of perceptual presence that analytic cubism sought to achieve in its practice of painting as a pure optical value. *Bebuquin II* strives for a similar state of psychological oblivion, although, like Braque's work from the 1920s, it arrives at that state through strategies of representational excess. Layering mnemonic image upon mnemonic image, *Bebuquin II* creates passages of resemblance between these strata that undermine the contours that separate one figure from another. In this respect, *Bebuquin II*'s "desperate attempt to get rid of hoary memory" (Einstein Archive, 8) continues the amnestic project of analytic cubism, but the strategy has changed: forgetting would now be realized not through the eradication of memory and its stock of mental imagery, but through a metastatic augmentation and endless accretion of the figures found in the depths of the mind.

Here *Bebuquin II* follows a mnemonic law fundamental to all signifying processes: the indelibility of the memory-trace. In an essay on the "art of forgetting," the semiotician and philosopher Umberto Eco explained that memories, once inscribed, cannot be expunged: "every expression determined by a semiotic sign function sets into play a mental response as soon as it is produced, thus making it impossible to use an expression to make its own content disappear. If the arts of memory are semiotics, it is not possible to construct an art of forgetting on their model."[6] Because signs will always inevitably evoke other signs, Eco notes, they cannot also be used to make signs disappear. To the contrary, as we saw in the previous chapter's discussion of paralipsis, the sign that is actively negated, like the phrase that is rhetorically disavowed, is only further reinscribed and affirmed through this very act of erasure. The expression "there is *no* rose," Abelard observed, will never fail to bring to mind a rose.[7] (Or, to cite an example from Einstein's own body of work: ~~*A Defense of the Real*~~ is still *A Defense of the Real*.) Irrespective of whether it is used affirmatively or negatively, then, the sign still continues to posit the existence of its referent, prompting Eco to conclude that there is no active method to forget the memory-trace that connects a signifier to a corresponding concept. Built out of mnemonic deposits that are by nature ineradicable, the human mind, to recall Freud's well-known analogy, is like the Eternal City in which all architectural constructions, no matter when they were built, persist in an impossible condition of simultaneity and spatial coextension.[8]

Despite the fundamental indelibility of the mnemonic inscription, Eco points out that the structures of memory can nonetheless be undermined by our overtaxing them. If the memory-trace connecting signifier and concept cannot be broken, it can still be détourned, blurred, and demented. It becomes possible, Eco writes, "to forget on account not of defect but of excess, just as, though it is not possible to destroy the meaning of an assertion pronounced aloud, it is possible to pronounce another assertion in the same moment, so that the two assertions are superimposed. There are no voluntary devices for forgetting, but there are devices for remembering badly: it is necessary to multiply the semiosis." Thus, he concludes, "one forgets not by cancellation but by superimposition, not by producing absence but by multiplying presences."[9] The mnemonic economy that Eco describes here is, to be sure, quite unlike Augustine's influential model of the human mind as a vast storehouse full of discrete parcel-like memories that can be referenced and accessed at any time: in contrast to Augustine's notion of memory as a "huge cavern" of empty space, memory is instead understood here like Freud's palimpsestic Eternal City, a compressed jumble in which every new trace is written on top of other preexisting mnemonic deposits.[10] Within the overinscribed space of the human mind, forgetting is achieved not by emptying out the cavern, but by cramming it with still more material.

This is how Einstein's autobiography tries to forget: through an incessant practice of recollection. With every iteration of a memory image, the previous trace is overwritten, inscribed each time into new associative fields that redirect the chain of reference along different lines. The consequences of this cumulative process for the system of mimetic realism are perhaps even more dire than was aesthetic modernism's phenomenological turn toward the materiality of the signifier. By "multiplying presences," to use Eco's phrase, *Bebuquin II* heaps sign upon sign until, collapsing on itself, the entire signifying order undergoes a process of desemanticization. Einstein characterized this strategy as "a remembering of the self taken to the point of annihilation" (Einstein Archive, 14).

The tactics of repetition and reinscription are visible throughout *Bebuquin II*, although most obviously in the system of dramatis personae, where Einstein puts into motion a rolling play of resemblance that blurs the boundaries between the individual figures. At times the protagonist of *Bebuquin II* is a character in the third person—named Beb or Laurenz—while at other moments Einstein constructs the narrative from a first-person perspective. These roles are continuously being recast in the text. In some of the working notes for *Bebuquin II*, for example, Einstein suggested that the birth of Laurenz should be realized "perhaps through the metamorphosis of someone else" (Einstein Archive, 8). This also explains the frequent references to reincarnation throughout his project notes, since the individual characters have no discrete points of origin and no personal fates, but instead beget one another through a series of shifts within the story. The ongoing process of recoding resembles the strategy that Einstein described, with reference to Braque, as an "accretion of form" in which "[e]very new deposit entails the forgetting and displacement of the preceding inventories of consciousness" (*Werke*, 3:283). With each additional accretion, with each reinscription of attributes, the contours containing the individual character grow less and less distinct and the figure begins to dissolve.

Just as Laurenz comes into existence "through the metamorphosis of someone else," *Bebuquin II* emerges through the metamorphosis of *Bebuquin.* This metamorphosis presents substantial challenges for the archivists and scholars of Einstein who, despite their impressive textological exertions, still haven't succeeded in convincingly outlining the boundaries of this autobiographical project, which was not a creation ex nihilo, but a return to a literary text from 1906, a text that *Bebuquin II* at once built upon and revoked. And if it is impossible to say when exactly Einstein began to write *Bebuquin II* (1925? 1906?), it is equally impossible to say if he ever would have finished it. Indeed, the textual prototype for these 1,300 discrete segments of writing would seem to be not the bound book—with a beginning, middle, and end—but the card catalog or the archival file, two strategies for organizing knowledge that permanently defer systematic conclusiveness. Writing about the note cards used by Michel Leiris, with whom Einstein edited the journal *Documents*, Denis Hollier observes, for example, that a "filing system is infinitely expandable, rhizomatic (at any point in time or space one can always insert a new card); in contradistinction to the sequential irreversibility of the pages of the notebook and of the book, its interior mobility allows for permanent reordering."[11] As Einstein explained in a letter written in 1923, shortly before he began to transform *Bebuquin* into *Bebuquin II,* his own words seemed to him perforce unfinishable, forever open to revision: "Everywhere in my writing I sense the fragment; I could continue revising every sentence that I write for my entire life."[12] And indeed, revisions to this ongoing project would continue until 1940, even then broken off only by its author's death.

Einstein's project to revisit and overwrite his earlier modernist work reflected a poetological impulse that was ubiquitous in the literature and art of the 1930s. As with Einstein, in many cases these authors reclaimed their previous experimental texts in order to embed them a second time within an autobiographical framework. Einstein's friend Gottfried Benn rewrote his legendary *Rönne-Novellen* (1916) as a memoir, *Lebensweg eines Intellektualisten* (*The*

Life's Journey of an Intellectualist, 1934), just as Walter Benjamin repeated many of the avant-garde *Denkbilder* from his *Einbahnstraße* (*One-Way Street*, 1926) in the autobiographical text *Berliner Kindheit um 1900* (*Berlin Childhood around 1900*, 1938).[13] Contemporaneous examples of this type of auto-anthologization can also be found in the visual arts, where Kasimir Malevich recapitulated in the early 1930s the entire artistic development of painterly modernism from Impressionism to cubo-futurism and suprematism at a furious pace, in some cases not just painting in the manner of these earlier styles but actually recreating specific works of his a second time; similarly, slightly later in the decade, Marcel Duchamp assembled a collection of miniature reproductions of his "classic" avant-garde works in a portable museum that he entitled, with reference to the gesture of double containment, the *Boîte-en-valise*.

Within a cultural atmosphere inclined to historical retrospection and aesthetic strategies of paradigm repetition, Einstein undertook a project of autobiographical anamnesis, although the goal of this endeavor was not to reconstruct the past, but to overload the circuitry of memory. If the interwar "return to order" is typically associated with a desire for regulation and submission to the psychic authorities, the repetitions that we find in *Bebuquin II* complicate this model of return-as-containment, suggesting to us that, to the contrary, procedures of repetition, when pushed to utter excess, actually enable an experience of radical novelty. As Einstein explained, the mature ego is propped up by a manageable and orderly mnemonic stock, a "little pension" of selfhood that provides mental continuity through a process of "psychic capitalization" (*Werke*, 3:97) but that also threatens to imprison the subject in a solipsistic loop of "slavish tautology." To escape from the curse of the ever-same and to restore the possibility of novelty and nonidentity, Einstein sought recourse in a state of consciousness unencumbered by this mnemonic pension. "Everything that is new," he wrote, "requires an extinguishing of memory, i.e. of consciousness and of the ego" (*Werke*, 3:305). Like contemporaries ranging from Shklovskii to Benjamin, Einstein elevated the figure of the child as a paradigm of precategorical consciousness, of a phenomenologically pure subject free from the burdens of habit and ingrained mental schemata. Because they haven't yet been disciplined by the symbolic systems that limit the perceptual world of the adult, children, he averred, are "completely inclined towards anti-naturalism" (*Werke*, 3:292) and therefore immune to representation's fraudulent reality effects.

And so where the typical autobiographical "ego-document" recollects the inchoate experiences of childhood so as to incorporate them into a stable adult narrative of selfhood, *Bebuquin II*, by contrast, revisits these earlier moments in order to commune with their precategorical chaos. Not all returns are returns to order. Einstein characterized the autobiographical exercise as a kind of *Infantiltraining*, a "training in infantilism" (Einstein Archive, 7) that reinstates the mode of consciousness that reigned before the child was subjected to the schematics of grammar, before the normativizing enterprise of education, before the purity of perception was subjugated to the conventions of representation—before, in short, "idiotization through intelligence" (Einstein Archive, 7). Thus it was through mnemonic overinscription that Einstein intended "to reconstitute childhood and to make its origins tangible through regressions" (Einstein Archive, 31). Repetition of the episodes of his autobiography became an instrument for Einstein to "stupefy [himself] back" (*zurückblöden*; Einstein Archive, 29) to a "wordless zone" of "primary experiences beyond language" (Einstein Archive, 7). Einstein's paradoxical model of a psychic economy in which more is less and advanced mnemonic accumulation results in the condition of speechlessness mirrors, moreover, a conclusion reached by Freud in his work on aphasia, namely that, those afflicted by this condition "suffer mainly from reminiscences."[14] They are expelled from the systems of language, from orders of symbolic representation, not because of forgetfulness, as one would assume, but because of a pathological surfeit of recollection that results in the sufferer's inability to erase her stock of memories. It is a psychic model that accounts simultaneously both "for the permanence of the trace and for the virginity of the receiving substance."[15] In the boundless recall of Einstein's anamnesis, the postsymbolic speechlessness of the overcongested adult mind becomes likewise indistinguishable from the presymbolic speechlessness of the child. From this perspective, the forgetting of language found in the aphasic is just the premature and aggravated onset of a natural aspect of senescence. In *Bebuquin II* the two poles of dotage and youth converge in the *Kindgreis* (Einstein Archive, 14), the oxymoronic figure of the "child-elder" that folds together the tabula rasa of youth and the mnemonic clutter of the aged mind.

The curious structure of *Bebuquin II*, in which self-inscription coincides with self-erasure, reminds us that the faculty that we call memory has a Janus-face. Indeed, in his *Lectures on Aesthetics*, Hegel insisted that there are two fundamentally different modalities of this retrospective consciousness, a difference that he parses using the terms *Gedächtnis* and *Erinnerung*, memory and recollection. On the one hand is *Erinnerung*, the dense and organic cache of mental experiences from which the subject crafts his psychological identity; in his gloss of Hegel's lectures, Paul de Man described this mode of symbolic internalization as an "inner gathering and preserving of experience."[16] On the other hand, memory (*Gedächtnis*) is a quasi-mechanical function that operates through "notation," "inscription," and "writing down," de Man proposed. If *Erinnerung* internalizes experience, *Gedächtnis* reverses this directionality, projecting and objectivizing the contents of the mind onto the external world. And far from enhancing our capacity to recall, the mnemonic aides and technics of inscription that serve *Gedächtnis* in fact inhibit the mental life of the subject, in Hegel's view, for they outsource recollection and thereby deaden the imagination, the faculty that governs the mental ordering of symbolic thought. Thus, according to Hegel, an excess of memory, of *Gedächtnis*, results not in total recall, but in its opposite, total forgetting. This deconstructive logic is encapsulated by de Man using a formula that is virtually identical to Einstein's own characterization of *Bebuquin II* as a "remembering of the self taken to the point of annihilation": "memory," de Man wrote, "effaces remembrance (or recollection) just as the I effaces itself." Thus, "in order to have memory, one has to be able to forget remembrance and reach the machinelike exteriority, the outward turn, which is retained in the German word for learning by heart, *aus-wendig* lernen."[17]

For this reason, the best way to forget something is to write something down and memorize it. Einstein designated this process as a *Veräußerung der Schrift* (Einstein Archive, 7), a phrase that captures at once both the physical act of inscribing and giving material form to a memory (an "*exteriorization* through writing") as well as the experience of psychic estrangement that results from an act of exteriorization that gives memory a life independent of its author (an "*alienation* through writing"). For Einstein, the autobiographical enterprise entailed a double gesture of commemoration and annihilation,[18] with each of the 1,300 sheets of paper that accompanied him during his wanderings in exile blotting out another moment of his own biography. Thus it is that consigning memory to writing does not impede forgetting, but enables it, even actively undermines the fitness of organic recollection and hastens the author's progress toward a state of mental oblivion. This rule, in fact, was corroborated by the early comparative anthropological researches that informed Einstein's writings on non-Western art and culture. As Lucien Lévy-Bruhl pointed out in his study *How Natives Think* (*Les Fonctions mentales dans les sociétés inférieures*, 1910), a book of immense importance to Einstein, members of societies that do not rely on written language for the transmission of cultural knowledge have much more powerful faculties of memory than those who have writing at their disposal.[19]

Einstein characterized his autobiographical "training in infantilism" as a "search for a lost childhood between leaves and a forgetting of what has been learned" ("die suche nach der verlorenen kindheit zwischen blaettern und vergessen des erlernten"; Einstein Archive, 7). There is a telling ambiguity in these words. On the one hand, the "leaves" in this phrase, the *blaetter*, would seem to refer specifically to the pivotal episode in *Bebuquin II* that Einstein called the *blaetterbegraebnis*, or the "burial in leaves." In this scene of primitive sacrifice, which was inspired by the accounts of anthropologists such as Lévy-Bruhl, the children in the story gather together in the forest to smother the child prince beneath a mountain of decaying organic matter. But, beyond this reference to a particular episode within the narrative, the phrase *blaetterbegraebnis* also contains a metapoetic reflection on the project of the autobiographer, for in German, the *blaetter* are of course also leaves of paper. Einstein's *blaetterbegraebnis* thus refers not just to the sacrifice of the child prince, but also to the suffocation and burial of the author's ego under 1,300 pages of dead biographical matter. The phrase "die suche nach der verlorenen kindheit zwischen blaettern und vergessen des erlernten" thus assumes a second aspect: translating the word *blaettern* in this phrase as a verb rather than a noun—entirely permissible, since here, as in almost all of the typewritten segments of *Bebuquin II*, Einstein avoids using capital letters—the project becomes a search for a lost childhood that is conducted by leafing through sheets of paper and, in this act of leafing, forgetting all that he has learned.

Einstein's characterization of *Bebuquin II* as a "search for lost childhood" is also an unambiguous nod to Marcel Proust's monumental anamnesis *In Search of Lost Time*, a book that exhibits a similarly perilous proximity between memory and forgetting. In a 1929 review of the novel, Benjamin struggled to come to terms with the puzzling structure of Proustian *mémoire involuntaire*, a mental process that is unconscious and thus, it would seem, highly subjective, and yet also exhibits profoundly machinelike qualities. Memory belongs to an apparatus of language that is both psychologically alien and physically exterior to the thinking subject. "The important thing to the remembering author," Benjamin wrote in his review, "is not what he experienced, but the weaving of his memory, the Penelope work of recollection. Or should one call it, rather, a Penelope work of forgetting? Is not involuntary recollection, Proust's *mémoire involuntaire*, much closer to forgetting than what is usually called memory? And is not this work of spontaneous recollection, in which memory is the woof and forgetting the warp [*in dem Erinnerung der Einschlag und Vergessen der Zettel ist*], a counterpart to Penelope's work rather than its likeness?" (*Schriften*, 2:311; *Writings*, 2:238). The curious image proposed by the final sentence of this quote can be translated two ways. By referencing the *Einschlag* ("woof") of recollection and the *Zettel* ("warp") of forgetting, Benjamin invokes the conceit of the "fabric" of remembrance, a metaphor consonant with the image of Penelope at work at the loom. Remove the thematic connotations of weaving, however, and the words present a different picture, one closely aligned with Hegel's analysis of recollection (*Er-innerung*) as an inner psychic process and memory (*Gedächtnis*) as a written, external record that facilitates forgetting: in *mémoire involuntaire* the organic act of *Erinnerung*, which produces an

Einschlag (an impact, an internalized trace), is interlaced with *Zettel* (a slip of paper, an external memory-trace) and thus, for Benjamin, comes precariously close to the process of forgetting (*Vergessen*).

The Dead Zone of Modernism

Earlier we observed that Einstein's account of the transition from analytic to synthetic compositional practices, which he described critically in his writings on cubism and realized textually in his autobiography, can be mapped onto the relationship of modernism to interwar realism more generally. These widespread structural transformations in the aesthetic field were the subject of his devastating theoretical broadside against modernism, *The Fabrication of Fictions*. Written at the same time as *Bebuquin II*, this text despairs of the political failure of the modernist project, whose great error, Einstein observed, was to have placed too much faith in the faculty of the imagination and its cultural agent, fiction, as resources for transforming reality. If once the imagination had provided a noninstrumentalized space of fantasy and subjective freedom that was distant from the pressures of the present and, for this reason, could function as a preserve of potentially revolutionary impulses that were unrealizable in everyday life, this faculty had, under the modernist regime of *l'art pour l'art*, distended inordinately to the point of severing all connection to reality. The imagination, Einstein explained, had become like a "bacillus" that breeds in the hiatus between the subject and the external world, its symbols and metaphors reproducing uncontrollably until they eclipse all external referents (Einstein Archive, 9). Under these conditions, which elevated fictionality as an autotelic value, the sign ceases to function as a mediator of experience. Under the aesthetic rule of modernism, Einstein wrote, the "poems and pictures of the imagination are stored in a dead zone; they exist only as long as one renounces reality."[20] With the establishment of this dead zone, "there is in fact no correspondence between the impressions that enter consciousness and the sequence of hallucinated signs" (*Werke*, 3:21). To be sure, Einstein came to write with such insight and passion about the failure of modernism's poetics of the imagination because it was a failure that he recognized in his own vita, where the romance with fictionality had trapped its author in a simulacral existence, cut off from the world and lacking a collective language. Looking back from the 1930s, Einstein lamented the fact that he had "lived in metaphors and never had contact with primary existence" (Einstein Archive, 38).

The collusion that Einstein discerned between the imagination and the practices of aesthetic modernism appears in the texts of his contemporaries as well, most notably the phenomenological analyses of the imagination that Jean-Paul Sartre published in the late 1930s. Central to Sartre's theory of the imagination was the notion that this faculty is invariably a negative one. Against the models of consciousness proposed by Descartes, Hume, and Leibniz, who asserted the identical nature of image and sensation, Sartre argued in *The Imagination* (1936) and *The Imaginary* (1940) that mental images do not correspond causally to any sensory content and, indeed, can be formed only by severing the connection with the outside world. For this reason, the imagination is structurally incompatible with, and even opposed to, the phenomenological act of perception.[21] Sartre illustrated this "privative, negative character of the image"[22] by analyzing the act of imagining his friend Pierre: "My image of him is a certain manner of *not* touching him, *not* seeing him, a way he has of *not being* at such [and such] a distance, in such [and such] a position. The belief, in the image, posits the intuition, but does not posit Pierre. The characteristic of Pierre is not to be non-intuitive, as one might be tempted to believe, but to be 'intuitive-absent,' [which is to say] given as absent to intuition. In this sense one can say that the image has wrapped within it a certain nothingness" (*Imaginary*, 14). For this reason, Sartre explained, the act of mental representation should not be mistaken as "presentifying" an object that just happens to be absent (*Imaginary*, 182), since the process of imagining actively negates and absents the real, existing referent that it represents. "The negative act is constitutive of the image," he observed (*Imaginary*, 183). For Sartre, then, imagining Pierre was a way of obliterating his friend's actual being and presence. Thus, in contrast to the perceiving consciousness, which posits its object as existent and present, the imagining consciousness posits its object as a nothingness, or *le néant*. It "nihilates" things (*néantiser*) in order to represent them. "To posit an image," Sartre summarized, "is to . . . hold the real at a distance, to be freed from it, in a word, to deny it" (*Imaginary*,

183). Through this process of cognitive subtraction, the phenomenal world is delivered over to that of mental representation and the perceiving subject is transformed into a thinking one, a manipulator of signs. But in this process, she is also denied the condition of ontological presence in the world that Sartre calls, following Heidegger, *in-der-Welt-Sein*.[23]

Like Sartre, Einstein considered the imagination to be a fundamentally negative faculty. It is by definition subtractive, he argued, and for this reason cannot posit, invent, or create. But whereas Sartre celebrated the imagination's challenge to the empirical exigencies of the present, discovering within its shattering of the world "as totality" (*Imaginary*, 184) a basis for liberation from matter and the pressures of *in-der-Welt-Sein*, Einstein, by the 1930s, had lost faith in the imagination as a vehicle of such liberation. For him, the imagination had instead become a prison house, a tautological grid in which signs continuously refer only to other signs. The imagination's strategies of mental "abbreviation" (*Abkürzung*), Einstein wrote, always entail an "omission" (*Weglassen*; *Werke*, 5:60) and an impoverishment of empirical experience that prompts "a flight from the present, a dearth of actuality" (*Fictions*, 120). Einstein discovered in the Sartrean mechanism of nihilation not subjective freedom but objective violence, an obliteration of experiential reality.

As Einstein drifted away from applied art criticism in the 1930s—his monograph on Braque from 1934, for example, has only the most tenuous relationship to the actual artworks he was commissioned to discuss—he grew increasingly invested in more general, sociological frameworks for understanding how the institutions of art function. And increasingly he came to see these institutions as fundamental obstacles to radical political transformation. Having become the locus for the imaginary enactment and neutralization of subversive revolutionary impulses, art played a social function that, according to Einstein, was inevitably reactionary.[24] Like Herbert Marcuse, whose 1937 essay "The Affirmative Character of Culture" argued that all art perpetuates alienated social relations because it provides a site for the symbolic resolution of repressed needs,[25] Einstein saw art as a conservative, socially stabilizing force. Even works with a pronounced social-critical stance perpetuate the status quo, he argued.

"The fact is that [artists] diverted important energies into the aesthetic instead of allowing the art event and its energies to pour into life" (*Fictions*, 66). Because these revolutionary impulses had been redirected away from the real sites of political conflict, people have become "incapable of revolt," their subversive impulses having already been "abreacted aesthetically." As a means to sublimate dissent, symbolic critique had become an ersatz for actual political change, prompting Einstein's final and unambiguous conclusion: "despite its revolutionary gesture, all art is conservative" (*Fictions*, 244).

Thus although Einstein and Sartre both provide a similar analysis of the functioning of modern art, their respective assessments of the political consequences of these imaginary acts of negation could not be more different. Nowhere is this disagreement more evident than in their contrasting stances on Stéphane Mallarmé, whom each crowned as the premier poet of modernist negativity. While Sartre exalted Mallarmé's hermetic lyrics and even credited the poet as the source of his philosophical concept of nothingness,[26] Einstein condemned these structuralist language games as socially solipsistic and semantically tautological, as a life-negating intrusion of *der Néant*. The "socially negative character of this poetry is obvious," he observed (*Fictions*, 113). Having abandoned the communicative function of language, Mallarmé valorized punning over meaning, endophoric allusion over external reference. "Mallarmé leaps from a tenuous motif to a remote metaphor in order to separate himself and his poem from the current reality and from the *sensus communis*" (*Fictions*, 113).[27] Modernists such as Mallarmé "were very proud of their negative orientation and their sterile solitude," Einstein wrote. "Opposing the imagination to the real, they elevated the former far above every naïve experience" (*Fictions*, 322). Such poets "absorbed (annihilated) individual positive experiences (in the interval of the imagination) and positive facts in abstract formulations ever more violently. Hence modern liberal culture became shapeless [*gestaltlos*]" (*Fictions*, 79).

To explain the mechanisms of the imagination and contextualize its ascent in recent art, Einstein offered his own phenomenological account of the reader's encounter with the modernist text. Here too his analysis is consonant with that

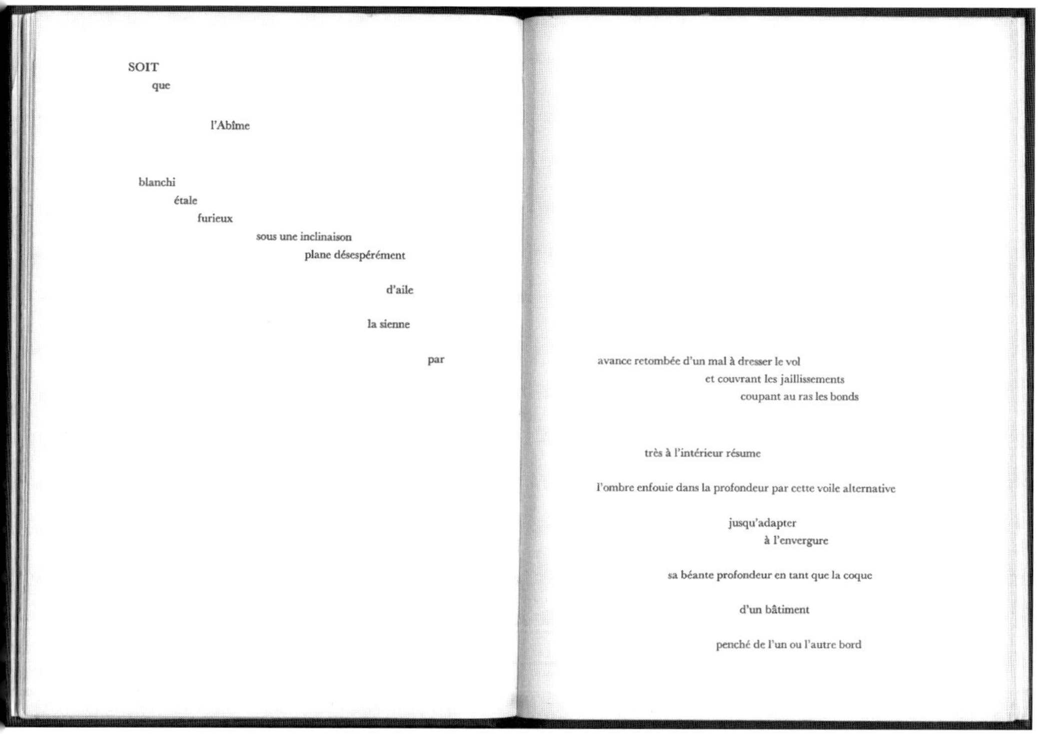

SOIT
que

l'Abîme

blanchi
étale
furieux
sous une inclinaison
plane désespérément

d'aile

la sienne

par

avance retombée d'un mal à dresser le vol
et couvrant les jaillissements
coupant au ras les bonds

très à l'intérieur résume

l'ombre enfouie dans la profondeur par cette voile alternative

jusqu'adapter
à l'envergure

sa béante profondeur en tant que la coque

d'un bâtiment

penché de l'un ou l'autre bord

Figure 4.3 Stéphane Mallarmé, *Un coup de dés* (1897).

of Sartre. Composed in a language attenuated to the point of silence, a poem by Mallarmé, for example, provides the reader with little sensuous data, prompting his retreat into the interior spaces of the mind (fig. 4.3). Confronted with these spare and rarefied lines, a "limited piece of positive reality is then supplemented by the imagination" (*Fictions*, 111). It is the labor of the imagination, in other words, to ink up the white page and, by filling in the text's omissions virtually, to reconstruct an absent aesthetic totality out of the heap of ambiguous fragments. "Every linguistic or visual communication contains organic or factual gaps [*organische und faktische Lücken*]; [in this regard, every artwork is a fragment that continues to have an effect by being completed by the observer]. It is precisely the sparseness of description that gives the intellectual the chance to fill out the patchy depiction through the imagination, through metaphor" (*Fictions*, 263).[28] As Einstein observes here, the process by which the imagination reconstitutes absent information is in no way specific to aesthetic experience alone. To the contrary, all "linguistic or visual communication" is invariably riddled with some "organic or factual gaps," hermeneutic omissions that require the addressee to connect the dots, as it were, in order to reconstruct the original message. In both art and other forms of communication, meaning is constituted subtractively, a law that the author Arno Holz illustrated in 1891 with the formula *art* = *nature* − *x*.[29]

Yet, as Einstein also insisted, under the rule of modernism, this quantity *x*—the "gap" (*Lücke*)—had become the very element that defined the artwork: "all artistic creation is characterized (negatively), by nihilism" (*Fictions*, 321). On this score, Einstein knew what he was talking about, having himself once been a leading voice in the school of modernist nihilism. *Bebuquin*, one reviewer noted in 1914, is uncompromising in its "resolute emphasis on the negative."[30] Its wrought and self-referential idiom demands extraordinary interpretive effort on the part of the reader to reconstruct the meaning of the lines. Like Mallarmé's poetry, *Bebuquin* provides a perfect illustration of Wolfgang Iser's dictum that "epistemologically fiction remains a blank."[31] Once the concrete basis for a *sensus communis*, the aesthetic encounter is privatized by these blanks, which, by triggering a flight from reality and a shift from perceiving to imagining, privilege the mental interior of the individual over collective experience. As an indication of the success and influence of modernism's paradigm of subtractive art, one need but glance at its contemporaneous aesthetic philosophy, which apotheosized the faculty of the imagination in important theoretical treatises such as Hans Vaihinger's 900-page *Philosophie des Als-Ob* (*Philosophy of As-If*, 1911).

According to Einstein, modernist negation took two forms, one sensory and one epistemological. The first is evident in the austerity of this art, its tendency to sparseness and abstraction. In Mallarmé's poetry, for example, this sensory negation is evident in the *néant* of the empty page and the rigorous constraint of the words themselves, which transpose the site of the aesthetic event from the artwork to the imagination of the reader. Modernism's will to anesthetize is even more manifest in the case of painterly abstraction, which, Einstein wrote, pushed the withdrawal of sensuous experience to its absolute limits. In contrast to his great enthusiasm for analytic cubist painting, which still maintained at least some degree of connection to external referents, Einstein never accepted the radical break with pictorial resemblance taken by Mondrian or Malevich, nonobjective painters whom he dismissed as "hygienists" and "ascetics," and whose works he derided as "ideals of a washroom civilization" (*Werke*, 5:238).[32] In an effort to purify the senses, he wrote, these strategies of "absolute" abstraction confined the body of the subject to a limited set of discrete sensory channels: "The effect of today's artworks is based on restricting the field of vision and the spectrum of sensation" (*Fictions*, 78). This process of sensory confinement—a perceptual constriction that would soon find its most brilliant advocate in that great hygienist of vision and enthusiast for pure opticality, Clement Greenberg—was, according to Einstein, the aesthetic corollary to those baleful and soul-destroying processes of rationalization that were choking the life out of modern culture. Having followed to its conclusion the morbid drive to optical purity, movements such as neoplasticism and suprematism had arrived at a state of sensory autism. "Seeing was now idiotized into a specialization," Einstein summed up (*Werke*, 3:219).

This sensory rarefaction had deleterious effects on the human organism, Einstein wrote. By restricting aesthetic experience to a limited number of perceptual channels, modernism had resulted in what he called *Organverengung*, the confinement of sensation to a single organ. This "purely optical encounter," he wrote, cripples the "meaningful complexes of consciousness," resulting in the "pathogenic overloading of one [particular] organ" and the "partial destruction of the individual" (*Werke*, 3:230). As one perceptual psychologist similarly observed in 1930, the experience of pure opticality is fundamentally *widersinning*—literally, "contrary to the senses"—and leads not to a condition of phenomenological presence or grace, but to a state of delirium and psychic dissociation.[33] Its "no-space of sensory deprivation" drove embodied experience underground, into the unconscious.[34] Against painterly abstraction's will to sensory specialization, which he derided as mere "sight" (*Sicht*), Einstein's later writings championed a composite mode of perception that he called "vision" (*Vision*), an intersensory chiasmus that ballasts perception with bodily substance and embeds experience in the firm ground of reality.[35]

Modern art's sensory negation was matched on an epistemological register by strategies of semiotic demotivation, methods that we have already encountered in the previous discussion of analytic cubism's subtractive logic. Enabled by the negative faculty of the imagination, modernism was by its very nature critical, Einstein argued, and thus incapable of creating new forms or positing new realities. As evidence for his claim, consider one of the cornerstones of modernist poetics, the device of "estrangement" made famous by Shklovskii as *ostranenie* or by Brecht as *Verfremdung*, whose purpose is to distort, and thus call awareness to, the mechanisms of signification that would remain otherwise unnoticed in mimetic artworks. In this operation, the modernist text constitutes itself as an inflected, or denaturalized, version of a realist one in which resemblance functioned intuitively and unproblematically. Thus the fragmentary construction of *Bebuquin*, for example, can be understood as the determinate negation of the integral totality of the realist novel, just as the same text's syntactic *glissement* across the surface of language also operates as the determinate negation of the psychological depth found in nineteenth-century narratives of *Bildung*. For this reason, Fredric Jameson has argued that "all modernistic works are essentially simply cancelled realistic ones." They are "not apprehended directly, in terms of their own symbolic meanings, in terms of their own mythic or sacred immediacy, . . . but rather indirectly only, by way of the relay of an imaginary realistic narrative of which the symbolic and modernistic one is then seen as a kind of stylization."[36] Because they are by their constitution beholden to the tradition of realist texts that precede them, all modernist texts are, in essence, simply realist texts of a different order. Thus, it is not the case that modernism has given up mimetic reference, only that its reference is one of a higher order: instead of pointing to extra-aesthetic reality, it points to the realist artwork. Behind every Proust is a Balzac, behind every Malevich a Repin. And so, for all its rarefaction and hermetic obfuscations, Mallarmé's blank page still cannot fail to be meaningful against the background of a literary tradition that has shaped the reader's interpretive horizon.

For this reason Einstein often compared modernist art to an apophatic theology, a structure of knowledge that arrives at truth through strategies of negation. In the same way that "one can speak of a negative theology, one can also speak of an art that is oriented toward negation," he observed in his book on Braque (*Werke*, 3:206); and in *The Fabrication of Fictions*, he similarly took note of "the affinity between [a] nihilistic aesthetic and the negative theology of mystics" (*Fictions*, 113). As Lyotard has argued in a series of essays, modernism's eschewal of embodiment and positive knowledge aligns it with the Kantian sublime, a borderline experience that, in contrast to the affirmative apprehension of the beautiful, is disclosed through a "negative presentation, or even a non-presentation."[37] Einstein's comparison of abstraction to negative theology is echoed, moreover, in Pavel Medvedev's contemporaneous polemic against aesthetic modernism, which the Russian literary critic dismissed as an "apophatic method" (*апофатический метод*), a mode of negative knowledge. In his 1928 study *The Formalist Method in Literary Criticism*, which took aim at the critical methods of the Russian formalists as well as the artistic production of their futurist allies, especially the *zaumniki*, Medvedev discussed strategies of modernist apophasis in a series of chapters on the subject of "negation" (*отрицание*). There he took issue with the opposition that futurism and formalism had established between everyday, communicative language and its negative image, poetic language: the "definition of the distinctive features of poetic language was developed in such a way that each of the basic indicators [*признаки*] of communicative language would have an opposite sign [*знак*] in poetic language. The basic concepts of the formal method—'transrational language,' 'deautomatization,' 'deformation,' 'making difficult'—turn out to be merely negations that correspond to the various indicators of everyday, practical language." "Thus," he reasoned, "the formalists did not define poetic language by what it is, but by what it is not." Medvedev's conclusion, like that of Einstein, was that this parasitic approach to aesthetic form could never be "creative," since, as he puts it, the "lexicon, grammar, and even the basic themes of the message have already been prepared beforehand."[38]

To be fair, the modernist paradigm of negative aesthetics had already reached a point of exhaustion even before Einstein and Medvedev rendered their verdict on modern art. After decades of use the same old devices of estrangement, deformation, and so forth had lost their critical function and devolved into a blind, contentless reflex. Or, to be more precise: their critical function was intact, but critique itself had since forfeited its privileged relationship to radical politics. As Brecht put it in 1930, "the avant-garde has capitulated, but it has not died." Even Adorno, that die-hard defender of negative aesthetics, would admit in a piece on the aging of modernism that, by 1927, this art's critical method had become ritualized and was recuperated as status quo. With the formalization of dissonance and estrangement as standard procedures in art, modernism's critical posture had turned into a "radicalness for which nothing is any longer at stake," as Adorno put it.[39] Indeed, if anything is to be learned from the illustrious career that modernism enjoyed in the West during the cold war, where abstract art was enlisted as a cultural cipher for the "values" of freedom, democracy, and consumer capitalism, it is that there is nothing inherently progressive about strategies of aesthetic negation, which are just as susceptible to dogmatization and political instrumentalization as was the realist art of the Eastern Bloc. But as we have already seen, Einstein's indictment of modernism goes even further than this, arguing that symbolic critique, by sublimating subversive tendencies within the contained sphere of art, comes to function as a substitute for actual political transformation. Modernism, in other words, is reactionary not despite but because of its radical posture. Thus, in his later writings, Einstein argued that this art had engendered "heroes of critique and dwarves of will" (Einstein Archive, 43), a race of artists whose submissiveness paved the way for the rise of totalitarianism.[40] Indeed, for Einstein, National Socialism was the very embodiment of modernist negativity. Taunting those who continued to enthuse about painterly abstraction, he predicted in *Bebuquin II* that if "Hitler were a cubist—and he will become one—then you would all be exhilarated" (Einstein Archive, 41).

According to Einstein, the apophatic logic of modernism doomed its art to cultural passéism. For all its avowed commitment to artistic innovation, and for all its bluster about breaking radically with the past, modernism remained structurally beholden to the preceding aesthetic models that it challenged. The artistic legacy circumscribed virtually every move of the modernist, whose deconstructions and demotivations of the aesthetic field, Einstein argued, were carried out automatically and without reflection. These artists "had an enormous capital of memories and visual traditions at their disposal, which stirred within them like shadows," he wrote. "The rebellious heirs were shadowed by a blurry mass of artistic forms, faded symbols and formulas that rolled along mechanically" (*Fictions*, 23).[41] One of the most obvious symptoms of the historicist character of modernism, Einstein observed, was the movement's stylistic heterogeneity. Barred from inventing new aesthetic constructions or positing affirmative form, the retrospective modernists, he wrote, were "forced into unholy eclecticism" and into rearranging "the second-class leftovers of multiple styles" (*Werke*, 3:202). These epigones were the "late descendants" of an "overformed" and "overeducated" civilization (*Werke*, 3:303). Modernism's negation of style was subsequently radicalized in the 1920s by its successors, the avant-garde movements that were distinguished aesthetically by their stylistic plurality. And while modernism and the avant-garde cannot be equated, for Einstein the two movements nonetheless shared the same logic of negation, a logic that, in both cases, was reflected formally in an absence of stylistic markers. Indeed, one encounters the same constitutive absence across the individual avant-gardes, irrespective of national context or political agenda: writing about Gruppe 1925, one of the most important constellations of German New Objectivity writers, Helmut Lethen, for example, confirms the very "impossibility of forming a coherent unity under the sign of 'Objectivity'";[42] likewise, Rosalind Krauss notes that the "formal heterogeneity" of French surrealism presents the critic with a "series of contradictions which . . . strike one as being irreducible" and concludes that "it is precisely *style* that continues to be a vexing problem for anyone dealing with surrealist art";[43] and already in 1923, Sergei Tret'iakov observed that Russian futurism "was never a school. It was a socioaesthetic tendency, the strivings of a group of people whose shared point of contact was not even positive tasks [*положительные задачи*], not a precise understanding of their 'tomorrow,' but rather a hatred for their 'yesterday and today," an inexhaustible and merciless hatred."[44]

Rather than work to create new collective forms of expression, the avant-garde had instead created a consciousness of style as such. As Peter Bürger noted in his influential account of this cultural formation, "[t]here is no such thing as a Dadaist or surrealist style. What did happen is that these movements liquidated the possibility of a period style when they raised to a principle the availability of the artistic means of past periods."[45] Indeed, the growing awareness of style as such in the 1920s prompted the birth of stylistics, a discipline that emerged at this time as the academic corollary to the avant-garde's metahistorical consciousness and took as its object of study those orphaned aesthetic devices that had lost their motivated relationship to society. For Einstein, the condition of stylistic pluralism reflected the general processes of cultural transvaluation set in motion by bourgeois liberalism, whose specious ecumenism and ahistorical universalism served to cover up the historical fact of the subject's atomization. "Liberal society could not develop a style," he wrote, "since it excluded the collective from the process of artistic production" (*Fictions*, 136). In contrast to those societies in which the psyche of the individual is "completely exteriorized" and "objectivated [*versachlicht*]" (*Werke*, 4:336) in a collective and culturally binding artistic style, the clearing-house of bourgeois liberalism relativized each individual artistic device as just one means among many. Like the commodity form upon which liberal society is based, these styles—all equally available and interchangeable—became subject to the rule of universal equivalence. In this regard, Einstein considered the deterioration of cultural norms and lack of community within liberal society to be a precondition for the stylistic pluralism of the avant-garde.[46] A "loosely knit fabric of paradoxical and contradictory tendencies inserted itself in the place of a unified culture," he observed (*Fictions*, 59).

Thus, when Einstein denounced modernism and the avant-garde in the 1930s, his attack was aimed not at any particular technical feature of these artworks (abstraction, facture, etc.) but at the loss of a coherent cultural matrix that would render these devices meaningful, the loss of a spontaneous correspondence between artistic style and social norms. As previous chapters of this book have shown how, after modernism, artistic devices such as linear perspective and narrative portrayal no longer possessed the spontaneous, privileged relationship to the subjective categories of experience and structures of consciousness that they enjoyed in previous epochs. Unmoored from their cultural fundament, such devices now lacked a corresponding *Weltanschauung*, as Einstein noted, and were no longer current. The "*endurance* of [artworks] resides in a succession of interpretations that are each current at their given moment. Herein lies the question of whether they can once again be made 'current,' i.e. whether they can be adapted to the present, to today's *Anschauung*. But the old [artwork] degenerates now into a phenomenon that is merely aesthetic" (*Werke*, 4:433). With their decommissioning as cultural *dispositifs*, these techniques were downgraded to mere aesthetic "style," "device," or "method." Thus, in 1923 Shklovskii, like Einstein, connected the autonomization of aesthetic devices with processes of social transvaluation and its resulting existential disorientation: "Once there was a top and a bottom, there was time, there was matter. / Now nothing is certain. Method rules over all else in this world. / Method was devised by man. / Method. / Method left home and started living on its own. [. . .] In art, too, method leads an independent life."[47] Under modernism, art grew defiant and self-willed, taking on a life of its own and becoming thoroughly alien to its creators.

Strictly speaking, there is no evolution within artistic method, Einstein argued, no linear development from cave painting to photography, since the technical arsenal of devices has remained fundamentally the same since the dawn of art. Artistic devices do not themselves change. What changes, rather, is the social formation that activates particular artistic techniques at certain historical intervals and removes them from cultural circulation at others. "We observe mutations," Einstein wrote in 1939, "although we still haven't ever found an explanation for why men become bored, discard one heritage, one inventory of forms, and accept a different trend. Obviously most of the time the new trend is celebrated as an improvement; and yet we are hardly more advanced than the painters of Altamira. The only thing that has changed is attitude and intention

[*Haltung und Absicht*]" (*Werke*, 4:371). For the scholar of art, understanding this historical dynamic required a methodological reorientation from formalist analysis to a sociology of art, a reorientation that was reflected in Einstein's own turn in the 1930s toward art as a document of "collective social history" (*Werke*, 4:354). To be sure, formalist analysis could provide a useful catalog of artistic strategies, but it could not locate these devices within the totality of culture or explain the social interests that drove the symbolic territorialization of aesthetic form.

For Einstein, then, drawing formal contrasts between, say, abstraction and figuration was ultimately irrelevant, or at least secondary, since the more fundamental question concerned the social motivation of these devices and whether these devices were organized in a style that was culturally binding and collective. Style, he insisted, was a "meta-artistic phenomenon," the authority of which transcends issues that were merely aesthetic in nature (*Werke*, 4:336). Recalling Shklovskii's observation from chapter 1, we are reminded that terms such as modernism and realism are just red herrings: "There is no such thing as nonobjective art. There is only motivated art or unmotivated art." Thus, when texts such as *Bebuquin II* and *The Fabrication of Fictions* call for a new "mythical realism," Einstein has in mind not a particular form of figuration or specific strategy of narration, but the emergence of a general style that, by interlocking subjective categories of thought and objective structures of sensation in single epistemic edifice, could overcome the liberal society's anomic condition of "masses without a collective culture" (*Werke*, 4:319). Artistic style had in fact always been closely intertwined with the expression of collective identity. During the era of the great nation-states in the nineteenth century, for example, the "search for style was identical with the desire for national identity."[48] Given the close connection between artistic style and mechanisms of social belonging, it makes sense that the deterioration of the nation-state toward the end of the century, followed by its complete ideological delegitimation in the First World War, would be reflected in the stylistic eclecticism of modernism, an avowedly 'internationalist' movement. After the implosion of the nation-state paradigm, the search for style and aesthetic motivation—which is to say, the search for a new realism—became, for Einstein, an urgent political project, even if it was unclear to him which configuration of community—trade union, class, race, generation, family, tribe, etc.—was robust enough to succeed the nation as the guarantor of collective identity. This connection between style and community in fact reappears across the populist discourses of interwar realism, from the appeals to *Volkstümlichkeit* in German Popular Front circles to the consecration of *народность* as one of the four conceptual pillars of socialist realism in Russia.

Mythical Realism and the Trampling Gesture of Representation

In his efforts to understand the new patterns of collective identity emerging within modern industrial society after the collapse of nationalist ideology, Einstein was increasingly drawn, as we know, to the methods of anthropology, a discipline already familiar to him from his research on non-western art. Like his *Documents* colleagues Georges Bataille and Michel Leiris, who enlisted ethnographic methods to analyze the collective myths, sacred geographies, and tribal filiations operating just below the surface of proper bourgeois society,[49] and like the British Mass Observationists, who founded a movement of "ethnography at home" in response to the 1936 abdication crisis of the "tribal leader" King Edward VIII,[50] Einstein turned to anthropology as a framework for developing a materialist theory of culture. Thus, an interview with the author about his recent work yielded the following report, which appeared in the *Chicago Tribune* in January 1931: "While making his ethnological study of the African negro, Dr. Einstein conceived the idea of applying the same scientific methods to the European white man, and among several new books he is at present engaged in writing is an *Ethnologie du Blanc*, in which he investigates, very seriously though perhaps a trifle sarcastically, the creation of myths, superstitions and erotic customs among the Europeans, treating them as if they were an extinct race."[51] The *Ethnologie du Blanc* mentioned in these lines was none other than *Bebuquin II*, of course, a text that was at once both an archaeological excavation of an "extinct race" and an autobiographical "necrologue of the ego."

Einstein patterned his autobiography after the speech genre of myth. Beyond his general enthusiasm for 'primitive' paradigms, there were three concrete reasons for his decision to follow the model of myth, one narratological, one tropological, and one textological. At the level of narrative design, myth observes a circular temporal structure that Einstein, following cubist parlance, called *das Simultané*. As he proposed in several of the outlines for *Bebuquin II*, his autobiography was to open with a "cosmogony," which is to say that the story would have no proper, discrete point of origin, no actual narrative beginning. As we saw earlier, Einstein proposed that the protagonist of his autobiography come into being not punctually, through the defining event of birth, but "perhaps through the metamorphosis of someone else." Cosmogonic myth similarly complicates the conceptual category of origins, since it is neither within nor outside historical sequence, but is instead situated at the zero hour of temporality and spans the transition from a cyclical state of eternal recurrence to linear, calendrical time. This cosmogonic paradigm was particularly important for the author of autobiography, Einstein observed, because of its close approximation of the primary processes of the Unconscious, which "take place in different and conflicting strata at the same time, i.e. they form a polymorphic *simultané*" (*Werke*, 3:325).

Since *Bebuquin II* was never completed, we can only speculate about how Einstein envisioned depicting this "cosmogonic" time in the final work. Nonetheless, the last piece of prose that Einstein published, a 1930 "fragment of a novel" that belongs to the constellation of texts around *Bebuquin II*, offers us a clue.[52] The fragment in question culminates in a series of psychosexual tableaux focusing on Persephone, queen of the underworld and daughter of Demeter. It is a significant choice of conclusions, for the cosmogonic myth of Persephone concerns the advent of worldly time as dictated by the solar cycle: as a consequence of Persephone's abduction, her mother Demeter divided the seasons and set in motion historical time, establishing the basic rhythm of human labor. With one foot in the eternal time of divine existence and the other in the linear time of human endeavor, the myth spans two incompatible conditions of experience. This conflicted temporality is visible in the Homeric hymn that served as Einstein's source, exemplified in the scene where Demeter hears the cry of Persephone as she is carried off by Hades:[53]

> Against her will he seized her and on his golden chariot
> Carried her away as she wailed; and she raised a shrill cry.
> Calling upon father Kronides, the highest and the best
> . . .
> The peaks of the mountains and the depths of the sea resounded
> With her immortal voice, and her mighty mother heard her.
> A sharp pain gripped her heart, and she tore
> The headband round her divine hair with her own hands.
> From both of her shoulders she cast down her dark veil
> And rushed like a bird over the nourishing land and sea,
> Searching . . .

To the modern reader, the most puzzling aspect of this scene must be the fact that Demeter already wears a black veil, a sign of grief, when she hears Persephone's cry. Paradoxically, she is in the process of mourning her daughter's loss at the very moment that she learns of Persephone's abduction, and casts down her veil in order to search for her.[54] In this cosmogonic time events take place in a state of "drunken simultaneity" (*besoffene Gleichzeitigkeit*; *Werke*, 3:113), to use Einstein's phrase.

"All time flows in both directions—full of contradictions," Einstein once observed early in his career in 1908 (*Werke*, 4:122). But if before, in a negative inversion of the unidirectionality of realist novel, Einstein's modernist texts insisted upon the reversibility of linear time—an appropriation from relativity theory popular in the modernist literature of the early 1900s—*Bebuquin II* instead overlays temporal strata on top of one another in the manner of ancient myth. In his autobiography, time is distinguished not so much by its reversibility as by its simultaneity. The narrative complexes in the text depict several phases of action at once, giving rise to what Einstein called, in an analysis of Hesiodic myth, "polymorphic event-ensembles" (*Werke*, 3:273). For Einstein, the objective here was not, as before, to cancel out the unidirectional linear design of the realist text through a determinate temporal inversion, but to repeat and reinscribe the individual episodes of his life, each time with a new variation, giving rise to a *simultané* that muddled the causal schemes of time-based narrative. The author's stand-in Beb is murdered as a child, for example, only to commit suicide later in life. At the text's syntactical level, Einstein demanded that the "concatenation of words must fuse together contrasting temporal strata" (*Werke*, 4:163). Needless to say, this cosmogonic circularity complicated the task of the storyteller immensely, who had no place to begin his narrative. So rather than open his autobiography with a punctual and distinct beginning, Einstein instead began with a metamorphosis, titling the first chapter "The Second Coming and Reincarnation" (Einstein Archive, 7). "The end overtakes the beginning," he wrote in 1930 (*Werke*, 3:94). As a result of this scrambling of the temporal priority of events, it becomes unclear to the reader at moments in the text whether Einstein is writing, for example, of his youth in Karlsruhe in the 1890s or of his recent exile in Paris in the 1930s. As if to symbolize this suspension of linear time through a concrete motif, Einstein writes into *Bebuquin II* a scene depicting the destruction of a watch—not once, but three times. It is what Einstein called a "vacation from causality" (*Werke*, 3:232).

The circularity of Einstein's text reflects a structural law of the autobiographical anamnesis, which, strictly speaking, can never have a precise and localizable origin. Within an autobiographical account, the beginning is always receding from sight, since the author's own birth is a vanishing point that can never be recalled and, by its very nature, is excluded from depiction. As the autobiographer comes closer to her origin, subjectivity falters, and the perspective becomes more eccentric and exterior. Like a bending hyperbola, the narrative line traced backward is diverted outward as it approaches the earliest years of life, which are available only secondhand, through narratives offered by relatives or documentary records such as photographs. At the very point of psychogenetic origin, therefore, we encounter an enigmatic absence of selfhood, a purely passive object that can be known only obliquely, in the third person. Thus, like myth, autobiographical inquiry forecloses the possibility of narrative beginnings, and is consequently forced to repetition and circularity. And it is the same at the other narrative pole of autobiography, where the hyperbola bends outward yet again, this time away from a conclusive ending. Autobiographies are perforce unfinishable, Philippe Lejeune writes, since concluding such an account would in effect require documenting one's own death.[55] By the very logic of his inquiry, then, the autobiographer—a "non-novelist," Einstein insisted (*ein Nichtromancier*)[56]—is denied two of the most basic elements of narrative form, a beginning and an end. As a result, autobiographies are necessarily cyclomythic by design, and cannot partake of the linear plotted structure of the novel.

The same patterns of contradiction and excess that were realized in narrative terms through the devices of temporal synchrony and circularity appear as well in the text's tropological system, where Einstein superimposes figures one upon the other to create what he called, in his study of Braque, a "*simultané* of rationally discrepant figural signs" (*Werke*, 3:325). Searching for ways to mitigate the ineluctable linearity of verbal language, Einstein made extensive use of poetry, which, as is well known, privileges the metaphoric image (paradigmatic axis) over narrative metonymy (syntagmatic axis).[57] In the roughly thirty poems that were integrated into this "lyrical novel," as he occasionally called his autobiography, Einstein took full advantage of the combinatory potential of the German language, connecting substantives to one another to form bizarre and internally contradictory compound nouns that seem, in many cases, to describe events rather than objects: *Fruchtgetöte* ("fruit-kill"), *Genitalienmeeting* ("genital-meeting"), *Scheibentrübung* ("pane-clouding"). With words such as these Einstein gives an impression of spatial simultaneity that is otherwise available only the visual arts. Indeed, he discovered similar strategies of temporal compression in the later etchings of Braque, especially his illustrations of Hesiodic myths such as *Themis and Hera*: "These figures are pure condensations," Einstein observed, in which "an ensemble or a *simultané* of mythical complexes are collected in a single figure that breaks through rational conventions of figuration" (*Werke*, 3:325). Appropriating this method for *Bebuquin II*, Einstein reinscribes again and again scenes and figures that are similar, although never perfectly identical, and in the process of replaying them undermines the reader's certainty whether the second appearance is an iteration at all or if it instead comprises an entirely different scene.

The tropological overinscription of *Bebuquin II* establishes a network of correspondences linking characters to one another in a continuous play of likeness and difference that blurs the contours separating individual figures. But it is not just the distinct identities of the figures that is erased through these rolling metamorphoses. The repetition also suspends the basic distinction between character and setting, since, with each transformation, the character is embedded into additional fields of association, incorporating new attributes and objects into the figure. For this reason, the spatial setting of *Bebuquin II* was immensely important for Einstein, who drafted several key sections of the book under the heading "Landscape." No mere background for the story, these topographic inventories served as hieroglyphs of *Bebuquin II*'s characters and, at many moments in the text, even displace the actors themselves. Time and narrative event become absorbed into space, rendering "all phases from prehistory to a visionary future in a single landscape" (Einstein Archive, 7). By depicting "[i]ndividuals e.g. as landscape," and, conversely, "objects and trees and rivers as actants," as Einstein proposed in one working note for the project (Einstein Archive, 10), *Bebuquin II* would sabotage the conceit of integral personhood upon which traditional narrative was based. Within the context of an autobiography, moreover, this dissolution of narrative character into landscape takes on a more profound aspect, since the character being dissolved is none other than the author himself. The geological self-portraits of *Bebuquin II* reflected Einstein's "desire . . . to sink back into a mineral existence" (Einstein Archive, 18). With reference to the famous essay by Roger Caillois, Einstein's autobiography could thus be described as a "psychaesthenic" narrative, a story that assimilates its author into a surrounding setting composed of mineral formations, landscapes, and architectural spaces. This spatialization of character was an appropriate device for a necrologue of the ego, since, as Einstein wrote in *Documents*, "exteriority of a landscape signifies the destruction of the self" (*Werke*, 3:41).

Like Braque's etchings, in which the addition of each new line threatens to throw the entire composition into a state of delineation, Einstein's repetition of figures in *Bebuquin II* ultimately leads to a state of disfiguration. "Time is amassed over the course of reading," he explained in his letter to Kahnweiler: time "functions as differentiation. Which means no repetition of events" (*Werke*, 4:161). Anticipating Deleuze's analysis from *Difference and Repetition*, which, as we saw in the introduction, describes iteration as a challenge to the fixity of conceptual identity and an event that unmoors the grid of representation, Einstein explains in his letter that perfect formal identity does not in fact exist, since the repetition of forms leads to the perception of difference, not of sameness. Within *Bebuquin II*, the process of reinscription opposes the work of realist representation by destabilizing the contours of the figures and draining them of their vividness. Through continuous repetition and transformation, Einstein mobilizes representation against itself, troping its figures into a state of oblivion and conceptual nonidentity, a state of semiotic collapse from which it becomes possible to break through the mnemonic screen of signs into an authentic perception of the world. "The only means to grasp the living [is] through an acceleration of metamorphoses," he observed.[58] It is precisely because he erases nothing from his autobiography that the cumulative effect of these metamorphoses is, paradoxically, that of erasure. "Ultimately every excessive addition to memory triggers an automatic forgetting" (*Werke*, 3:277). This convergence of overinscription and oblivion, of archiving and expunging, was a mechanism that, moreover, Einstein claimed to discern everywhere in interwar European culture, which, in a kind of autoimmune reaction to "civilization overload" (*Werke*, 3:303) and being "historified to death" (*tödlich vergeschichtet*; *Fictions*, 140), had begun to delete its own record and return to a state of primitive *in-der-Welt-sein*.[59]

Thus, as Einstein wrote to Kahnweiler, reading is not simply a process of accumulation, since at the same time it also entails a "corollary forgetting or wearing out of what has already been read" (*Werke*, 4:161). To read, in other words, is also to overwrite. This is a process that de Man characterized as a "trampling gesture," a gesture that undermines the faithfulness of memory and that subverts the primary violence of figuration. The repetition of tropes, he explained, "enacts the necessary recurrence of the initial violence [of positing a figure]: a figure of thought, the very light of cognition, obliterates thought. . . . Each of the episodes forgets the knowledge achieved by the forgetting that precedes it. . . . The repetitive erasures by which language performs the erasure of its own positions can be called disfiguration." The end result of this reinscription is "the form of a pseudo-knowledge which is called forgetting."[60] Figuration works the same way in *Bebuquin II*: first in an act of positing and then in an act of "corollary forgetting," first as inscription and then as "wearing out." Here Einstein reveals just how fragile is the tropological economy of mimetic realism, which requires figuration in order to produce the illusion of verisimilitude, but which can tolerate only so much figuration before it lapses into irreality.

Neither properly modernist nor realist, the strategies of figuration found in *Bebuquin II* are instead closer to a poetics of the grotesque, a method in which, as Einstein explained in 1926, a "closed figure" is opened up, "cleaved apart by contrasts" (*kontrastierend zerspalten*) and made nonidentical with itself (*Werke*, 4:171). Although Einstein's words here may appear to invoke the strategies of aesthetic fragmentation used by modernist authors such as Mallarmé, the figural dehiscence that we find in the grotesque is in fact utterly inimical to the modernist fragment, which works by invoking an absent aesthetic totality in the reader's mind and thus, in the end, exercising the faculty of the imagination. To the contrary, the grotesque's surfeit of figuration overwhelms and paralyzes the imagination. This was why Benjamin contrasted the excess of the grotesque with the subtractive powers of the imagination in a short note of 1921. He observed there that "genuine imagination is unconstructive, purely de-formative [*rein entstaltend*]—or (from the standpoint of the subject) purely negative" (*Schriften*, 6:115; *Writings*, 1:280). It "creates no new nature," he continued. "Pure imagination, therefore, is not an inventive power" (*Schriften*, 6:117; *Writings*, 1:282). By contrast, the grotesque "does not de-form [*entstaltet*] in a destructive fashion but destructively over-forms [*überstaltet*]," Benjamin proposed (*Schriften*, 6:115; *Writings*, 1:280). The distinction that Benjamin draws here maps onto the transition, within Einstein's work, from *Bebuquin* to *Bebuquin II*, a transition in which *Entstaltung* becomes *Überstaltung* and the negations of the imagination give way to the accumulations of the grotesque.

Again and again in the art and literature of the interwar period we encounter this same "trampling gesture" of representation, this same process of *Überstaltung*. If modernism interrogated mimesis through calculated sensory impoverishment and epistemological critique, interwar art, by contrast, supercharged mimesis, as it were, but in ways that were no less inimical to the traditional realist enterprise. Whether in the eclectic miscellany of characters that populate its novels, in the motivic jumble of late-synthetic cubism, or, as we will soon see, in the "overcoding" of Heartfield's photomontages, the art of this period aspired not to strip down reality but to outstrip it. All of the phrases that circulate around socialist realism, for example—"Life has become better, comrades, life has become more joyous" or "more alive than the living"—reflect an extravagant, technicolor, hypersaturated art that strives to be more "real" than reality itself.[61] If, according to Arno Holz, the formula for art in 1891 was *art* = *nature* − *x*, the formula in 1930 would now read *art* = *nature* + *x*, as the author Alfred Döblin proposed in a talk on Holz and the "new naturalism."[62]

Through strategies of repetition Einstein cultivated a form of representation that dismantles the primary opposition between sensation and semiosis upon which modernism and realism were both equally based. As de Man noted, the process of figural reinscription "does not fit within the symmetrical structure of presence and absence,"[63] a structure that, as we have already seen, was fundamental to the Sartrean opposition between perception and imagining. But, far more than Sartre, the name that must be mentioned here is that of Ferdinand de Saussure, whose structuralist doctrine can be read as the poetological breviary of the modernist project, whether in the visual or the verbal arts: just as analytic cubism illustrates perfectly the structuralist model of signification in painting,[64] the work of Mallarmé, the great poet of the *Néant*, provides a consummate literary example of Saussurian doctrine, which defined the sign negatively, as a purely relational unit whose meaning is predicated on its difference from other signs in the same system. As Einstein points out, this apophatic structure of knowledge means that experience and cognition can never coincide. "We moderns are maniacs of distinction [*maniaken der unterscheidung*]," he wrote with disgust (*Werke*, 4: 234). Indeed,

Einstein's endless tirades against the imagination and negative modernism read like attacks on the model of consciousness posited by structural linguistics, in which the "prison-house of language," to use Jameson's apt phrase, precludes the possibility of a primary encounter with reality or history: "Arrested concepts give rise to moribund contrasts," he writes, "which is how language hurls us into a much more intense existential conflict; like images, words intensify conflict (dialectics). Thus the dialectics of being are intensified conceptually through linguistic expression and grammatical contrasts that cannot be reconciled. On the other hand, with its mechanisms, language degrades us into speaking machines, just like the mechanicity of ideas that is reflected in philosophy" (Einstein Archive, 12). Against the modernist "mania" for structural distinction, Einstein argued that the real world lacks this grammar of contrasts: in actuality there are no binary oppositions, "there are only transitions [*Übergänge*]" (Einstein Archive, 12).

The repeated operation of inscription that is evident in the imagery of *Bebuquin II* can also be observed also at the textological level of Einstein's work, where we discover another "trampling" of representation. Here again he draws inspiration from the speech genre of myth, which lacks a point of origin. An inherently collective textual form that is attributable to no particular author, myth emerges as if through an emanation of the communal psyche. As a result, it is not ratified by the "author function" that, as Foucault showed, has served in the modern era to secure the meaning of the text by limiting the "dangerous proliferation of signification."[65] Indeed, proliferating is something that myth does extremely well. As its passes from mouth to mouth and across generations, myth adapts with each new formulation to the exigencies of the present, a fact that makes it at once both timeless and utterly contemporary. By nature textually promiscuous, its protean and robust archetypes—"floating signifiers," as Lévi-Strauss called them[66]—resurface in all sorts of collective representations from folk tales to urban legends. It was precisely for this reason that André Jolles, with reference to myth's second-hand nature, translated *μῦθος* as "transmitted narrative" ("überlieferte Erzählung") in his *Basic Forms* of 1930.[67] These transmissions have neither author nor Ur-text, and thus thwart attempts to prioritize any single version of the text as the original. The textological puzzle that results is exemplified by Franz Kafka's treatment of the Prometheus myth in the early 1920s, which recounts four different and mutually incompatible accounts of the Titan's exploits and produces through their juxtaposition the kind of exegetical surplus—the "dangerous proliferation of signification"—for which his work is so famous. Like *Bebuquin II*, which, in a single stroke, both retold and erased its predecessor *Bebuquin*, Kafka's treatment of myth makes clear that the act of narrative transmission invariably entails not just retelling previous versions of the story but also modifying and thus *un*telling them in the very act of narration.

In addition to its inherent collectiveness, myth also appealed to Einstein because of its peculiar cognitive structure, a structure that the philosopher Friedrich Schelling called "tautegorical." Myth, Schelling wrote, "has as its object that of which one can only say that it is."[68] Since sign and concept are inseparable, indeed identical, in mythical speech, its contents cannot be assimilated to codes and meanings external to it. It contains no abstract message, but is instead valid only in and for itself. In this regard the tautegory of myth differs essentially from allegory, a mode of interpretation that is exemplified in the Bible, whose bipartite structure sets up a closed circuit of prefiguration and fulfillment, and which generates meaning by eliding the discrepancies between the individual narratives of the Old and New Testaments. In the narrative syllepsis of allegory, all divergences are reconciled within a third master plot. By contrast, myths cannot be resolved with one another to produce a definitive and final version, but can only be described in their own terms. There is no master narrative behind Kafka's four renditions of Prometheus's story, only a continuous play of similarity that connects the texts laterally. According to Samuel Coleridge, whose thought about myth developed in close exchange with Schelling, allegory thus expresses "a different subject but with a resemblance," whereas tautegory expresses "the same subject but with a difference."[69]

Given its tautegorical structure, all attempts to divest myth of contradiction, difference, and inconsistency—all efforts, in other words, to convert *mythos* into *logos*—are fundamentally misguided, because they misconstrue the function of myth, whose purpose is not to be universal and abstract (in the manner of conceptual logic), but to be constructive and useful. "Through its syntactical and semantic organization," the anthropologist Jean-Pierre Vernant observed, "the language employed by myth in itself represents a way of arranging reality, a kind of classification and setting in order of the world, a preliminary logical arrangement, in sum an instrument of thought."[70] In this regard, the mythical sign follows a mode of thinking that is fundamentally dissimilar from that of modern rationalism. Instead of operating vertically, connecting material sign to abstract concept, tautegory operates laterally, linking signs to other signs in a network of similitude. It was a mode of thought that Lévy-Bruhl famously characterized as *prélogique*, and that he juxtaposed to conceptual abstraction: "Prelogical mentality is essentially synthetic. By this I mean that the syntheses which compose it do not imply previous analyses of which the result has been registered in definite concepts, as is the case with those in which logical thought operates. In other words, the connecting-links of the representations are given, as a rule, with the representations themselves."[71]

Picking up on Lévy-Bruhl's account, Einstein argued for the utter contemporaneity of mythical thinking in society today: "there exists not only the *prélogique* which governed man before his hypertrophic rationalization; there also exists a *postlogique* that swells with the damming of forgotten forces" (*Werke*, 3:308). Despite belonging to opposite poles on the hierarchy of cultural evolution, these two systems of thought were, for Einstein, indistinguishable. "In this way two opposed phases bear an astonishing resemblance to one another," he observed about the curious convergence between the earliest configurations of human society and the most advanced technical civilization (*Fictions*, 111). Like the *prélogique* of the "early primitive," the *postlogique* of the "late primitive" tends toward a synthetic mode of signification that is fundamentally inimical to the structuralist sign, with its analytic system based on contrast, distinction, and critical reason. Indeed, as we will see in the next chapter, this apparently premodern mode of signification, which privileges lateral patterns of similitude over vertical relations of reference, is in fact the sign-structure that comes to dominate systems of representation at the moment of historical transition into spectacle society during the 1920s.

To be sure, there were also concrete political exigencies that precipitated Einstein's turn to mythical thinking in the 1920s and '30s. Confronted with the successes of fascist political formations across Europe, artists of the Left—those "heroes of critique and dwarves of will"—were forced to reconsider their apophatic methods, since, as was becoming increasingly clear, this one-sided allegiance to the negative had ceded powerful resources to politically reactionary groups. Critique, it seemed, was incapable of animating the hearts of humanity as myth can.[72] Recognizing that leftist art had been too slow in mobilizing the forces of fantasy and libido, voices within the Popular Front such as Ernst Bloch insisted that mythical schemes should not simply be dismissed as regressive and irrational primitivisms, for these collective utterances potentially also contained blueprints for new social configurations, even if their utopian wish-contents were often articulated in distorted idioms. Myth "does not belong to the order of comprehension, as the sign does, but rather to that of affectivity and desire," noted Vernant.[73] It was for this reason that Einstein deemed myth to be more viable a platform for revolutionary activity than the negations of aesthetic modernism. "Only a positive doctrine that provides a clear goal . . . can lead to revolution ([can] engender actions, since actions are determined by their end)" (*Fictions*, 33). Although modernism's critical project may once have served a progressive political agenda, this art's negations had devolved into contentless and reactive *épater la bourgeoisie* tactics, when it needed instead to be fomenting revolution. The final lines of *The Fabrication of Fictions* thus proclaim that the task of art is not "to reject reality, but to recreate it collectively. Art will once again have place in this project if it participates humbly in the production of a new reality" (327).

In its renewed concern with the affective dimension of revolutionary art, Einstein's program of "mythical realism" aligned with the objectives of socialist realism, even if its author never accepted the formalization of socialist realism as academic neoclassicism, which he derided as an "embarrassing" "comedy of revenants" (*Fictions*, 91, 254).[74] Indeed, one of the sources for the socialist realist program had been the so-called philosophy of god-building (*богостроительство*), proposed already decades before by Maxim Gorky and Lunacharsky in an effort to breathe life into the rarefied philosophical abstractions of dialectical critique. Founded not upon the promise of salvation in the hereafter but upon humanist values to be realized within the living rituals of an ethical community, this antitranscendental religion included a mythological pantheon of embodied socialist values. In contrast to Lenin, an inveterate disciple of the dialectic who, in his faithfulness to the *Bilderverbot* of Marxist theory, eschewed positive figurations of socialist utopia and instead measured objective political progress only in negative terms (e.g. as the atrophying of the state apparatus), Gorky and Lunacharsky sought to provide concrete representations of the society to come.[75] And so, just as Schelling had once championed the foundational tautology of myth as an alternative to Hegel's apophatic method, whose march to truth and certitude proceeds along the path of logical negation, these early architects of socialist realism established mythical figuration as a cornerstone of a positive revolutionary philosophy.[76] Even if Lenin managed officially to eradicate god-building from the Bolshevik agenda, this secularized theology nonetheless returned after his death in the "positive heroes" (*положительные люди*) of the socialist realist pantheon[77] and in the importance that this art places on highly ritualized behaviors.[78] Indeed, mythological tautegory is at the very core of the socialist realist project, whose pageant of fatuous ideologemes, empty slogans, and formulaic epithets is closely related to the forms of phatic speech found in religious ritual. Such "floating signifiers" may be the "disability of all finite thought," Levi-Strauss explained, but, as sites of collective libidinal investment, they are also "the surety of all art, all poetry, every mythic and aesthetic invention."[79]

In an attempt to uncover these communal sites, Einstein embarked on an *Ethnologie du Blanc*, a personal autobiography that was at the same time a collective psychomythography. As he proceeded to inventory the contents of memory, peeling away its sedimented layers one by one, he discovered that he was writing not a personal memoir but a "novel about a generation or an epoch" (as he once characterized *Bebuquin II*).[80] Confirming in this way the structural law of autobiographical inquiry, whose vantage, as we saw earlier, is paradoxically deflected outward as it progresses into the deeper recesses of the individual psyche, Einstein descended into a world made of Jolles's "transmitted speech," a world of authorless clichés and secondhand utterances. In the course of writing, Einstein again and again likened himself to a phonographic record, a mechanical medium for an inauthentic language whose origin lies elsewhere. Speech is not expressive in *Bebuquin II*, but is rather a kind of haunting, a dispatch from the preceding generations now long dead. Beb becomes a "phonograph for spirits, a haunted house, a passageway for spirits," Einstein wrote (Einstein Archive, 48). Like the other "lifetime prisoners of a phonographic society that has long been bankrupt," Beb is but an echo of voices that preceded his entry into subjectivity and selfhood (*Werke*, 3:114).

This reliance on the prefabricated schemes of myth connects Einstein's "necrologue of the ego" to another autobiographical project undertaken in the mid-1930s, Michel Leiris's *Manhood*. Like *Bebuquin II*, Leiris's book effaces the "authentic" author of autobiography, replacing him with a subject whose behavior is rigorously schematized and whose language is likewise fashioned out of readymade phrases. From its very first lines, which initiate a cold and radically unfeeling inspection of Leiris, *Manhood* seeks to repatriate the most intimate contents of his psyche to a presubjective condition of reified exteriority. Echoing Einstein's "desire . . . to sink back into a mineral existence," Leiris thus characterized *Manhood* as a "symbolic attempt at mineralization."[81] This petrification of the self commences with an exposition of a set of mythological themes, "the frame—or the fragments of a frame—within which everything else has been set."[82] A series of rigid, impersonal postures, these archetypes establish the ineluctable course that his life must take. Everything that follows upon them unfolds as if prophesied. So, for example, when Leiris falls in love, his object choice has already been anticipated, indeed exhaustively diagrammed, by the mythical figure of Judith. Whether in his childhood infatuation with "Tante Lise," in the first adult love that he experiences for his "initiatrix" Kay, or in his later obsessions with certain prostitutes, Leiris, "throat cut" and "penis inflamed," is always destined to play Holofernes to their Judiths.

Such "classical themes," as Leiris called these archetypes, are standard tropes in the figurative idiom of the return to order. But if critics of interwar art have hastily condemned these revenants as regressive nostalgia, as the primitivizing reaction of a technical civilization longing to recover some authentic mode of existence, the neoclassicism that we find in *Manhood*, by contrast, is neither authentic nor originary but profoundly clichéd and counterfeit. Leiris transforms the archetypes of antiquity into a morbid statuary. "Marble attracts me by its glacial temperature and its rigidity," he wrote. "I actually imagine myself stretched out on a slab (whose coldness I feel against my skin) or bound to a column. Sometimes it seems to me I could formulate my desire by saying I lusted after a body 'cold and hard as a Roman building.'"[83] These antique themes provided Leiris no vitality. A devotee of Baroque theater, he staged his neoclassical statuary as a Racinian play of frozen tableaux that were propped up by mechanical reproductions and secondhand fictions. Leiris's deepest, most personal desire, he confessed, is to live alongside a trompe-l'oeil wife in a trompe-l'oeil house with a trompe-l'oeil log that burns in a trompe-l'oeil fireplace.[84]

In this regard, the myths and classical themes that populate Leiris's psyche are no different than the debased industrial commodities that play a central role in structuring the desire of the Western subject. And these too appear at the beginning of the text, where they are cathected by the young Michel in the manner of tribal fetishes, at once both collective and public but also deeply personal and secret. From the heraldic emblem that brands the stove *La Radieuse* to the hypnotic image of a rajah taken from a popular illustrated magazine, his fantasy life is pieced together from mass-produced articles "as a sort of photomontage," the author proposes.[85] These mundane commodities are objects of intense psychic investment, sites of what Leiris famously identified as "the sacred in everyday life."[86] In the same way that his romantic pursuits will recapitulate the story of Judith and Holofernes, his understanding of infinity—one of the deepest metaphysical enigmas of his being—was already prefigured by a Dutch cocoa tin that sat on his childhood breakfast table and featured on its label a picture of the same cocoa tin, and on the label of that tin yet another tin, and so on, in infinite regress.[87] The matrix of individual comportment and even of the structures of thought itself conform to the contours established by industrial commodities and the idiom of advertising, which, as the basic units and language in the collective mythology of the modern world, provide the preliminary architecture for young Michel's developing ego.

Thus, in *Manhood*, as in *Bebuquin II*, the author's archeological quest to discover his own unique point of origin yields only an exhibit of artifacts and ideologemes that predated his arrival in the world. For both writers, this venture to recover the collective contents of the individual psyche would become an ongoing process, interminable like the psychoanalysis that first prompted Leiris to write *Manhood*. Both projects in fact set their authors on a course of endless self-auditing—and self-erasure—that ended only with their respective deaths. In the case of *Bebuquin II* this enterprise was cut off by its author's suicide in 1940 as he was fleeing the Nazis, but for Leiris the process of autobiographical inventorying continued for another fifty years. Tellingly, the next volume that Leiris would publish after *Manhood* bore the title *Biffures*, a word that means both "scratches" and "erasures" and that, in an echo of *Bebuquin II*'s poetics of *Überstaltung*, or "overformation," suggests the dual process of writing on top of an existing record while simultaneously crossing out, canceling, the previous installment through the very act of reinscription.

Einstein and Leiris's discovery that autobiography does not recount a personal story, but, to the contrary, disintegrates into a collective narrative recalls the position of the philosopher Georg Misch, whose introduction to the epochal eight-volume *History of Autobiography* (1907–1969) quotes Dilthey's observation that, "[a]s a species, man dissolves into the process of history."[88] Approaching his origin, the author of *Bebuquin II* begins to blend psychaesthenically into the surrounding environment and events of the society from which he emerged. "I will become this epoch, these people," he wrote of the project (Einstein Archive, 4). Einstein depicts this dissolution into the collective process of history through the endless chains of metamorphosis that continuously modify his character's contours. He writes, for example, of the "manycreaturedmanydestiniedmanysexed body of little Laurenz" (Einstein Archive, 19), an open creature who merges with the figure of Lissi in a blur of "transvestism" and "hermaphroditism" (Einstein Archive, 4). Together these human transformers discover an eroticism that exceeds the sexual encounter, an ecstatic transport made possible by the innate plasticity and indeterminateness of the human form. Whereas all other organisms on this planet are confined to a closed anatomy that is alterable only by the slow hand of evolution, humans "are able to sprout like plants or be inert like minerals, to radiate like stars or extinguish like moons. Which is to say that man is the acrobat of the worldly states that emanate from him. . . . man is the play of ceaseless metamorphoses that emerges in dreams" (*Werke*, 5:268).

Einstein borrowed this notion of the human as a structurally open, undefined being from contemporary biology, which, as we have already seen, also informed the constructivist paradigms of philosophical anthropology. If animal species dissolve into the process of morphological evolution, man, by contrast, dissolves into the process of history, as Dilthey observed. "[D]estabilized by the basic discoveries of biology" (*Werke*, 5:158) and recent scientific "efforts to alter and modify man" (*Werke*, 3:579), the classical humanist image of the body as closed, universal and timeless had been definitively overturned, Einstein argued. Once a being with a fixed essence, man "was no longer [an] image of order, no longer a stable model, but a bundle of processes" (*Werke*, 5:163) and an "an aggregate of functional relations" (*Werke*, 5:158). With the deterritorialization of man's image, the human body went from being a fixed substance to being a "passage" (*Werke*, 3:339), from a hierarchically organized and integral totality into a historical "hodge-podge" of disparate parts (Einstein Archive, 19). Here too Einstein discerned a resemblance between advanced industrial civilization and primitive cultures, who also viewed the human form as a tentative project. Like his distant ancestors, contemporary man "does not believe in the constancy of his body," he wrote (*Werke*, 3:338). The only difference, he continued, is that primitive man dissolves the individual body through totemic identification and ritual magic, whereas modern man modifies the human form through surgical enhancement and technical prostheses.

But man's biological indeterminacy is not just a physical or anatomical matter. Indeed, when Bataille wrote in a 1930 *Documents* article that "[m]an's architecture is not simple like that of animals and it is not even possible to say where he begins [*où il commence*]," he identified an anthropological enigma that was temporal as well.[89] As impossible as it is to say *where* the plastic body of man begins and ends, it is no more possible to say *when* the individual subject begins historically, Einstein observed. "At first the individual contains 1000 destinies" (Einstein Archive, 19), which society bequeaths to her in the form of "mnemonic matter" (*Erinnerungsmassen*; *Fictions*, 140). As we observed in chapter 2's discussion of Leroi-Gourhan's "operational sequences," human beings inherit from their social milieu not just an abstract syntax of time, but also the determinate contents of this temporal edifice, a cache of collective and transindividual memories. Building on Leroi-Gourhan's analysis, the philosopher Bernard Stiegler consequently observes that the "temporality of the human, which marks it off among other living beings, presumes exteriorization and prostheticity: there is time only because memory is 'artificial,' becoming constituted as already-there *since* its 'having been placed outside of the species.'" Man, he concludes, is an animal whose "historial, nonlived past can be inherited inauthentically."[90] In Einstein's *Ethnologie du Blanc*, this inauthentic mnemonic legacy takes the form of the collective scripts, myths, and symbols that reduce autobiographer to a human phonograph. The more this machine turns inward, the more its self-auditing is deflected outward and dissolves into the process of history.

Freud had encountered the same core enigma of "where man begins" while investigating infantile amnesia, a phenomenon that enshrouds early experiences up to around the seventh year. According to Freud, this curious absence of memory was attributable to a law of human development that he called the *zwei-zeitiger Ansatz*, or "beginning twice over." This theory, which reappears in a number of Freud's texts, proposes that the human child, unlike other young animals, undergoes a second birth years after its first, when the individual enters into the collective social frameworks of family and community. In contrast to the first, biological birth, which marks the infant's punctual arrival into the world, the second is the culmination of an exceptionally long period of physical development and psychic enculturation. This protracted period of "extra-uterine gestation," to use the term of the Swiss zoologist Adolf Portmann, gives the human multiple points of origin. Like Nietzsche, who defined man as the "not yet determined animal," Freud argued that this diphasic developmental structure is the evolutionary innovation that distinguishes humans from other creatures:

"postponement and the beginning twice over are intimately connected with the history of hominization [*Geschichte der Menschwerdung*]," he wrote. "Human beings appear to be the only animal organisms with a latency period and sexual retardation of this kind" (*Werke*, 16:180; *Standard Edition*, 23:75). For Freud, this notion of a "beginning twice over" explained the phenomenon of early childhood amnesia, which stems from the adult's incapacity to recall the period before her birth into society and history, that is, to recall a purely organic, creaturely existence before the acquisition of productive gestures, technology, and symbolic thought. It is an amnesia, moreover, that appears in Einstein's autobiography as an absence of narrative origin, an absence that imposes a cyclomythic structure on his text.

According to this diphasic developmental law, the life span of the subject is both longer and shorter than her organic existence in the world: longer, because this second birth inducts the subject into collective cultural technics whose historical duration far exceeds that of individual; and shorter, because this second, social birth recommences development years after physical birth. Like many of his contemporaries, Einstein used the word "generation" to designate these social frameworks into which the individual is born. With this key term, which recurs throughout *The Fabrication of Fictions* but especially in *Bebuquin II* (a "novel about a generation or an epoch"),[91] Einstein identified both an organic process of individual procreation ("the act or process of reproducing a living organism") as well as the larger social units into which people are assimilated ("all of the people born and living at about the same time, regarded collectively"[92]). It is a word whose use exploded during the interwar period in an attempt "to understand, by borrowing directly from the realm of biology, the exchange of forms between mental and social currents."[93] As Karl Mannheim noted in his famous 1928 essay "On the Problem of Generations," the phenomenon of generation is a key concept to understanding the unique developmental pattern of the human, whose course of growth and individuation proceeds by "incorporating itself into a group" (*das Hineinwachsen in eine Gruppe*).[94] If the duration of every other animal on this planet is measured exclusively in terms of organic life spans, only the human's is also measured in terms of generations. As Dilthey had explained, man alone dissolves into the process of history.

According to Freud, the evolutionary facts of man's premature birth and extra-uterine gestation constitute the biological foundation of the need for love and intimacy.[95] As a naturally relational being, the human organism requires for its ontogenetic development an affective community, a generation of peers. But, Einstein observed, something in this evolutionary program had miscarried in recent history, and with catastrophic results: "This generation was incapable of experiencing community in any form," he noted in *Bebuquin II* (*Einstein Archive*, 7). It is indeed significant that the conservative philosopher Arnold Gehlen, when confronting this same evolutionary pattern, came to a very different conclusion from Freud, arguing in his 1940 opus *Man* that the human infant's entry into the world in an unfinished state was the psychogenetic origin not of the desire for intimacy but of the need for authority and regulation. If, for Freud, the unfinished animal required community for completion, for Gehlen, the "deficient being" (*Mängelwesen*) was a "being of discipline" (*Zuchtwesen*) and a creature driven by a compulsion for constraint (*Formierungszwang*).

The two widely divergent conclusions that Freud and Gehlen drew from the same evolutionary mechanism reflect, with remarkable precision, the historical transition that Germany faced during the interwar period, when the biological capacity for intimacy and collective experience was channeled into the masochistic desire to submit to a totalitarian order defined by "Blood and Soil." In his famous study of the behavior and mental life of the National Socialist male, Klaus Theweleit defined these fascist subjects as the "not-yet-fully-born" (*die nicht zu Ende geborenen*).[96] Raised in a Wilhelminian society that denied them the possibility of realizing the desire for intimacy within secure social relations, this generation was left with an unstable drive economy that made them susceptible to fascist demagoguery. As Theweleit explained, these subjects responded to the overwhelming anxiety about the dissolving contours of selfhood with a pathological fortification of the ego that only further inhibited the possibility of experiencing stable affective bonds. Refused a second birth into that form of social collectivity known as "generation," this group's capacity for love was deformed into a need for discipline. The result, to repeat Einstein's conclusion, was that "this generation was incapable of experiencing community in any form."

It was in search of these collective forms that Einstein initiated his autobiographical project in the mid-1920s, hoping through this *Ethnologie du Blanc* to arrive at the cultural myths that defined his generation. As we have seen, this project was also an exercise in self-erasure. As time went on, Einstein's desire for collective experience grew increasingly radicalized until the point when, disclaiming his literary pursuits entirely, he joined the Durruti Column, in whose ranks he fought for two years during the Spanish Civil War. It is uncertain whether or not Einstein continued to work on *Bebuquin II* during these years, but his descriptions of existence within the syndicalist commune certainly reflect the desideratum of his autobiographical project. In one of his final published texts, Einstein praises Buenaventura Durutti for banning the pronoun *I* from language: "The Durutti Column knows only collective syntax. These comrades will teach the academics to restore the collective meaning of grammar. Durutti understood profoundly the power of anonymous labor. Namelessness and communism are one and the same" (*Werke*, 3:459). In the same way that, as Einstein explains here, Communism strives toward a state of anonymity, autobiography repatriates the *I* to a "collective syntax." Communism and autobiography are parallel projects of self-effacement, as Il'ia Ehrenburg proposed in 1925, when he observed that "good communists have no biography."[97] For this reason, Einstein explained, the destruction of the self, this auto-thanatography, was not a morbid impulse, since, to the contrary, the death of the ego is a birth into community. It is a form of socialization, registered in the shift from the *I* to the *we*. Just as the individual undergoes multiple births into society, so too are there multiple deaths, equally social, that precede the final gasp of breath. "In our language, then, we should say that death, like birth, is accomplished in stages," Lévy-Bruhl explained.[98] For Einstein, *Bebuquin II* was one of these stages.

5

The Secret Always on Display: Caricature and Physiognomy in the Work of John Heartfield

When socialist realism first appeared, nobody knew quite what to make of it. It may be difficult for us today to imagine that this artistic movement, which eventually became so rigorously schematized and so ruthlessly administered, could have originally been so provisional in its conception, but at the time of its appearance few people understood the meaning of this aesthetic departure. Emerging out of a miscellany of realisms that circulated in the aesthetic discourses of the interwar period, this new variety of realism triumphed over these various rivals, from "proletarian" to "romantic" realism, to receive the official imprimatur of Soviet state institutions in 1932, the year that all independent artistic organizations were officially liquidated. With the subsequent backing of the Comintern, socialist realism was vigorously promoted internationally, although there too the exact provisions of this aesthetic fiat remained elusive and open to an array of interpretations. Thus, in a letter to his friend Brecht written immediately after the August 1934 First Soviet Writers' Congress in Moscow, Sergei Tret'iakov, for example, attempted to summarize the proceedings of this congress, where the tantalizing phrase "socialist realism" had been invoked again and again, but, failing to provide a workable synopsis of the new doctrine, wrote simply, "I am afraid that my German doesn't permit me to express myself clearly enough. But I must emphasize that there are a series of essentially new positions which need to be discussed and studied."[1]

The problem, of course, was not with Tret'iakov's German, a language that he spoke quite well. Tret'iakov's exceedingly precise mind was confused, rather, because socialist realism in 1934 could neither be explicated conceptually by its theorists or nor delimited stylistically by its practitioners.[2]

And yet, it is perhaps precisely because of this conceptual poverty that socialist realism would prove to be such a voracious doctrine. Equipped with a supremely capacious—and thus endlessly protean—theoretical rubric under which to work, socialist realist artists looked back across the long history of aesthetic forms for the forebears of their practice. In this regard, the official liquidation of all distinct artistic schools from the late constructivism of Oktiabr' to the absurdism of OBERIU was in fact a prerequisite for the emergence of socialist realism not just legally but also conceptually, since this new practice positioned itself as the heir to *all* these various movements and to the panoply of aesthetic techniques they had at their disposal. After the atomization of all individual artistic schools, socialist realism began to pick over the remnants of their styles, combining and conjugating these aesthetic devices at will. Symptomatically, it was the issue of the *Erbe*, or artistic legacy, that became a locus of debates in the German-speaking circles of the Popular Front, where cultural producers argued over which of the various cultural legacies should be salvaged and put to use.[3] In a May 1934 *Pravda* editorial on socialist realism written with Party bureaucrat Pavel Iudin, the author Aleksandr Fadeev captured this posthistorical mindset succinctly when he declared that "the most important task facing art in the era of socialism is the task of synthesis." "We need a great summary art," they enjoined, "an art of great historical synthesis."[4] Socialist realism, we could conclude, was the aesthetic program of a society undergoing a process of dramatic cultural and symbolic recoding.

Socialist realism was less an independent and recognizable artistic movement than a logic of cultural supplementarity, a logic that established itself by qualifying preexisting aesthetic traditions that were already familiar and known. Even if not conceptually exponible, by referencing a previous body of art, this aesthetic cipher became at least empirically demonstrable. Lacking any founding charter of its own, socialist realism assimilated strategies from previous artistic movements, foremost among which were, of course, the epic narrative and figurative painting of the nineteenth century. For this reason, despite socialist realism's outspoken rhetoric of expressiveness and creativity, the appropriationist directive of this work in fact observes a reproductive logic similar to the one found in photography. Like the latter, socialist realism proceeds by reframing its subject and transforming it into a higher-order representation, an image of what existed before.[5] The much-heralded organicism of socialist realism is thus belied by its pastiche practices. Indeed, no less an authority than Louis Aragon, the founder in 1932 of the Association of Revolutionary Writers and Artists, observed that "socialist realism made its first appearance in photomontage, born in the least realistic of the arts."[6]

Given the filiation that he discerned between socialist realism and photomontage, it is not surprising, moreover, that Aragon, a vociferous champion of the new appropriationist realism, was also responsible in 1935 for writing the first major critical essay on the work of John Heartfield. And in fact, few artists are better suited to confirm Aragon's insight about the origins of socialist realism. The work of the German photomonteur, who was most famous for his satirical covers of the *AIZ* (*Workers' Illustrated News*) and book covers designed for his brother's Malik Press, found particular resonance within the cultural politics of the Popular Front at a moment when the emerging socialist realist program was establishing itself, in effect, by annexing preexisting artistic traditions. After a period of work in the crucible of Berlin Dada, in 1924 Heartfield began to distance himself from the apophatic practices of this avant-garde, eventually becoming one of the most popular political artists in German Communist circles and abroad. If Heartfield's early Dada work circulated in that plastic "space of anguish" which, as we saw in the previous chapter, Lyotard associated with critical abstraction and the avant-garde's aesthetic of the death drive, after 1924 he started reconstructing an integrated space of pictorial illusion that, instead of repulsing the desire of the spectator, now ensnares this desire and locks it into the "erotic unity" of the representational field.

This shift from avant-garde fragmentation to realist representation (in Lyotard's terms: from the death drive to the pleasure principle) could be integrated into the familiar narrative about interwar art's return to notions of aesthetic harmony and totalization, if only Heartfield's "realism" weren't in fact so blatantly heterodox, even aggressively so. Like much early socialist realist work, whose logic of assembly relied on appropriation and pastiche, Heartfield constructed his photomontages almost exclusively out of readymade imagery plagiarized from a variety of contemporary bourgeois, fascist, and revolutionary print media. These prefabricated elements function like the reified mythological imagery in Leiris's *Manhood*, privileging the mechanical reproduction that is anterior to artistic expression, the serial copy behind the original. (Not by chance did Leiris characterize his autobiography as "a sort of photomontage.") Even at the level of language usage, Heartfield availed himself of readymade constructions, incorporating a variety of linguistic clichés such as puns, popular sayings, and propaganda slogans into his graphic work. From the imagery to the phraseology, everything in his work is secondhand. These strategies of quotation and intertextual reference prompted Ernst Bloch in 1938 to compare Heartfield's photomontages with Brecht's *Fear and Misery of the Third Reich*, a play that, as chapter 3 demonstrated, was assembled out of a stockpile of newspaper clippings and fragments of "reported speech."[7] On rare occasion Heartfield would himself produce a photograph that his composition lacked, but these staged elements were the absolute exception, since it was essential to his second-order practice that the pictures and slogans in his photomontages were already in wide circulation within the popular imaginary, and thus readily recognizable as reproductions stolen from other sources.

Heartfield's use of visual and linguistic cliché throws new light on what Aragon called, in his 1930 "Challenge to Painting," the inherent "morality of collage": "Plagiarism is necessary. Progress involves it. It adheres closely to an author's words, makes use of his expressions, erases a false idea, replaces it by a correct one."[8] Overturning the romantic myth of the solitary artistic genius who creates work *ex nihilo*, the secondhand techniques of collage reveal that art is always a collaborative production. Collage is "moral," as Aragon puts it, because it defies authorial copyright, and is inherently collective in nature. Ideological mainstays of bourgeois art such as the notions of artistic creation and personal expression have little purchase in Heartfield's photomontages, based as they are on the work and words of others. Though one could point to the biographical origins of Heartfield's dependence on "reported speech"—the artist was unusually inarticulate as both a writer and a speaker[9]—his silence was not so much that of a failed wordsmith but that of a mimic and a moralist. It is a silence that recalls the reticence of the journalist and consummate stylist Karl Kraus, who, just after the outbreak of the First World War, announced: "Expect no words of my own from me. Nor would I be able to say anything new, for in the room in which one writes there is such noise, and at this time one should not determine whether it comes from animals, from children, or merely from mortars. . . . Let him who has something to say come forward and be silent!"[10]

Heartfield's mimetic appropriations, should not, however, be confused with the aesthetic negations of the avant-garde. If, as the previous chapter demonstrated, the avant-garde strove, through strategies of semiotic demotivation, to arrive at a condition that György Kepes eloquently identified as "the zero point of the meaning-organization,"[11] Heartfield's work in the mid-1920s picks up where this deconstructive project terminated, seeking to remotivate the conventions of representation through the practices of pastiche. At this moment the avant-garde's relentless *de*coding of the conventions of mimetic illusionism yields, as we will soon see, to a zealous *over*coding of these same devices. Drawing widely and liberally from the technical resources developed in the great traditions of European art, Heartfield borrowed styles and compositional devices from their original contexts in order to embed them in new semantic fields. In the 1935 essay, "John Heartfield and Revolutionary Beauty," Aragon, for example, situated the photomonteur's work within a venerable genealogy of high art and the aesthetic discourse of idealist philosophy. Delivered on the occasion of Heartfield's show at the Paris Maison de la Culture, Aragon's talk gestured to the "centuries of painting" from which Heartfield drew, taking note, for example, of the remarkable resemblances between the photomonteur's work and that of Chardin.[12] In a review of the same Paris exhibition, the art critic Paul Westheim likewise pointed to the resonances between the works hanging in the

Maison de la Culture and the show by Francisco Goya concurrently on view at the Bibliothèque Nationale.

Aragon and Westheim's efforts to inscribe Heartfield's work into the august lineage of the cultural *Erbe* may have been standard rhetorical maneuvering for the Popular Front era, but the embrace of tradition in Heartfield's case was particularly notable in light of his previous cultural liquidationism. In the notorious 1920 polemic penned with Georg Grosz, "The Art Scoundrel" ("Der Kunstlump"), Heartfield had called for the destruction of the masterworks hanging in the institutions of high art, which the two pilloried as the idle pastime of an elite circle of esthetes. The journals in which Heartfield worked early in his career such as *Die neue Jugend*, where he came into contact with Franz Jung, and *Der blutige Ernst*, which was published by Carl Einstein, led him to the aggressive anti-aesthetic stance of Berlin Dada. And yet, as was also the case in the trajectories of Jung and Einstein, this phase of aggressive semioclasm and formal interrogation was followed by a return to order in which Heartfield began to engage once again with the techniques and cultural values of high art. Prompted—so the legend goes—by his encounter with Grosz, Heartfield may have destroyed all of his canvases and definitively renounced painting in 1915, but the slogan emblazoned over the doorway of his installation at the 1929 *Film und Foto* show in Stuttgart enjoined his viewers to "Paint with the Photo!" (*Male mit dem Foto!*)—a slogan that captures the curious sublation of the artisanal and photomechanical that, as we just saw, Aragon regarded as the very essence of socialist realism.

Caricature and Overcoding

Of all of the diverse sources in the history of Western art plundered by Heartfield, one particular artistic forebear was of paramount importance: the nineteenth-century lithographer and caricaturist Honoré Daumier. The corrosive satirist of French bourgeois society had a distinct appeal for the militant Communist Heartfield, whose admiration for the caricaturist suggests more than just an attempt at cultural legitimation. Having been introduced to Daumier's work by his "paternal friend" Eduard Fuchs, one of the leading collectors and historians of caricature, Heartfield, who otherwise wrote quite little, celebrated Daumier's work in two essays from the time of the Nazi dictatorship, "Daumier, More Alive Than Ever!" (1937) and "Daumier in the 'Reich'" (1942).[13] The reasons for his attraction to Daumier are multiple. Some commentators, for example, have noted resemblances between the two artists at the level of formal design, in some cases even mapping out entire series of one-to-one equivalences between specific works of the German photomonteur and his French "source."[14] But perhaps even more appealing for Heartfield, who designed photomontages for the popular press, was Daumier's status as one of the first media artists working in the emerging world of modern journalism and its public sphere. Often created in response to current events, Daumier's caricatures regularly appeared alongside news items in the daily press under the rubric *Actualités*. As Fuchs observed, the rise to prominence in the 1830s of lithography and caricature as new "possibilities for reproduction" was buoyed by two developments: the proliferation of means of technical reproducibility and the structural massification of society. "It was not just technical developments that needed to be advanced; the victory of the masses over the individual had to be equally decisive, and the populace, in all of its strata, had to be recognized as an important determinant."[15] For Heartfield, whose most famous photomontages circulated on book covers and in the pages of the weekly *AIZ*, Daumier's legacy exemplified a politically *engagée* art made for the new urban, mass audiences using the means of the modern media.

A visual idiom used by both Daumier and Heartfield, caricature is closely associated with the practice of montage. Although Heartfield himself never directly connected the two in his writings, their kinship was made explicit by the Soviet filmmaker Eisenstein, who, like Heartfield, wrote repeatedly on Daumier after turning away from the radical montage experiments of the mid-1920s. The fact that caricature regularly displaces montage in Eisenstein's later writings underscores the filiation, even structural equivalence, between the two techniques, one explicitly figurative and another that was coded as mechanistic. Indeed, caricature became a pivotal term in Eisenstein's negotiations between realism and the avant-garde because it shortcircuits the hackneyed opposition between organic figuration and fragmentary montage. Take his reading of Daumier's 1851 lithograph *Ratapoil Offers His Arm to the Republic* (fig. 5.1),

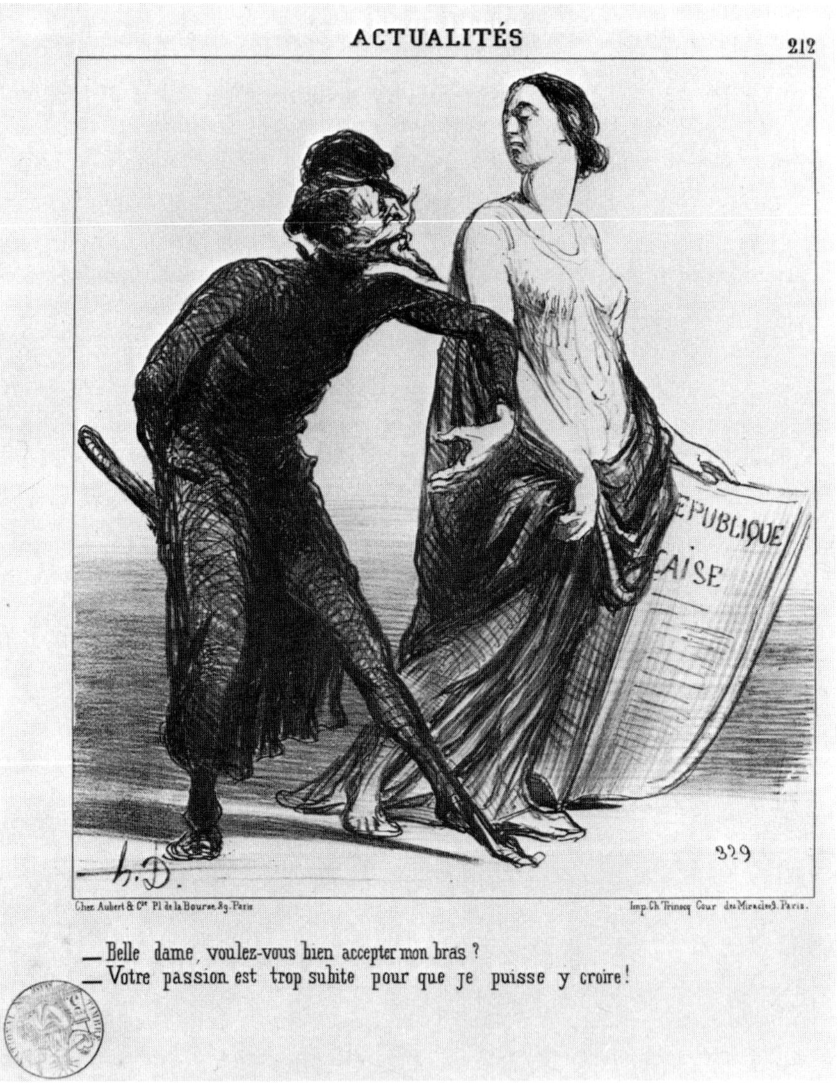

Figure 5.1 Honoré Daumier, *Ratapoil Offers His Arm to the Republic* (1851).

where Eisenstein uncovers a montage construction hidden just below the surface. "By the law of *pars pro toto*," he observes, "from the position of the foot you mentally extrapolate the attitude which the entire figure should be taking up at that moment. The same applies to the knee, the neck, and the head, so that in effect the figure drawn in this way is interpreted as if it were six successive 'frames' of the same figure in the various sequential phases of movement" (*Montazh*, 159; *Works*, 2:111). Like Baudelaire before him, Eisenstein praises Daumier's talent for creating a visual dynamism that explodes the static equilibrium of the closed figure. Noting how the caricaturist truncates a sequence of six distinct movements into a single posture, he reveals an entire cinematic sequence in Ratapoil. This discovery explains the Soviet filmmaker's keen interest in caricature, a form of depiction that, as one expert noted much later, utilizes an inherently "filmic mode of perception."[16] The secret to the "fabulous mobility" of Daumier's figures, Eisenstein wrote, can be attributed to "the fact that various parts of the bodies of [his] figures are depicted in spatial situations (positions) that vary temporally" (*Montazh*, 522; *Works*, 1:165). By collapsing a series of postures into the silhouette of one figure, Daumier has captured an entire chain of events—an entire narrative—in a single frame.

Whereas it seems at first glance that Daumier is depicting a conventional figure here, Eisenstein thus argues that Ratapoil's individual body is in fact a multiple. Cautioning the viewer against being taking in by this body's specious holism, Eisenstein explains that Daumier's achievement "lies in the fact that despite the difference between the stages of movement in the various limbs, they contrive to retain an overall impression of the *wholeness* of the total figure. . . . It is quite obvious that in this picture his arm is 'anatomically' broken at the elbow. . . . [T]he phases of the scene are deployed between groups of participants who are, in essence, depicting *the successive stages of a single act*" (*Montazh*, 159–160; *Works*, 2:111). Examining the physiques of Daumier's figures carefully, the spectator discovers that these bodies are in fact anatomically impossible. In his analysis of temporality in the graphic arts, Florenskii called this aspect *coincidentia oppositorum*, explaining that the compression of time within a static image produces a dramatic impression of "anatomical contradiction" within its figures."[17] Such bodies, Eisenstein observed, may "contrive to retain an overall impression of the *wholeness* of the total figure," and thus at least superficially resemble the organic figures found in realist art, but they are in fact fractured and broken. The same disintegration of the human body found in Daumier's caricatures prompted Benjamin to the insightful remark that "no one has depicted bodily enervation and debility as fascinatingly as Daumier" (*Schriften*, 2:500; *Writings*, 3:281). But what Benjamin reads as physical debility Eisenstein interprets as a condition of multiplicity. Like Brecht's *gestic* actor, these figures have been taken apart, combined with others, and then reassembled. According to the Soviet filmmaker, the "anatomical spatial disproportion of the parts" in Daumier's bodies, which gives these physiques their fractured quality, points toward a new montage practice that is fragmentary and mechanical at the same time that it is holistic and natural (*Montazh*, 522; *Works*, 1:165).

It is hardly a coincidence, then, that Eisenstein began frenetically to draw caricatures at the same time that he renounced the aggressive montage cutting of his early works such as *Strike* and *Potemkin*. For the practice of caricature offered a continuation of montage by other means—means that were, at least superficially, in closer concert with the humanist idiom of the day. At a time when the radical montage practices of experimental film were increasingly under attack by the advocates of the new proletarian realism, Eisenstein, in a brilliant move, turned to caricature as a model for a purely organic mode of montage that sublated the distinction between the fragment and the whole, the mechanistic and the anthropomorphic. His later films make increasing use of caricature to supercharge the image and create what he designated as "conflict within the frame" (*внутрикадровый конфликт*). In this way, despite their extremely static mise-en-scène, films such as *Ivan the Terrible* still manage to produce an impression of utmost tension and dynamism. The segmented bodies that Eisenstein drew in his studies for films like *Ivan* (fig. 5.2) closely resemble those found in Daumier's caricatures: "The way the arm and the leg, the torso and the extremities correlate in their common movement *is not the same*—the way they are *linked up*, or interconditioned, is different from the way they are in normal organic movement."[18] When correctly composed, "a single shot will explode into a chain of shots" in

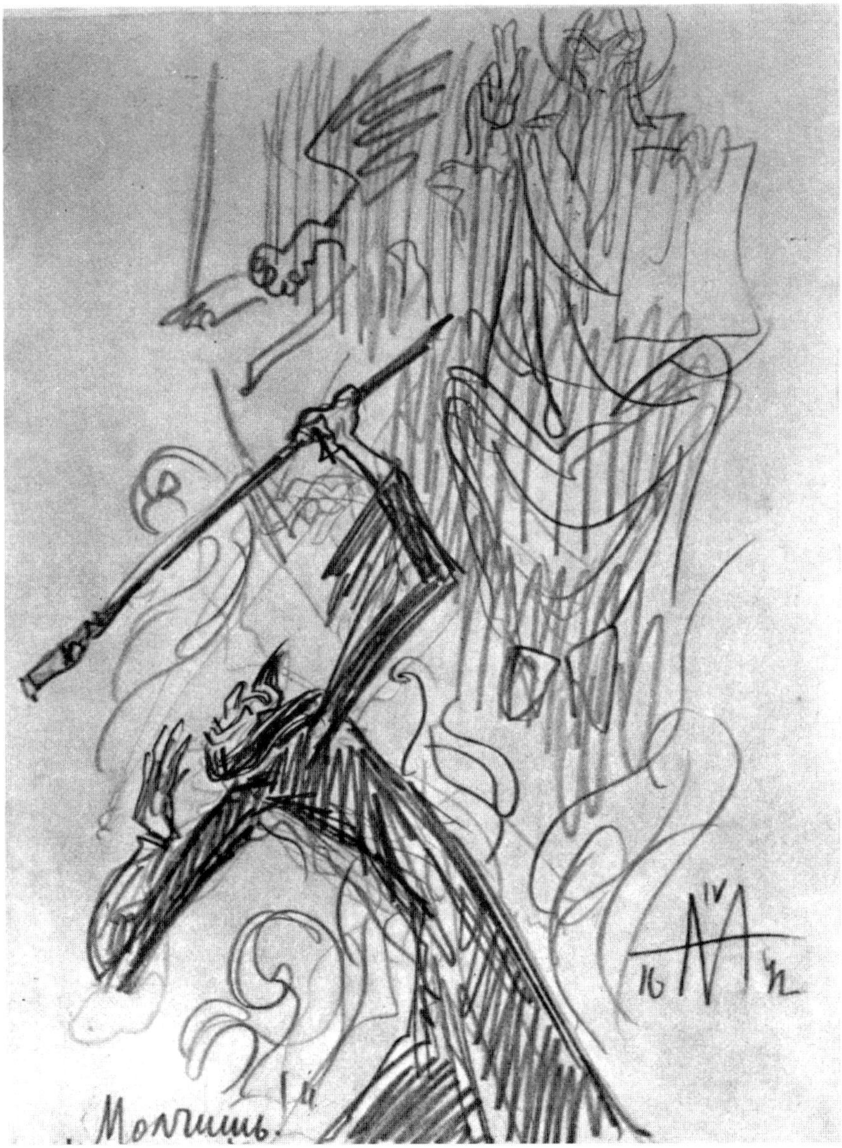

Figure 5.2 Sergei Eisenstein, drawing for *Ivan the Terrible* (1942). Russian State Archive of Literature and Art.

the mind of the viewer (*Montazh*, 106; *Works*, 2:56), releasing a compressed kineticism that projects, in Eisenstein's famous phrase, "beyond the shot" (*за кадром*).

Eisenstein's analysis of montage procedures in caricature bears no less upon the work of Heartfield. The latter's immensely successful 1928 election poster for the German Communist party, *A Hand Has 5 Fingers* (*5 Finger hat die Hand*; fig. 5.3), for example, utilizes the same dynamic technique of fracture and reassembly found in Daumier's caricatures. One of many works in which Heartfield takes up the iconography of the hand, this poster depicts the instrument of manual production as an agent of political representation. While the visual impact of the poster seems initially to spring from the simple, graphic starkness of the solitary hand, upon closer examination, the singularity and unicity of the hand gives way to a complex concert of elements, both linguistic and graphic. The poster enacts a series of semantic displacements allegorizing the movement from the individual to the collective on multiple registers: first, the splayed fingers together comprise the basic instrument of manual labor, the symbol of the industrial working class; by casting a vote, in turn, the isolated laboring hand is socialized and integrated into the political collective; finally, Heartfield's hand acquires a verbo-linguistic aspect and learns to speak, as it were: the count of the fingers, as the poster proclaims, also correspond to the abstract number five (the designation for Communist Party on the 1928 ballot), making this mute appendage into a means of expression and an organ of calculation. In this poster, the hand simultaneously labors, legislates, and communicates.

It is important too that the subsumption of the individual into the collective—the device that Eisenstein designates as *pars pro toto*—is never completed or closed in Heartfield's poster. The hand remains open and internally segmented, like a poised spider. In his 1936 monograph on the photomonteur's work, Tret'iakov touched upon this aspect in Heartfield's work using terms resonant with Eisenstein's analysis of *Ratapoil*: "For the sake of expressiveness, Heartfield adjusted the photograph of the hand itself, extending the fingers where necessary and then dislocating the thumb even more sharply [*резче*] to the side," he writes about *A Hand Has 5 Fingers*.[19] As with Daumier's bodies, which, Eisenstein observed, are "'anatomically' broken," Heartfield's hand has been segmented and then

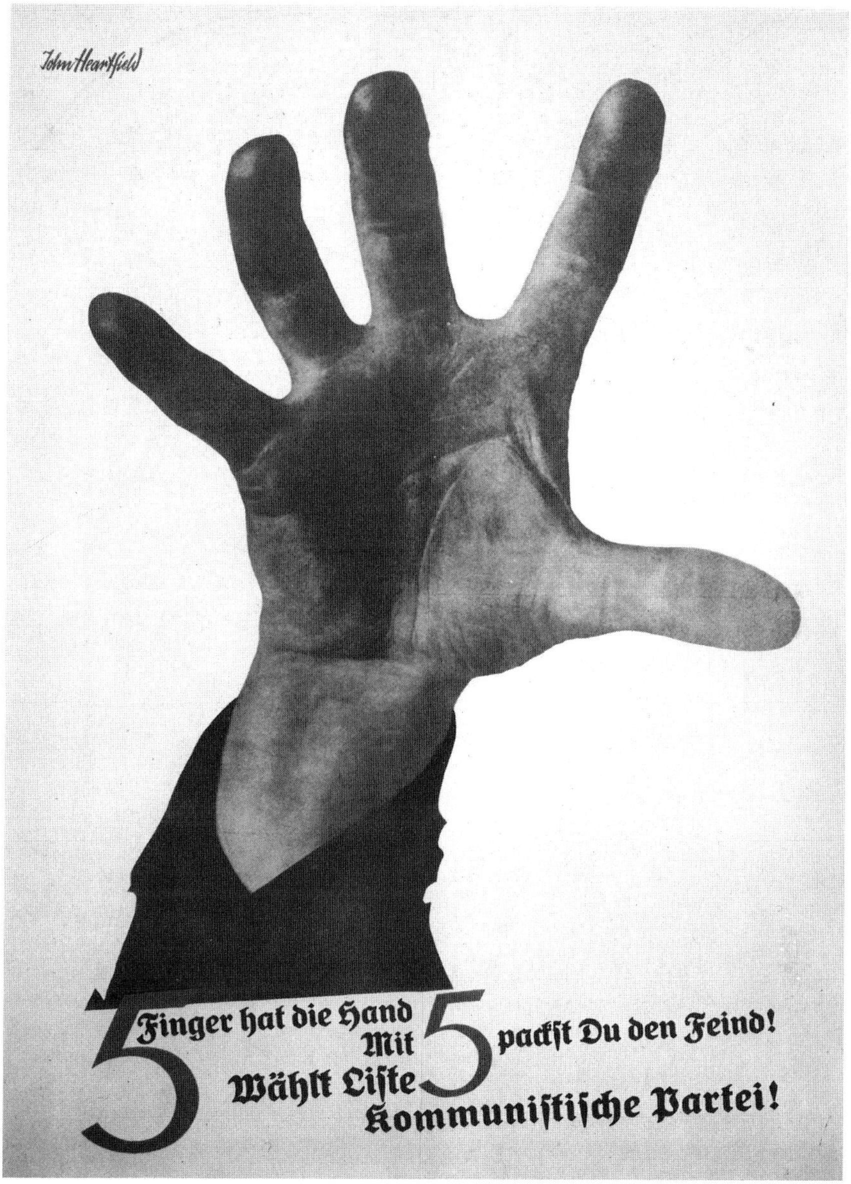

Figure 5.3 John Heartfield, *A Hand Has 5 Fingers* (1928). © 2012 Artists Rights Society (ARS), New York/VG Bild-Kunst, Bonn.

sutured back together to create a new pictorial totality. Despite its seemingly unified gestalt, then, the hand turns out to be a deft orchestration of several discrete photo-elements, a compound figure that is assembled through a process of montage. The quality of "expressiveness" (*выразительность*) that Tret'iakov imputes to the hand designates the same experience of temporal compression and logical contradiction that Eisenstein perceives in Daumier's caricatures.[20] The *coincidentia oppositorum* of the hand explodes, like a filmic sequence, into an entire series of hands. This decompression reverses the allegory of political representation by dissolving the collective figure into multiple individuals.

While the stark composition of *A Hand Has 5 Fingers* may seem at first glance to be relatively straightforward, closer analysis thus reveals an intricate network of interlocked visual and linguistic elements. The polyvalence of Heartfield's work becomes all the more apparent when the poster is compared to the work of other photomonteurs such as Gustav Klutsis. For all its graphic impact, the constructivist design for *All Men and Women Workers: To the Elections of the Soviets!* (1930, fig. 5.4), for example, lacks the elaborate network of semantic interdependencies and slippages found in Heartfield's election poster, where the verbal and the visual continuously inflect one another. In Klutsis's constructivist poster, image and caption mirror each other perfectly in a closed and univocal semantic system. For this reason, when Klutsis found his work repeatedly compared with that of Heartfield in the early 1930s, the juxtaposition was rarely to the benefit of Klutsis, whose posters, under the ascending star of socialist realism, were denounced as formalist because they were optically more striking but rhetorically less ambitious than Heartfield's.[21]

Where Dada photomontage once sought to demotivate the sign semantically—Peter Sloterdijk has called this the "semantic cynicism" of Dada[22]—the works that Heartfield began to produce after 1924 inclined instead toward a condition of rhetorical and hermeneutic surplus. In his 1936 monograph on Heartfield, Tret'iakov christened this technique *переосмысливание*, a neologism that we could translate as "*re*coding," but, since the Russian prefix used here also implies an action taken to the point of excess, could also be rendered in English as "*over*coding" or "*over*semanticization." Tret'iakov considered this surplus the

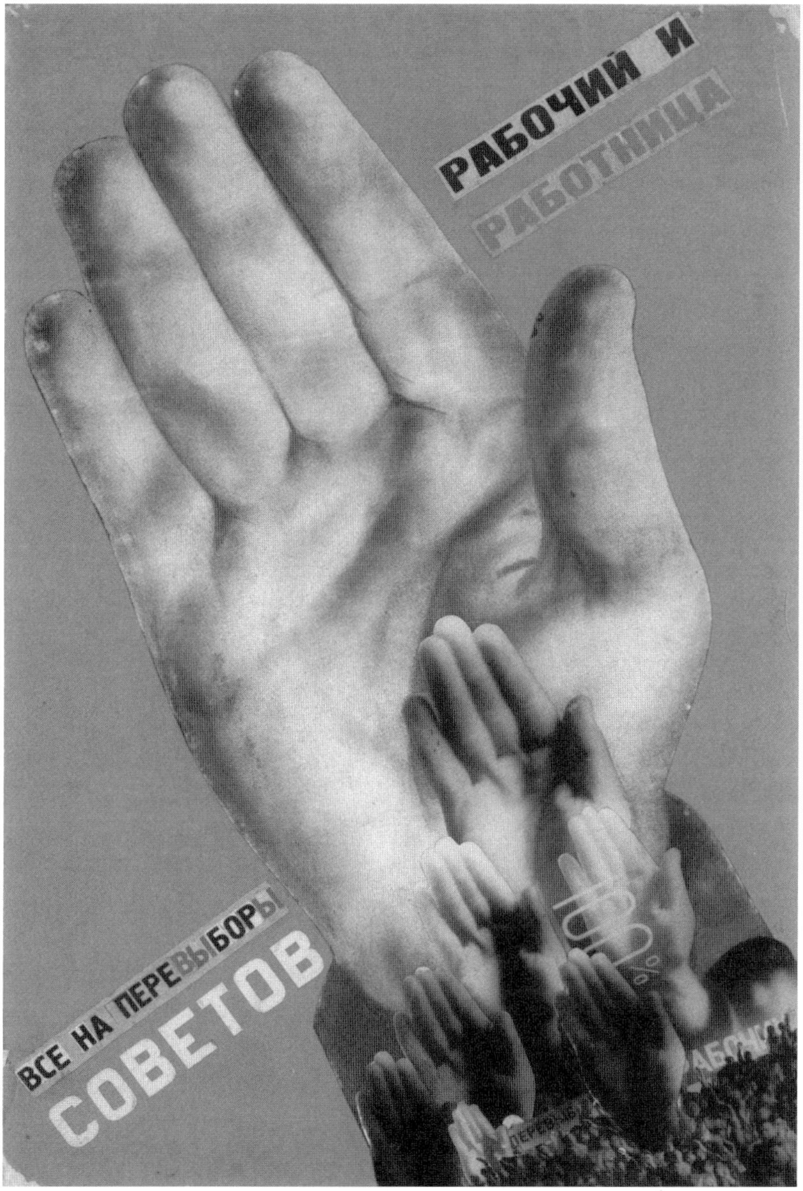

Figure 5.4 Gustav Klutsis, *All Men and Women Workers: To the Elections of the Soviets!* (1930). © 2012 Estate of Gustav Klutsis/Artists Rights Society (ARS), New York.

very sine qua non of photomontage: "photomontage begins where mechanical juxtaposition is replaced by mutual inflection, where an overcoding of the photograph takes place, where we see before us multiplication rather than addition."[23] Simply putting together an assortment of photo-fragments does not in and of itself constitute photomontage, Tret'iakov wrote, since this is a process of mere accumulation. One speaks of photomontage only once these pieces have been assembled in a way that supercharges the image semantically, giving rise to dynamic visual impressions and a multiplicity of potential interpretations. When putting his compositions together, it was important to Heartfield that he not erase the original context in which the image first appeared, but instead superimpose onto this first connotative field a second series of associations that inflect and transform the original object semantically. Heartfield always worked with found photographs and readymade language because semantically unmarked images and words lacked the plural meanings he required and were therefore useless to him. He required a palimpsest, not a tabula rasa. Thus, where Dada strove for semantic nihilism (fig. 1.1) and constructivism semantic univocity (fig. 5.4), Heartfield's later photomontages instead court semantic excess, resulting in what Tret'iakov called "overcoding," or what Günther Anders, in his review of Heartfield's 1938 show in New York, likewise called "polyvalence" (*Vieldeutigkeit*).[24]

Such strategies of overcoding are the very essence of caricature, a word that derives from the Italian verb *caricare* ("to load," "to burden") and that has come to designate a supercharging, or exaggeration, of an object's distinctive features. The French term for caricature, *portrait charge*, or "loaded likeness," conveys this same aspect. For this reason, in his comprehensive history of caricature, Fuchs defined his subject by this quality of excess: within a caricature, he observed, objects are necessarily "freighted too heavily" (*zu stark belastet*).[25] Here the strategies of caricature overlap with those of the grotesque, an idiom that, as we saw in the previous chapter, Carl Einstein used extensively in his autobiography. Indeed, much like *Bebuquin II*, Heartfield's photomontages employ the protocols of mimetic realism, although they follow these scripts to a point of excess, exploding the tightly regulated economy of pictorial illusionism by a process of figural "trampling."

Heartfield crowds multiple figures into a single body without, however, fully harmonizing them. These compound physiognomies can be resolved logically only when they are projected across the axis of time—decompressed, as it were, in the mind of the spectator. The process of "multiplication," as Tret'iakov calls it, recalls the proto-cinematic quality of Eisenstein's caricatures, in which an individual figure explodes into an entire series of postures. It was for this reason that the critic Aleksei Fedorov-Davydov sensed in Heartfield's work a particular temporal condensation and narrative overdetermination that was at conflict with its graphic clarity: "Despite its pithiness and simplicity, and despite the simultaneity with which the viewer perceives it, [Heartfield's work] is unquestionably narrative, at least insofar as it triggers a complex sequence of logical associations and forces the spectator to ponder it at length."[26] Like Daumier's *Ratapoil*, Heartfield's overcoded image demands that the viewer unspool the figure cinematically, a process that Fedorov-Davydov described as an "unfolding [*развертывание*] of the events in time."[27]

Because, as Fedorov-Davydov argued, all of these works open onto a narrative dimension, there is no facet of Heartfield's photomontages uncontaminated by language, no space of purely optical perception. Even in those works bearing no textual caption, or in those lacking the verbal puns for which Heartfield was so famous, the linguistic is never far off. Consider *The Loyal Subjects* (*Die Untertanen*), a photomontage depicting a petty-bourgeois family standing before a military parade, which appeared in the 1929 volume that Heartfield published with Kurt Tucholsky, *Deutschland, Deutschland über alles* (fig. 5.5). Compared with his later covers for the *AIZ*, which, like baroque emblems, set up an elaborate rhetorical complex consisting of *inscriptio*, *pictura*, and *subscriptio*, the structure of *The Loyal Subjects* seems relatively straightforward. With their backs to the viewer, a family stands passively in the foreground, taking in the impressive spectacle of the troops marching before them. The composition anticipates *Forced Supplier of Human Matériel* (*Zwangslieferantin von Menschenmaterial*, 1930), a work that generates meaning, as Tret'iakov pointed out, through the collision between two spatial vectors, the horizontal one above and the vertical

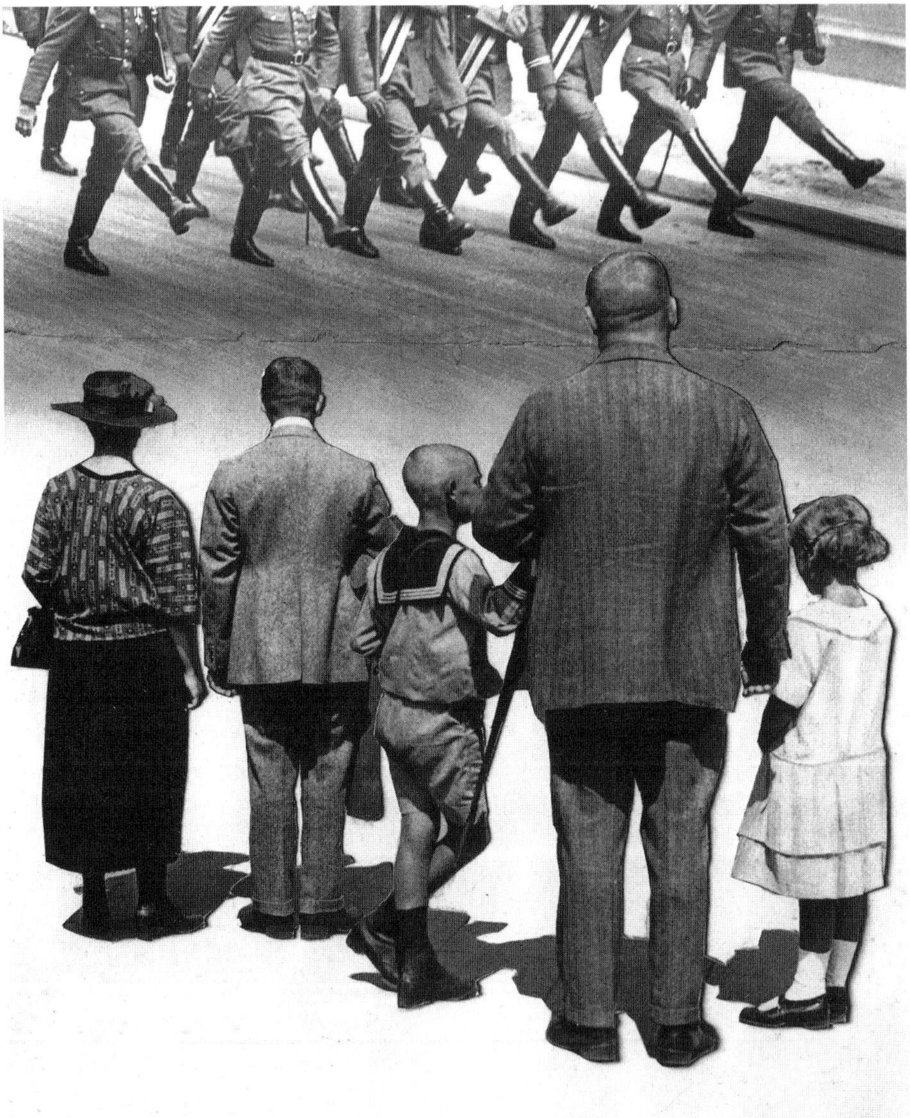

Figure 5.5 John Heartfield, *Die Untertanen*, from *Deutschland Deutschland über alles* (1929). © 2012 Artists Rights Society (ARS), New York/VG Bild-Kunst, Bonn.

one below. Encoded as two distinct moments in time, these two axes posit a kind of before-and-after sequence: in *Forced Supplier*, a pregnant proletarian below carries the child that she will soon bear, who is already dead on the battlefield above, while in *The Loyal Subjects*, a son wears a sailor costume in a dress rehearsal of his approaching assimilation to the military machine on display before him. Heartfield delivers an entire narrative within a single image. This literary aspect explains the curious presence of language even in his works that make no use of words. Although it has no caption, although it doesn't contain a single letter, *The Loyal Subjects*, for example, invokes the graphemic signifier at the top of the image, where the legs of the goose-stepping troops are iterated serially, giving this lateral phalanx a distinctly typographic appearance, like a headline of inverted *V*s. Flowing from left to right, the line of troops observes the spatial orientation of the written word, which, in European print culture, has always commanded the horizontal axis. This latent rhyme between the limbs and the letter would become even more pronounced later that year when Heartfield redeployed *The Loyal Subjects* on the cover of a Münzenberg publication, with the legs now appearing directly adjacent to the title of the magazine (fig. 5.6).

Certainly one of the most productive conceptual approaches for understanding the dynamics of meaning within the hybrid scripto-visual spaces of photomontage would be Freud's model of the dream-rebus. Circulating among the deeper psychic registers where "word-presentation" (*Wortvorstellung*) and "thing-presentation" (*Dingvorstellung*) are indistinguishable, the dream spans together linguistic signs and image signs. Already in *The Interpretation of Dreams* (1900), Freud discerned a structural resemblance between the dream and the visual practices of montage when he opened his investigation of the dream-work with a description of an oneiric rebus: "a house with a boat on its roof, a single letter of the alphabet, the figure of a running man whose head has been conjured away."[28] Freud's words read like a description of a surrealist montage *avant la lettre*. Elaborating upon this filiation between montage and the dream, some have subsequently claimed that montage more closely conforms to the structure of fantasy and the preverbal primary processes than does abstract, logical language.[29]

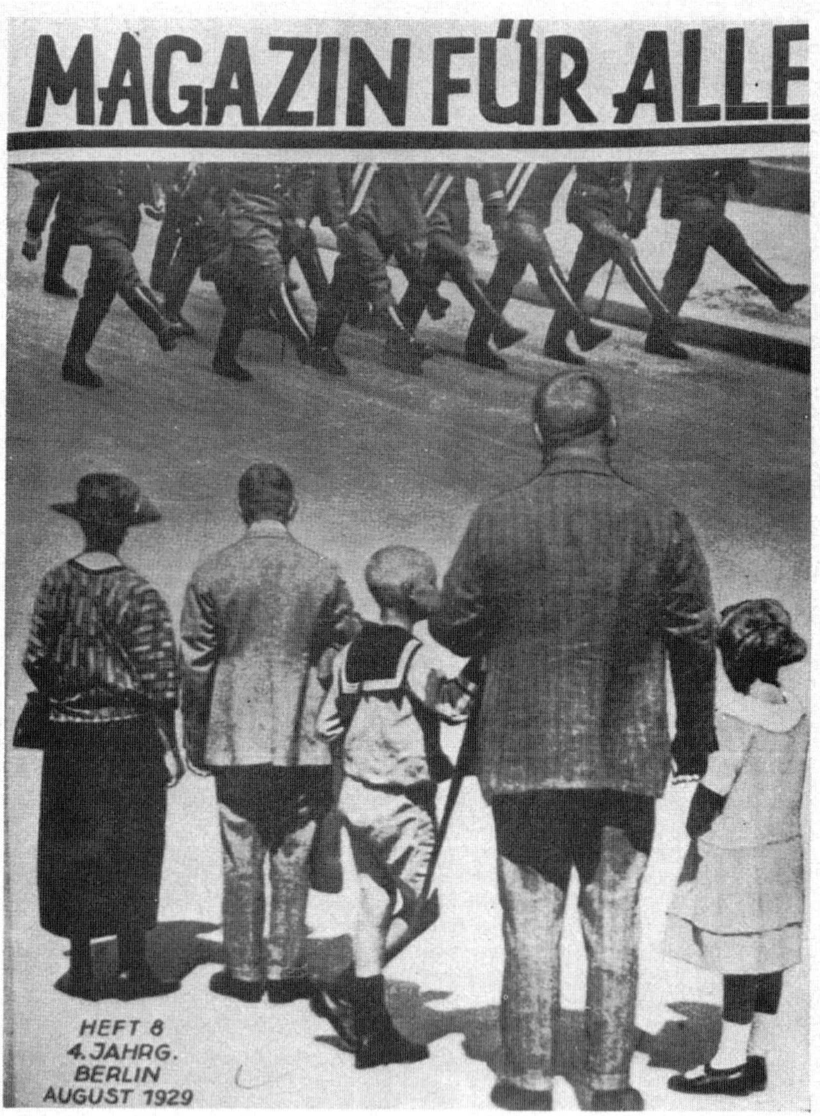

Figure 5.6 John Heartfield, *Die Untertanen*, on cover of Münzenberg's *Magazin für Alle* (1929). © 2012 Artists Rights Society (ARS), New York/VG Bild-Kunst, Bonn.

It is not surprising, then, to discover in psychoanalytic accounts of the dream the same paradoxical temporality, and the same strategies of figural compression, that we have been developing over the previous pages. In words that echo Eisenstein's reading of Daumier's caricatures and Fedorov-Davydov's analysis of Heartfield's photomontages, Lyotard, for example, observed that "the oneiric or quasi-oneiric stage" perforates the achronism of figural representation with the sequentiality of verbal discourse, resulting in the "possibility of the incompossibles, occupation of a single space by several bodies or of a single body in several positions, simultaneity of the successive, consequently, approach of a timelessness which will be the chronical pendant of this 'topological' space."[30]

The structural resemblance between the dream and montage is confirmed by the discovery, within Heartfield's work, of both of the primary mechanisms for transcoding between sign and image that are native to the dream, namely, condensation and displacement. As an example of the former we can cite his famous 1932 *AIZ* cover, *The Meaning of the Hitler-Salute: Millions Stand Behind Me!* (fig. 5.7). As is typical for Heartfield's work, the point of departure for this montage is a press photograph that was already in wide circulation, a picture of the Führer performing his signature salute before a mass of troops.[31] Pulling this clichéd motif out if its original context, a military inspection, Heartfield then recodes the gesture as a financial transaction. The gist of the piece hinges on the word *millions*, which, in Hitler's famous phrase, designated the multitudes that support him, but which now, after Heartfield's semantic *détournement*, refers to the millions of marks paid by the consortium of German industrialists who poured capital into the National Socialist Party after 1928. Like a Wittgensteinian duck-rabbit, the word "million" compresses two distinct meanings into a single lexeme, producing the effect that Tret'iakov called "overcoding." In his study of jokes, Freud dwells at length on words such as these that are generated through a dream-like process of condensation, citing as an example an anecdote in which a speaker characterizes her treatment by the wealthy Solomon Rothschild as being "quite famillionaire"—a *Mischwort* ("composite word") made out of the distinct words *familiar* and *millionaire* (*Werke*, 6:17; *Standard Edition*, 8:19). Eisenstein too foregrounded the use of

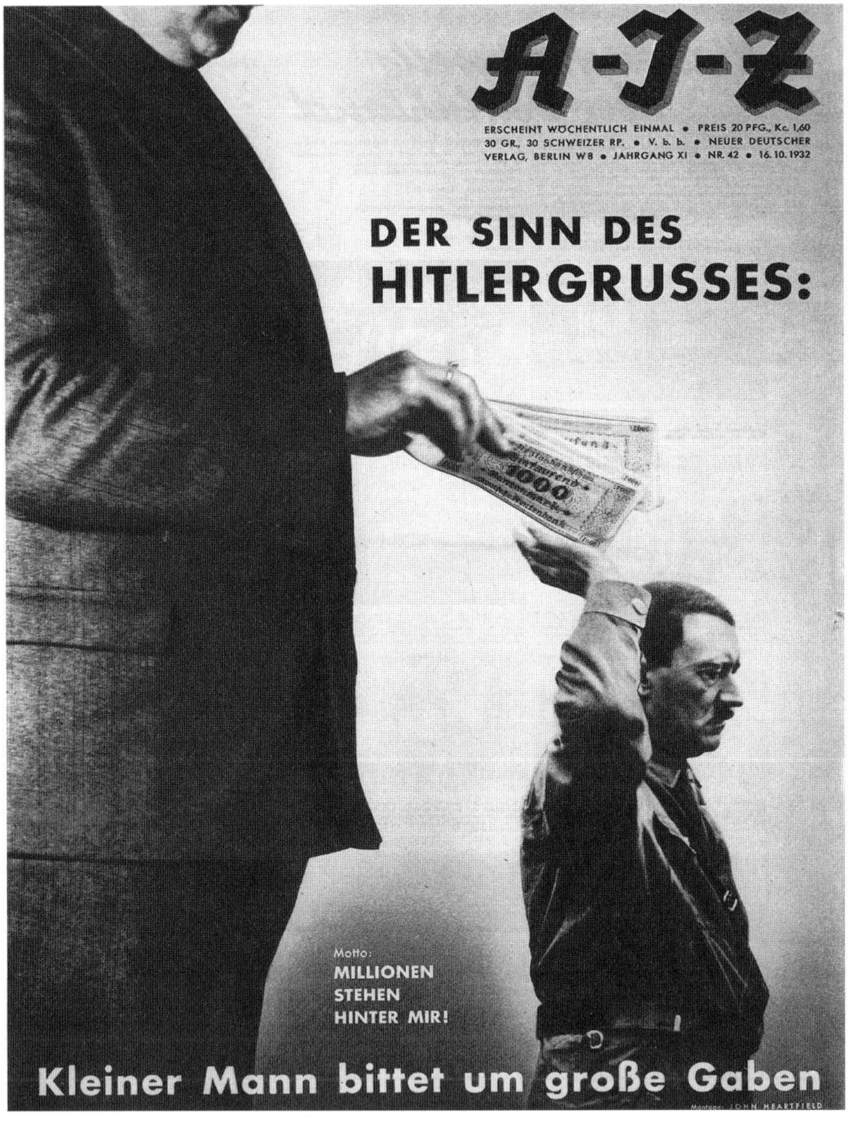

Figure 5.7 John Heartfield, *The Meaning of the Hitler-Salute: Millions Stand Behind Me!* (1932). Image courtesy the Research Library, Getty Research Institute, Los Angeles. © 2006 Artists Rights Society (ARS), New York/VG Bild-Kunst, Bonn.

hybrid words in his 1938 essay on montage, where he argued that Freud's bizarre portmanteaux captured the monteur's technique of semantic condensation:[32] *Kleptorumania* (kleptomania + Rumania), *Cleopold* (Cleo + Leopold), *alcoholidays* (alcohol + holidays).[33] Like the single frame that explodes into a full-blown cinematic sequence, the semantic compression of *millions* in Heartfield's photomontage begets an elaborate commentary on the support base of the National Socialist Party. This grafting of millions (of marks) onto millions (of supporters) dramatically transforms the valence of the piece's visual elements in turn. Once the dual aspect of the "millions" has been grasped by the spectator, Hitler's entire comportment and countenance change as well: suddenly his famous salute no longer looks turgid and imperious but appears flaccid and receptive; his mien is no longer stern and exacting, but downcast and defeated. The charismatic and popular Führer is unmasked as the passive pawn of monopoly capital.

Strategies of displacement are no less common in Heartfield's photomontages, whose complex chains of associations often rely on concrete visual forms to provide the intermediary semantic links between words. Fluidly combining word-presentation and thing-presentation, these compound visual assemblages realize the representational strategies that are detailed in Freud's discussion of the rebus. Here words acquire concrete sculptural values to become "a plastic material with which one can do all kinds of things" (*Werke*, 6:34; *Standard Edition*, 8:34). As a corollary to Freud's formula, one could cite as well Aragon's enthusiastic discovery, in his 1930 essay on collage, that "painters are truly beginning to use objects as words."[34] In the photomontages of Heartfield, where the act of reading is never wholly separate from that of seeing, the word's plastic quality is no less significant, no less expressive of meaning, than is its abstract, lexical dimension. As the Formalist Grigorii Vinokur pointed out in an important 1924 essay "The Language of Typography," the form of a typeface, the use of capital letters, the relative sizes of fonts to one another, the spatial hierarchy of the page, and so forth, are all graphic signals whose contributions to the meaning of the printed word are just as important as intonation and gesture are to the meaning of the spoken utterance.[35] So, for example, in his 1931 book cover for Upton Sinclair's *Mountain City*, translated into German under the title *So macht man Dollars* (*How to make dollars*), Heartfield twice exploits the sculptural values of the capital *S* at the beginning of the title, transforming it first into a dollar sign, which in turn becomes a ladderlike scaffold that the bourgeois figures scramble up in an allegory of capitalist competition (fig. 5.8). These two displacements transform the abstract taxonomy of language into a physical figure, discourse into perception.[36]

The pertinence of the psychic devices of condensation and displacement for an analysis of works such as *The Meaning of the Hitler-Salute* and *How to make dollars*—one could elaborate endlessly on these two examples using Freud's psychic machinery—indicates that there may be more at stake in the use of montage than mere technique or style. Indeed, montage is not just an artistic strategy of assembly, but an instrument of thought itself, albeit one whose materialist modality differs fundamentally from that of the purely verbal sign. Again and again Heartfield was praised in the 1930s by critics who marvel at his ability to motivate photographic material semiotically, to transform the image into a sign without recourse to abstract conceptual discourse. Anders, for example, rhapsodized about how Heartfield "*creates signs out of the visible fragments* that he combines,"[37] just as Aragon, in his narrative of Heartfield's return to meaning after Dada, wrote that the "pieces of photos he had arranged in the past for amazement and pleasure, now under his fingers began to *signify*."[38] Similarly, in the Soviet context, Heartfield's montage strategies were regularly compared to a process of cognitive induction whereby thought advances from the perception of the isolated sensory datum to the synthetic judgment. One critic, for example, admired Heartfield's particular talent for "artistic generalization" (*художественное обобщение*) that "reorganizes contingent relations, separating the important and typical from the secondary and particular."[39] Fedorov-Davydov likewise observed that Heartfield's photomontages bestow "the form of generality and regularity to the individual and the particular."[40]

Tellingly, the word used by Heartfield's Russian commentators to designate this process of cognitive induction, *обобщение* ("generalization"), is the same term that is utilized in Eisenstein's writings to identify the materialist mode of thought found in montage. Earlier in the twentieth century, *обобщение* was typically paired and contrasted with the term *абстракция* ("abstraction"),

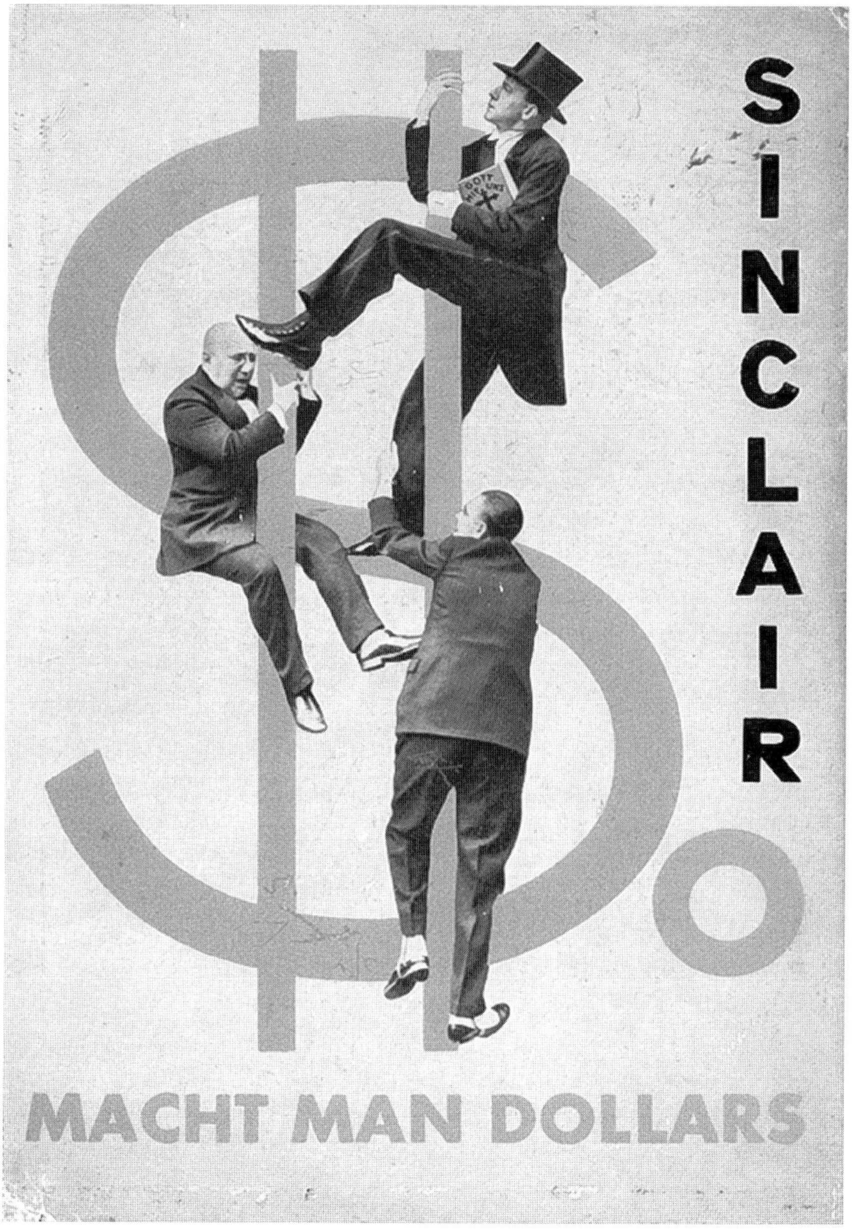

Figure 5.8 John Heartfield, book cover for *So macht man Dollars* (1931). Courtesy of Galerie Bassenge, Berlin. © 2012 Artists Rights Society (ARS), New York/VG Bild-Kunst, Bonn.

which was associated with the metaphysics of the verbal sign as explicated by structural linguistics. Eisenstein, for one, famously likened the inductive strategies of montage "generalization" to the forms of signification found in the writing systems of Asian languages, whose ideogrammatic characters functioned at once as both picture and sign. And in his later essays, he insisted that montage was not a mere technical device—something specific to cinematic production—but could be discovered in all forms of art and materialist thought, from poetry and literature to theater and painting. As opposed to the top-down movement of abstract, deductive logic, montage proceeds, Eisenstein explained, by bringing together two sensuously concrete signifying elements, whose collision creates an "unexpected juncture" (*нежданный стык*) from which an idea springs forth. Herein lay the essential distinction between, on the one hand, *generalization*, which is a mode of sensuous signification that preserves the material heterogeneity of the elements that it connects, and, on the other, the Enlightenment's model of linguistic *abstraction*, which, aspiring to a condition of semiotic transparency, valorizes the ideational content of the signified over the empirical particularity of the sign. The rationalist discourse of abstraction would eventually culminate, at the turn of the twentieth century, in the Saussurian doctrine of semiotic arbitrariness and its corresponding poetological system, a modernist movement that, as the previous chapter argued, absolutized the imagination and its power to nihilate sensuous particularity. If, in the structuralist model of meaning, which Voloshinov insightfully dubbed "abstract objectivism," cognitive abstraction is achieved through the subsumption of the concrete token into the conceptual taxon, montage generalization arrests the vertical movement of this semiotic, creating meaning instead through lateral connections among the material tokens themselves.

Among the various visual idioms in which this strategy of cognitive generalization can be found, the language of caricature has always ranked among the most important. In this regard, caricature is nothing less than a philosophical device, Adorno suggested. Writing in 1939 about Daumier's works, he explained that these drawings grant a "very special status to the concept of the type: in each image of the *particular*, as rendered in an outsized nose or a set of bony shoulders, an image of the *general* is to be captured at the same time, much the same way that Balzac, in describing Nucingen, tends to present his eccentricities as those of the species of the banker in general."[41] Adorno's words here, which are strikingly resonant with Eisenstein's discussions of montage, claim caricature's vocation to be that of bridging the chasm between empiricism and idealism that has grown insuperable in the modern world. Successful caricature discovers lateral systems of likeness among the features of individual specimens and articulates these connections through the calculated exaggeration (*caricare*) of their distinctive characteristics, thereby arranging the manifold chaos of lived experience into an orderly body of knowledge. Through its visual embellishments and systematic distortions, which posit resemblances among the most disparate of phenomena, caricature creates networks of association among material forms without recourse to abstract conceptualization.

THE PHYSIOGNOMIC DIVIDUAL

Such systems of material correspondence have, since the seventeenth century, been the subject matter of the science known as physiognomics. A field of study whose fortunes since the Baroque have been closely tied to the practice of caricature, physiognomic analysis seeks to situate the features of the unique specimen within a general code of visual morphemes and replicable elements, in order to uncover underlying structural resemblances that cut across a group of individuals. If, as we just saw, Adorno discerned in caricature a movement from the particular to the general, in his subsequent discussion of physiognomic analysis he observed the same process of connecting specimen and type, albeit now in a reversed polarity: the "physiognomic gaze, which extravagantly highlights the distinguishing detail in contrast to featureless uniformity, has no other purpose than to rescue the particular within the general," he wrote.[42] Although the study of physiognomics has a long tradition extending back to antiquity, the field burgeoned in the nineteenth century in response to urbanization and the emergence of mass society, which generated an acute psychological need for orientation in the contingent and socially deterritorialized conditions of metropolitan existence. Within this social context, physiognomics provided a lexicon for translating the anonymous face into a set of meaningful signs, thereby rendering navigable the impersonal sea of bodies that were encountered in urban life on a daily basis. Thus, for example, as the narrator of E. A. Poe's celebrated short story "The Man of the Crowd" (1840) gazes upon the undifferentiated throng of London's inhabitants, he explores physiognomic perception as a practice that connects the general to the particular: "At first my observations took an abstract and generalizing turn. I looked at the passengers in masses, and even thought of them in their aggregate relations. Soon, however, I descended to details, and regarded with minute interest the innumerable varieties of figure, dress, air, gait, visage, and expression of countenance."[43]

As a recent spate of scholarship on the subject has shown, physiognomic analysis, which had always been intimately connected to the social structures of mass industrial society, exploded once again during the interwar period to become a dominant hermeneutic paradigm.[44] Indeed, if physiognomics had previously limited itself to the analysis of the figure and the face, in the Weimar era networks of physiognomic resemblance expanded far beyond the human body to embrace all sorts of phenomena, both organic and inorganic. The writings of authors ranging from Béla Balázs and Ernst Jünger to Kracauer and Benjamin abound with references to the "physiognomies" of everything from consumer articles and natural landscapes to vehicles and artworks. Everywhere people looked in the 1920s, a human countenance looked back at them. On one level, the sudden ubiquity of the physiognomic model during this period reflects a widespread desire to give a human face, as it were, to the artifacts of technical civilization. As this book has shown, this will to anthropomorphize was typical of the interwar years. Yet the prevalence of physiognomics in the discourse of Weimar Germany was much more than just a popular humanist trope. No longer just a complex of family resemblances among people, at this moment physiognomics became the foundation for an entire structure of knowledge. Indeed, as we will see, the meteoric ascent of the physiognomic sign during the interwar years reflected a global transformation within systems of signification as they shifted away from the linguistic semiotic that had earlier reached its apogee in the poetics of modernism.

Heartfield's contemporaries often located his work within this new semiotic model. Ranging over statements made about the photomonteur, it is typical to encounter the claim that Heartfield "interprets physiognomies," as one photographer who worked with Heartfield put it.[45] In a discussion of his famous 1933 *AIZ* cover *Goering: Executioner of the Third Reich* (fig. 5.9), Heartfield himself insisted that "an image of Goering with an effective caption forces the viewer to consider his physiognomy, his features."[46] Heartfield's choice of examples here is particularly apt. The real impact of *Goering* is not the result of the superadded caption, which details one of the many abuses of the Reich's justice system by the Nazis; nor is its visual effectiveness entirely attributable to the shocking collection of butcher's attributes that the photomonteur gives to Goering—ax and apron, spattered with blood. The most striking and unforgettable feature of the photomontage is instead physiognomic: the dislocation of Goering's shrieking head. Although the intervention here is technically quite minimal, by shifting his head forward, Heartfield completely transforms the disposition of Goering's face. As a result of this subtle displacement, the head of Goering, now thrusting forward rather than upward, no longer falls in with the vertical alignment of the human body. This violation against the erect posture of man unmasks Goering as a beast in human guise, a quadruped that has reared up in mimicry of human posture. Suddenly the spectator no longer looks upon Goering as one looks upon a human face, as a sum of distinctive and individual traits, but instead regards the Nazi officer as a representative of an animal species. Heartfield trades in the gaze of the humanist for that of the zoologist. Like the famous sketches by Charles Le Brun exploring resemblances between human faces and species of fauna (fig. 5.10), the photomonteur's physiognomic intervention animalizes Goering's face. The effect of this translation is so total, so startling, that Heartfield even disclaimed in small print below the image that he had not in fact altered his subject's features at all: "Goering's face is taken from an original photograph and has not been retouched." Rather than distort or rearrange the facial lineaments themselves—expanding the mouth out into a maw, say, or stretching the nose into a snout—he instead alters the spectator's perceptual framework itself, invoking the physiognomic gaze so that

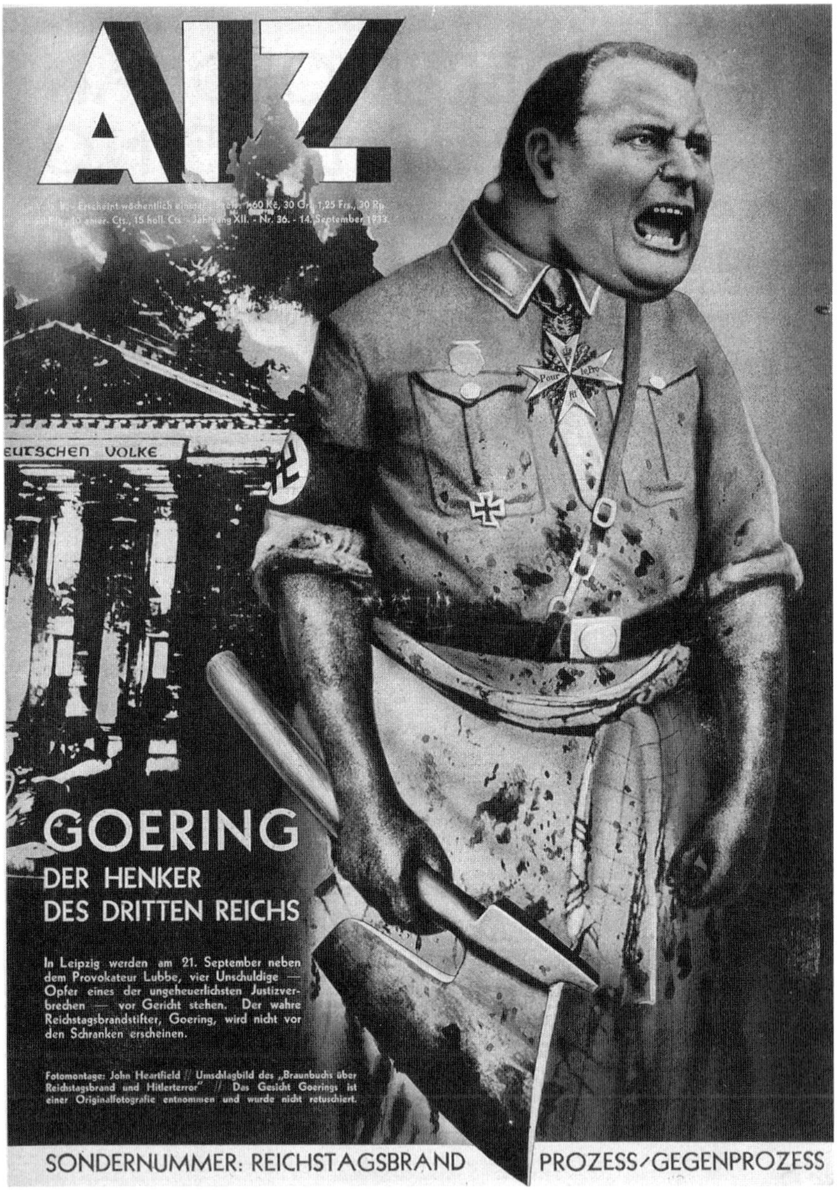

Figure 5.9 John Heartfield, *Goering: Executioner of the Third Reich* (1933). Image courtesy the Research Library, the Getty Research Institute, Los Angeles. © 2012 Artists Rights Society (ARS), New York/VG Bild-Kunst, Bonn.

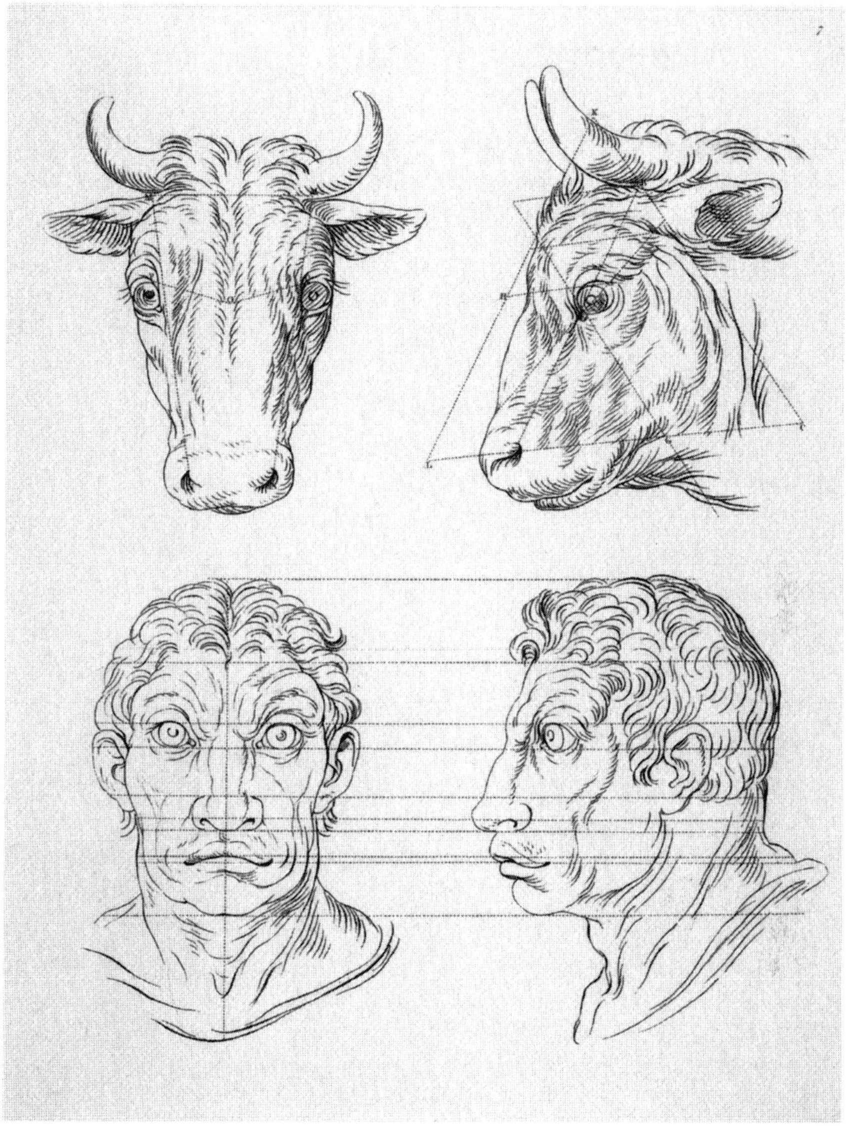

Figure 5.10 Charles le Brun, *Deux têtes de boeuf et deux têtes d'hommes en relation avec le boeuf.* Louis-Jean-Marie Morel d'Arleux, *Dissertation sur un traité de Charles Lebrun concernant le rapport de la physionomie humaine avec celle des animaux*. Paris, Chalcographie du Musée Napoléon, 1806.

the image of Göring reads as a type not a person, an animal breed not an individual human. What results is a complex allegory of Germany's self-destruction at the hands of the Nazis: Goering is at once both the executioner and the beast to be slaughtered.

To be sure, the resurgence of physiognomic depiction during the interwar years was a deeply ambivalent cultural phenomenon, found among artists of diverse political stripe who, despite their partisan differences, shared a common disdain of the ideology of bourgeois humanism. So, for the left, social physiognomy provided a way to envisage the collective subject, while the right essentialized physiognomic into a racist pseudo-science, developing a biological discourse that was eventually used to justify the eugenic policies of the National Socialists. In both cases, however, it is clear that the human face that returns in interwar art is now a serialized structure, no longer an inviolable locus of individuality but an assemblage of coded elements that undermines all claims to uniqueness. Nowhere was the physiognomic assault on the ideology of individualism better exemplified than in August Sander's *Face of Our Time* (1929). This famous portrait atlas of Weimar Germany has two radical aspects. First is the objective and scientistic style of Sander's photography, which, free of all sentimentalizing, captured his sitters with utter indifference as if they were biological samples under a microscope. These photos lay bare the human face, denying it any possibility of equivocation or concealment. Still more striking, however, was Sander's subsequent arrangement of these individual specimens within a grand social taxonomy, which unfurls a series of physiognomic likenesses laterally across the faces of his subjects (figs. 5.11, 5.12). As the viewer pages through the book, Sander draws attention to the networks of similitude that cut across the social strata, blending the individual faces together and integrating the unique human countenance into a portrait of the mass subject. Cultural conservatives such as Max Picard, a staunch defender of humanist ideals and the author of *The Limits of Physiognomy* (1937), were appalled by the serial quality of the faces in photo-books such as Sander's, which Picard denounced in a 1932 review:

> as we leaf past the faces, [it is] as if the border separating one face from the other also vanishes; we do not see the individual face in

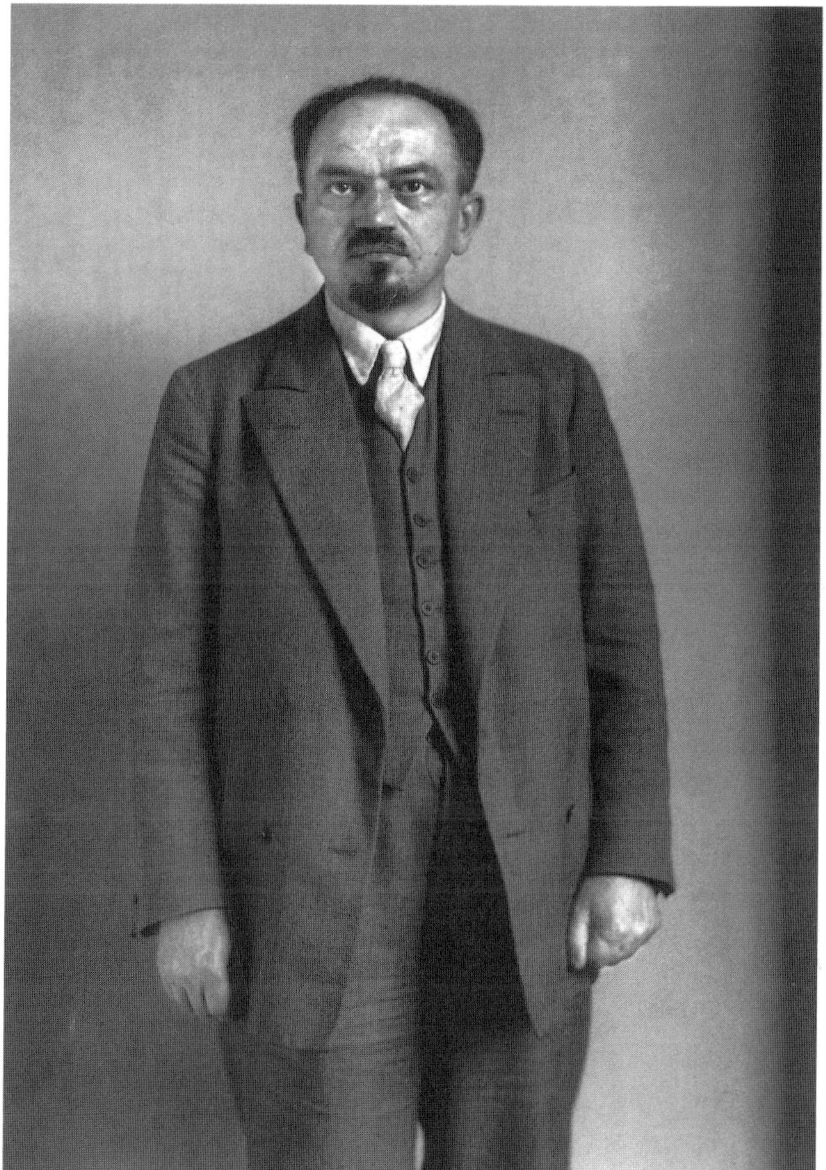

Figure 5.11 August Sander, *Communist Leader* (1929). © 2012 Die Photographische Sammlung/SK Stiftung Kultur—August Sander Archiv, Cologne/Artists Rights Society, New York.

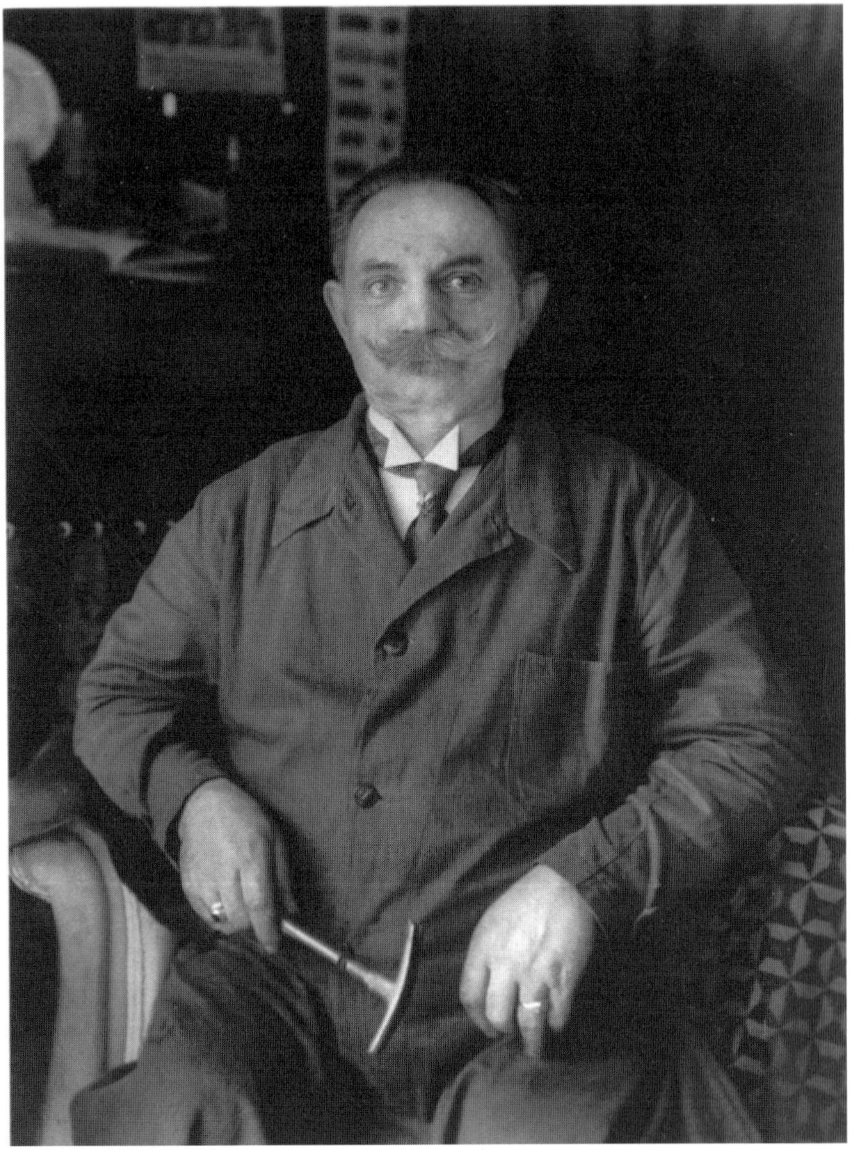

Figure 5.12 August Sander, *Master Upholsterer, Berlin* (1929). © 2012 Die Photographische Sammlung/SK Stiftung Kultur—August Sander Archiv, Cologne/Artists Rights Society, New York.

> and for itself; turning onto a new page, we continue to see in the face that opens before us a piece of the one that we have just leafed past, and at the same time we anticipate the face that is to follow; one face blurs into the next; the faces roll past us as if on a film strip. . . . These cinematic books of faces are like an apparatus that loosens the fixed image of the face: instead of teaching us how to hold a face fast, they teach us how to take it apart and make it to disappear.[47]

Even more objectionable than the cold, scientific idiom of these portraits, even more anti-humanist than Sander's overexposure of the face, Picard wrote, is the placement of these photographs within a serial system that, positing lateral correspondences between the sitters, gathers all of the distinct faces together into a single "face of our time." Specific traits—the particular arc of an eyebrow, the attitude of a hand, a creasing of the eye—reappear again and again throughout the book, connecting all of the sitters together in a vast taxonomy of central European civilization.

Such sequences of similarity are the stock-in-trade of physiognomic signification. Heartfield's most aggressive photo-caricatures push such patterns of resemblance to the point of absolute equivalence, where the face is reduced to a matrix of serialized signs. In one work, for example, the head of a bourgeois is replaced with an empty zero (fig. 5.13); in another, a judge is transformed into an automaton who mindlessly executes the letter of the law (fig. 5.14). In absorbing utterly the individual face into the abstract type—and indeed, here, into the typeface—such photomontages realize the violence inherent to all caricature, which, as the psychoanalyst Ernst Kris and E. H. Gombrich observed in a 1940 pamphlet, divides the face into iterable graphemes as a "means to annihilate [the sitter's] individuality." If "the very word 'in-dividual' means inseparable," Kris and Gombrich propose, caricature's parsing of the face transforms the heroic individual into a dividual.[48]

Heartfield radicalized this strategy of physiognomic "dividuation" in his notorious back cover for the 1930 Malik translation of Upton Sinclair's *Money*

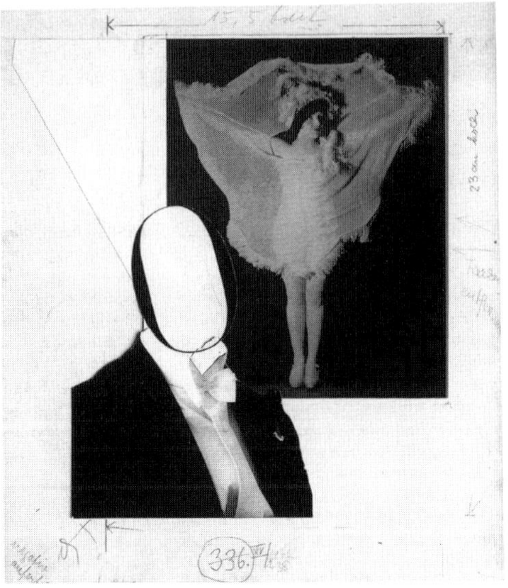

Figure 5.13 John Heartfield, *This? This is the Age, It Cries out for Satire*, from *Deutschland Deutschland über alles* (1929). © 2012 Artists Rights Society (ARS), New York/VG Bild-Kunst, Bonn.

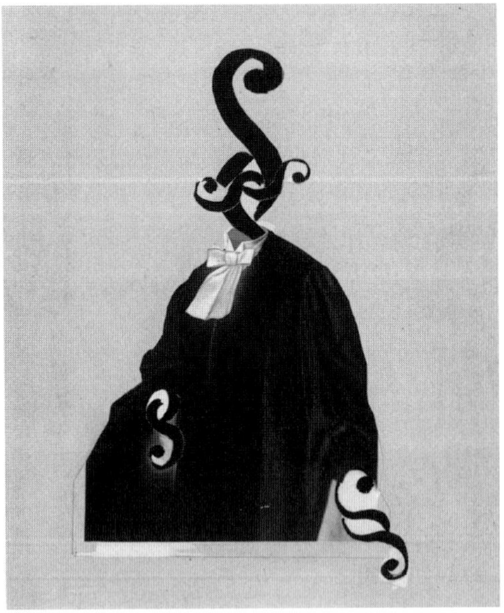

Figure 5.14 John Heartfield, *I only Know Paragraphs*, from *Deutschland Deutschland über alles* (1929). © 2012 Artists Rights Society (ARS), New York/VG Bild-Kunst, Bonn.

Writes. A study in the economics of literature, *Money Writes* (1927) was a critique, in Sinclair's words, of "my own tribe, the men and women of letters who sit perched upon the apex of sophistication and look with scorn upon all mass emotions."[49] On the back of this broadside against the caste of "human urchins," as Sinclair described these writers, Heartfield reproduced, without any identifying caption, a picture of the German author Emil Ludwig relaxing with his family on the terrace of their Swiss estate (fig. 5.15). Here Heartfield's choice of photographs was doubly motivated. On the one hand, Ludwig was immensely successful financially and thus a perfect representative of that class of literary condottieri who spin words into gold. At the same time, the subject matter from which this particular author had made his fortune as a writer was itself deeply ideological, for Ludwig achieved literary fame in the 1920s as the premier writer of psychological biographies, producing in that decade alone bestsellers on Goethe, Bismarck, Napoleon, Michelangelo, and Lincoln. As Kracauer observed in his essay "Biography as an Art Form of the New Bourgeoisie," written the same year Heartfield produced his cover for *Money Writes*, Ludwig was the most influential and prodigious promoter of the ideological cult of the great individual.[50]

Although Malik Press had legally acquired the rights to the publicity photo of the Ludwig family, the author litigated to have the photo removed from the book cover, invoking the "right to one's own image" (*das Recht am eigenen Bild*) and claiming damage to his person.[51] This law had been put in place at the turn of the century, when legal theorists confronted increasing anxiety around the loss of control over technically reproduced images of private citizens in photography and cinema.[52] The "right to one's own image" sought to reassert the ontological privilege of the subject over his likeness, the unique original over his simulacrum. Importantly for the Ludwig case, however, there was one notable exception to this law: the "person of contemporary history" (*Person der Zeitgeschichte*) was not given the same legal immunity against duplication that was granted to private individuals, since the general public, it was claimed, had a right to be informed about these popular personages. Ironically for Ludwig, then, the success of his lawsuit to remove the image from Sinclair's book hinged on his ability to demonstrate that he was *not* a "person of contemporary history."

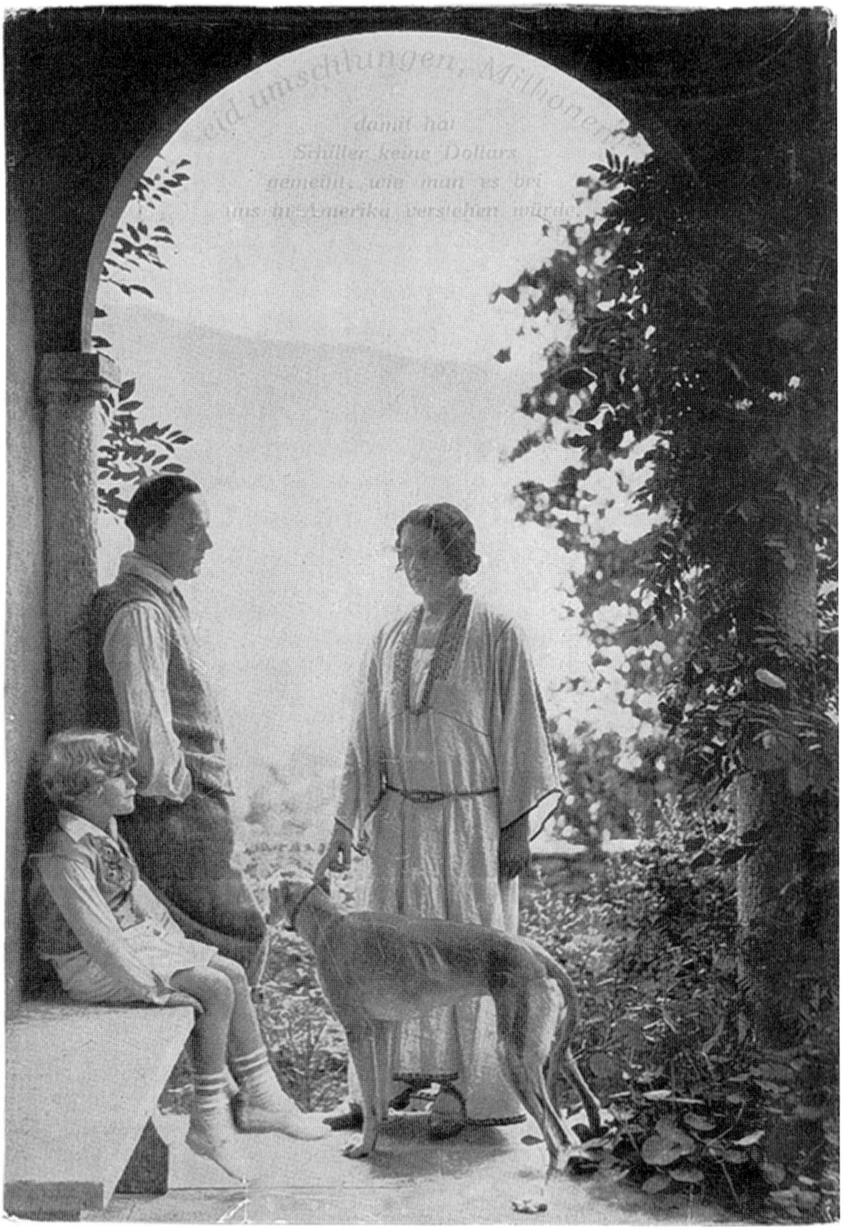

Figure 5.15 John Heartfield, original back cover of *Das Geld schreibt* (1930). Courtesy of Galerie Bassenge, Berlin. © 2012 Artists Rights Society (ARS), New York/VG Bild-Kunst, Bonn.

To win his case, Ludwig, the ideologue of the great individual, had to show the world that he was himself not a figure of any significance. He, unlike the heroes of his biographies, had to prove that he was himself a nobody.

Rather than become embroiled in Ludwig's lawsuit, Heartfield elected simply to censor his work, removing from the back cover the heads of the entire Ludwig family, together with their dog (fig. 5.16).[53] He was forced, as Tret'iakov recounted, to design the image "*без личностей*"—a Russian phrase meaning "without identifying" the subject, but also "without personality" or even "without the individual" tout court. Here Heartfield's particular strategy of de-facement is especially canny, for instead of simply concealing the faces of his subject, he physically punched out the heads from the photograph, leaving behind in each one's stead a uniform oval hole through which the reader could see the text of Sinclair's book below. He thereby turned the image into a kind of picture-puzzle, inviting the viewer to an imaginary game in which each of the cut-out heads could be slotted into any of the other holes in the image, including, most insultingly, the one on the dog's body. Each identity, human and animal, became completely interchangeable. In this way, the system of family resemblances among the Ludwigs yielded to relations of sheer equivalence.

This second version of the cover, which was understandably "even more insulting to the German censors and to the writer than before it was corrected," as Tret'iakov noted, demonstrates the threat that generalization poses to the individual and to the conceit of humanism generally.[54] Brecht, too, encountered this very lesson the same year as Heartfield, when the agit-film he made with the communist Ernst Ottwalt *Kuhle Wampe* was censored, surprisingly, not because it showed its audience the real misery of working class existence—which it did—but because it showed this misery in terms that were all too general and schematic, because the characters were not sufficiently individuated. "I reproach your depiction for not seeming sufficiently *human*," the censor informed Brecht. "You have not depicted a person but, well, to put it frankly, a type. Your unemployed worker is not a real individual, not a person made of flesh and blood, and distinct from every other person, with his own particular worries, particular joys and finally his own particular fate" (Brecht, *Werke*, 21:459).

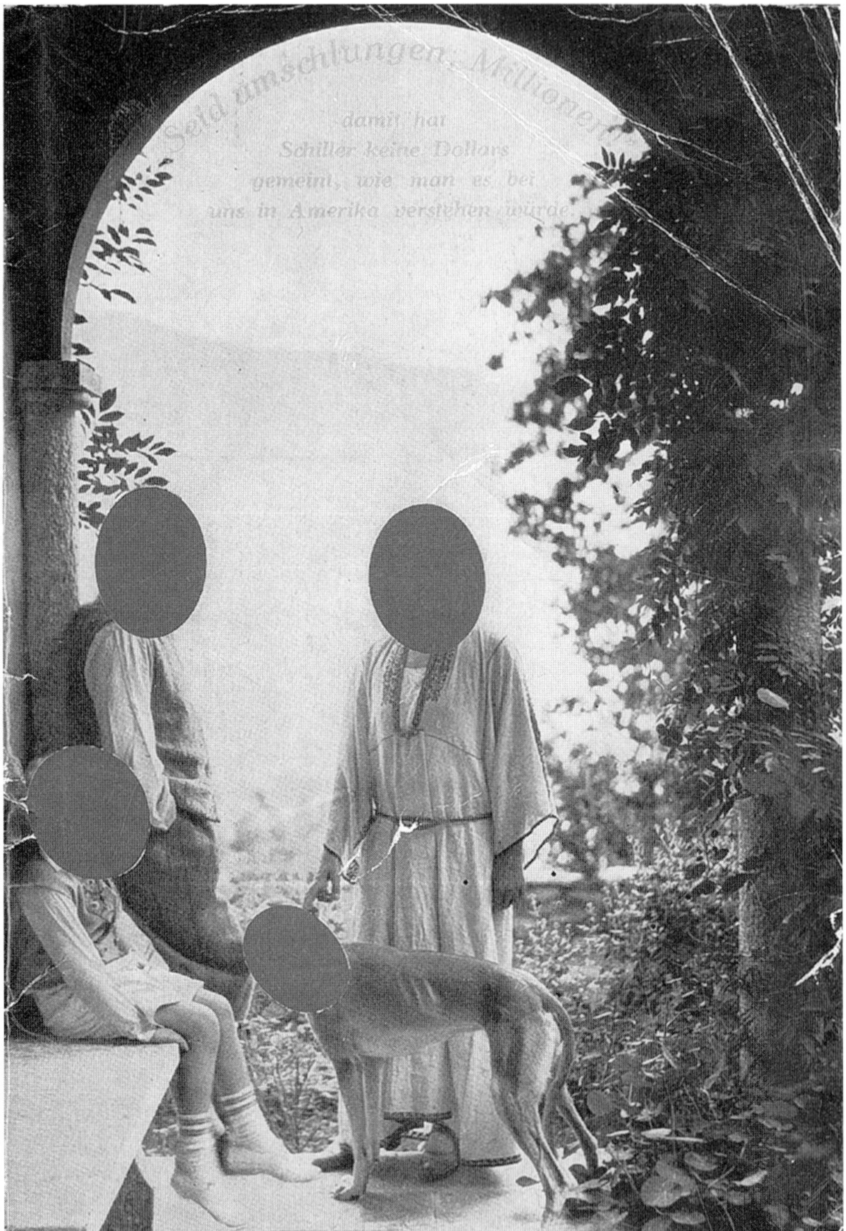

Figure 5.16 John Heartfield, censored back cover of *Das Geld schreibt* (1930). Courtesy of Galerie Bassenge, Berlin. © 2012 Artists Rights Society (ARS), New York/VG Bild-Kunst, Bonn.

As the art historian Wilhelm Waetzoldt pointed out his *Art of the Portrait* (1908), a study that was formative for Heartfield's thinking about physiognomy,[55] the genre of portraiture, like physiognomics, mobilizes those relations of similitude that in German are called *Ähnlichkeiten*.[56] In the book's key chapter, "The Problem of Similitude"—a section which Heartfield explicitly referenced in a talk on portraiture—Waetzoldt explained that relations of *Ähnlichkeit* are of a general semiotic nature, relevant not just to the activity of the portraitist but also to the very operations of visual representation. For Waetzoldt, the portrait cultivates the same patterns of likeness that can be found in many other strategies of depiction, although no other pictorial genre establishes the particular bond between image and subject quite so powerfully. Here Waetzoldt drew a categorical distinction between the *Abbild*, a mere copy that remains ontologically secondary and subordinate to the original, and the *Bildnis*, or portrait proper, which replaces relations of reference with networks of similitude. Whereas the copy is grounded and stabilized in a system of external reference, the portrait's patterns of similitude, by contrast, are dynamic and mutable (*Kunst des Porträts*, 122–130). Relations of *Ähnlichkeit*, Waetzoldt explained, are never static, but vary over time. He wrote, for example, of the paradox of the portrait's "*becoming* similar" (*das Ähnlich*werden) to its model, and referenced cases in which the original model "disappears completely" behind its representation (*Kunst des Porträts*, 94). For this reason, just as much as a portrait resembles its sitter, the sitter can also come to resemble her portrait. According to Waetzoldt, the purpose of the *Bildnis* is not to duplicate the face perfectly, then, but to investigate the structural laws that organize the face and to extrapolate from them a likeness that gives expression to this visual isomorphism. Thus, if the *Abbild* delivers an accurate facsimile of the original person, the *Bildnis* instead delivers a prototype, a matrix of common analogies shared by the sitter and the image.

If Waetzoldt's attempt in "The Problem of Similitude" to outline a non-referential relationship between object and image raises sweeping questions about the nature and mechanisms of representation generally, why then does he limit the ambit of his analysis to the face and to genre of portraiture specifically? This is because, he suggested, the human face constitutes such an incredibly rich repository of these correspondences. It exhibits a degree of organization unparalleled among phenomena. Although other parts of the body are also organized according to structural patterns and morphological laws, the face alone "condenses the organizational principle [*Organisiertheit*] of the human figure" (*Kunst des Porträts*, 35). This structuration can indeed be found scattered in all living organisms, but, Waetzoldt added, it is only in the human face that this organizational principle finds its most cogent and robust articulation. With reference to Georg Simmel's 1901 essay "The Aesthetic Significance of the Face," which argued that the defining quality of the face was the "integral connectedness of its features," Waetzoldt thus concluded that "within the human figure the face possesses the highest degree of integrality" (*Kunst des Porträts*, 36). As evidence of the extreme degree of organization found in the face, he cited the fact that the smallest alteration to a single feature, whether through injury or distortion, will destroy the entire balance of the facial system. Indeed, Waetzoldt continued, there is "a kind of reciprocity" (*eine Art Wechselwirkung*) among all of the face's various parts (*Kunst des Porträts*, 102). Semiotically speaking, we could say that the face is a highly motivated construction.

Waetzoldt's analysis of the problem of similitude suggests, then, that the face exemplifies a structure of knowledge, albeit one that differs fundamentally from that of the linguistic sign, which operates strictly within a referential system of meaning. Whereas in the science of structural linguistics the sign is always a secondary image of the referent, physiognomic correspondences are not subject to this dualist distinction between original and copy. As a result, they are more dynamic, more open to revision, than the stable, vertical relations of reference established by the structuralist sign. But this does not mean that this network of material *Ähnlichkeiten* is unsystematic, random, or associative. As Waetzoldt forcefully demonstrated, quite the opposite is the case: the relations of similitude captured in the human face are in fact the very apex of *Organisiertheit*. "The organization of the face is a strong one," Deleuze and Guattari insist, echoing Simmel and Waetzoldt. "We could say that the face holds within its rectangle or circle a whole set of traits, *faciality traits*, which it subsumes and places at the service of signifiance and subjectification."[57] If, for structural linguistics, connections between phenomena are established by common membership in a universal category (e.g., all writing implements that make marks with graphite are grouped together as "pencils"), the relations of similitude established by physiognomic correspondence lack this abstract taxon, moving instead horizontally, from face to face and thing to thing. Physiognomic thinking is heuristic rather than definitional, demonstrable yet not exponible. Thus, in his account of *Ähnlichkeit*, Waetzoldt describes a form of knowledge that cannot be circumscribed by abstract discourse: "By 'similitude' we mean a relationship among the contents of consciousness that is fundamental to the coherence of our system of mental representation [*Vorstellungsleben*]—a relationship that cannot be defined more precisely, but can only be demonstrated by experiencing it" (*Kunst des Porträts*, 85). It may not be possible to communicate these relationships to others using definitional language, but this imperviousness to discourse does not condemn similitude to the realm of subjectivism and personal intuition. To the contrary, the experiential aspect of similitude underscored by Waetzoldt recalls the structure of aesthetic judgment itself, a category of knowledge whose modality, to be sure, differs fundamentally from that of critical reason, but which nonetheless constitutes a universal and generalizable form of experience that, following Kant, becomes the basis for an embodied *sensus communis*.[58]

Buoyed by the proliferation of the physiognomic sign, research on the relations of similitude surged during the interwar period, as we earlier observed. Benjamin, for one, made remarkable forays into this territory with two texts from 1933, "Doctrine of the Similar" and "On the Mimetic Faculty." In these essays, Benjamin described a contest between two structures of signification: a mimetic one established on relations of similitude ("magical correspondences") and an arbitrary one based on the abstract linguistic signifier ("an agreed-upon system of signs").[59] The historical evolution of human thought can be summarized as a shift from the former to the latter, he proposed. Whereas once, in antiquity, mimetic correspondences could be detected everywhere—in stars, entrails, runes, dances—the aptitude for perceiving these connections had vastly atrophied by the modern era, leaving only the abstract sign to organize experience and make sense of the world. While the ability to perceive correspondences can still be observed in its full potency in the mimetic behavior of children, Benjamin noted, the adult continues to see these systems of similitude consciously only in faces. With the increasing disenchantment of the world, the structure of knowledge contained in these networks of likeness falls into disrepute, banished into the occult spheres of clairvoyance and magic, downgraded to pseudo-sciences such as graphology and astrology. Under the conceptual regime of the linguistic sign, physiognomy becomes the only remaining sphere where it is still possible to experience these networks of analogy in a fashion that is at least somewhat systematic. The perception of similitude in other phenomena having become fleeting, oblique, and random, the face is the only remaining vestige of an entire semiotic system.

For all its brilliant insights, Benjamin's analysis of *Ähnlichkeit* is fettered by the esoteric idiom of these essays, which characterize similitude as a form of "linguistic magic" and liken physiognomy to a pre-lapsarian, naturally motivated mode of signification.[60] Turning eastward, however, we find a less obscure, more materialist account of the same phenomenon in the contemporaneous research of the developmental psychologist Lev Vygotsky, whose 1934 opus *Thinking and Speech* analyzes the issue of similitude in a manner that is both theoretically precise and experimentally demonstrable. In this text, Vygotsky, like Benjamin, set about correcting a certain linguistic bias within current models of cognition that wrongly privilege, as he put it, the "purely verbal aspect" of higher mental activity.[61] Vygotsky explained that humans utilize two distinct modes of thought. On the one hand is thinking by means of the concept (*понятие*), which he equated with modern rationalism. Distinguishing categorically between material phenomena and the abstract plane of meaning, this dualist model understands ideation as a form of knowledge that proceeds by constructing categories or sets according to abstract definitions. From this perspective, which is promulgated in "contemporary linguistics," as Vygotsky noted—the Russian translation of de Saussure's *Course in General Linguistics* had appeared the previous year—higher thought is understood as a logical process of linking empirical particulars to general concepts.

Building on the recent research of the German developmental psychologist Heinz Werner, Vygotsky conducted experiments to ascertain the laws of a far more elusive and seemingly unsystematic mode of intellection that Vygotsky dubbed "thinking in complexes" (*комплексное мышление*). Like Benjamin, Vygotsky discovered this second mode of cognitive generalization in its purest form in the behavior of children, whose "leaps of thought," "unpredictable generalizations," and "decentered associations" he similarly admired (Vygotsky, *Myshlenie*, 137). The child does not think according to the abstract definitional categories of the adult, Vygotsky observed: she will be able to learn the words for "chair," "table," and "bed" relatively quickly, but the abstract taxon "furniture," which encompasses all of these concrete objects conceptually, will not be available to her until a much later developmental stage. Even when the child uses the words of the adult, then, she uses them in a way that is entirely incompatible with rationalist thought, for she organizes her experiences according to complexes and groups rather than concepts and classifications. Children and adults may share the same words, but, because their thoughts are patterned according to different structural laws, the correspondences in their speech are entirely superficial. Indeed, that children and adults can communicate at all with each other is a mere felicity, Vygotsky explained, since they are in fact speaking two completely different languages.

Unlike conceptual thought, in which all particular phenomena must share the same defining trait, or set of traits, in order to belong to an abstract class, thinking in complexes eschews the fixed definitions of formal logic, arranging knowledge instead into horizontal chains of similitude (*цепные комплексы*, or "chain complexes").[62] Within such a complex, he wrote, "the individual links are connected together dynamically and temporally so that they form a single chain in which meaning is transferred [*перенос значения*] across the separate links of this chain" (*Myshlenie*, 144). No single link in this sequence of laterally connected signs can encompass or exemplify the thought in its entirety, since the semantic effect, the production of meaning, is achieved here by a sequence of associations that moves along the entire length of the chain of signs. Each individual link within this semantic chain has some combination of the traits shared by other members of the group, but there is not necessarily any single trait common to them all. Because there is no one defining feature that all members of the group share in common, a chain complex "lacks any kind of core": the "end of the chain may have nothing at all in common with the beginning," Vygotsky observed (*Myshlenie*, 135).

Whereas the child thinks exclusively by means of complexes, the adult utilizes both systems of cognition, even if she does not recognize it. "The speech of adults is full of the vestiges of thinking in complexes," explained Vygotsky, who illustrates his point, significantly, using the example of family resemblance, specifically, the family name:

> The best example in our speech that uncovers the fundamental constructive law behind a given thought complex is the family name. Any family name such as "Petrov" encompasses a complex of individual objects that closely approximates the character of the complex found in children's thinking. In a way we could say that the child, when it arrives at a certain level of development, begins to think by means of family names, or, to put it differently, the world of individual objects is unified and organized for him by grouping them into distinct families that are connected to one another. (*Myshlenie*, 140)

The individual members of these physiognomic families, Vygotsky explained, cannot be subsumed into an abstract ideal type. Twice in *Thinking and Speech* he derided, for example, the composite photographs of Francis Galton, the Victorian anthropometrist who claimed to produce a comprehensive typological atlas of various "families" (Jews, consumptives, criminals, etc.) by superimposing photographic exposures of individual members of this class. He compared Galton's method to structuralist thought, which proceeds "in a mechanical fashion, summarily . . . by means of a gradual transition from the concrete to the abstract" (*Myshlenie*, 129). This method, however, effaces the concrete traits possessed by individual members of the "family," erasing all empirical particularities to arrive at an image of an abstract type that does not in fact exist in reality.

The difference between thinking in concepts and thinking in complexes can be illustrated using the following table:

	traits
	1. ABCD
members	2. CDEF
	3. EFGH

Confronted by three phenomena with overlapping combinations of traits A through H, experimental subjects using concept-thinking approach the task of classification differently that those using complex-thinking. For the former, phenomena 1 and 2 would be grouped together in the category defined by the traits CD, just as phenomena 2 and 3 would belong together in the category "EF," while phenomena 1 and 3 could not be reconciled within a shared abstract class since they have no single trait in common. This is not the case, however, in complex-thinking, which would group 1 and 3 together based on a likeness that is mediated by member 2. In the case of complex-thinking, meaning is not contained within the abstract conceptual category CD or EF, but is instead displaced across the entire chain of objects, in which the qualifying features change from one link to the next. Thus, whereas thinking in concepts maps out phenomena in abstract taxonomies, thinking in complexes arranges phenomena into sequences. In his own investigations of similitude, Ludwig Wittgenstein would consequently liken the latter signifying structure to a rope: "We find that what connects all the cases of comparing is a vast number of overlapping similarities, and as soon as we see this, we feel no longer compelled to say that there must be some one feature common to them all. What ties the ship to the wharf is a rope, and the rope consists of fibres, but it does not get its strength from any *fibre* which runs through it from one end to the other, but from the fact that there is a vast number of fibres overlapping."[63] Complex-thinking, as exemplified by the experience of family resemblance, is structured not like a grid, but like a thread—and a potentially infinite thread at that, since the introduction of additional members doesn't just expand the parameters of the group quantitatively, but transforms the very compositional law of the complex. With each new encounter, complex-thinking mutates and adapts.

Within the various attempts to understand the difference between complex-thinking and concept-thinking, that is, between a physiognomic and a linguistic semiotic, there is a tendency to regard the former as spontaneous and naturally motivated, in contrast to the latter, which is considered to be conventional and culturally specific. If thinking in complexes is a modality of embodied cognition that is exemplified in the still largely preverbal thought of children, then the capacity to use abstracts concepts, it seems, must be a later psychogenetic development acquired only with the enculturation of the adolescent. Benjamin, for example, in his attempt to distinguish an image-based form of mimetic thought from the logical taxonomies of abstract language, certainly inclined to map this difference onto the respective spheres of biology and culture. But similitude is not quite the prelapsarian, naturally motivated semiotic that Benjamin claimed it to be. Indeed, complex-thought is no more spontaneous, no less socialized or collective, than is abstract discourse. The child, Vygotsky observed, "does not construct its own complexes freely. It finds them already prefabricated in the process of understanding the speech of the other [*чужая речь*]. It does not select the individual concrete elements freely, incorporating them at will into any given complex" (*Myshlenie*, 152). Thus, experimental research conducted by one of Vygotsky's followers has demonstrated that, even without having yet acquired the formal framework of language, the precategorical thought of children nonetheless follows an organized system of "event structures" and social "scripts" that she shares with other members of her culture.[64] Despite its desultory and spontaneous appearance, then this experiential syntax of encounter is no less structured, methodical, or conventionalized than abstract conceptual thought.

We have already encountered one conceptual model for understanding complex-thinking in chapter 2's discussion of "operational sequences," the term used by Leroi-Gourhan to designate the basic repertoire of work gestures upon which the technical activity, social memory, and symbolic thought of a given culture are based. As Vygotsky and his colleague Aleksandr Luria themselves discovered while they were researching the effects of modernization on perception among the rural peasantry of Soviet Uzbekistan in 1931–1932, a culture which tended to organize knowledge into these sorts of functional sequences. The largely illiterate population that they were studying, which was uninitiated into the forms of categorical thought enabled by the written word, avoided theoretical classification and preferred instead to use concrete, situational thinking. Asked to group several objects together based on relations of similitude, for example, their subjects staged these things in a specific scenario of encounter, imagining how they could be used in a concrete operation. Thus, when presented with pictures of a hammer, a saw, a log, and a hatchet and told to group together the objects that were "similar" (in Uzbek: *ukhshaidi*; in Russian: *сходный*), a number of their subjects replied that all four objects were necessary and that such a division was impossible. Having expected their subjects to group the hammer, saw, and hatchet together under to the generic concept of "tool," and to reject the log as a member of a different group, Luria and Vygotsky were surprised to find that their subjects instead linked these objects together into a chain-complex. The peasants did not think taxonomically, but operationally. "All four of them fit together here!" one insisted. "The saw should be used to saw the log, the hammer should be used to strike it, and the hatchet has to chop it. And in order to chop the log up well, you need the hammer! You can't remove anything from this group. There isn't anything you don't need."[65] On the basis of such responses, Luria and Vygotsky deduced two distinct modes of thought, an abstract-classificatory one, which they associated with the linguistic sign, and a concrete-situational one, which they associated with visual thinking. Using terms consonant with those of Heartfield's Soviet commentators, they then designated these two modalities of thought abstraction (*абстракция*) and generalization (*обобщение*), respectively.[66]

It is in the latter's bonds of similitude that we discover the semiotic proper to Heartfield's photomontages. These strategies of cognitive "generalization" do not observe the monosemantic relationships found in static, definitional logic, but instead follow a chain of correspondences that move across signifying elements. Earlier in this chapter we touched on the syntax of these sequences in our discussion of Heartfield's use of condensation and displacement, two devices that link signs together through a structured series of transformations and distortions. Recalling the montaged rebus described by Freud in his dream book, it would be absurd to contend that the house with a boat on its roof "means" the figure of the headless man in the same way that the lexeme HORSE "means" a maned mammal that gallops and neighs, and yet the parts of the rebus are still ineluctably connected to one another within a single semantic complex. Heartfield's photomontage *The Face of Fascism* from 1928 provides another illustration of this lateral mechanism (fig. 5.17). Projecting a skull onto the somber face of Mussolini, here Heartfield depicts the architect of Italian fascism as the Grim Reaper, unmasking the death drive behind Il Duce's vitalist rhetoric of regeneration. If the technique of photographic superimposition was used in Galton's work to produce an abstraction out of individual faces, *The Face of Fascism*, by contrast, retains the recognizability of Mussolini's features. The resulting dual countenance exemplifies what could be called, after Einstein, a "metamorphotic" image, a visual passage that merges two distinct forms without, however, erasing either of them. Heartfield further freights this transition between Mussolini and the death's-head with additional meanings by positioning it within what Fedorov-Davydov called "a complex sequence of logical associations," a certain narrative-causal dimension encoded here onto the picture's diagonal axes. Situated at the center of the work, Mussolini becomes the visual copula connecting the various events in the photomontage's four corners. Mediating between the grimacing bourgeois that lurks behind him at the top left and the corpses strewn before him at the lower right, Mussolini functions as a catalyst between these two states, a transducer that converts capital into death. On this cognitive register, thought functions through what Vygotsky called *перенос значение*, a semantic *glissement* along an entire chain of phenomena. Here the logic of assembly in Heartfield's photomontages, which have long been compared to the ornate word-image complexes of the baroque emblem, recalls the compositions of the sixteenth-century artist Giuseppe Arcimboldo, whose paintings, Barthes once proposed, provide a visual synopsis of an elaborate chain of physiognomic transformation that was comparable, Barthes also noted, to a system of family resemblances (fig. 5.18).[67] These portraits "are, all in all, merely the visible space of a transmigration which leads,

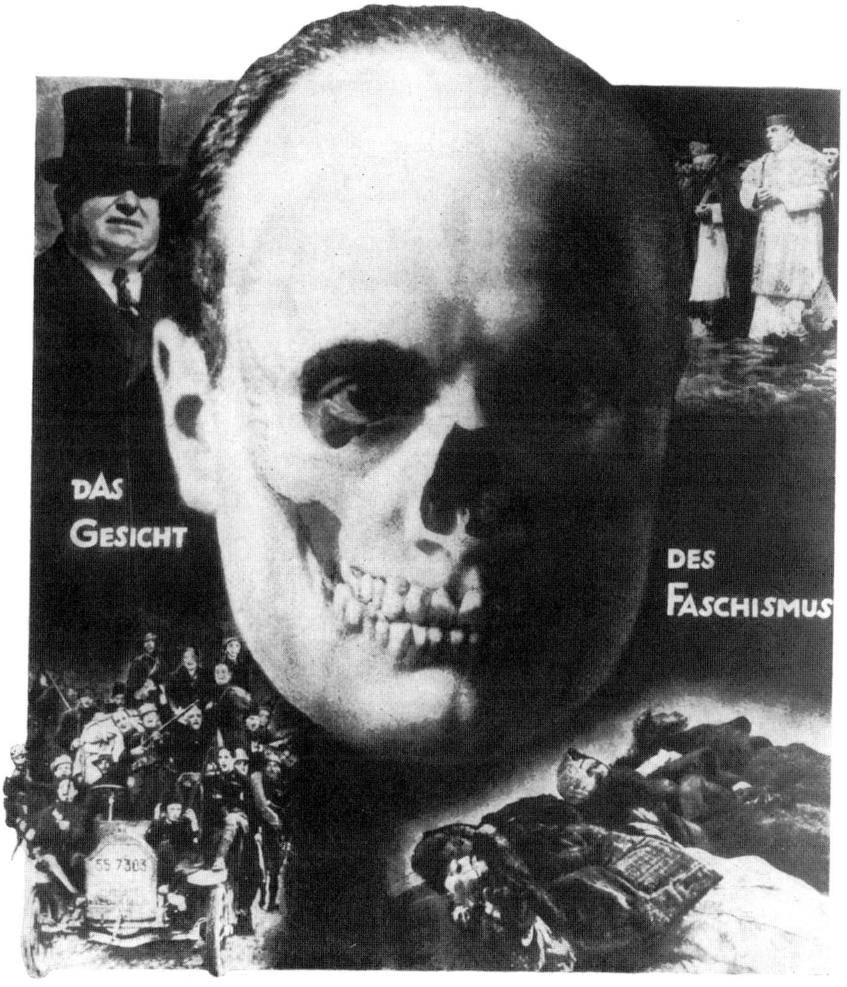

Figure 5.17 John Heartfield, *The Face of Fascism* (1928). © 2012 Artists Rights Society (ARS), New York/VG Bild-Kunst, Bonn. Akademie der Künste, Berlin, Kunstsammlung, Heartfield 3869; photograph: Roman März.

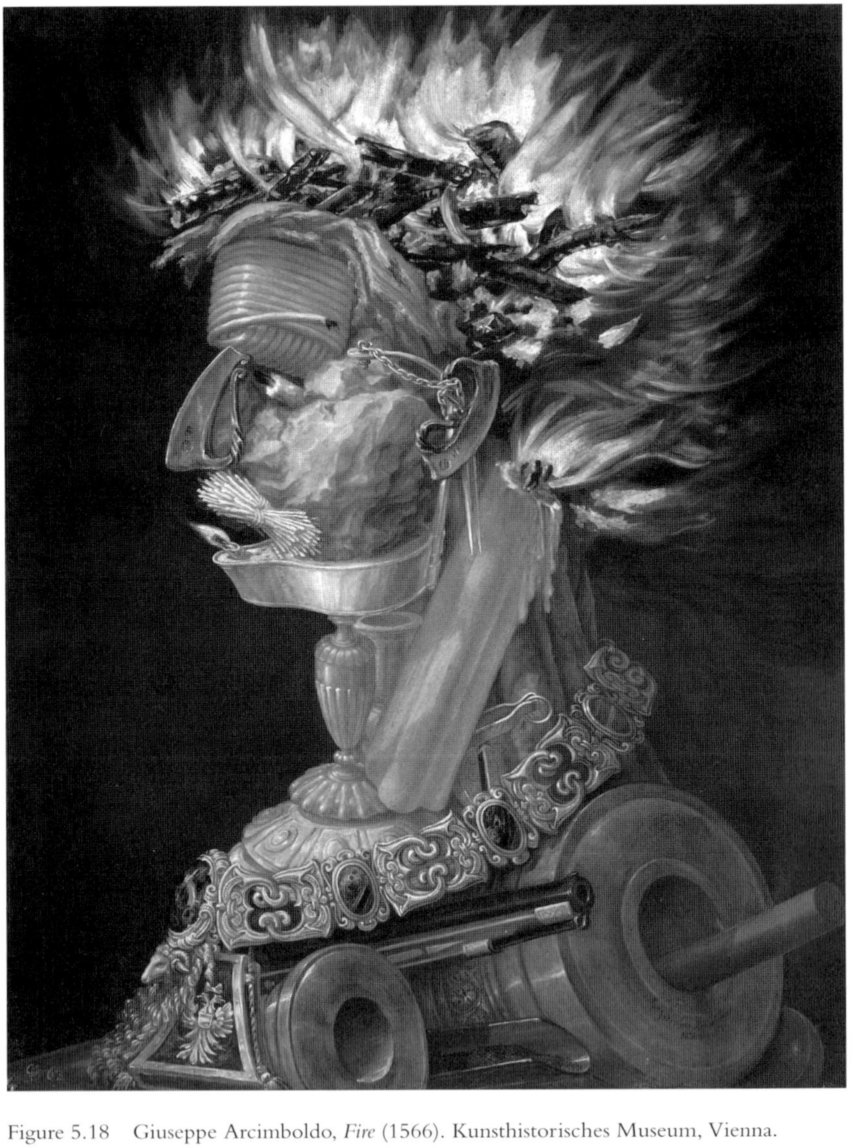

Figure 5.18 Giuseppe Arcimboldo, *Fire* (1566). Kunsthistorisches Museum, Vienna.

before our eyes, from fish to water, from the faggot to the fire, from the lemon to the pendant, and finally, from all substances to the human face."[68]

It is unnecessary to enumerate still more examples of these transformational chains in Heartfield's photomontages, which other scholars have already identified and amply explored using the conceptual rubric of "metamorphosis."[69] The question that remains, however, is why the physiognomic sign, as exemplified in Heartfield's post-1924 work, returns from its exile in the twilight regions of occult pseudo-science to become once more a paradigmatic structure of knowledge during the interwar years? There are two interrelated answers to this question. The first, which we have already touched upon, regards the resurgence in physiognomic thought as a reaction to the exhaustion of the structuralist model of signification. Here a perfect case in point would be developments in the work of Ludwig Wittgenstein, whose growing dissatisfaction with the linguistic bias of the philosophy of mind prompted a turn to the semiotic of similitude around 1933. If the rigorous mathematical systems of the *Tractatus Logico-Philosophicus*, written in the trenches of First World War, exemplify the structuralist paradigm and its valorization of formal logic, by the 1930s Wittgenstein was no longer convinced of the adequacy of this abstract, classificatory account of meaning and began to consider how cognitive procedures such as combining and likening also contributed to the organization of experience. Eventually, of course, in his *Philosophical Investigations*, he would compare these chain-complexes of "overlapping similarities" to physiognomic systems of "family resemblance," or *Familienähnlichkeit*.

But the ascent of similitude and physiognomics in the 1920s was more than just an immanent cultural auto-correction to the overextension of the structuralist model of meaning and its poetological corollary, aesthetic modernism. The physiognomic turn also reflected a new historical development during the interwar years: the transition from a symbolic economy based on the referential sign to one based on the simulacrum. This global mutation in the structure of signification was caused by the saturation of everyday life with technical media such as photography and film, means of serial reproduction that subverted the ontological distinction between original and copy on which the classical semiotic order had been based. To be sure, these analogical recording media had existed already for many decades, but, as Guy Debord noted, it wasn't until around 1927 that the quantitative proliferation of these technologies tipped over into a qualitative transformation, giving rise to the society of the spectacle.[70] In the wake of this new machinery of representation, new signifying practices emerged that linked phenomena and signs through lateral relations of likeness rather than vertical relations of denotation.[71]

Max Picard, the Platonist critic who, as we saw earlier, recoiled in horror before *Face of Our Time*, considered Sander's physiognomic atlas a symptom of the baleful loss of reference that confronts modern society:

> The photographic world has penetrated into everything today. It is not tied to any object; it is already there before the arrival of the object to be photographed; no human being is even needed; one photo photographs the other. It is no longer necessary for anything to take place since everything has already been *photographed beforehand*, prior to its occurrence. The event trails behind the photo, stumbling, like a pale imitation of the photo. (The photos in the illustrated press all look this way: not like reports about events that have taken place, but like a set of instructions stipulating that events should take place in a certain manner.)[72]

Here Picard observes that the physiognomic sign, as deployed in the work of Sander, corresponds structurally to a world of mass media images in which the ontological priority of the referent over its sign has been inverted, leading to condition in which even the seemingly most spontaneous and natural phenomenon is already thoroughly mediatized. In this simulacral state "everything has already been *photographed beforehand*," Picard notes. Instead of depicting actually existing things and events, as naturalist art once endeavored to do, portraiture and figurative art now project matrices of resemblance, nodes of correspondence between reality and its representation. Art no longer seeks to depict life but to generate its prototype. As a result, the figures peopling this art become synthetic, transitional, and, to recall Tret'iakov's analysis of Heartfield, overcoded. This scrambling of the hierarchies of reference gives rise to an epistemic quandary that Katerina Clark has insightfully characterized as the "modal schizophrenia" of early socialist realism, an artistic practice that strove to capture in a single stroke both "what is" and "what ought to be."[73] Waeztoldt conveys this same logical paradox when he writes of the portrait's "*becoming* similar" (*das Ähnlich*werden) to its model and of the cases in which the referent "disappears completely" behind its representation. Thus, despite manifest stylistic parallels between the realism of the nineteenth century and that of the interwar period, there remains the crucial difference that the former is firmly based in the semiotic paradigm of representation while the latter, by contrast, is an art of a simulacral order.

The epistemic distinction between the representational semiotic and a semiotic of similitude was mapped out by Michel Foucault, first in his genealogy of the structuralist paradigm, *The Order of Things*, and then in subsequent essays such as *This Is Not a Pipe*. In these texts, Foucault observed a transformation in the nature of the sign taking place in the first half of the twentieth century that restored the cultural authority of analogy and physiognomy, modalities of thought that had been suppressed with the emergence of the classical episteme in the seventeenth century. He characterized the difference between resemblance and similitude, between the structuralist sign and the simulacrum, in the following way:

> Resemblance has a "model," an original element that orders and hierarchizes the increasingly less faithful copies that can be struck from it. Resemblance presupposes a primary reference that prescribes and classes. The similar develops in series that have neither beginning nor end, that can be followed in one direction as easily as in another, that obey no hierarchy, but propagate themselves from small differences among small differences. Resemblance serves representation, which rules over it; similitude serves repetition, which ranges across it. Resemblance predicates itself upon a model

> it must return to and reveal; similitude circulates the simulacrum as an indefinite and reversible relation of the similar to the similar.[74]

Importantly, Foucault linked the reemergence of the semiotic of similitude not to aesthetic modernism—as some commentators have proposed[75]—but to the *decline* of the modernist program, which, he pointed out, had never in fact broken free of the classical episteme. As the previous chapter noted, high modernism's logic of negation meant that, for all its radicality, the movement remained confined to a territory that was already circumscribed by the realist representational episteme. Modernism, Foucault explained,

> is, in fact, the strict unfolding of Western culture in accordance with the necessity it imposed upon itself at the beginning of the nineteenth century. It would be false to see in this general indication of our experience, which may be termed "formalism," the sign of a drying up, of a rarefaction of thought losing its capacity for re-apprehending the plenitude of contents; it would be no less false to place it from the outset upon the horizon of some new thought or new knowledge. It is within the very tight-knit, very coherent outlines of the modern *episteme* that this contemporary experience found its possibility; it is even that *episteme* which, by its logic, gave rise to such an experience, constituted it through and through, and made it impossible for it not to exist.[76]

In its campaign to estrange and denaturalize the conventions of nineteenth-century realism, modernism's formalist critique may have exposed the finitude and arbitrariness of the representational semiotic, but, as Einstein made clear in his analysis of this apophatic poetics, it never successfully escaped from the prison-house of the structuralist sign. This escape would become possible only with the waning of the system of representation that distinguished between the referent and its image, a system that was succeeded by a semiotic based on similarities that circulated freely between matter and sign. This new semiotic, which recognized the fluid kinship between language and the world, resembled, as Foucault noted, a "uniform layer, in which the *seen* and the *read*, the visible and the expressible, were endlessly interwoven."[77]

For Foucault, the artistic strategy that best exemplified this simulacral condition could be found in the image-text rebuses that René Magritte first began to paint in 1925, around the same moment when Heartfield himself started experimenting with chiasmic amalgams of photos and words. Despite this convergence of artistic strategy, there nonetheless remains a crucial distinction between these two montage projects that is reflected in their radically disparate attitudes toward the task of communication and questions of intersubjectivity. Although Magritte and Heartfield both proceed by interlacing thing-presentation (*Dingvorstellung*) with word-presentation (*Wortvorstellung*), to recall our Freudian terminology, each constructs the rebus to quite different ends: while Heartfield designed his mechanical photomontages for mass circulation in the popular press, Magritte's paintings, by contrast, lack this social disposition at the level of both content and technique, and instead seek to capture on canvas a private and dream-like emanation of the unconscious. Indeed, the difference between these two artistic projects can be compared to the difference between the joke and the dream, two psychic phenomena that, as Freud pointed out, are beholden to the same transformational laws of condensation and displacement[78] but that have entirely different social orientations: whereas the joke is a collective speech genre destined for transmission, for recounting to others, the dream is a solipsistic utterance fashioned deep in the recesses of the sleeper's mind, where the psyche is unfettered by any "concern for intelligibility" (*Rücksicht auf Verständlichkeit*), Freud observed.[79] As Foucault noted in his remarks on Magritte, "it is in dream that men [are] at last reduced to silence."[80] If these silent paintings induce withdrawn contemplation, Heartfield's works, conversely, provoke boisterous laughter. With good reason, then, critics in the 1930s compared the structure of Heartfield's rebuses to that of the joke,[81] just as Eisenstein's later theorization of montage, which resonates so powerfully with these works, borrowed much more from Freud's joke book than from the more famous study of dreams.[82] This commitment to intersubjective dimensions of discourse, evident in Heartfield's preference for the dialogical joke over the introverted dream, can be observed as well in his standard technique of assembling works solely out of visual and verbal material that was already circulating in the public imaginary and that was consequently recognizable and familiar to all who viewed them. In contrast to an easel painting, a Heartfield photomontage is to be read not as personal artistic expression, but as collective utterance.

And while this second-order practice of reconstellating the authorless signs of mass culture indeed demonstrates Heartfield's dedication to the democratic ideals of populism and collaborative production—what Aragon called the inherent "morality of collage"—it also responds to a transformation in the relationship between knowledge and power that took place in the 1920s. If in the classical bourgeois public sphere of the eighteenth and nineteenth centuries power operated in secrecy and darkness,[83] it operates under the refeudalized conditions of the modern mass media instead through the mechanisms of celebrity and display. Changing their strategies of ideological manipulation, the vested elites of the interwar period no longer strove, or even bothered, to cover up their will to domination, but instead conducted their misdeeds in plain view. Rather than conceal its motives, power now broadcasts them in a blinding media blitz. Detonating an "information bomb" that submerges consciousness under a cascade of imagery, reports, disclosures and data,[84] the masters of spectacle today provide not too little information about the world, but too much. Interwar Germany possessed no mysteries, no secrets, since all aspects of this society of the spectacle were already on open display.

As Peter Sloterdijk has suggested, Weimar culture had unprecedented access to knowledge about itself and correspondingly developed a remarkable capacity for self-reflection: today this "nudist era"—an "era of exposure" and "open secrets"—"stands before us as the most self-aware epoch in history."[85] Paradoxically, however, this self-awareness and the general accessibility of knowledge in this period did not create the conditions for political enlightenment in the traditional sense of the word. Indeed, it seems that just the opposite was the case, and that the refeudalized public sphere, or *Öffentlichkeit*, provided ideal conditions in which false consciousness was able to thrive: the "signature of the whole era," Adorno observed about Weimar Germany, was that "human beings are not simply deceived by ideology but rather obey the Latin saying and want to be deceived."[86] In his 1929 study of the white-collared masses (the *Angestellten*), the newly emergent class of information proletariat that would contribute significantly to the National Socialist electoral success four years later, Kracauer offered similar reflections on the paradoxical structure of modern false consciousness, which, he explained, beguiled not through deception but through sheer obviousness. "Even the radical intellectuals cannot easily get behind the exoticism of the everyday. And the white-collared employees themselves? They are least conscious of their situation. But surely their existence is spent in full public view [*in voller Öffentlichkeit*]? Just like the 'Letter to Her Majesty' in Edgar Allan Poe's tale, it is precisely its public nature [*Öffentlichkeit*] that protects it from discovery: nobody notices the letter because it is out on display."[87]

As Kracauer points out, the obliviousness of the white-collared employees is matched by the ineffectuality of the "radical intelligentsia," the political avant-garde entrusted with the task of ideological exfoliation and political enlightenment. What he touches upon here is, moreover, an impasse faced by critique itself, which no longer has any traction, or indeed any object, in a culture of "open secrets" where everything is already on display. As the most famous analyst of *Öffentlichkeit* Jürgen Habermas has observed, within a modern culture saturated with technical media, "publicity loses its critical function in favor of a staged display; even arguments are transmuted into symbols to which again one can not respond by arguing but only by identifying with them."[88] Thus, if the traditional strategies of leftist critique presumed, first, that hidden social realities were at work below the surface of everyday appearances and, second, that ideological enlightenment would result from the revelation of these obfuscated truths, this method of *Ideologiekritik* is rendered ineffectual within a society that has nothing to hide. Indeed, ideology can no longer even be properly defined as "false consciousness"—as a distortion of reality or as a suppression of knowledge about the actual state of affairs—since knowledge and information have now become the very medium and expression of power. Even worse, within spectacle society the revelations of injustice performed by classical *Ideologiekritik* can themselves be politically reactionary. As Guy Debord noted, the purpose of disclosing secrets is to "make domination more respectable, never to make it more comprehensible. They are the privilege of *front-row spectators* who are stupid enough to believe that they can understand something, not by making use of what is hidden from them, but *by believing what is revealed*!"[89] The skepticism of Kracauer and Debord echoes the consternation of Carl Einstein, who, as the previous chapter showed, grew disillusioned with the reified critical posturing of his leftist contemporaries—"heroes of critique and dwarves of will"—which had devolved into a blind, contentless reflex. Indeed, again and again in *Realism after Modernism* we have encountered this same response to the atrophy of the public sphere's critical function, evident not just in Heartfield's use of found imagery, but also in Reger's refusal to designate *Union of the Strong Hand* as a *roman à clef*—a genre that implied something concealed and hidden from view, when in fact all of Reger's materials were taken from public sources—and also in Brecht's technique for writing *Fear and Misery of the Third Reich*, which was pieced together out of secondhand material taken from the mass media.

Under the condition of spectacularity, Weimar Germany took leave of the epistemic configuration that Paul Ricoeur dubbed a "hermeneutics of suspicion," an analytical system for which "the fundamental category of consciousness is the relation hidden–shown."[90] This hermeneutic orientation had come into being with the structuralist semiotic, Foucault observed, and was subsequently systematized in the critical science of ideology, the "knowledge of all knowledge" that made it possible to connect the sign and its meaning through an act of interpretation. In response to the representational semiotic's structural need to locate the obscured signified ("meaning") that lurks behind every arbitrary signifier, the science of ideology had kindled an insatiable hermeneutic quest to uncover the suprasensible truth behind the world of appearances. But as the metaphysical gap between sign and referent closed in the 1920s, so too did the era of ideological judgment and false consciousness. At this moment, the interpretive paradigm of *criticism* yielded to that of *commentary*, to use Foucault's terms.[91] No longer concerned with the project of ideological demystification, the hermeneutical impulse would now be redirected toward the surface of culture and its "absolutely superficial secret,"[92] toward "gestures instead of being," as Karl Jaspers wrote in 1931.[93] In the culture of the interwar period, manifest evidence trumps latent motives just as facticity trumps ideology; in the same way that the visual hieroglyph eclipses the linguistic sign, so too the category of appearance eclipses authenticity; and just as behaviorist models overtake those of ego psychology, functionalism overtakes ontology. In sum: the paradigm of expression cedes priority to *Sachlichkeit*.[94] This reversal of the values of surface and depth, this cultural turn toward exteriority, was demonstrated in the new status enjoyed by physiognomic resemblance, a signifying structure that flattens the distinctions between sign and referent in the manner of the mythical tautegory (which, as we saw in the previous chapter, "has as its object that of which one can only say that it is").[95] The import of physiognomic judgment within a signifying regime based on relations of similitude was recognized already by Waetzoldt, whose *Art of the Portrait* invoked the turn outward with a verse of Goethe:

> Nichts ist drinnen; nichts ist draußen
> Denn was innen, das ist außen
> So ergreifet ohne Säumnis
> Heilig öffentlich Geheimnis.
>
> Nothing "inside" or "out there,"
> The "outer" world is all "in here."
> This mystery grasp without delay,
> This secret always on display.[96]

Of course, if there is one thing that the case of Heartfield forcefully demonstrates to us, it is that cynicism was not the only alternative to *Ideologiekritik*, indeed, that the failure of the critical impulse had not put an end to the project of radical political transformation in Weimar Germany. His work suggests instead that the locus and strategies of political engagement had shifted away from the legerdemain of Kracauer's "radical intellectuals" towards the surface of culture. Indeed, seldom did Heartfield reveal anything to his audiences that they did not already know: few could be surprised to discover either that the agenda of the propertied class is to accumulate wealth by expropriating the labor of others, since this is the basic mechanism of capitalist profit, or that the goal of fascism's choreography of power and adulation of the Führer was the political and psychological subjection of the populace. Such things were all too plain to see. At the level of artistic technique, too, Heartfield took the side of the obvious, using the language and imagery of public media that were already widely disseminated, elements that were not just public, but avowedly and militantly clichéd. Here the corrective to false consciousness proceeds not through the revelation of new information—the uncovering of a hidden signified—but through the manipulation and reorganization of a teeming mass of information already at hand. After 1924 this became the central strategy of Heartfield's montage practices, which, rather than demotivating the semiotic code in the manner of Dada montage, now sought, as Tret'iakov explained, to *re*code or *over*code the sign. For Heartfield, ideology and knowledge were to be found not behind signs and representations, but between them, as a syntax of assembly. Renouncing the structuralist paradigm, which remained intrinsically metaphysical in both its affirmative and negative cultural instantiations (i.e., in the aesthetic projects of both the nineteenth-century realists and their modernist critics), his second-order art turned to physiognomic analysis as a means to intervene in this syntax, to rearrange the networks of sign aggregation that were organized in accordance with the interests of power.

6

Into the Entomic Age: A Coda on Ernst Jünger's *Glass Bees*

Consider two images that, despite the eighty-year span between them, perform the same rhetorical operation, that of glorifying a technological marvel through contrast with a living creature: from 1921, a dynamo component so massive that it dwarfs the mortal technician who services it (fig. 6.1); from the late 1990s, a chain of gears so minuscule that a spider mite would barely notice them (fig. 6.2). The first, a photograph taken by Lewis Hine, displays a monstrous rotor that has been removed from its housing and propped, upright and frontal, against the darkness of the factory background. Only a few distant visual incidents—some windows and fluorescent tubes—perforate the shadowy space behind and establish a set of deep, receding orthogonals. Otherwise the industrial form at the center completely dominates the scene. To the right of this colossal steel anemone, Hine has set up a bright flash, whose light diffuses across the metallic surfaces of the disc and fades into the inky setting at the left. The narrative conceit of the photo seems evident enough: with rod and ruler in hand, the technician has mounted the giant rotor in order to assess some aspect of its features, perhaps to gauge the wear on the disc. Yet something about this act of calibration is implausible. It is all too posed. Standing off-center to the left so that the camera has an unobstructed view of his performance, he seems not so much to measure, but appears instead to demonstrate the gesture of measuring.

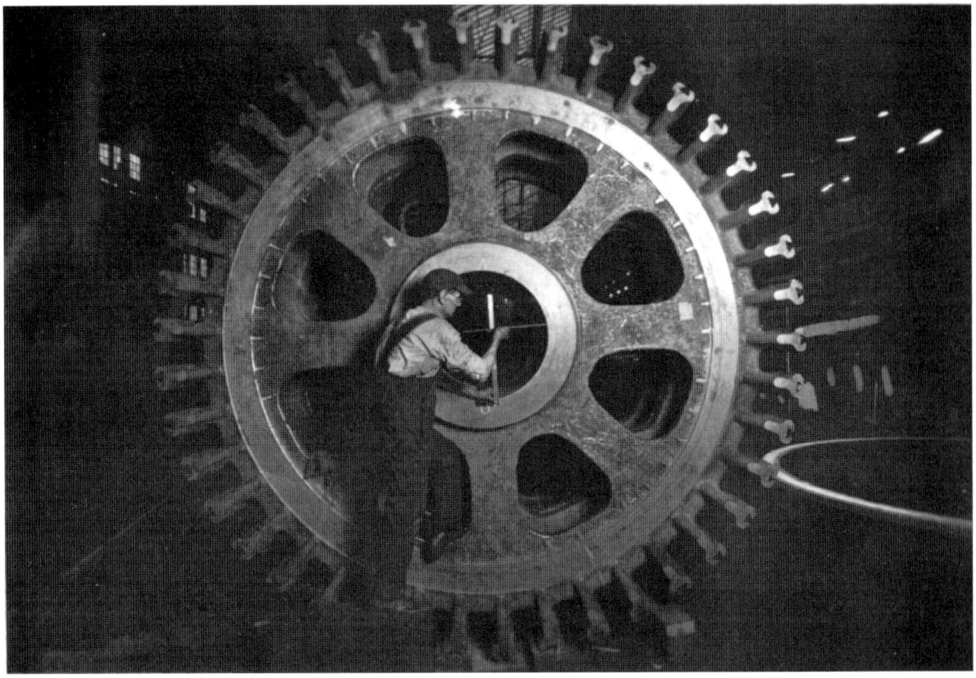

Figure 6.1 Lewis Hine, *Man at Dynamo* (1921). Courtesy of George Eastman House, International Museum of Photography and Film.

The ruler that the technician displays is an old and familiar trope within scientific photography. In his photographs for the U.S. geological surveys of the 1860s and 1870s, for example, Timothy O'Sullivan regularly included such devices to indicate the scale of the objects he recorded. In Hine's photograph, however, another ruler is present, which introduces a second scale: this is the scale of the technician himself, whose body conveys the relative size of the dynamo to the spectator. In this regard, the apt nineteenth-century precursor would be not O'Sullivan but Maxime Du Camp, the amateur photographer who, in his 1849–51 tour of Egypt and the Near East with his friend Gustave Flaubert, regularly included human figures in his pictures in order to convey the

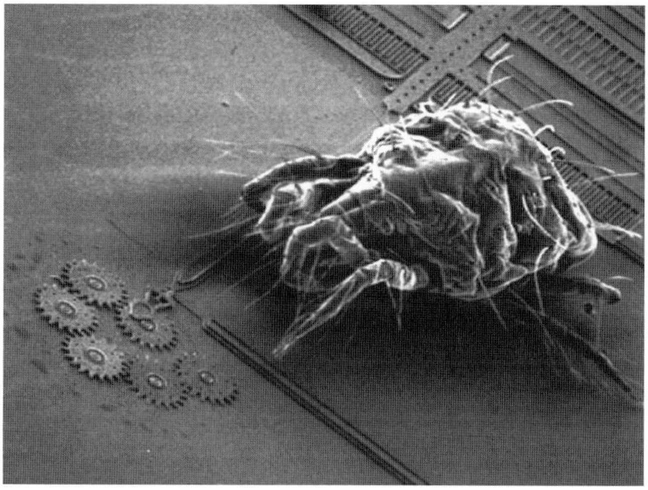

Figure 6.2 Spider mite and nanogear chain (late 1990s). Courtesy of Sandia National Laboratories.

scale of the ancient monuments he was documenting (fig. 6.3). As Alberti had long before suggested in his treatise *On Painting*, the placement of the human form within a perspectivally integrated pictorial field establishes, immediately and intuitively, the relative sizes of the other objects contained in this field: "Since man is the thing best known to man, perhaps Protagoras, by saying that man is the mode and measure of all things, meant that all the accidents of things are known through comparison to the accidents of man."[1] Nature may be chaotic and contingent, Alberti explained, but at least some of its accidents have human contours.

Thus the presence of the technician's body in Hine's photograph does another thing: by providing the spectator with a familiar point of reference, this figure humanizes the technical artifact on display. As the viewer's surrogate, the technician anchors the scale of this extraordinary object in that of his body—the phenomenological ground of perception and thought common to all viewers of the photograph—and makes this otherwise purely abstract technical

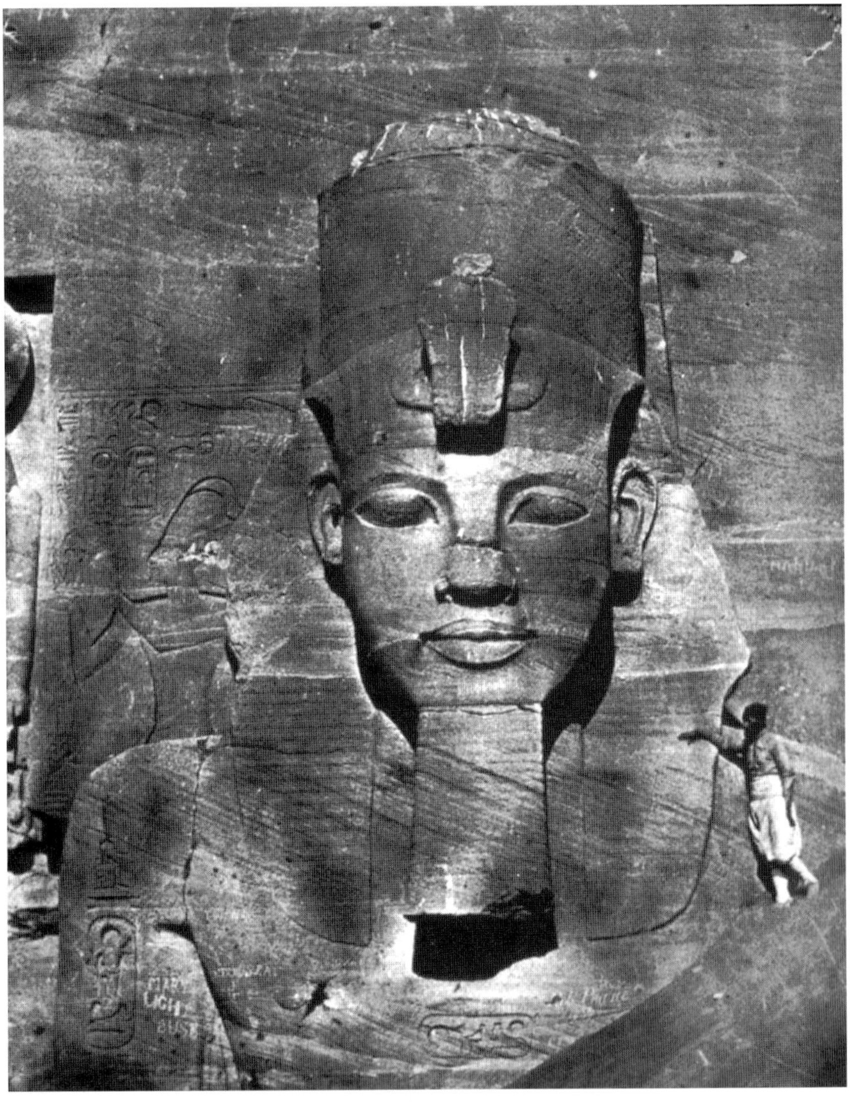

Figure 6.3 Maxime Du Camp, *Abu Simbel* (1850). Image copyright © The Metropolitan Museum of Art. Image source: Art Resource, New York.

form intuitively knowable and familiar. Without this human anchor, the rotor would be a visual ornament of uncertain dimensions, yet another manifestation of the decontextualized technological fetish that was the stock-in-trade of New Objectivity photography.

Herein lies its crucial different with the second image (fig. 6.2). Made at the end of the last millennium with a scanning electron microscope (SEM), the latter picture too relies on a zoomorphic gauge to indicate the relative scale of the technological wonder, but here the experiential aspect is all but blocked off to the spectator. A spider mite stands in for the technician. Gone is the most intuitive and expressive of measures, the human body, replaced by the mute carapace that hovers to the right. Mediated through an anatomy and a sensorium radically unlike our own, the *Umwelt* of the mite, to invoke biosemiotician Jakob von Uexküll's term, is inaccessible to the human imagination. The mite's body may help to contextualize the fantastical scale of the tiny nanomechanism, but it is a context, and a measure, that unfolds far beyond the natural spatiotemporal parameters of human existence. The disorienting effects of the alien scale are further compounded by the ambiguity of the spatial relations in the SEM image. Unlike the high-contrast values and deep recessional space of Hine's photograph, the flat, uniformly focused, and evenly illuminated visual field here fails to indicate visual relations that could situate the body of the spectator within the "anthropocratic" space of one-point perspective.[2] This image has no depth, nor any of the standard devices (converging orthogonals, horizon line, etc.) used by post-Renaissance optical theory to humanize space. Thus, it is not just the anatomy of the mite that renders inhuman the scene depicted; so, too, does the visual technology behind it.

The substitution of the insect for the human body in these images marks an epistemic threshold that separates the 1920s from the 1990s. This chapter examines a remarkable and farsighted document of this transition, Ernst Jünger's *Glass Bees* (1957). Written at a moment almost exactly between Hine's photograph and the SEM image, Jünger's science-fiction novel limns vividly this shift from the mesoscopic scale of the human to the microscopic scale of the insect, a metamorphosis in the technological order that, as this book has endeavored to demonstrate, was already underway in the first half of the twentieth century but was completed only with the advent of the atomic age, when all standards of measurement were recalibrated in accordance with nonanthropomorphic units. As we will see, this intersection between metric reform, on the one hand, and the establishment of a technological system that displaces man as the standard for measurement, on the other, constitutes the historical background for Jünger's *Glass Bees.* Once this threshold was passed, the "accidents of things," to repeat Alberti's formula, could no longer be known "through comparison to the accidents of man."

By the time Jünger's novel appeared, innumerable other texts, from Weber's writings on rationalization to Husserl's *Crisis of European Sciences*, had already called into question the collusion of instrumental reason, abstract mathematization, and the impoverishment of experience. And like them, *Glass Bees* attributed the existential dysphoria of modernity to a particular will to quantify and measure—processes of deterritorialization that convert inhabited space and time into a series of indifferent and purely notional units of universal equivalency. Symptomatically, the protagonist of Jünger's novel carries with him a book by Flavius Josephus, the ancient historian and author of *Jewish Antiquities* who claimed that it was no less villainous a figure than Cain himself, the wicked son of Adam and Eve, who was responsible for the invention of weights and measures. Through this citation, Jünger insinuated that metrification represented nothing less than a second expulsion from Eden.[3]

However, Jünger's book does not simply rehash familiar laments linking rationalization and, concomitantly, measurement to the loss of social value and to cultural deterioration. To the contrary, *Glass Bees* suggests that metrification in and of itself is not pernicious. Measurement, strictly speaking, entails nothing more than comparing the magnitudes of two objects using a third as a constant. This third term constitutes what systems theorist Niklas Luhmann discerningly called the *Einheit der Differenz*. This equivocal phrase, which can be variously translated as "unit of distinction" or "unity of the difference," reveals the dual logic of this unit/y: the unit of distinction makes it possible to discriminate between two objects, to tell them apart, at the same time that it also insists on their ultimate dialectical unity vis-à-vis a third object. For Jünger, the decisive element in any act of measurement is precisely this third object, the unit that mediates the comparison.

THE METRICS OF *GLASS BEES*

In the 1950s, when the human dimensions of the older industrial order were definitively displaced by the atomic scale and the body ceased to serve as the unit of difference, *Glass Bees* spelled out, in the direst of terms, the cultural and anthropological challenges that would attend this process of technical recalibration. Part essayistic treatise on technology, part autobiographically inflected narrative, Jünger's book recounts two days in the life of Richard, a decommissioned cavalry officer who has returned from military service to a technological civilization in which the ancient values and precepts of the warrior have lost their purchase. Richard's melancholic response to the disappearance of the martial code reflects an estrangement that pervades many of the postwar writings of Jünger, who had served enthusiastically as an officer in the Great War, but then, in the following World War, found himself morally disoriented and ultimately revolted by the abstract calculus of modern technological warfare. Returning home, the protagonist in *Glass Bees* quickly comes to the realization that he is no more fit for civilian life in the technical age than he had been for combat, not because he is incapable of shedding the habits of the soldier but because he feels ill prepared for a society in which mechanization has all but completely obliterated the difference between war and peacetime. The prophetic scenario envisioned by Jünger, in which these two spheres have become indistinguishable, anticipates the media genealogies proposed much later by Paul Virilio and Friedrich Kittler, who, tracing the origins of contemporary mass media to a variety of warfare technologies, have demonstrated the inextricability between the military, economic, and technological complexes.[4]

The setting for *Glass Bees* is a globalized dystopia in which all geographical specificities and phases of historical development have converged into a single undifferentiated gray territory. This vague zone does, however, have one distinguishing feature: it is in a state of perpetual civil war. This is the fate of technological civilization, in which the cadres of soldiers have been superseded by an army of police. In his early Weimar works like *Storm of Steel*, Jünger celebrated the front line as a zone of 'infinite danger,' but this radiant nihilism was tempered by the brutality of the Third Reich. By the 1950s, the author was far less sanguine about a zone of danger that had metastasized into all civilian sectors. In the postwar period, when danger had become indistinguishable from disaster, Jünger waxes nostalgically in texts such as *Glass Bees* about a time when the threat to existence could still be contained on the front. Confronted with what the sociologist Ulrich Beck aptly phrased the postwar "risk society," his noble-warrior protagonist becomes a dropout.[5] "A retired cavalryman cuts a poor figure in the middle of these cities, where the neighing of a horse is no longer heard. . . . Words had lost their meaning, and even war was no longer war. [Richard's late mentor] would turn in his grave if he could hear what they called war nowadays. After all, peace wasn't peace anymore either" (*Werke*, 15:462).[6] Confused and sickened by the new techno-industrial order, the unemployed Richard refuses integration into its ranks and so becomes instead its casualty, "like a man from a bygone era who has been placed at a traffic intersection" (*Werke*, 15:516).

Concerned, however, about his wife Theresa's welfare, Richard agrees to one final job interview, this time for the firm of the entrepreneur Giacomo Zapparoni. One of the numerous allusions in *Glass Bees* to E. T. A. Hoffmann's fantastic tale *The Sandman*, the enigmatic Italian Zapparoni is a manufacturer of robots who specializes in two particular types of automata: android actors whose hyperverisimilitude has revolutionized the entertainment industry and microscale robots that carry out a variety of useful tasks from sorting money to removing pollen from the air. Both species of robot, Richard also notes, can be "repurposed" for more sinister vocations such as surveillance or military deployment.

When Richard shows up at the Zapparoni plant dressed in a threadbare suit and with a growling stomach, he is escorted to the inventor's house at the heart of the facility. There he is surprised to find a modest and manifestly low-tech dwelling whose contents, he estimates, predate the middle of the eighteenth century. What make the strongest impression on Richard are the distinctly human proportions of the dwelling and its grounds, in complete contrast with the industrial sprawl that encircles it. Richard recognizes in Zapparoni's home a product of the earliest metrological standards, taken from the era before the French Revolution, when the dimensions and attributes of objects were compared using hands and outstretched arms, and the carrying distance of a one's voice served as a unit to parse space. "One sensed the old measurements: the foot, the ell, the inch, the rod" (*Werke*, 15:497).

Unlike modern units of measurement whose high degree of abstraction facilitates the comparison of qualitatively heterogeneous substances—take the meter, which can be used to measure both the depth of a well and the thickness of an electrical filament—primitive metrics do not reflect arbitrary units. Jünger once noted in a diary entry that a fathom, a brace, a stone's throw, and an hour's walk are all "magnitudes of a natural variety"; as a result, they are "perceptually intuitive" (*anschaulich*) in a way that, say, the centimeter, kilometer, and kilogram are not (*Werke*, 3:379). What makes earlier conventions of measurement such as yards, feet, inches, and fingers by nature intuitive is that they are anthropomorphic, derived from the limbs of the body and intimately bound to the contexts of daily existence. Such units of measurement triangulate all of worldly spatial extension through the body, translating, in effect, every object into a scaled portrait of the human figure. In anthropometric systems of measure, the body serves as the universal *Einheit der Differenz*, to repeat Luhmann's term: while it posits the human body as a term of distinction between two objects, it also covers over the incommensurability of the objects by humanizing them. What is more, this act of portrayal extends beyond our static limbs to encompass our labor capacities as well. Many of the oldest units of agrarian measure, for example, correspond to the area of land that can be tilled by a person in a single day (e.g., the German *Morgenland*, the Russian *обжа*, the French *arpent*, and the Italian *giornata*). Such units are in essence condensed figurations of labor processes. For this reason Witold Kula, a Polish economic historian, has characterized these older units of measure as "representational."[7] Mensuration, his analysis suggests, is not only a method of quantification; it is an act of depiction.

If every measurement is at the same time a tacit depiction, then it is critical to know what a given metric depicts. Indeed, their referents may be surprising. After a few minutes outside Zapparoni's house, Richard begins to suspect that the harmonious proportions of this preindustrial artifact are only dissimulated and that this antediluvian paradise is in fact infested with machinery. Only gradually, almost belatedly, does he become aware of the eponymous glass bees, tiny robots that are gliding about gathering honey. That he did not notice them earlier strikes him as strange. After observing them through a mysterious pair of field glasses conveniently found nearby—another allusion to *The Sandman*—Richard speculates that the bees had slipped by unnoticed not because of their tiny size but because he lacked a frame of reference for the scale of these machines. "Judging their relative size was difficult because the objects in question were outside of the realm of experience and had no corresponding norm in consciousness. Without experience there can be no measure" (*Werke*, 15:517). The minuscule machines perplex the naked eye because they do not refer to anything from the realm of everyday experience. Richard likens these robots to bees, but even that analogy, he admits, is a poor approximation. Cognitively speaking, they "represent" nothing—at least nothing that is known, familiar, or human.

For millennia, the human body had been the basis not just for mapping out space, but also for building technological forms. Even when not explicitly endowed with a human countenance (as was the case in many famous eighteenth-century examples, from the writing boy of Jaquet-Droz to von Kempelen's Turkish chess player), the machine had nonetheless been modeled on the body since the first flushes of industrialization. In his 1877 *Outline for a Philosophy of Technology*, Ernst Kapp characterized technical invention as a method of "organ projection" (*Organprojektion*) through which cultures construct the limbs and instruments that their members lack at birth but require for survival. Conceived in the throes of the second Industrial Revolution, this definition of technology insisted that tools and machines were in essence supplements to natural human organs. Jünger characterized this generation of machine as "prostheses that imitate limbs and that replace, refine and multiply their functions. The hammer is a fist; the shovel is a hand that digs; the mill that pulverizes grain assumes the labor of the teeth" (*Werke*, 8:500). Such machines were conceived in the image of their masters. This belief in "the 'humanity' of the machine," to borrow a phrase from Heinrich Hauser's 1928 book *Interaction with Machines*, underwent a dramatic—and final—surge in the Weimar period.[8] An illustration from Fritz Giese's *Psychologie der Arbeitshand*, published the same year as Hauser's book, offers a pithy summary of this conception of tools as representations, extensions, and amplifications of their operator's limbs (fig. 6.4). And yet changes in the composition of the forces of production were already underway during the interwar period that would bring to an end the technological order that for centuries had taken the human form as its basis. In *Technics and Civilization* (written in 1930–31), Lewis Mumford, for example, predicted that in the current

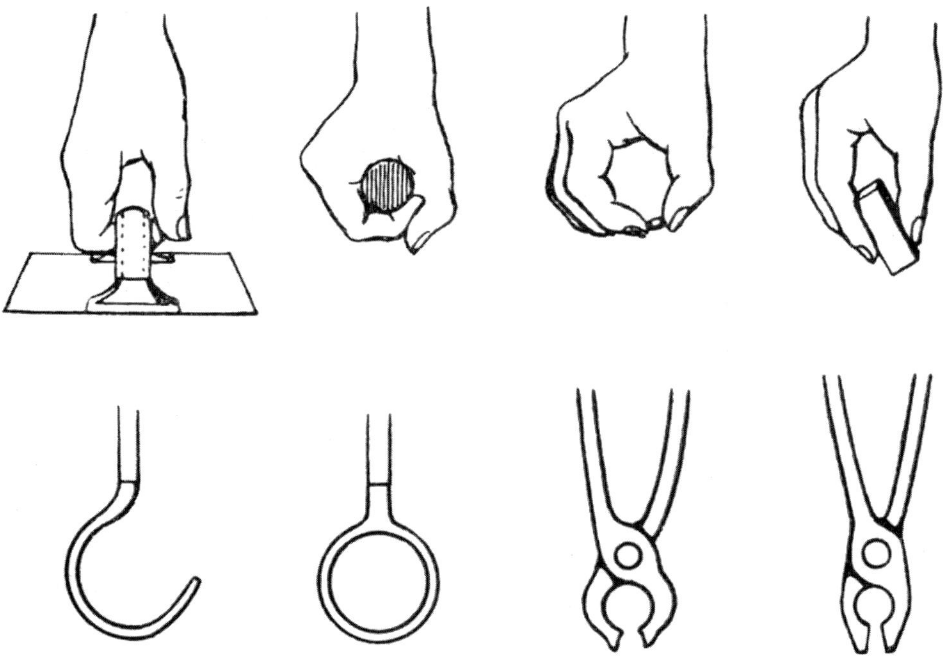

Figure 6.4 Hook-, ring-, and pincer-grip. From Fritz Giese, *Psychologie der Arbeitshand* (1928).

"neotechnic" age the technological artifact will become ever smaller. The latest technological order, he noted, is postindustrial and microscopic.[9]

Zapparoni's robotic bees mark the definitive break with the anthropomorphic technologies that had dominated throughout the industrial age. Whereas our mental map of space was once mediated by feet and fathoms, and our instruments were once modeled after operations performed by our own limbs—and bore accordingly the indelible, if only imaginary, imprint of the human form—in a world of glass bees the cognitive relationship we have to the environment around us, and even to our own bodies, is triangulated through devices that are decidedly something other than human. This new technological wave observes the logic not of Kapp's "organ projection" but of Ernst Bloch's "de-organization" (*Entorganisierung*),[10] a term that denoted not a movement toward chaos—that is, not *dis*organization—but a process of cultural deanthropomorphization discernible in those new technologies whose components have no prototypes in the anatomy and organs of the human body.

Thus a second technological visitation occurs at the Zapparoni plant, a vision more lysergic even than the glass bees. Richard notices—again, only gradually—that the pond next to the house is sown with bright red objects. He discovers that they are severed ears. The depot of dismembered human parts is a grim sign of the times, the aristocratic warrior speculates, yet one that is ultimately all too foreseeable, a gruesomely fitting complement to the posthuman, deorganized technology of the glass bees.

> The brutal display of the severed limbs had stunned me. But it was an inevitable motif in this context. Didn't it perforce go hand in hand with technical perfection and with the intoxication that this perfection brought to an end? Has there ever been at any period in the history of the world so many dismembered bodies, so many detached limbs, as in ours? For time immemorial mankind has waged wars, but I can't recall a *single* instance in the entire *Iliad* when the loss of an arm or a leg is reported. (*Werke*, 15:520–521; emphasis in original)

If the pathologically armored bodies of Jünger's Weimar writings revealed their author's anxiety about the fragility of the human body in the face of modern warfare, in postwar works such as *Glass Bees* it is technoscientific progress and invention rather than weaponry that threaten to violate the organic soundness of the human frame and obviate the classical aesthetic that Jünger associates with antiquity and texts like *The Iliad*.[11] In *Glass Bees,* the deorganization of technology produces the deorganization of the body: "We sense an attack on our bodily integrity, on our proportions. That our arms and legs are in jeopardy is not yet the greatest danger" (*Werke*, 15:521). The worst is yet to come. For the anatomization and dismemberment of the body is only the prelude to its final state when it will be converted into a purely notional quantity. Just as all that remains of the horse in the contemporary metropolis is a value abstraction quaintly termed "horsepower," human beings, too, will soon follow in their fate, replaced by apparitions that bear their name but not their likeness. The techno-entrepreneurial spirit "wanted to calculate using manpower just as it had already long been calculating using horsepower. It wanted units that were equivalent and divisible. To achieve this, man would have to be eliminated just as the horse had been eliminated before him" (*Werke*, 15:547).

In his reference to *The Iliad* Jünger posits a contrast between classical antiquity and the present that underscores a critical distinction between Greek technological thought and our own. These two epochs mark the most extreme points of antithesis between anthropomorphic and nonanthropomorphic technological paradigms. Georg Lukács, for example, suggested that the primitiveness of Greek science and engineering reflected an economy that was based exclusively on slave labor. The autonomization of machinery through scientific rationalization and invention was unthinkable in a society whose forces of production always had a human face.[12] In "Some Remarks on the Forms and Limitations of Technological Thought among the Greeks," Jean-Pierre Vernant advanced a similar thesis, albeit without the Marxist framework. There Vernant argued that for the Greeks technology always operated on analogy with human organs. The technological "*organon* transmits and amplifies man's force rather than acting by virtue of its own internal structure and producing an effect through a mechanism of a type different from human exertion."[13] Like Lukács, Vernant suggested that this mentality ultimately prevented the Greeks from becoming technical innovators. Hence, both note, the vast discrepancy between the astounding achievements of Greek philosophical thought and the poverty of their technical standing.

This belief in the inalienably human origin of force and energy further explains the centrality of causality in Greek scientific thought, since it was the category of causality that allowed them to establish a fundamental distinction between humankind and artifact. Aristotle argued in *Physics*, for example, that natural beings have within themselves an immanent source of change and action, whereas such "self-causality" is alien to technical (i.e., artificial) forms. In contrast with natural beings, which the Greeks considered to be autotelic, technology had a cause that was external to it. Technical forms were necessarily instrumental or utilitarian. This division would again be rehearsed in the distinction drawn much later between organic and inorganic bodies, between biology and mechanics. For the Greeks, the cause, or motive principle, of a technical mechanism was always to be found in the natural force of the human operator whom it served as an instrument. Machines that had their own source of energy were considered not *techné*, but *thaumata*, quasi-occult objects of marvel and wonder.[14] Even in the philosophical discourse of antiquity, then, technology was anthropic by nature, derived from and dependent upon the human.[15]

At the other end of this arc are Zapparoni's automata (*automaton* = "acting of itself"), which have inverted the determinative relationship between the human and the artifact. Mortal bodies no longer serve as the prototypes or kinetic agents for these constructions that effortlessly surpass humanity. These avatars do not copy or resemble their masters. In fact, they are easily distinguished from their human counterparts by a degree of perfection that is fundamentally inhuman:

> their faces were more brilliant, more flawless; their eyes of a larger cut, like precious stones; their movements slower, more graceful and, when excited, also more violent and faster than anything we

> have experienced . . . these figures did not simply imitate the human form; they took it beyond its potentials and its scale. (*Werke*, 15:511)

And although this autarkic generation of androids does not imitate the human, it has nonetheless kindled the converse mimetic ambition in its creator. These robots possess a mien that "became the model for human actors who adapted themselves to it" (*Werke*, 15:448–449). In Jünger's book, technological artifice has advanced to the point where the distinction between first and second nature no longer obtains. Here the Baroque logic of the simulacrum takes over and man is remade in the image of his creation, as Benjamin predicted in *The Origin of the German Tragic Drama:*

> where art so firmly occupies the centre of existence as to make man one of its manifestations instead of recognizing him above all as its basis, to see man's existence as the eternal subjects of its own creations instead of recognizing him as its own creator, then all sane reflection is at an end. And whether, with the removal of man from the centre of art, it is Nirvana, the slumbering will to life, which takes his place, as in Schopenhauer, or whether it is the "dissonance become man" [*Menschwerdung der Dissonanz*] which, as in Nietzsche, has created both the manifestations of the human world and man himself, it makes no difference; it is the same pragmatism.[16]

Lacking the natural harmony of the human form, Zapparoni's android is precisely this "dissonance become man." If, among the Greeks, cause and force were always immanent to the human whose pneuma quickened the mechanical construction, now it is the construction that animates the man and, in the process, reformats him according to nonanthropometric scales. Such technology, Richard notes, "gave a new measure to man" (*Werke*, 15:543). This pseudomorph rejects the balanced and symmetrical proportions of natural man and makes the latter instead into the subject of its own creation.

Entomic Prototypes

Like many texts of the 1950s, *Glass Bees* bears the imprint of the atomic age. Popular discourse in Germany and elsewhere was dominated at the time by anxieties about the bomb and the threat it posed to the survival of the human species. But it was equally unclear whether humankind and long-established notions of the human would survive even if the human race could avert physical annihilation. In innumerable texts, from Günther Anders's *Die Antiquiertheit des Menschen* (1956) to Karl Jaspers's *Die Atombombe und die Zukunft des Menschen* (1958), public intellectuals in Germany voiced their disquiet about technologies that rendered humanity and its scale obsolete. The "radiation industry," to quote a passage from Bloch, "would perfect the de-organization of technology, of technology which is no longer Euclidean, to the remotest extent: it would jut out of our mesocosmic world into one that that is immeasurably different, not just into one that is subatomic, but also one that is macrocosmic."[17] Much like *Glass Bees*, Bloch's lament about the loss of the mesocosmic reflects a prevailing concern about changing standards of measurement and scale.

The composition of these texts coincided with the most extensive reform of the metric system since its establishment in 1791 after the French Revolution. Jünger wrote *Glass Bees* at the moment when time and space, the long-standing Kantian a priori absolutes of experience, lost their intuitive foundations in quotidian existence and began instead to be regulated by units of measure established on the invisible scale of atomic phenomena. For example, with the invention of the first atomic clock in 1949, the passage of time no longer reflected the movement of the earth around the sun and the alternation of day and night, but came to be determined instead by rates of atomic decay. Spatial extension was likewise deprived of its earthly referent in 1960, when the prototype meter in Sèvres, France, which had been defined in 1791 as a portion of the circumference of the earth, was abandoned and replaced by the most notional of formulas (1,650,763.73 wavelengths of the orange-red emission line in the electromagnetic spectrum of the krypton-86 atom in a vacuum). Before these changes, human beings had by constitution been earth-bound creatures whose perceptions were grounded in the regular movements and finite dimensions of their planet, a natural, knowable object. The earth, Hannah Arendt wrote in 1958, is "the very quintessence of the human condition."[18] But, she continued, the launch into space one year earlier of the first earth-born object, *Sputnik*, had shaken humanity's phenomenological categories, which were rooted in a telluric frame of reference.

One of the most significant scientific developments at this moment was the emergence of the nanoscale. From the iron megamachinery that had dominated the industrial age, science and engineering now turned to inner space and microscopic metrics. The advent of nanoscience is customarily dated to December 29, 1959, when the physicist Richard Feynman delivered a talk entitled "There's Plenty of Room at the Bottom."[19] In this presentation, Feynman envisioned a host of tiny, self-replicating robots manipulating matter at the atomic scale. He also announced the creation of two prizes named after himself, one that would go to the first person to construct a 1/64-inch electric motor and another to the first person to shrink the type on a standard page of paper to 1/25,000 of its original size. Commentators have not failed to point out that Feynman's talk, epochal though it surely was, owed much to ideas and hypotheses circulating in the popular imagination long before 1959, and that key features of Feynman's predictions can be traced to science-fiction sources of the previous decade. *Glass Bees* did not appear in English until 1960 and thus can't be counted among these sources, but the two visions clearly share a common inspiration. For Jünger's science fiction novel about a world infested with micromachinery, Feynman's nanotechnology delivered the science to suit the fiction.[20] Jünger's novel about a zone in which "molecules were being controlled" (*Werke*, 15:541) in fact prefigures multiple topics that dominate current debates about nanotechnology: nanoscience as a space of infinite danger;[21] uncertainty about our ability to maintain control over self-replicating "Lilliputian robots" (*Werke*, 15:426);[22] the replacement of traditional scientific methods by what Bruno Latour has called "technoscience";[23] the inversion of the causal distinction between representing and intervening;[24] the reduction of the human body to a construction site or a collection of parts;[25] and, concomitant with this violation of the body's holistic integrity, declarations about the obsolescence of the human tout court.[26]

One particular convergence between Jünger and contemporary nanoscientists is their shared preoccupation with the volatility, on the scale of single atoms, of the boundary between the natural and the artificial.[27] Animal cells, the building blocks of organic life, are already hundreds of times larger than the objects addressed by nanoscience.[28] As a consequence, at this scale the laws of biology and mechanics, which emerged from the distinction between life and technology, here enjoy parity. The division that Aristotle established between the autotelic human being and its instrument, between natural life and fabricated artifact, loses its purchase in the realm of individual molecules. As nanotech guru Eric Drexler has concluded, the organization of matter at the molecular level causes "the distinction between hardware and life . . . to blur." For this reason, nanologic is ultimately, one scholar proposes, "a cyborg logic, imploding the separation between the biological and the technological, the body and the machine."[29]

If the conventional distinction between life and death breaks down with physical diminution, it becomes clear why, for Jünger, the harbinger of the new technological order would assume the form of a mechanical bee. Indeed, insect life has long attracted attention from philosophers who were captivated by its curious blurring of organic and inorganic. Descartes, for example, referred to insects as "natural automata."[30] The same ambiguous aspect motivated Roger Caillois's fascination with insects first in the autobiography he penned at the age of twenty and then in his essays on the praying mantis and psychasthenia. Jünger evidently learned much from his acquaintance and fellow "entomophile" Caillois.[31] In a direct citation of Caillois's writings from the 1930s, Jünger celebrated insects as "ideograms" that reveal the porosity of the boundary between the living and the mineral. In his memoir *Subtle Hunts* (1967), the insect's hard chitinous exoskeleton occasions meditations on the transitions where life (Jünger favors the Greek word *bios*) both absorbs and is itself absorbed by inorganic matter. "Bones and teeth, shells and armor, stingers and pincers" all testify to dead matter's service to the living: "There is no such thing as 'dead' rock. . . . Chalk is situated on the border between the two domains that we divide into life and death. It is often difficult to distinguish stone from flesh; stone appears to blossom in the coral reefs" (*Werke*, 10:218).

Like *Subtle Hunts*, *Glass Bees* revived the trope of the "organic construction" (*organische Konstruktion*) familiar from Jünger's Weimar text *The Worker.* But the existential stakes and psychological repercussions of this figure are entirely different in the postwar text. Whereas Jünger celebrated the organic construction in 1932 as the vehicle for a vitalistic subordination of matter to the human will, in *Glass Bees* the same phenomenon triggers epistemological uncertainty, paranoia, and insanity. In another allusion to Hoffmann's *Sandman*, the uncanniness of the automata is linked to the derangement of those who encounter them. The narrator Richard recalls, for example, an anecdote about a desperate young man who committed suicide after having fallen in love with an automaton that was incapable of requiting his feelings. Little wonder, too, that Caretti, the man who previously held the job for which Richard is applying, disappeared forever after having been driven mad from hallucinations that left him unable to distinguish between natural entities and phantasmata.

Jünger's hypothesis that the first stirring of the future science would manifest itself in a species of mechanical bees was hardly just the invention of a novelist reaching for a lively conceit. Jünger was in fact an authority on insects. A trained entomologist who, having studied zoology for several years in Leipzig after World War I, continued working informally as a naturalist throughout his life, he had, by the time of his death at the age of 102, conferred his name in the Linnaean taxonomy to several shellfish and butterflies, a single-celled organism, and no fewer than six beetles, including a subspecies of tiger beetle (fig. 6.5). He even felt that his achievements as a naturalist would confer more posthumous glory on him than his literary works.[32] Given his qualifications and achievements as an internationally recognized entomologist, Jünger's prediction that the atomic age will be an entomic one must be heeded.

A product of his profound familiarity with the mechanical principles that underlie insect anatomy, the filiations that Jünger discerned between nanostructures and insect form reflected the knowledge that both observe the same structural laws of scaling. The relationships among the components of an organized

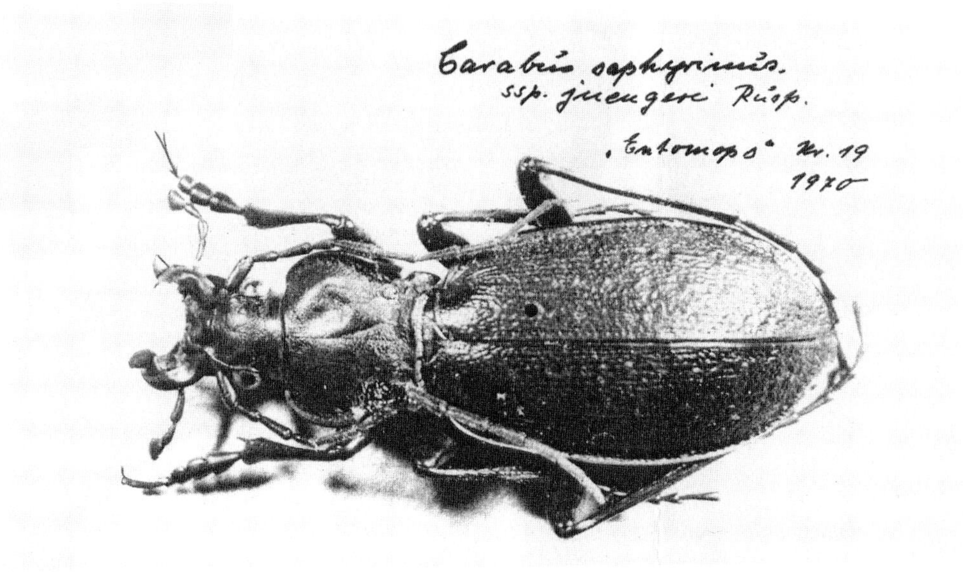

Figure 6.5 *Carabus saphyrinus juengeri.*

system, whether biological or inorganic in nature, must be modified with changes of magnitude. For designers of microelectromechanical systems (MEMS), this means that the laws of Newtonian-scale physics that govern mesoscopic masses such as the human body become less relevant as machines approach the size of individual molecules. As a consequence, the mechanical components developed in the industrial age on analogy with the muscular and circulatory systems of larger vertebrates—conveyer belts, piping, gear drives, derrick cranes, and so on—must be replaced on the smaller scale by quantum mechanisms that are engineered in accordance with different structural principles.

At this magnitude, the tectonics of the insect body offer a persuasive and practicable template. Jünger was not alone in this insight: long before the nanotech revolution, the evolutionary biologist J. S. Haldane had explained in an elegant essay from 1927 titled "On Being the Right Size" that two fundamental principles govern downward scaling: as objects become smaller, gravity becomes less important; at the same time, surface tension—the result of van der Waals cohesion between molecules—increases in significance.[33] To a spider, being dropped down a thousand-yard mine shaft would be of little consequence, but for a human it would be fatal. Conversely, a healthy human being has no trouble lifting himself from the bathtub, although a fly, once it has broken the surface of a body of water, is in most cases doomed. A specialist in biometry, Haldane understood that organized systems cannot simply be transposed from one scale to another without affecting their functionality and viability. Tellingly, insects served already in 1927 as paradigmatic illustrations of these laws of scaling.

Haldane's observations about gravity and surface tension have subsequently been recognized as the two most important laws that account for differences in the performances of meso- and nanophenomena. Based on these principles of scaling, recent research has concluded that nanomachines cannot simply be designed as downsized versions of mesoscopic artifacts but must instead originate as "bottom-up" technologies. Hence the unsoundness of the proposal to shrink human instruments to microscopic dimensions.[34] Instead, the anatomy of the insect today informs the "bottom-up" design of MEMS that, like the insect body, convey materials by means of liquid circuits rather than closed circulatory systems. The architecture of the insect hemocoel, or body cavity, provides a compelling blueprint for the construction of microfluidic devices (fig. 6.6). This is because the transportation of blood within an arthropod's fluid-filled hemocoel is actuated chiefly by means of percolation, diffusion, and van der Waals cohesion rather than by pump circulation through discrete blood vessels. Unlike the vertebrate anatomy that serves as the model for conventional machinery, the internal cavity of the insect is not threaded with tubes and pumps that regulate blood flow to the individual parts of the body. Instead, the insect's organs float in a tank of fluid hemolymph. On the microscale, the closed circulatory systems that vertebrates use to transport blood long distances would be not just superfluous but actually unviable. Bioengineers have consequently concluded that optimal MEMS should utilize the same principles to distribute materials as those used in the insect body.[35]

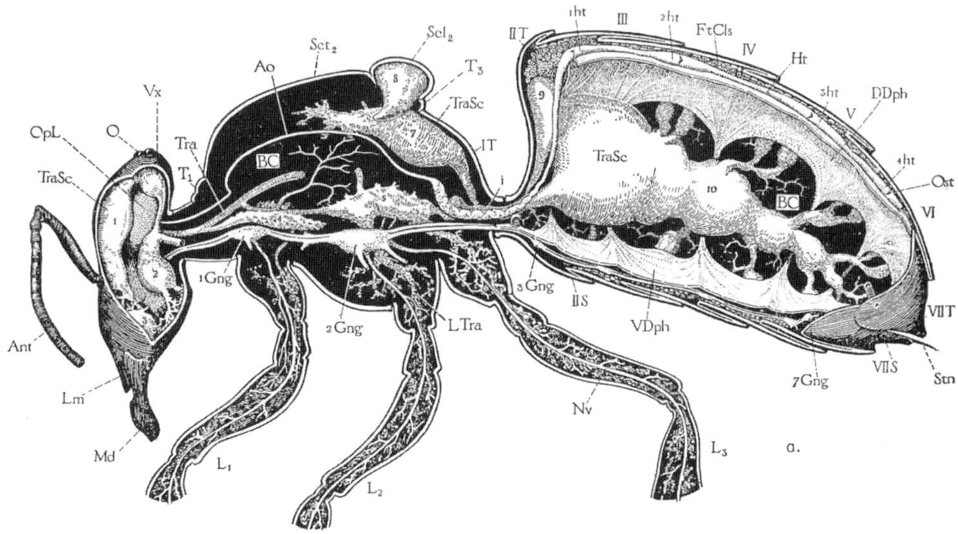

Figure 6.6 The nervous and open circulatory system of *Apis mellifica*. From Hermann Weber, *Lehrbuch der Entomologie* (1933).

That the laws of scaling govern both the physiology of insects and the architecture of MEMS may explain why Jünger would confer an entomic aspect to atomic technology, but this does not yet answer why, in 1957, he would select a honeybee rather than some other insect as the herald of this future world. The answer can be found in the honeybee's newfound status in the 1950s as a natural prototype for the modern microprocessor. Since Hesiod and Aristotle, the honeybee hive had served poets and philosophers as an emblem of civic organization and political order,[36] but in the 1950s extensive scientific research into the social life and swarm intelligence of the bee added new dimensions to its ancient metaphorical value. With the explosion of interest in its communicative capacities, *Apis mellifera* was transformed from a paradigm of civic virtue to an exemplary number cruncher and information processor. Leading this development was Karl von Frisch, the German zoologist who declared in a 1956 article that "the language of the bees is on a higher level than the means of communication among birds and mammals with the exception of man."[37] Substantiated by decades of research on the dances bees use to transmit information about the location of food sources, von Frisch's research became by the end of the 1940s one of the most sensational discoveries of entomology and cognitive ethology. A three-month lecture tour through the United States in 1949 and the publication of the lectures the following year as *Bees: Their Vision, Chemical Senses, and Language* secured the renown of von Frisch's theories about bee language.[38]

In *Bees*, von Frisch demonstrated that forager bees are able kinesthetically to transmit information about the location of food sources to their hive-mates through a series of dancelike movements. Behaving much like pointer breeds of dogs, foragers orient themselves on the honeycomb toward the food source and perform a "dance" into which are encoded variables that indicate the relative distance of the food source, up to 1,250 meters, from the hive (fig. 6.7). Statistical analysis of the accuracy of bee language suggested that bee comprehension, in the words of two researchers, "may not compare unfavorably with the performance of human beings when given complicated instructions." In fact, apian directions to hive mates were notably more accurate than human phrases such as "northeast by east."[39] Differentiations within bee language turned out to be so sophisticated that researchers came across dialectal distinctions between various species. Expanding on von Frisch's experiments, his student Martin Lindauer even discovered that bees use a version of the "dance" to reach a consensus about the location of a future hive: presented with a number of possible choices, the swarm intelligence of the hive arrives at a collective decision using the dance-system in a manner comparable to human voting. Haldane, a former member of the Communist Party, had himself conducted experiments on bee language and declared that the discovery of this democratic process among bees was more significant to the history of human politics than even Rousseau's *Social Contract*.[40]

Enthusiasm over the implications of honeybee language was hardly limited to ethological circles. Linguists, too, were fascinated by what was widely regarded to be "the most significant example of versatile communication known in any animals other than our species."[41] In a 1952 essay discussing von Frisch's

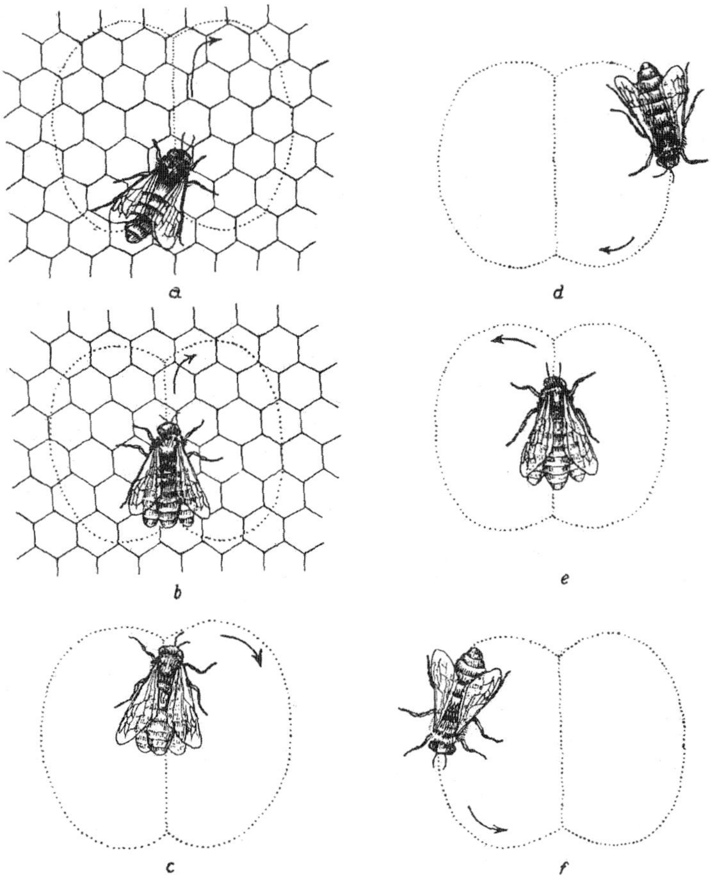

Figure 6.7 The waggle dance of the bee. From Karl von Frisch, *Aus dem Leben der Bienen* (1948).

work, the structural linguist Émile Benveniste marveled at the discovery of highly complex language among insects, which were hardly considered to be very far up on the evolutionary chain. Honeybee language belied the assumption that animals are incapable of communication on the order of human speech. According to Benveniste, the only qualitative distinction between human and honeybee language is that the latter knows no second order of transmission; in other words, the message cannot be reproduced by another bee that has not already seen for itself what is being announced (e.g., the location of the food source).[42] Benveniste consequently reasoned that bees communicate using signals rather than abstract symbols. Their language was, he concluded, bodily and contagious, not cognitive and conventional.

But others who were inclined to more behaviorist models of communication would not recognize even this nominal distinction between human and honeybee language.[43] In a 1963 review of the work of von Frisch and Lindauer, the semiotician Thomas Sebeok argued that honeybee language offered evidence to support Roman Jakobson's case for the existence of a panchronic linguistic system that was composed of universal distinctive features.[44] Citing Jakobson's observations about "the direct homology between the logic of molecular and phonemic codes," Sebeok saw honeybee communication as confirmation of a unified and all-embracing theory of language.[45] Ahead of the genome-mapping projects of the 1990s, bee communication became proof that informational codes were common to all forms of animate being and could be found at all levels within these beings from the cellular to the systemic. Jakobson claimed that certain linguistic structures could be discerned at the molecular level even in inorganic entities.

Listening to the wordless dance of *Apis mellifera*, scientists in the 1950s thus overheard the cosmic language of all creation. Behind the curtain of silence that enveloped mute matter, von Frisch had picked up the murmurings of a natural world teeming with signals and messages. Sebeok likened the student of animal communication to a "cryptologist" who deciphers the myriad flows of information pulsing through nature.[46] The apparent discovery of a transcendental language that encompassed all phenomena from biological genetics to molecular structures and abstract human logic gave new actuality to the romantic aspiration to decipher the universal Book of Nature.

In the 1950s, this romantic science went by the name of cybernetics, and the bee, a tiny modulator of informational flows, was given the title of nature's archetypal microprocessor. With direct reference to Shannon and Weaver's 1949 *Mathematical Theory of Communication*, Haldane and the geneticist Helen Spurway proposed that communication between bees provided the "perfect example" of "etiological cybernetics."[47] The symbolic language of these tiny microprocessors, they wrote, "is like that of an analogical calculator such as a slide rule or a speedometer, which represents one continuously variable magnitude by another. The human symbolism is like that of a digital computer such as an ordinary calculating machine or a mileometer, which represents it by one of a discrete series of symbols."[48] Other scientists too regarded bee communication through the optic of cybernetics. Referring to von Frisch's research, the linguist Charles Hockett suggested in 1959 that the bee could be compared to an analog computer (fig. 6.8)—although, he added, this resemblance also accurately

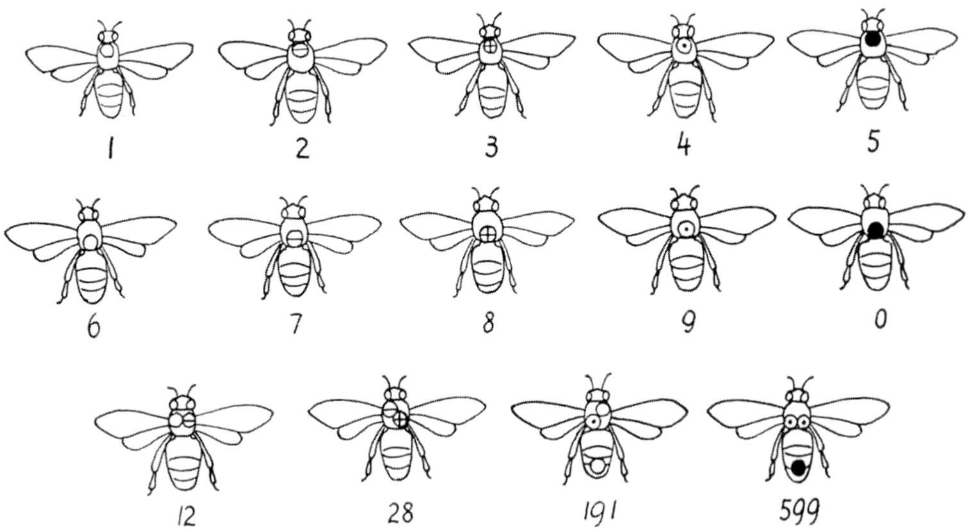

Figure 6.8 Von Frisch's code for identifying bees. From Karl von Frisch, *Bees: Their Vision, Chemical Sense, and Language* (1950).

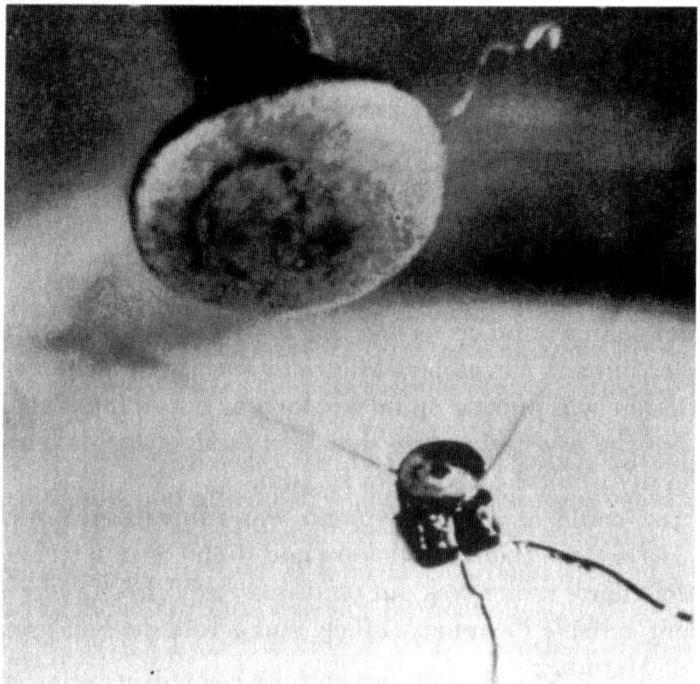

Figure 6.9 William McLellan's 1/64-inch micromotor, which won the first Feynman Prize in 1960.

reflected the limitations of analog systems: "An analog computer is often beautifully adapted for a narrow function and worthless for anything else. Just so, bees can talk about nectar and hive-sites; humans can talk about anything."[49]

As an enthusiastic entomologist, Jünger could scarcely have been unaware of such momentous developments within the discipline that was his lifelong passion. Given the insect's status, already in the 1920s, as an object lesson in those principles of mathematical scaling that would subsequently become fundamental criteria informing the design of MEMS and nanotechnologies, and given, three decades later, the explosion of research into honeybee language that established the bee as an exemplary microcomputer, it cannot be surprising that future

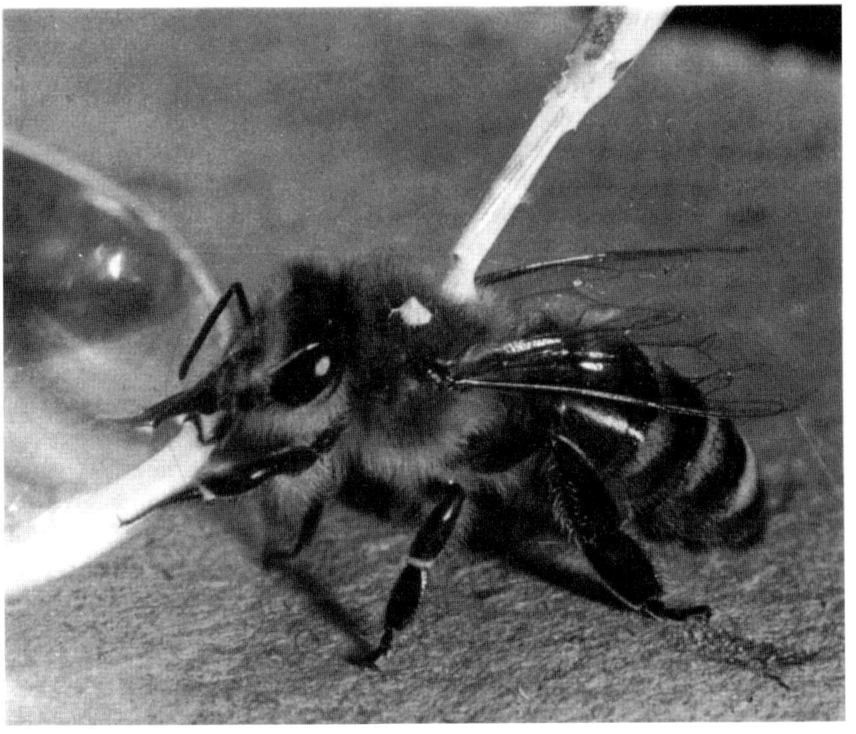

Figure 6.10 A bee is given the number 16. From Karl von Frisch, *The Dance Language and Orientation of the Bees* (1967).

science takes on the likeness of the glass bee in Jünger's 1957 novel. Indeed, bees figure prominently in a number of the author's postwar meditations on technology. He discerned that this insect, both in its architecture and in its capacity as an information processor, was a model machine for the atomic age (figs. 6.9, 6.10).

But the insect's displacement of the human as the paradigmatic technical form of the era had drastic implications. The philosophical emblem at the core of Jünger's science fiction novel *Heliopolis* (1949) illustrates his prognosis: in a scene among apiaries, the narrator and a beekeeper contemplate the lessons that humanity could learn from bees, and conclude that these creatures will force us to revise "the old adage that man is the measure of all things" (*Werke*, 15:208). In *Glass Bees*, the final consequence of the new metric order is the disarticulation of the human form into a combinatory scheme of discrete objects: after the revelation of the glass bees follows the discovery of the depot of spare organs. When insects become the measure of all things, the fate of the human is clear: it was inscribed long ago at the etymological origin of *entomon*, which, like *atom*, has as its root the Greek word meaning "to cut." Aristotle had christened these tiny creatures "en-toma" (Lat. "in-sectum") precisely because they struck him as beings that were divisible into distinct segments. The human frame, however, cannot sustain this segmentation as the insect's can: "Has there ever been at any period in the history of the world so many dismembered bodies, so many detached limbs, as in ours?" Richard asks.

For Jünger, the startling otherness of the insect world was compounded by its perceptual virtuality. Its unfamiliar scale, over which presides a set of physical laws alien to vertebrate experience, constitutes a zone that can be accessed only indirectly with the aid of mediating technologies like microscopes. Because the insect world is all but invisible to the unenhanced eye, it becomes inextricable from the mechanical contrivances that render it perceivable. Jünger's entomological memoir, *Subtle Hunts*, in fact begins with young Ernst acquiring the hardware that grants entry into the realm of insects. (The book's first line: "The hunt could begin: Father had given us the equipment for Christmas" [*Werke*, 10:11].) In *Glass Bees*, Richard similarly requires a pair of field glasses to observe Zapparoni's glass bees. Here Jünger dwells on the unease that proliferates in the interval separating spontaneous human vision from vision that is mediated through equipment. The variance between the two has existential implications: in unassisted vision we perceive an object, whereas in mediated vision we encounter only its representation. Zapparoni's field glasses bring the glass bees optically closer at the same time that they render the bees ontically more remote.

Drawing on a similar line of thought, Lukács once suggested that optical instruments can be distinguished by the degree to which they either observe or transgress the parameters of experience that are established in quotidian human existence. "Glasses do not deanthropomorphize," he explained, "while the telescope and the microscope do, since the former just distorts the normal relations within the everyday life of the whole person, while the latter reveals a world that is inaccessible to the human senses."[50] Telescopes and microscopes—portals respectively to the macro- and microcosm—do not belong to the perceptual organon native to our species. Such devices are inhuman, Lukács suggests: they "deanthropomorphize." Thus, as we saw in the opening SEM image (fig. 6.2), it is not just the microtechnologies themselves that institute alien proportions, but the very instruments of visualization that make these forms perceptible.

When Richard observes that Zapparoni's universe of micromechanisms "was just on this side of pure fantasy" (*Werke*, 15:428), he anticipates current concerns about the dubious perceptual status of nanoentities.[51] Because our natural organs lack access to this world, bodies on the nanoscale have no sensual quiddity independent of their visualization through mediating machines: they exist only as representations, as phantoms. Take the SEM image of the gear chain and the spider mite again: unlike optical photography, the SEM does not actually "see" the specimen but uses a stylus to determine its surface contours and then translates the resulting information into an image that is legible to our senses. The same data that were used in this case to generate a three-dimensional image of the mite could just as easily be rendered in a series of numbers, a graph, or a value map. More like a fax machine than an optical camera, the SEM scans its sample in a raster pattern rather than capturing its likeness.[52] The SEM image is thus a highly mediated articulation of preestablished systems of discourse, cultural conventions, and objectivated knowledge and ideology. As one scholar notes, "aesthetic factors (e.g., picture style and quality), epistemological factors (e.g., picture interpretation and artifact identification), and social factors (e.g., collective decisions on goals and standard practices) all play roles in determining the meaning of an electron microscope picture."[53] In the end, the nanoscale remains a realm of quasi-objects, of phenomena that occupy an ambiguous zone between natural fact, technological fabrication, and psychological projection. Figurality thus becomes an occupational ineluctability for those dealing with phenomena that are accessible only through "deanthropomorphizing" technologies such as the SEM. On the nanoscale, the quantum physicist Niels Bohr once observed, "We are suspended in language."[54] In *Glass Bees*, this purely speculative realm with seemingly no reference to natural experience or familiar scales constantly threatens to devolve into solipsism and derangement.

"Without experience there is no measure," Richard notes as he surveys the bees through Zapparoni's field glasses. The insect's usurpation of man as the measure of all things is, however, a future that Jünger's protagonist will refuse. Defying the mind that "negates the free, unspoiled human figure" (*Werke*, 15:547), Richard insists that the human body must remain an indivisible and holistic Gestalt. At the end of the book Zapparoni refuses to give the job to Richard, who is himself in resigned agreement that he is too old-fashioned for the new technologies. The last person to hold the position went insane, after all, and Richard has no desire to suffer the same fate. Jünger nonetheless reserves a happy end for Richard, to whom Zapparoni offers a different job as an arbitrator of disputes among his employees. This line of work should pose significantly fewer ethical and psychological challenges to Richard, who has by now demonstrated that he is far more suited for the world of people than that of technical invention. After receiving an advance from Zapparoni, Richard's final deed in the book, conspicuous in its bathos, is an act of consumer therapy that puts everything back in its (human) place: "I . . . purchased for Theresa a lovely summer dress with red stripes that reminded me of the one she had on when I first encountered her. It fit her like a glove; I knew her measure precisely" (*Werke*, 15:554–555).

Notes

Introduction

1. I write here not of modernism's *end* during the interwar period, but of its *withdrawal* because, of course, the paradigms of aesthetic modernism ebbed during these years only to be reborn in the postwar era with perhaps even more cultural authority and force than before. One of the important contributions of the group of scholars constellated around the journal *October* has been their sustained, collaborative theorization of modernism's repetition in the visual arts. For a formalist perspective on the multiple deaths of abstract painting, see Yve-Alain Bois, "Painting: The Task of Mourning," in *Painting as Model* (Cambridge, Mass.: MIT Press, 1990), 229–244; Benjamin Buchloh provides a historical materialist account of this phenomenon in "The Primary for the Second Time: A Paradigm-Repetition of the Neo-Avant-Garde," *October* 37 (1987): 41–52; Hal Foster approaches the phenomenon of paradigm repetition through the psychoanalytic model of "deferred action" (*Nachträglichkeit*) in *The Return of the Real: The Avant-Garde at the End of the Century* (Cambridge, Mass.: MIT Press, 1996); and Rosalind Krauss provides a structuralist "etiology" of modern art's signature device in "Grids," in *The Originality of the Avant-Garde and Other Modernist Myths* (Cambridge, Mass.: MIT Press, 1985), 8–22.

2. Thorstein Veblen, *The Theory of the Leisure Class: An Economic Study of Institutions* (New York: Modern Library, 1934), 163. As Hal Foster observes in chapter 2 of *Prosthetic Gods* (Cambridge, Mass.: MIT Press, 2004), the human body that was connoted in high arts such as easel painting would necessarily be that of a "proper subject," i.e., a vertical body that has been territorialized according to a valorized set of cultural hierarchies and distinctions.

3. Erwin Panofsky, *Perspective as Symbolic Form*, trans. Christopher S. Wood (New York: Zone Books, 1991), 72. Although Panofsky has little to say specifically about contemporary artwork, his essay's historical narrative suggests intriguing parallels with the development of modern art. Recapitulating a history of art that closely resembles the trajectory of painterly modernism, he

observes in section III, for example, that linear perspective's illusion of space could only be constructed after painting had achieved a condition of radical flatness.

4. Roland Barthes, "Lesson in Writing," in *Image, Music, Text*, trans. Stephen Heath (New York: Hill and Wang, 1977). Similarly, Jameson writes that "character function and situation are in narrative—and thereby in narrative analysis as well—virtually inseparable. . . . One might go on, from this point, to argue the ultimate irreducibility of narrative as such; or, taking it from a different angle, the inevitable anthropomorphism of even our most seemingly abstract conceptual categories." Fredric Jameson, *Brecht and Method* (London: Verso, 1998), 101–102.

5. José Ortega y Gasset, "The Dehumanization of Art," in *The Dehumanization of Art and Other Writings on Art and Culture* (New York: Doubleday, 1956), 11.

6. Jean-François Lyotard, "The Sublime and the Avant-Garde," in *The Inhuman* (Stanford: Stanford University Press, 1991), 89–108.

7. Maurice Merleau-Ponty, "Cézanne's Doubt," in *Sense and Non-Sense*, trans. Hubert L. Dreyfus and Patricia Allen Dreyfus (Evanston: Northwestern University Press, 1964), 16.

8. Gilles Deleuze, *Cinema I: The Movement-Image*, trans. Hugh Tomlinson and Barbara Habberjam (Minneapolis: University of Minnesota Press, 1986), 81.

9. Guillaume Apollinaire, "On Painting," in *The Cubist Painters*, trans. Peter Read (Berkeley: University of California Press, 2004), 9.

10. Herbert Marcuse observes that the historical transition from the individual to the mass subject during the Weimar era precipitated a flattening, or shrinkage, of the ego, which was no longer able to sustain itself as distinct from the id and the superego. The situation "in which the ego and superego were formed in the struggle with the father as the paradigmatic representative of the reality principle—this situation is historical: it came to an end with the changes in industrial society which took shape in the inter-war period." At this moment, the nuclear family as a site of socialization was replaced by the mass media, schools, political parties, consumer lifestyles, and other group identities that assumed management of the ego's functions. As a result of this transformation, Marcuse observes, the task and methodology of psychoanalytic criticism must change correspondingly: "The analysis of the ego turns into *political* analysis where individuals combine in masses, and where the ego ideal, conscience, and responsibility have been 'projected,' removed from the realm of the individual psyche and embodied in an external agent." Herbert Marcuse, "The Obsolescence of the Freudian Concept of Man," in *Five Lectures: Psychoanalysis, Politics, and Utopia*, trans. Jeremy Shapiro and Shierry M. Weber (Boston: Beacon Press, 1970), 46; 48.

11. Adolf Behne, *The Modern Functional Building*, trans. Michael Robinson (Santa Monica: Getty Research Institute, 1996), 128.

12. Walter Benjamin, *Gesammelte Schriften*, ed. Rolf Tiedemann and Hermann Schweppenhäuser, 7 vols. (Frankfurt: Suhrkamp, 1991), 6:132; hereafter referenced and abbreviated in text as *Schriften*, followed by volume and page number.

13. See Hal Foster's discussion of "traumatic mimesis" as a survival strategy in "Dada mime," *October* 105 (2003): 166–176. Rejecting the prevailing conception of Dada as an art movement motivated by purely critical impulses, Foster discerns within Dada ambivalent forms of mimetic adaptation that are "not nihilistic so much as immunological" (170).

14. Helmut Lethen's work over the last two decades has made critical contributions to recovering the connections between the cultural production of the interwar years and their subtending anthropological models. See *Cool Conduct: The Culture of Distance in Weimar Germany*, trans. Don Reneau (Berkeley: University of California Press, 2001). Recent contributions that build on Lethen's pathbreaking work include *Leben und Geschichte: Anthropologische und ethnologische Diskurse der Zwischenkriegszeit*, ed. Thomas Keller and Wolfgang Eßbach (Munich: Fink, 2006); and Gregor Streim, *Das Ende des Anthropozentrismus: Anthropologie und Geschichtskritik in der deutschen Literatur zwischen 1930 und 1950* (Berlin: de Gruyter, 2008).

15. Ludwig Steinecke, "Wissenschaft und Weltanschauung," *Die literarische Welt* 7, no. 2 (May 15, 1931): 1.

16. Arnold Gehlen, *Der Mensch: Seine Natur und seine Stellung in der Welt*, in *Gesamtausgabe*, ed. Karl-Siegbert Rehberg, 7 vols. (Frankfurt: Vittorio Klostermann, 1993), 3:4; *Man: His Nature and Place in the World*, trans. Clare McMillan and Karl Pillemer (New York: Columbia University Press, 1988), 4.

17. Gehlen, *Der Mensch*, 3:14; *Man*, 12.

18. See especially M. Bakhtin, "Avtor i geroi v esteticheskoi deiatel'nosti," in *Estetika slovesnogo tvorchestva* (Moscow: Iskusstvo, 1979), 7–180; trans. Vadim Liapunov as "Author and Hero in Aesthetic Activity," in *Art and Answerability: Early Philosophical Essays*, ed. Michael Holquist (Austin: University of Texas Press, 1990), 4–256. See also Tzvetan Todorov, "Philosophical Anthropology," in *Mikhail Bakhtin: The Dialogical Principle*, trans. Wlad Godzich (Minneapolis: University of Minnesota Press, 1984), 94–114.

19. Oskar Negt and Alexander Kluge, *Geschichte und Eigensinn I: Geschichtliche Organisation der Arbeitsvermögen* (Frankfurt: Zweitausendeins, 1981), 17.

20. In an essay that examines citizenship through the lens of philosophical anthropology, Balibar observes that "the human subject is able concretely to meet the essence of its 'humanity' only within a *civic*, or *political*, horizon in the broad sense of the term." Here he revives Aristotle's definition of man as *zoon politikon*, "the being naturally living by and for the city." "Subjection and Subjectivation," in *Supposing the Subject*, ed. Joan Copjec (London: Verso, 1994), 7, 8.

21. "The history of Being is the history of its inscription in technicity," observes Stiegler in *Technics and Time I: The Fault of Epimetheus*, trans. Richard Beardsworth and George Collins (Stanford: Stanford University Press, 1998), 4. Although Stiegler makes no explicit references to Arnold Gehlen, he has, in effect, extrapolated many of the arguments found in philosophical anthropology through a synthesis of Heidegger's existential phenomenology and the paleoanthropology of André Leroi-Gourhan. See Leroi-Gourhan's opus, *Gesture and Speech*, trans. Anna Bostock Berger (Cambridge, Mass.: MIT Press, 1993).

22. Béla Balázs, "Sachlichkeit und Sozialismus," *Die Weltbühne* 24, no. 52 (1928): 917.

23. Luiz Costa Lima, *Control of the Imaginary: Reason and Imagination in Modern Times*, trans. Ronald Sousa (Minneapolis: University of Minnesota Press, 1988).

24. An epithet that emerged in the late 1920s to describe the neoclassical idiom that began to reappear in the art of the interwar period, the phrase "return to order" is now applied generically to designate a wide variety of figurative art after the avant-garde, from the Italian *pittura metafisica* to German *Neue Sachlichkeit*. On interwar neoclassicism, see Kenneth Silver, *Esprit de Corps: The Art of the Parisian Avant-Garde and the First World War, 1914–1925* (Princeton: Princeton University Press, 1989), and Romy Golan, *Modernity and Nostalgia: Art and Politics in France between the Wars* (New Haven: Yale University Press, 1995). When compared to the radical experimentalism and semioclasm of preceding avant-garde movements, this figurative art is dismissed by critics such as Silver and Golan for a perceived obeisance to traditional conventions of aesthetic depiction. This contrast between an inherently "innovative" avant-garde and a "conservative" realism, however, is open to revision from both sides: on the one hand, as the later development of abstraction in the postwar period shows, formalism is itself just as susceptible to ideological dogmatization as figurative art; on the other hand, as *Realism after Modernism* seeks to demonstrate, interwar figuration reconfigured existing devices of anthropomorphic realism in remarkably innovative ways.

25. Fredric Jameson observes that, for Bloch, the *Kulturerbe* was "less a system of precepts than a sum of possibilities." In Ernst Bloch, et al., *Aesthetics and Politics*, ed. Ronald Taylor (London: Verso, 1980), 13–14.

26. Gilles Deleuze, *Difference and Repetition*, trans. Paul Patton (New York: Continuum, 2004), 330–381.

27. Viktor Shklovskii, *Tetiva: O neskhodstve skhodnogo* (Moscow: Sovetskii pisatel', 1970).

28. The mechanism of evolutionary retardation essential to both Engels's and Freud's understanding of human development is, I would argue, identical to the one found in Gehlen's definition of the human. Engels discussed the "hominization" of the ape though labor in the 1876 essay "The Part Played by Labour in the Transition from Ape to Man [*Menschwerdung des Affen*]," in *Dialectics of Nature*, trans. Clemens Dutt (New York: International, 1940). In *Moses and Monotheism* Freud observes about the curious temporality of human development that "the postponement of sexual life and its diphasic onset [in two waves] are intimately connected with the history of hominization [*die Geschichte der Menschwerdung*]." "Der Mann Moses und die monotheistische Religion," in *Gesammelte Werke*, ed. Anna Freud, 18 vols. (Frankfurt: Fisher, 1999), 16:180; hereinafter abbreviated and referenced in text as *Werke*, followed by volume and page number. *Moses and Monotheism: Three Essays*, in *The Complete Psychological Works of Sigmund Freud*, ed. and trans. James Strachey, 24 vols. (London: Hogarth Press, 1995), 23:75; hereinafter referenced in text as *Standard Edition*, followed by volume and page number. For a more detailed discussion of the "diphasic onset" (*zweizeitiger Ansatz*) of human development, see chapter 4 of this book.

29. Peter Sloterdijk, *Critique of Cynical Reason*, trans. Michael Eldred (Minneapolis: University of Minnesota Press, 1987), 389.

30. Bertolt Brecht, "Über den formalistischen Charakter der Realismustheorie," in *Werke: Grosse kommentierte Berliner und Frankfurter Ausgabe*, ed. Werner Hecht et al., 30 vols. (Frankfurt: Suhrkamp, 1988), 22:439; hereinafter referenced in the text as *Werke*, followed by volume and page number.

31. Walter Benjamin, *Selected Writings*, ed. Marcus Bullock and Michael Jennings, 4 vols. (Cambridge, Mass.: Harvard University Press, 1996), 2:769; hereinafter abbreviated and referenced in text as *Writings*, followed by volume and page number.

32. Andrew Hewitt, *Fascist Modernism: Aesthetics, Politics, and the Avant-Garde* (Stanford: Stanford University Press, 1993).

33. Walter Gropius, "László Moholy-Nagy 1895–1946," in *Moholy-Nagy*, ed. Krisztina Passuth (Dresden: Verlag der Kunst, 1982), 446–447.

34. Leo Löwenthal, "Die biographische Mode," in *Schriften*, ed. Helmut Dubiel, 5 vols. (Frankfurt: Suhrkamp, 1980), 1:235.

1 The Myth Reversed: Perspectives of László Moholy-Nagy

1. "It must be noted," Kemény wrote, "that Moholy-Nagy has nothing to do with Suprematism. . . . Suprematism has attained a maximum of creative potential, of the inherent necessity of creation; Moholy-Nagy has achieved a minimum of creative potentiality and one sees in his work the maximum of non-creative aesthetics, of external and contrived sterility. . . . Moholy . . . who is eclectic and derivative, has a[n] . . . insignificant role within the essential outcome of new Constructivist art as within Suprematism. . . . Moholy merely represents the outward organization-fetishism of a poor intellect—without economy and precision." Alfred Kemény, "Comments," trans. Mátyás Esterházy, in *Moholy-Nagy*, ed. Krisztina Passuth (London: Thames & Hudson, 1985), 394–395.

2. The Soviet photographer Aleksandr Rodchenko was tarred with the "formalist" brush when his photographs were compared with those of Moholy-Nagy on the pages of *Sovetskoe Foto* in 1928. See Rodchenko's defense, "Downright Ignorance or a Mean Trick?," trans. John E. Bowlte, in *Photography in the Modern Era: European Documents and Critical Writings, 1913–1940*, ed. Christopher Phillips (New York: Metropolitan Museum of Art, 1989), 245–248.

3. František Kalivoda, "Postscript to the Special Issue of *Telehor* on Moholy-Nagy," in *Moholy-Nagy*, 430.

4. In "The Armed Vision Disarmed: Radical Formalism from Weapon to Style," Abigail Solomon-Godeau, for example, argues that Moholy-Nagy co-opted the revolutionary projects of the Russian avant-garde, and neutralized these agitational techniques by formalizing them as aesthetic devices. In *Photography at the Dock: Essays on Photographic History, Institutions, and Practices* (Minneapolis: University of Minnesota Press, 1991).

5. Moholy-Nagy, "Photography Is Creation with Light," in *Moholy-Nagy*, 304. Trans. mod.

6. Hubert Damisch, *The Origin of Perspective*, trans. John Goodman (Cambridge, Mass.: MIT Press, 1995), 446.

7. Erwin Panofsky, *Perspective as Symbolic Form*, trans. Christopher Wood (New York: Zone Books, 1993), 72.

8. Damisch, *Origin of Perspective*, 424.

9. Panofsky, *Perspective*, 41. Italics added.

10. In this regard, this chapter follows the lead of Yve-Alain Bois, who has written compellingly on the use of axonometric perspective in the work of El Lissitzky. As we will see, axonometry is but one of several para-perspectival systems with which the avant-garde experimented in the 1920s. See Bois, "Lissitzky, Malevich, and the Question of Space," in *Suprématisme* (Paris: Galerie Chauvelin, 1977), 26–46; "Metamorphoses of Axonometry," in *Daidalos* 1 (September 1981): 41–58; "El Lissitzky: Radical Reversibility," *Art in America* (April 1988): 161–181; and "From – ∞ to + ∞: Axonometry, or Lissitzky's Mathematical Paradigm," in *El Lissitzky: Architect, Painter, Photographer, Typographer* (Eindhoven: Municipal Van Abbemuseum, 1990), 27–34.

11. Damisch, *Origin of Perspective*, 42.

12. It is a curious paradox that linear perspective, itself a symbolic instantiation of "modern 'anthropocracy,'" in fact excludes the very form that was the condition for its existence: while perspective may excel at rendering architectural volumes, Alberti, for one, recognized early on its inadequacy for depicting organic forms such as the human body. Margaret Iversen notes that "Alberti's veil, described in his *On Painting*, was designed precisely to deal with irregular bodies, such as the human figure, which do not lend themselves to perspective construction." "The Discourse of Perspective in the Twentieth Century: Panofsky, Damisch, Lacan," *Oxford Art Journal* (2005): 198.

13. On New Vision photography and perspective, see Wolfgang Kemp, "Das Neue Sehen: Problemgeschichtliches zur fotografischen Perspektive," in *Foto-Essays: Zur Geschichte und Theorie der Fotografie* (Munich: Schirmer/Mosel, 1978). For an introduction to New Vision photography generally, see Christopher Phillips, "Resurrecting Vision: The New Photography in Europe between the Wars," in *The New Vision: Photography between the World Wars* (New York: Metropolitan Museum of Art, 1989). On perspective in contemporaneous Russian photography, see Leah Dickerman, "The Radical Oblique: Aleksandr Rodchenko's Camera-Eye," *Documents*, no. 12 (spring 1998): 23–34.

14. Maurice Merleau-Ponty, "Eye and Mind," in *The Primacy of Perception*, trans. William Cobb (Evanston: Northwestern University Press, 1964), 167.

15. Damisch, *Origin of Perspective*, 45.

16. Moholy-Nagy, *Vision in Motion* (Chicago: Paul Theobald, 1947), 118; hereinafter referenced in text as *Vision in Motion*. As Panofsky points out, linear perspective is a profound distortion of physiological vision, although its great appeal is that it applies these distortions systematically and consistently: "the modern vanishing-point construction distorts all widths, depths and heights in constant proportion, and thus defines unequivocally the apparent size of any object, the size corresponding to its actual magnitude and its position with respect to the eye. That is precisely the enormous advantage of the modern method, precisely why it is so passionately pursued" (*Perspective as Symbolic Form*, 40).

17. Jurgis Baltrusaitis, *Anamorphic Art*, trans. W. J. Strachan (Cambridge: Chadwyck-Healey, 1977).

18. Hubert Damisch, *A Theory of /Cloud/: Toward a History of Painting*, trans. Janet Lloyd (Stanford: Stanford University Press, 2002), 134. In "'normal,' 'scientific,' 'rational,' practice," Damisch writes, "perspective functions as a technique for appropriating reality and setting it in order, a technique that has been said to correspond to the establishment of an 'adult' relationship with the world. But that same technique, those same principles can be used in precisely the *opposite way*, for hallucinatory or disconcerting purposes (for *delusion* or deception, as opposed to illusion). This history of perspective cannot be solely identified with that of artistic 'realism'" (133). Anamorphosis, he continues, constitutes precisely this hallucinated distortion of the perspective paradigm. "Rather than annihilating the system, anamorphosis works at its systematic deregulation, and does so—it must be emphasized—using the means of the code itself" (134). Anamorphosis, Damisch concludes, represents "a kind of *reductio ad absurdum* of the *aporia* into which perspective leads when it is reduced to solely its linear components" (136).

Damisch's discussion of anamorphosis in *Theory of /Cloud/* echoes that of Jean-François Lyotard, whose *Discourse, Figure*, published one year prior, argued that anamorphic distortion challenges the structural model of Renaissance perspective, albeit not by negating the system outright, but by multiplying, relativizing, and thus demotivating it. "The principle of the anamorphic picture consists in the play of two imbricated spaces: what is recognizable in one space is not recognizable in the other. The good form of representation is deconstructed by the 'bad' forms," he notes. According to Lyotard, then, anamorphosis is not an alternative to perspectival representation, but is instead an event *within* the grid of representation that, by producing an awareness of difference, causes the system to buckle (*Discours, figure* [Paris: Klincksieck, 1971], 378).

19. On the "entfesselte Kamera" in cinema, see Jacques Aumont, "The Variable Eye, or the Mobilization of the Gaze," trans. Charles O'Brien and Sally Shafto, in *The Image in Dispute: Art and Cinema in the Age of Photography*, ed. Andrew Dudley (Austin: University of Texas Press, 1997); Karl Prümm, "Das schwebende Auge: Zur Genese der bewegten Kamera," in *Medien und ihre Technik: Theorie Modelle Geschichte*, ed. Harro Segeberg (Marburg: Schüren, 2004).

20. Renate Lachmann, "Die 'Verfremdung' und das 'Neue Sehen' bei Viktor Schklovskij," *Poetika* 3 (1970): 226–249.

21. Máriusz Rabinovzsky, "The Photographer Man" (1930), in *Moholy-Nagy*, 425.

22. W. Warstat, "Die 'entfesselte Kamera' und die 'produktive Photographie.' Zu den Ideen Professor Moholy-Nagys," *Deutscher Kamera-Almanach* 19 (1929): 44–45.

23. Nikolai Tarabukin, "Foto-mekhanika," *Al'manakh proletkul'ta* (Moscow: 1925), 106. An edited version of this essay was published later that year as the final chapter in Tarabukin's book *The Art of the Day*, and has been translated into English by Rosamund Bartlett in *October* 93 (summer 2000): 57–77. Since the passages I discuss here do not appear in the later version, I must forgo page references to the English text.

24. Ibid., 108.

25. Lyotard, "Representation, Presentation, Unpresentable," in *The Inhuman*, 123–124.

26. Moholy-Nagy, "Photography Is Creation with Light," 302.

27. Andreas Haus examines the wide range of techniques that Moholy-Nagy used to make photograms in his excellent essay "Lichtgestaltung und Neues Sehen: Die fotografischen Aspekte in Moholys Kunst und Theorie," in *Lászlo Moholy-Nagy: Fotos und Fotogramme* (Munich: Schirmer-Mosel, 1978), 21.

28. Viktor Shklovskii, *Sentimental Journey: Memoires 1917–1922*, trans. Richard Sheldon (Ithaca: Cornell University Press, 1970), 233.

29. György Kepes, *The Language of Vision* (Chicago: Paul Theobold, 1944), 205.

30. For Moholy-Nagy, as for Marx, the mimetic claims of photography are subordinate to its function as a material force of production. Indeed both Marx and Moholy-Nagy distinguished categorically between the camera obscura, which is an image-making device, and photography, which is an industrial technology of production. Marx's only mention of photography appears in a chapter entitled "The Machine and Modern Industry" from *Capital*, where he discusses photography as a form of industrial machinery, not a means of image production.

31. Moholy-Nagy claims to be describing *Kino-Glaz*, but he seems, rather, to be confusing a whole series of distinct scenes from *Man with a Movie Camera*. This correction is ultimately superfluous, however, since Moholy-Nagy admits in a footnote that the scene he "recalls" here does not in fact exist in *any* of Vertov's films: "That Vertov did not shoot this scene in its possible perceptual succession is a mark of his subtlety."

32. Gilles Deleuze, *Cinema I*, 81.

33. Ibid., 60. On Vertov's inhuman photography, see François Zourabichvili, "The Eye of Montage: Dziga Vertov and Bergsonian Materialism," trans. Melissa McMahon, in *The Brain Is the Screen: Deleuze and the Philosophy of Cinema*, ed. Gregory Flaxman (Minneapolis: University of Minnesota Press, 2000), 141–152.

34. Carl Einstein, *Georges Braque*, in *Werke*, ed. Rolf-Peter Baacke, 5 vols. (Berlin: Medusa, 1980–1996), 3:263; hereinafter referenced in text as *Werke*, followed by volume and page number.

35. Moholy-Nagy, "In Defense of Abstract Art," in *Moholy-Nagy: An Anthology*, ed. Richard Kostelanetz (New York: Praeger, 1970), 45.

36. Moholy-Nagy, "Space-Time and the Photographer," in *Moholy-Nagy*, 349.

37. Paul Virilio, *Negative Horizon: An Essay in Dromoscopy*, trans. Michael Degener (New York: Continuum, 2005), 116.

38. Ibid., 151–152.

39. Ibid., 110.

40. Moholy-Nagy, "Dynamic-Constructive System of Forces," in *Moholy-Nagy*, 290.

41. Ibid.

42. Moholy-Nagy, "On the Problem of New Content and New Form," in *Moholy-Nagy*, 287.

43. Decrying verticality as a "ghetto," Virilio also argues against the skyscraper. "Paul Virilio and the Oblique: Interview with Enrique Limon," in *Virilio Live*, ed. John Armitage (London: Sage, 2001), 54. At moments, Virilio and Claude Parent's collaborative architecture, which works almost exclusively with oblique angles, recalls that of Moholy-Nagy. See *The Function of the Oblique: The Architecture of Claude Parent and Paul Virilio, 1963–1969*, ed. and trans. Pamela Johnston (London: Architectural Association Publications, 1996); and "After Architecture: A Conversation with Paul Virilio and Sylvère Lotringer," trans. Michael Taormina, *Grey Room*, no. 3 (spring 2001): 32–53.

44. Peter Yeadon, *Kinetic Reconstructive System*, 2005. Moholy-Nagy's *Kinetic Constructive System* and Yeadon's 2005 animation are discussed in Oliver Botar, *Technical Detours: The Early Moholy-Nagy Reconsidered* (New York: The City University, 2006), 170–177.

45. Siegfried Giedion, *Space, Time, and Architecture* (Cambridge, Mass.: Harvard University Press, 1967), 356.

46. Jean-Marc Offner and Agnès Sander, "For a Geometry of Trajectories. An Interview with Paul Virilio," *Flux*, no. 5 (July–September 1991): 48–54.

47. Walter Gropius, "László Moholy-Nagy 1895–1946," in *Moholy-Nagy*, 432.

48. On the connections between Moholy-Nagy and Malevich, Lissitzky, and Rodchenko, see the essays in *Laslo Mokhoi-Nad' i russkii avangard*, ed. Sergei Miturich (Moscow: Tri kvadrata, 2006).

49. Nikolai Tarabukin, "Eccentric Space and Hyperspace in Painting," trans. Lev Chaim, *Experiment*, vol. 3 (1997), 288–291. Tarabukin's talk on reverse perspective was part of his ongoing research for the book *Philosophy of Icons*. In Russia, reverse perspective was closely associated with the native idiom of icon painting, and as a result was esteemed for being close to popular tradition.

50. Clemena Antonova and Martin Kemp note:

> To make sense, reverse perspective has to be the reverse of something. The obvious implication is that it is reversing the rules observed in linear perspective. In that sense, the term is extremely misleading both on historical and philosophical grounds. Although there were perspectival systems of representation in classical antiquity, Eastern Orthodox art can hardly be thought as an immediate, deliberate, and polemic response to forms of art so culturally remote. On the other hand, if the reversal is defined with respect to Renaissance linear perspective, as generally happens, it is necessary to point out that reverse perspective had been in existence long before what it was supposedly reversing. . . . In practice, the question comes down to whether the major characteristics of linear perspective can be legitimately opposed to those of Eastern Orthodox pictorial space, and vice versa, or whether we are dealing with two completely different pictorial phenomena requiring different frames of optical and conceptual reference. (Clemena Antonova and Martin Kemp, "'Reverse Perspective': Historical Fallacies and an Alternative View," in *The Visual Mind II*, ed. Michele Emmer [Cambridge, Mass.: MIT Press, 2005], 400–401)

51. El Lissitzky, "A. and Pangeometry," trans. Mary Whittall, in *El Lissitzky: Life, Letters, Texts*, ed. Sophie Lissitzky-Küppers (London: Thames & Hudson, 1968), 353.

52. Like Malevich's *Black Square*, which can be read either as a figure within the pictorial field or as a form painted on top of the surface of the canvas, Lissitzky's pyramid illustrates the degree zero of pictorial space, suspended between the pictorial illusion of representational painting and the plastic material of the support structure. The spatial ambiguity of the square, which oscillates between projection and recession, is discussed in Viktor Shklovskii's 1919 essay "Prostranstvo v zhivopisi i suprematisty," in *Khod konia* (Moscow/Berlin: Gelikon, 1923), 90–100; "Space in Painting and the Suprematists," in *Knight's Move*, trans. Richard Sheldon (London: Dalkey Archive Press, 2005), 58–64.

53. Lissitzky, "A. and Pangeometry," 353.

54. Although the 1920 essay was not published until after Florenskii's death, his lectures on the subject of reverse perspective were well known and a standard point of reference for those working on the issue of perspective in Russia in the 1920s. His VKhUTEMAS lectures from 1924 to 1925 have been published under the title *Analiz prostranstvennosti i vremeni v khudozhestvenno-izobrazitel'nykh proizvedeniiakh* (The Analysis of Spatiality and Time in the Visual Arts) (Moscow: Progress, 1993). These fascinating lectures address a number of topics central to the development of the Russian avant-garde at that moment, including the composition–construction debates at INKhUK (The Institute of Artistic Culture) and the postulates of production art.

55. Pavel Florenskii, "Obratnaia perspektiva," in *Izbrannye trudy po iskusstvu*, ed. I. Andronik and M. Trubacheva (Moscow: Izobrazitel'noe iskusstvo, 1996), 47; "Reverse Perspective," in *Beyond Vision: Essays on the Perception of Art*, ed. Nicoletta Misler, trans. Wendy Salmond (London: Reaktion, 2002), 254. Florenskii's arguments about reverse perspective are elaborated in Lev F. Zhegin's *Iazyk zhivopisnogo proizvedeniia: Uslovnost' drevneva iskusstva* (The Language of Painting: On the Conventionality of Ancient Art) (Moscow: Iskusstvo, 1970).

56. Florenskii, "Obratnaia perspektiva," 14; "Reverse Perspective," 207.

57. Florenskii, "Obratnaia perspektiva," 39; "Reverse Perspective," 242.

58. Tarabukin, "Eccentric Space and Hyperspace in Painting," 290.

59. David Bethea, "Florenskii and Dante: Revelation, Orthodoxy, and Non-Euclidean Space," in *Russian Religious Thought*, ed. Judith Kornblatt and Richard Gustafson (Madison: University of Wisconsin Press, 1996), 126.

60. For similar reasons, Meyer Schapiro would later discover the device of reverse perspective, for example, in the disquieting lines of *Wheat Field with Crows* by Van Gogh, an artist whose fate within criticism has been to incarnate painting *non compos mentis*: "the perspective network of the open field, which he had painted many times before, is now inverted; the lines, like rushing streams, converge toward the foreground from the horizon, as if space had suddenly lost its focus and all things turned aggressively upon the beholder." Meyer Schapiro, "On a Painting by Van Gogh," *View* 9 (fall 1946), quoted in Rudolf Arnheim, "Inverted Perspective in Art: Display and Expression," *Leonardo* 5 (1972): 133.

61. Jacques Lacan, "Of the Gaze as *Objet Petit a*," in *The Four Fundamental Concepts of Psychoanalysis*, ed. Jacques-Alain Miller, trans. Alan Sheridan (New York: W. W. Norton, 1978), 72.

62. Clemena Antonova offers an excellent précis of scholarship on the subject in "On the Problem of 'Reverse Perspective': Definitions East and West," *Leonardo* 43, no. 5 (2010): 464–469; and in the article coauthored with Martin Kemp, "'Reverse Perspective': Historical Fallacies and an Alternative View."

63. Friedrich Theodor Vischer, *Kritische Gänge*, ed. Robert Vischer, 2 vols. (Leipzig: Verlag der Weissen Bücher, 1922), 2:31. F. T. Vischer's son, Robert, similarly characterizes the experience of *Einfühlung* in terms of a "transposition [*Versetzung*] of the center": "My ideo-sensory ego is transposed into the *interior* of an object where it experiences the character of this object's form from the inside out. I am in the moon and look down at myself with a wistful gaze." "Der ästhetische Akt und die reine Form," in *Drei Schriften zum ästhetischen Formproblem* (Halle: Niemeyer, 1927), 48. Here Robert Vischer seems to be indebted to the progenitor of philosophical anthropology, Gottfried Herder, whose 1778 *Plastik* characterized empathy as a transposition, or *Versetzung*, of the psychological center of subjectivity. It is in the Vischers' technical and physiological approach to *Einfühlung*, which takes as its point of departure the human organism's innate capacity for mediality—for perception through inorganic objects—that we find articulated already in the nineteenth century some of the most interesting issues and problematics of later media theory. This strain of empathy theory resurfaces, for example, in Ernst Jünger's analysis of a "second consciousness" (*das zweite Bewußtsein*) in modern media societies. Writing in 1934, Jünger observed that the photographic camera, like other "artificial sense organs" (42), cultivates an "ever-increasing ability to see oneself as an object" (38). This eccentric perspective and the "progressive objectification of life" (41) are the consequences of the suffusion of everyday existence with media technologies such as photography, radio, and film. See section 14 of *On Pain*, trans. David Durst (New York: Telos Press, 2008). Four years earlier, Jünger, like Robert Fischer, had illustrated this same experience of mediatized self-contemplation, of "second consciousness," with a scene of gazing back at oneself from the moon. This mobilized vision was the origin of what Jünger tellingly identified as the "stereoscopic gaze"—a vantage that, as we will see shortly, is closely associated with the experience of reverse perspective. In his 1930 "Sicilian Letter to the Man in the Moon," he notes that "our greatest efforts are dedicated to the stereoscopic gaze, which perceives the more secret, dormant corporeality of things." "Sizilischer Brief an den Mann im Mond," in *Sämtliche Werke*, 22 vols. (Stuttgart: Klett-Kotta, 1979), 9:20; hereinafter abbreviated and referenced in text as *Werke*, followed by volume and page number.

64. In "Inverted Perspective in Art," Rudolf Arnheim, for example, argued that, while linear perspective is particularly well suited to depict objects situated on the same horizontal plane as the viewer, reverse perspective must assume a vantage at least slightly above the objects it depicts.

65. Oskar Wulff, "Die umgekehrte Perspektive und die Niedersicht," in *Kunstwissenschaftliche Beiträge August Schamarsow gewidmet*, ed. Heinrich Weizäcker (Leipzig: 1907), 19.

66. Arnheim, "Inverted Perspective in Art," 128. It is significant that Arnheim's essay focuses on Picasso's use of inverse perspective in works from the 1930s and after. He discusses the device in *Two Girls Reading* from 1934 and *Birdcage and Playing Cards* from 1937, which is to say, Arnheim

sees reverse perspective as a key aspect of Picasso's *post*cubist work. The programs of analytic and synthetic cubism, by contrast, still seem to attempt an outright *negation* of linear perspective.

67. Moholy-Nagy, "Space-Time and the Photographer," in *Moholy-Nagy: An Anthology*, ed. Kostelanetz, 65. The version of this 1943 essay that is published in Kostelanetz's book contains passages expurgated from the version printed in Passuth's book.

68. See Jean Clair, "Opticeries," *October* 5 (1978): 101–112; and "Duchamp and the Classical Perspectivists," *Artforum* 16 (March 1978): 40–49.

69. Moholy-Nagy, "Photography Is Creation with Light," 304.

70. Alfred Neumeyer, "Zur Raumpsychologie der 'Neuen Sachlichkeit,'" in *Zeitschrift für bildende Kunst* 61, no. 37 (1928), 66; hereinafter abbreviated and referenced in text as "Raumpsychologie."

71. Panofsky, *Perspective as Symbolic Form*, 67.

72. Ibid., 49.

73. Wieland Schmied, *Neue Sachlichkeit und Magischer Realismus in Deutschland 1918–1933* (Hannover: Fackelträger, 1969), 27, 26.

74. Here Neumeyer seems to follow the argument of Franz Roh in his famous account of New Objectivity painting, *Nach-Expressionismus* (1925). In a chapter entitled "The New Space," Roh discusses the "Raumwucht" ("spatial force") that has arisen in post-Impressionist painting, which "juxtaposes the very close with the very distant." These paintings, Roh observes, "press forcefully into the foreground, but at the same time reach far into the distance": "Everywhere today the image emphasizes the space of proximity, which waxes and surges into the foreground. Moreover, all foreshortenings (which could have been placed in the middle- or back-ground) are perceived to thrust forward rather than recede backward." *Nach-Expressionismus: Magischer Realismus* (Leipzig: Klinkhardt & Biermann, 1925), 54–55. This "thrust forward" conveys the impression of reverse perspective.

75. Oswald Spengler, *The Decline of the West*, trans. Charles Francis Atkinson, 2 vols. (New York: Alfred Knopf, 1926), 1:63–64.

76. Ibid., 1:176. Spengler's stereometric model of space reappears in Heidegger's 1950 lecture entitled "Das Ding" ("The Thing"), which argues that abstract space does not antedate the material thing as its precondition, but that the thing, rather, calls space into being as a concrete field of force. Martin Heidegger, "Das Ding," in *Gesamtausgabe*, ed. Friedrich-Wilhelm von Herrmann, 16 vols. (Frankfurt: Vittorio Klostermann, 2000), 7: 165–184; "The Thing," in *Poetry, Language, Thought*, trans. Albert Hofstadter (New York: Harper & Row, 1976), 165–182. As Heidegger argues here, space does not contain the thing, as Descartes proposed; instead it is the thing that, paradoxically, itself contains space. Heidegger's famous example is that of a jug, a vessel that engenders space as a cavity within its body, giving form, as it were, to a void. "The vessel's thingness does not lie at all in the material of which it consists, but in the void that it holds" ("Das Ding," 171; "The Thing," 169). The jug, we could say, modulates and folds space. From this conception of space as the nonent Heidegger draws an epistemological distinction between the

thing and the object, *das Ding* and *der Gegenstand*: whereas the thing engenders its own space-time and is thus purely immanent and nonequivalent, the object stands opposite the subject (the "over-againstness" of the *Gegen-stand*) within a preexisting grid of representations and ideas. The "uniform distancelessness" of homogeneous, geometral space is what makes the circulation and exchange of objects possible ("Das Ding," 167; "The Thing," 166). Because the thing, unlike the object, dwells within its own spatial envelope, it resists this circulation *qua* sign. Among things, Heidegger continues, man doesn't enjoy the sovereignty he has in the Kantian space of objects. "In the strict sense of the German word *bedingt*, we are the be-thinged, the conditioned ones" ("Das Ding," 182; "The Thing," 181).

77. It is highly probable that Florenskii read Spengler's book, which was immensely popular in Russia in the early 1920s when Florenskii was lecturing on perspective and space in painting. On the reception of Spengler in Russian art circles in 1921–22, see Maria Gough, "The Death of the Object," in *The Artist as Producer: Russian Constructivism in Revolution* (Berkeley: University of California Press, 2005), 121–149.

78. Florenskii, *Analiz prostranstvennosti i vremeni*, 51.

79. Ibid., 23.

80. Ibid., 25.

81. Ibid., 6.

82. Florenskii, "Obratnaia perspektiva," 65; "Reverse Perspective," 269.

83. Anatolii Bakushinskii, "Lineinaia perspektiva v iskusstve i zritel'nom vospriiatii real'nogo prostranstva," *Iskusstvo*, no. 1 (1923): 213–261.

84. See also Bakushinskii's *Khudozhestvennoe tvorchestvo i vospitanie: Opyt issledovaniia na materiale prostranstvennykh iskusstv* (Moscow: Novaia Moskva, 1925).

85. A similar analysis is provided by Hans Jantzen in "Die Raumdarstellung bei kleiner Augendistanzen," *Zeitschrift für Ästhetik und allgemeine Kunstwissenschaft* 6 (1911): 119–123.

86. Many of these same distinctions will reappear the following year in *Perspective as Symbolic Form*, although in Panofsky's text they would be mapped out culturally along a North–South axis rather than an East–West one. Panofsky notes, for example, that Renaissance treatises on linear perspective explicitly forbade constructions with short perpendicular distances and instead recommended redrawing the scene at a greater distance. *Perspective as Symbolic Form*, fn. 149. Similarly, Panofsky explained that the Italians tended to depict vast, open spaces with centered vanishing points, while the Northerners, who were obsessed with mass and volume (i.e., stereometric perception), constructed closed, intimate scenes using oblique perspectives (69–70).

87. Martin Heidegger, "Die Zeit des Weltbilds," in *Gesamtausgabe*, 5: 69–104; "The Age of the World Picture," in *The Question Concerning Technology and Other Essays*, trans. William Lovitt (New York: Harper Torchbooks, 1977), 115–154.

88. Tobias Wilke, *Medien der Unmittelbarkeit: Dingkonzepte und Wahrnehmungstechniken 1918–1939* (Munich: Fink, 2010).

89. Although Moholy-Nagy's first photograms were, like Schad's schadographs, made outdoors using daylight paper, Moholy-Nagy quickly moved indoors, where he henceforth made his photograms with artificial lighting. Again and again Moholy-Nagy praised the superiority of artificial illumination to solar light. In his 1929 essay "Photogram and Frontier Zones," Moholy-Nagy called for the creation of "light studios" that could "replace the obsolete academies of painting." This would allow "creation with direct light" and liberate the artist from his beholdingness to the sun (*Moholy-Nagy*, 306). The goal, he wrote, was to strike a blow against the "sun-worshippers," whom he characterized as "old-timers" (*Vision in Motion*, 178). Here Moholy-Nagy's heliophobia reiterated Lissitzky's position that "the new light will give us new color and the memory of the solar spectrum will be preserved only in old manuals on physics" ("Suprematism in World Reconstruction," in *El Lissitzky*, 332).

90. Rabinovzsky, "The Photographer Man," 422–423.

91. Rosalind Krauss, "When Words Fail," *October* 22 (1982): 95–96.

92. Stereoscopic vision is inimical to the integrated space of linear perspective, which achieved the impression of spatial homogeneity only by limiting vision to a single, monocular channel. The function of the stereoscope is to produce not visual likeness, but the sensation of tangibility. Jonathan Crary, "Techniques of the Observer," in *Techniques of the Observer: On Vision and Modernity in the Nineteenth Century* (Cambridge, Mass.: MIT Press, 1990), 97–137.

93. Moholy-Nagy, "Response," in *Photography in the Modern Era*, 101. This piece was a rejoinder to an essay by Ernő Kállai claiming the incompatibility of photography and facture.

94. Ernő Kállai, "László Moholy-Nagy," in *Moholy-Nagy*, 415. Maurice Merleau-Ponty provides a similar analysis, suggesting that, for Cézanne, the object "is no longer covered by reflections and lost in its relationships to the atmosphere and to other objects: it seems subtly illuminated from within, light emanates from it, and the result is an impression of solidity and material substance. . . . [Cézanne] stated that he wanted to make of Impressionism 'something solid, like the art in the museums.'" "Cézanne's Doubt," in *Sense and Non-Sense*, 12.

95. Fritz Novotny, *Cézanne und das Ende der wissenschaftlichen Perspektive* (Vienna: Anton Schroll, 1938), 39. The spacecraft engineer and theorist of perspective Boris Rauschenbach (1915–2001) linked Novotny's analysis to reverse perspective in his 1986 study *Sistemy perspectivy v izobrazitel'nom iskusstve: Obshchaia teoria perspektivy* (Moscow: Nauka) (Perspectival Systems in the Graphic Arts: A General Theory of Perspective). Unfortunately, Rauschenbach's work on the depiction of space using linear and reverse perspective by and large duplicates Bakushinskii's analysis from the 1920s, without, however, citing Bakushinskii's important research.

96. Merleau-Ponty writes that "Cézanne's painting . . . reveals the base of inhuman nature upon which man has installed himself." "Cézanne's Doubt," 16.

97. Ibid., 14. Merleau-Ponty's analysis continues with the observation that "Gustave Geffroy's table stretches into the bottom of the picture, and indeed, when our eye runs over a large surface,

the images it successively receives are taken from different points of view, and the whole surface is warped."

98. Yve-Alain Bois, "Cézanne: Words and Deeds," *October* 84 (1998): 35.

99. In an interesting coincidence that would corroborate Moholy-Nagy's "New Vision" reading of Cézanne, Krauss's description of the haptic *Niedersicht* of New Vision photography reappears in a later analysis of Cézanne's painting, where, she argues, perception is similarly constituted in the downward glance. Her description of the phenomenology of Cézanne's painting is virtually identical to the "somatic setting" of New Vision photography: "one of the anomalies registered again and again in Cézanne's work is that as the perceptual array swivels out of the strictly vertical field of the diaphane—the plane of vision parallel to the painter's upright regard—and, approaching the plane where he stands, it slides away from the visual and into the ground that is beneath his very feet, the painter is then forced to drop his head and to look instead at the zone of his own body." "The Motivation of the Sign," *Picasso and Braque: A Symposium*, ed. Lynn Zelevansky (New York: Museum of Modern Art, 1992), 268.

100. Merleau-Ponty writes that the "distinctions between touch and sight are unknown in primordial perception. It is only as a result of a science of the human body that we finally learn to distinguish between our senses." "Cézanne's Doubt," 15.

101. Jonathan Crary makes a compelling case for aligning Cézanne with the mechanical eye in "1900: Reinventing Synthesis," in *Suspensions of Perception: Attention, Spectacle, and Modern Culture* (Cambridge, Mass.: MIT Press, 2001), 281–360.

102. Moholy-Nagy, "Modern Art and Architecture," in *Moholy-Nagy*, 339.

103. Moholy-Nagy, *Painting, Photography, Film*, trans. Janet Seligman (Cambridge, Mass.: MIT Press, 1969), 30. Trans. mod. This passage is taken from the 1922 essay "Production-Reproduction," trans. Caroline Fawks, in *Photography in the Modern Era*, 80. Here Moholy-Nagy echoes the program described by Raoul Hausmann in his essay "Biodynamic View of Nature" from the same year (1922):

> The significance of art and technology for human psychology can be found in their continuous capacity to renew its functional elements. It is the ultimate goal of all technical apparatuses to return [*zurückfallen . . . auf*] the acquired capacities back to man as new creative capacities for his organs. This is the goal of radio technology just as it is the goal of the aeroplane. ("Biodynamische Naturanschauung," *Scharfrichter der bürgerlichen Seele: Raoul Hausmann in Berlin*, ed. Eva Züchner [Berlin: Berlinische Galerie, 1998], 172)

On Hausmann's theories of perception and technology, see Bernd Stiegler's "Raoul Hausmanns Theorie der Optophonetik und die Erneuerung der menschlichen Wahrnehmung durch die Kunst," *Hofmannsthal Jahrbuch* 10 (2002): 327–356.

104. Friedrich Kittler, *Optische Medien: Berliner Vorlesung 1999* (Berlin: Merve, 2002), 32; *Optical Media: Berlin Lectures 1999*, trans. Anthony Enns (Cambridge: Polity Press, 2010), 36.

105. Panofsky, *Perspective as Symbolic Form*, 65–66.

106. Florenskii, *Mnimosti v geometrii* (Moscow: 1922). Most of this text was written in 1902, but §9, in which Florenskii seeks to rehabilitate the Aristotelian–Ptolemaic worldview, was written in 1922, on the occasion of 600th anniversary of Dante's death.

107. Ernst Mach, quoted in Pierre Kerszberg, "The Phenomenological Analysis of the Earth's Motion," *Philosophy and Phenomenological Research* 48, no. 2 (December 1987): 182.

108. Fred Hoyle, *Nicolaus Copernicus* (London: Heinemann, 1973), 79.

109. Sergei Kriklaev and Andrei Ujica, "Toward the End of Gravity," trans Sara Ogger, *Grey Room* 10 (1999): 49. As terrestrial creatures, Kriklaev explains, it is inevitable that the earth is the basis for our worldview: "it seems to me that you do look more often at Earth [than into the depths of space], since it is our home. . . . If someone were born on the Moon and had lived most of their life there, he or she would look toward the Moon more than somewhere else" (57).

110. Here three texts are key: "The World of the Living Present and the Constitution of the Surrounding World That Is Outside the Flesh" (1931); "Foundational Investigations of the Phenomenological Origin of the Spatiality of Nature" (1934); and the latter's pendant, "Notes on the Constitution of Space (Continuation of the Investigations on the Phenomenological Interpretation of the Copernican Doctrine)" (1934). See the essays and notes by Husserl translated and published as appendixes in Maurice Merleau-Ponty, *Husserl at the Limits of Phenomenology, Including Texts by Edmund Husserl*, ed. and trans. Leonard Lawlor and Bettina Bergo (Evanston: Northwestern University Press, 2001). *Husserl at the Limits* also includes the important notes for a course taught by Merleau-Ponty in 1959–1960 on Husserl's *Origin of Geometry*. On the latter, also see Jacques Derrida's study of the same text by Husserl, which was written one year after Merleau-Ponty's lectures: *Edmund Husserl's* Origin of Geometry*: An Introduction*, trans. John P. Leavy (Lincoln: University of Nebraska Press, 1989). On geocentrism in the late writings of Husserl, see Juha Himanka, "Does the Earth Move? A Search for a Dialogue between Two Traditions of Contemporary Philosophy," *Philosophical Forum* 31, no. 1 (spring 2000): 57–83; and "Husserl's Argumentation for the Pre-Copernican View of the Earth," *Review of Metaphysics* 58, no. 3 (March 2005): 621–644.

111. *Husserl at the Limits*, 89.

112. David Rodowick, *Gilles Deleuze's Time Machine* (Durham: Duke University Press, 1997), 32.

113. Husserl, "Notizen zur Raumkonstitution," *Philosophy and Phenomenological Research* 1, no. 1 (September 1940): 29.

114. Ibid., 26.

115. Husserl, *Husserl at the Limits*, 153.

2 The Time of Capital: Three Industrial Novels

1. Like Ehrenburg, later scholars working on Reger's *Union of the Strong Hand* have focused their energies on determining the names of the actual persons who served as the sources for the

characters in the novel. Two of the most important discussions of Reger's novel each sedulously reconstruct the original historical references behind these characters. See Jost Hermand, "Erik Regers *Union der festen Hand*: Roman oder Reportage?" *Monatshefte für deutsche Unterricht, deutsche Sprache und Literatur* 57, no. 3 (1965); and Karl Prümm, "Nachwort," in Erik Reger, *Union der festen Hand: Roman einer Entwicklung* (Kronberg: Scriptor, 1976).

2. The leading commentator on German New Objectivity, Helmut Lethen, argued in an early critique of *Union of the Strong Hand* that Reger deliberately concealed the names of those working at Krupp. *Neue Sachlichkeit, 1924–1932: Studien zur Literatur des "Weißen Sozialismus"* (Stuttgart: Metzler, 1970), 73–89.

3. The letter from Ehrenburg's secretary, Anne Marie Ittmann, to Reger (October 12, 1931) as well as Reger's response (November 17, 1931) are in the Reger Archive of the Berlin *Akademie der Künste*, Mappe 55. Contents of the Reger Archive hereinafter referenced in text as Reger Archive, followed by file number.

4. "You will see that [the book] is not a novel in any strict aesthetic sense. But since it involves portraying typical processes and typical mental attitudes in the disguise of a novel, I have called it a 'Novel of Development' [*Roman einer Entwicklung*]. I do this in the hopes of echoing the 'Novel of Education' [*Erziehungsroman*] conceptually and provoking a sense for the contrast that exists between the 'Novel of Education,' which involves the formation of individual character, and what we have here, which is a genre that involves the formation of the strongest power-complex of our age." Resumé of *Union der festen Hand* for the Frankfurter Societätsdrückerei, Essen (May 1, 1930) (Reger Archive, 182).

5. "Vom Oberbürgermeister zum Generaldirektor," in Reger, *Kleine Schriften*, ed. Erhard Schütz, 2 vols. (Berlin, Argon: 1993), 1:272. Hereinafter referenced in text as *Schriften*, followed by volume and page numbers.

6. David Harvey, *The Limits to Capital* (London: Verso, 1999), 142–143.

7. Henry Ford, *My Life and Work* (London: Heinemann, 1923), 263. The fact that Ford makes these observations about the loss of a human scale in, of all places, an autobiography reflects a profound ideological *méconnaissance*, since autobiography, of course, is the leading genre for translating historical processes into a human scale.

8. Erik Reger, *Union der festen Hand: Roman einer Entwicklung* (Berlin: Argon Verlag, 1990), 452. Hereinafter abbreviated and referenced in text as *Union*, followed by page number.

9. Reger explained that the book is not about individuals, but social logics of organization: "It is about the mechanism, about the system. Later on it addresses: the system of the workers' councils, the welfare system, the wage labor system, the system of industrial concerns and rationalization, the system of domestic colonies, the system of quotas, the system of factory communities, the workers' household system, the system for employing capital, the system of political influence, etc." (Reger Archive, 182).

10. "Do not be fooled by the fact that this book is designated a novel on the title page," Reger announces in the first lines of his industrial novel (*Union*, 9).

11. Hermann Broch, "Das Weltbild des Romans," in *Dichten und Erkennen: Essays I* (Zurich: Rhein Verlag, 1955), 233.

12. Georg Lukács, "Reportage oder Gestaltung?" in *Werke*, 15 vols. (Neuwied: Luchterhand, 1971), 4:35–68.

13. Hegel, quoted in Georg Lukács, "Roman kak burzhuaznaia epopeia" (1935), in *Literaturnaia entsiklopediia*, 11 vols. (Moscow: Sov. Entsikl., 1929–1939), 9:808; German translation as "Roman," in *Disput über den Roman: Beiträge zur Romantheorie aus der Sowjetunion 1917–1941*, ed. Michael Wegner et al. (Berlin: Aufbau Verlag, 1988), 327.

14. Adolf Raskin, "Die Union der festen Hand" (1931), reprinted in *Der Scheinwerfer: Ein Forum der Neuen Sachlichkeit*, ed. Erhard Schütz and Jochen Vogt (Essen: Klartext-Verlag, 1986), 296, 293.

15. Walter Benn Michaels has written eloquently on this subject in his analysis of American naturalism at the turn of the century. See his discussion of the corporate entity and "natural persons" in "Corporate Fiction," which appears in *The Gold Standard and the Logic of Naturalism* (Berkeley: University of California Press, 1987).

16. See, e.g., Erik Reger, "Frühlingswiese," *Deutsche Allgemeine Zeitung*, April 19, 1925; and "Gartenbild am Ostertag," *Hannoverscher Kurier*, April 11, 1925.

17. Erhard Schütz, "'. . . der Wille zur Empfänglichkeit . . .' Erik Reger: Leben und Werk," in Reger, *Schriften*, 2:323.

18. On the paradoxical resurgence of nature at the heart of Germany's industrial complex, see Michael Jennings, "Agriculture, Industry, and the Birth of the Photo-Essay in the Late Weimar Republic," *October* 93 (2000): 23–56.

19. As Adorno explained, it is precisely where nature "appears to harden most profoundly within itself" that "concrete, living meaning" challenges the metaphysical unfolding of absolute spirit. "Die Idee der Naturgeschichte," in *Schriften*, 1:345–365. For a discussion of Adorno's talk, see Susan Buck-Morss, "Dialectics without Identity: The Idea of Natural History," in *Origin of Negative Dialectics* (New York: Free Press, 1977), 55, 56.

20. Lyotard, *The Inhuman*, 7.

21. These are the terms of Hans Blumenberg, whose book *Lebenszeit und Weltzeit* argues that the gap between global time and the time of organic existence has never been as great in the history of humankind as it is in late modernity. As he puts it, there is now more distance between the blades of the "scissors of time" (*Zeitschere*) than ever before. Hans Blumenberg, *Lebenszeit und Weltzeit* (Frankfurt: Suhrkamp Verlag, 1986).

22. Hannah Arendt, *The Human Condition* (Chicago: University of Chicago Press, 1958), 322.

23. Aristotle, *The Poetics*, in *Classical Literary Criticism: Aristotle, Horace, Longinus*, ed. and trans. T. S. Dorsch (Harmondsworth: Penguin, 1965), 41.

24. Roland Barthes, "Lesson in Writing," in *Image, Music, Text*, trans. Stephen Heath (New York: Hill & Wang, 1977).

25. Paul Ricoeur, *Time and Narrative I*, trans. Kathleen McLaughlin (Chicago: University of Chicago Press, 1990), 52.

26. Paul Ricoeur, "Initiative," in *From Text to Action: Essays in Hermeneutics II*, trans. Kathleen Blamey and John B. Thompson (Evanston: Northwestern University Press, 1991), 214.

27. On Jung's narration of the mass subject, see Annette Graczyk, *Die Masse als Erzählproblem: Unter besonderer Berücksichtigung von Carl Sternheims* Europa *und Franz Jungs* Proletarier (Tübingen: Max Niemeyer Verlag, 1993).

28. This was how Georg Grosz characterized Jung. Quoted in Walter Fähnders and Andreas Hansen, "Nachwort," in *Vom* Trottelbuch *zum* Torpedokäfer: *Franz Jung in der Literaturkritik, 1912–1963*, ed. Fänders and Hansen (Bielefeld: Aisthesis, 2003), 498.

29. Intermittently active in the finance sector even during his most radical years from the mid-1910s until 1924, Jung began to concentrate again on his work as a trade journalist when his literary celebrity began to wane in the mid-1920s. In 1927 he formed a journalists' bureau called *The German Economic Reports* (*Die deutschen Wirtschaftsberichte*), which profited from the trade connections he had established during his years working in Soviet Russia as a representative of Willi Münzenberg's *Workers International Relief* (IAH). In 1931 Jung founded a finance capital company and edited its journal (*Der Gegner*, or *The Adversary*), which became a leading organ of New Objectivity thought in cultural and economic sectors. The editor of the economic section of the Communist Party paper *Die rote Fahne* observed that Jung, with whom he worked closely, "was never lacking in talent for combining his abundant thoughts with one another; nor did he lack a creative knowledge of dealings within the area of world economy and international finance." Günter Riemann, quoted in Fritz Mierau, *Das Verschwinden von Franz Jung: Stationen einer Biographie* (Hamburg: Nautilus-Verlag, 1998), 199. On Jung's later activity in the economic sector see chapter 8 of Wolfgang Rieger, *Glückstechnik und Lebensnot: Leben und Werk Franz Jungs* (Freiburg: Ça-Ira-Verlag, 1987), 181–197.

30. Gertrud Alexander, "Die Eroberung der Maschinen," in *Vom* Trottelbuch *zum* Torpedokäfer, 126.

31. Ibid., 131–132.

32. Jung was never convinced that his industrial narratives should be designated "novels." Already in 1917 he published an article in the Expressionist journal *Die Aktion* voicing doubts that the "problem of economic relations" could be mastered using techniques of "good S. Fischer epic" like "representation" (*Darstellung*) and "plot" (*Handlung*) (Samuel Fischer, who owned one of the leading belletrist presses, published the likes of Thomas Mann and Hermann Hesse). Franz Jung, "Finanznovellen," in *Werke*, 14 vols. (Hamburg: Nautilus-Verlag, 1991), 1.2:186. Hereinafter referenced in text as *Werke*, followed by volume and page number.

33. He composed each of the volumes of *The Technology of Happiness* during two respective terms in prison: the first when he was detained for hijacking a ship and taking its crew to Russia, where he met with Lenin and Bukharin in the hopes of gaining official Soviet recognition for the syndicalist party that he had helped to found, the German Communist Worker's Party (KAPD); and the second while he sat in jail in Breda for his role as a KAPD agitator and terrorist in the March 1921 uprisings.

34. In a withering review of *The Technology of Happiness*, Gertrud Alexander, who otherwise wrote largely positive reviews of Jung's works, dismissed the second volume of the theoretical text as an "outrage" that "philosophizes into the blue sky" in an idiom even "more confused and bombastic" than its predecessor. Reprinted in *Vom* Trottelbuch *zum* Torpedokäfer, 123, 120, 122.

35. Jung's focus on reproductive labor and the social superstructure as sites for revolutionary struggle placed him in close proximity to the political program of the Russian Proletkul't movement. This affinity must have been evident to the Russians, because during Jung's 1922 trip to Moscow on assignment for Willi Münzenberg's *International Worker's Aid*, Boris Arvatov solicited contributions from Jung for a journal that he was editing for Proletkul't. See Jung's reference to Arvatov in *Werke*, 11:110.

36. On German neo-liberalism and *Vitalpolitik* after 1925, see Michel Foucault, *The Birth of Biopolitics: Lectures at the Collège de France 1978–1979*, ed. Michel Senallart, trans. Graham Burchell (New York: Palgrave Macmillan, 2008), 75–158.

37. Franz Jung, "Das Leben im Dunkeln" (1921), reprinted in *Gegner*, no. 1 (December 1999): 12.

38. "Capitalism is merely a coiling of life; dissolving and unraveling this knot is the first precondition to liberating life and achieving happiness" (*Werke*, 6:18). Here Jung's understanding of property as the obstruction of vital energies closely resembles arguments made by Carl Einstein that same year. In a manuscript entitled "Revolution Smashes through History and Tradition," Einstein defined property and objects as "calcified" tautologies that "rigidify into a myth of guaranteed continuity, into the drunken slumber of the mechanical." And like Jung, Einstein also praised the Bolshevik abolition of private property for unblocking the dense accretions of experience and time that had been "arrested [and] fixed in objects." "Revolution durchbricht Geschichte und Überlieferung," in *Werke*, 4:146; trans. Charles Haxthausen, *October* 107 (2004): 141.

39. Jung designates this inorganic rhythm within the mental apparatus the "Subconscious." His terminology here is significant: as Laplanche and Pontalis point out, the Subconscious (*das Unterbewußte*) implies "the idea of a '*second* consciousness,'" while Freud's preferred concept of the Unconscious (*das Unbewußte*) expresses "the topographical split between two psychic domains" (J. Laplanche and J.-B. Pontalis, *The Language of Psycho-Analysis*, trans. Donald Nicholson-Smith [New York: W. W. Norton, 1974], 431). Thus, unlike the Unconscious, which Freud understood as a distinct domain interior to the mental topography, Jung's term "Subconscious" implies a splitting of the psyche and the emergence of a second consciousness outside of the self. As Jung puts it, the "Subconscious" is a "third element" alien to the mind that is neither subject nor object (*Werke*, 6:24). Whereas the Unconscious is located subjacent to the conscious mind, the Subconscious is located beyond it, "exteriorized in property and capital" (*Werke*, 6:25).

40. On Gross's theorization of schizophrenia as psychic desynchronization, see Lois Madison, "Von der Synergetik zur Schizophrenie: Der Zeitfaktor bei Otto Gross," in *Bohème, Psychoanalyse & Revolution: 3. Internationale Otto Gross Kongress* (Marburg: Verlag LiteraturWissenschaft, 2003). Although numerous other borrowings from psychoanalytic theory can be found in Jung's work, his relationship to psychoanalysis is ultimately too complex to illuminate here. It is worth noting,

however, that at the time Jung was in jail writing *The Technology of Happiness*, he was also editing the works of his friend Gross, who had recently died.

41. Joseph Schumpeter, *Theorie der wirtschaftlichen Entwicklung* (Leipzig: Duncker & Humbolt, 1912).

42. Joseph Schumpeter, "Preface to the Japanese Edition of *Theorie der wirtschaftlichen Entwicklung*" (1937), in *Essays: On Entrepreneurs, Innovations, Business Cycles, and the Evolution of Capitalism*, ed. Richard Clemence (New Brunswick: Transaction, 1989), 166.

43. Joseph Schumpeter, "Karl Marx, der Denker" (1918), in *Beiträge zur Sozialökonomik*, ed. Stephan Böhm (Vienna: Böhlau, 1987), 91.

44. Like Marx, Schumpeter presumed, for the purpose of his analysis, "the absence of outside disturbances" to the capitalist system. Joseph Schumpeter, "The Explanation of the Business Cycle" (1927), in *Essays*, 25.

45. To justify this "purely economic" (*reinwirtschaftlich*) approach, Schumpeter offered the following, quite telling, analogy: although individuals die from a great number of causes, scientists still find it necessary to investigate the patterns and internal ordering of man's lifespan "in the absence of all lesions, by virtue of the working of the human organism." Joseph Schumpeter, *Business Cycles: A Theoretical, Historical, and Statistical Analysis of the Capitalist Process*, 2 vols. (New York: McGraw-Hill, 1939), 1:34.

46. Schumpeter, "The Explanation of the Business Cycle," 30.

47. Spengler, *The Decline of the West*, 2:507.

48. See *Turbokapitalismus: Gesellschaft im Übergang ins 21. Jahrhundert*, ed. Elmar Altvater, Oskar Negt et al. (Hamburg: VSA-Verlag 1997); and Edward Luttwak, *Turbo-Capitalism: Winners and Losers in the Global Economy* (New York: Harper, 2000).

49. Teresa Brennan, *Exhausting Modernity: Grounds for a New Economy* (New York: Routledge, 2000), 130–131.

50. Brennan observes that "agricultural commodities are more obliged to keep their natural forms and thus (it is implied) their natural time-cycles of reproduction." "Why the Time Is Out of Joint: Marx's Political Economy without the Subject," *South Atlantic Quarterly* 97, no. 2 (spring 1998): 271.

51. Richard Clemence and Francis Doody, *The Schumpeterian System* (Cambridge: Addison-Wesley Press, 1950), 19.

52. It would seem that acceleration and capture are in fact not opposed, but simply two modalities of the same time-binding force found everywhere in capitalist production. See Hartmut Rosa, *Die Beschleunigung: Die Veränderung der Zeitstrukturen in der Moderne* (Frankfurt: Suhrkamp, 2005), which argues that, in a dialectical reversal, the speed of early modernization and globalization has now turned into inflexibility and stasis.

53. John Bates Clark, "Review of *Theorie der wirtschaftlichen Entwicklung*," *American Economic Review* 3 (1912): 875.

54. Ibid., 873–874.

55. See Marshall Berman, "Goethe's *Faust*: The Tragedy of Development," in *All That Is Solid Melts into Air* (Harmondsworth: Penguin, 1982), 37–86.

56. Johann Wolfgang von Goethe, *Faust I*, trans. Peter Salm (New York: Bantam, 1985), lines 1687–1689.

57. In the working notes that include references to *Faust*, Jung concludes with the canny observation that "Happiness is everywhere; it is just in a bound state" (*Werke*, 9.2:462). Apt words for a prisoner.

58. For Foucault, too, the structural evolution of capitalism was related to a changing definition of time. Before the 1920s and '30s, bourgeois economic science had "constantly striven to neutralize [labor] by reducing it exclusively to the factor of time," Foucault observed. But during the interwar period economists such as the ordoliberal group in Germany finally recognized the limitations of this purely quantitative method, which left subjective patterns of time and habitus out of its abstract calculus of production. The ordoliberals sought to move beyond the opposition between capital and labor power by developing new sociological methods that addressed these subjective aspects of human capital. See especially Foucault's lecture from March 14, 1979 in *The Birth of Biopolitics*: 215–237; here: 220.

59. Jung's disparagement of organized worker's parties can be traced to his conflicts with the German Communist Party (KPD). Jung was briefly a member of the KPD from 1919 until his expulsion at the beginning of 1920, after which he helped to form the radical Left opposition party, the German Communist Worker's Party (KAPD). Hoping to gain the recognition of the Communist International for the KAPD, Jung and Jan Appel hijacked the ship *Senator Schröder* later that year to Murmansk in order to meet with Lenin and Bukharin; it was also under the charge of the KAPD that Jung went to Mansfeld in March 1921 to incite the general strike. Both initiatives reflected the spontaneist orientation of the KAPD, which, unlike the KPD, did not consider economic categories to be the exclusive determinant of revolutionary consciousness. Jung regarded the "division of classes according to the conditions of their economic activity" to be but a "secondary symptom" of authentic revolutionary struggle, the goal of which was to transform the conditions of everyday existence by reconfiguring social relations, dismantling the patriarchal family, and restoring labor to its nonalienated conditions (*Werke*, 5:10). Since the requisite economic conditions for revolution had already long ago been achieved in Germany, which had the most advanced industrial forces of production in all of Europe and was thus "overripe" for revolution, the KAPD concluded that the obstacles to revolutionary transformation could not be objective economic conditions, but must instead be subjective psychological ones. See the "Programm der Kommunistischen Arbeiterpartei Deutschlands" (May 1920), in *Syndikalismus und Linkskommunismus*, ed. H. M. Beck (Meisenheim, 1967), 407–417. In books such as *The Technology of Happiness* Jung thus eschewed the abstract economistic thinking typical of the KPD and spoke instead the languages of phenomenal experience, subjective solidarity, and psychological

transformation. Only changes in quotidian existence and consciousness would make the belated revolution in Germany possible. "I don't hesitate to say aloud," he wrote in 1919, "that the scope of class struggle will only expand after we have overcome the problematics of proletariat, capitalism and entrepreneurship. It will not conclude with the attainment of material goals or even with the realization of the communist slogan about guaranteeing the means of existence; rather, it will expand into forms of life and the experiential conditions of people in society" (*Werke*, 1.1:231).

60. Étienne Balibar confirms the insights of Jung and Brecht when he observes that the word *proletariat* "as a singular substantive which implies the representation of a personality responsible of a historical mission" "almost never appears in *Capital*." Étienne Balibar, "The Notion of Class Politics in Marx," trans. Dominique Parent-Ruccio and Frank R. Annunziato, *Rethinking Marxism* 1, no. 2 (summer 1988): 19, 18.

61. One review praised Jung for creating a language that is "scratched into the rhythm of the event" and "set in motion by the rhythm of the event." Paul Rilla, "Über Franz Jung" (1919), in *Vom* Trottelbuch *zum* Torpedokäfer, 136.

62. Gertrud Alexander, "*Die Eroberung der Maschinen*" (1923), in *Vom* Trottelbuch *zum* Torpedokäfer, 128.

63. Hans Ulrich Gumbrecht, "Rhythmus und Sinn," in *Materialität der Kommunikation*, ed. Hans Ulrich Gumbrecht and K. Ludwig Pfeiffer (Frankfurt: Suhrkamp, 1988), 715.

64. The everyday, Lefebvre wrote, is the theater of the interaction between "great indestructible rhythms and the processes imposed by the socio-economic organization of production, consumption, circulation and habitat." Henri Lefebvre, *Rhythmanalysis: Space, Time, and Everyday Life*, trans. Stuart Elden and Gerald Moore (London: Continuum, 2004), 73. In his analysis of social space, Lefebvre similarly observed that the history of space "begins . . . with the spatio-temporal rhythms of nature as transformed by a social practice." *The Production of Space*, trans. Donald Nicholson-Smith (Oxford: Blackwell, 1991), 117.

65. Lefebvre, *The Production of Space*, 205.

66. Lefebvre, *Rhythmanalysis*, 14.

67. Ibid., 51.

68. Ibid., 11.

69. Ibid., 52.

70. "In former times the period determining the break between one generation and the next . . . used to be fixed at thirty years. What is the lapse of time nowadays, how many years does it take for the past to be rejected and then forgotten, with the inevitable result: the possibility for subjects to be repeated? Ten years? Five? Even less? The speeding-up and telescoping of the cycle are obvious." Henri Lefebvre, "Tenth Prelude: Renewal, Youth, Repetition," in *Introduction to Modernity: Twelve Preludes, September 1959–May 1961*, trans. John Moore (London: Verso, 1995), 164–165.

71. Ibid., 165.

72. Lefebvre, "Eleventh Prelude: What Is Modernity?" in *Introduction to Modernity*, 211.

73. Robert Edwin Peary, *The North Pole*, with an introduction by Theodore Roosevelt (London: Hodder & Stoughton, 1910), 166–167.

74. A. A. Brill, "Piblokto or Hysteria among Peary's Eskimos," *Journal of Nervous and Mental Disease* 40, no. 8 (August 1913): 520, 519. Brill's chauvinistic analysis of "arctic hysteria" remained essentially unmodified in subsequent psychoanalytic accounts of the phenomenon. Zachary Gussow, for example, described piblokto in 1960 as a "hysteroid behavior" that is "psychologically primitive and infantile, but characteristically Eskimo." In "*Pibloktoq* (Hysteria) among the Polar Eskimo: An Ethnopsychiatric Study," in *The Psychoanalytic Study of Society*, vol. 1, ed. W. Muensterberger and S. Axelrod (New Haven: Yale University Press, 1960), 229, 233. A different group of researchers more recently characterized piblokto as a frenzied reaction of a traumatized ego that is arrested in the pre-Oedipal phase of development. See Edward Foulks et al., "Pre-Oedipal Dynamics in a Case of Eskimo Arctic Hysteria," in *The Psychoanalytic Study of Society*, vol. 8, ed. W. Muensterberger and L. Boyer (New Haven: Yale University Press, 1979), 41–69.

75. Although Jung makes no direct reference to Brill's text, several quoted passages in Jung's sketch are taken from Brill's interview with a man in Peary's expedition. Jung also incorrectly attributes some of Brill's commentaries to Peary's lieutenant, Donald Macmillan.

76. More recent studies of piblokto have inferred a causal "relationship between the appearance of 'pibloktoq' and the events of the early contact era," noting that the syndrome was in fact "made more frequent by contact with Euro-Americans." Lyle Dick, "'Pibloktoq' (Arctic Hysteria): A Construction of European-Inuit Relations?" *Arctic Anthropology* 32, no. 2 (1995): 13, 21.

77. Reinhard Koselleck, "Historia Magistra Vitae: The Dissolution of the Topos into the Perspective of a Modernized Historical Process" and "Historical Criteria of the Modern Concept of Revolution," in *Futures Past: On the Semantics of Historical Time*, trans. Keith Tribe (New York: Columbia University Press, 2004), 26–42; 43–57. Niklas Luhmann, "The Future Cannot Begin: Temporal Structures in Modern Society," *Social Research* 43, no. 1 (spring 1976): 130–152.

78. "These programs, drawn from an unchanging fund, are organized into sequences of stereotyped gestures whose repetition ensures the individual's normal balance within the social environment and his or her own psychological comfort within the group. . . . The individual's integration in society depends upon the smooth performance of these operational sequences in normal life." André Leroi-Gourhan, "Memory and Rhythms," in *Gesture and Speech*, 232.

79. Ibid., 228.

80. Ibid., 233.

81. Lewis Mumford, *The Myth of the Machine I: Technics and Human Development* (New York: Mariner Books, 1971).

82. Structurally such cultures are no less complicated than European society, however, for they compensate for their restricted temporal horizon through the complexification of social and environmental relations. See Luhmann, "The Future Cannot Begin."

83. Max Weber, *The Protestant Ethic and the Spirit of Capitalism*, ed. Talcott Parsons (New York: W. W. Norton, 2009), 54.

84. Ibid., 53.

85. Ibid., 71.

86. Ibid., 71; 25.

87. Wolfgang Rieger, *Glückstechnik und Lebensnot*, 68.

88. See Jacques Derrida's discussion of Nietzsche in "Otobiographies: The Teaching of Nietzsche and the Politics of the Proper Name," in *The Ear of the Other: Otobiography, Transference, Translation*, trans. Peggy Kamuf (Lincoln: University of Nebraska Press, 1988), 1–40.

89. Jean-François Lyotard, *Libidinal Economy*, 162. Here Lyotard is commenting on Aristotle's observation that "What money does for us is to act as a guarantee of exchange in the future: that if it is needed now, it will take place as the need arises."

90. Bourgeois society, as it emerged in the eighteenth and nineteenth centuries, "has been a revolutionary society with a strong structural emphasis on time and corresponding simplifications of social and environmental relations." One of these "simplifications," Luhmann writes, is "the antistructural postulate of equality." "The Future Cannot Begin," 151.

91. Ibid. As Joseph Vogl has likewise suggested, money (qua credit) assumes the rhetorical structure of a *promise*, albeit a promise that can never be fulfilled without imperiling the system as a whole. See Vogl, "1797: Geld als Versprechen," in *Die Ordnung des Versprechens: Naturrecht—Institution—Sprechakt*, ed. Manfred Schneider (Munich: Fink, 2005), 313–332. Here Vogl explains that when paper currency was severed from its material guarantor, the gold standard, this modernization of the economic system introduced a potentially "ruinous loss of reference" (325). Having previously been connected to stocks of gold held in the national treasury, money now lost its representational character and became self-referential. To avoid collapse, this tautological system could only be sustained through permanent deferral of payment—by projecting an endless cycle of exchange across the axis of time. The loss of reference was thus counterbalanced by a "temporalized self-reference," Vogl observes. As a promissory note, money is "a prompt and a reminder of a deferred reciprocity, of an open circle that awaits completion" (314). This temporalization opens onto an endless future, understood as a rolling cycle of exchange, the conclusion of which would result in the collapse of the system. Ultimately, "the power of this continuously open future indicates the lack, an essential absence, that is at the displaced center of this movement: circulation takes place not by means of progressive compensation, but through the endless proliferation of a debt that can never be amortized—a temporalization that is realized in a system that operates perpetually until further notice" (327). Toward the end of his essay, Vogl connects this open system with a libidinal economy that recalls Jung's "technology of happiness": "Credit represents the insatiability of needs" (328).

92. Lawrence Leshan, "Time Orientation and Social Class," *Journal of Abnormal and Social Psychology* 47, no. 3 (July 1952): 591. Leshan's research triggered a host of sociological studies in the 1950s on "DGP," or the "deferred gratification pattern." Focusing on the class variances in the temporal frameworks used by the individual to evaluate her own behavior, these researchers

investigated how confidence in the predictability of the future and the experience of temporal continuity contribute to the individual's scheme of action. Interviews with schoolchildren suggested that middle-class children plan more and have longer-term goals, delaying immediate gratification in order to increase their reward. Renunciation for future gain is a practice that presumes the surplus of resources and stored wealth that create a cohesive and structurally sound temporal edifice. Within unpropertied classes, by contrast, "one does not frustrate oneself for long periods or plan actions with goals far in the future. The future generally is an indefinite, vague, diffuse region and its rewards and punishments are too uncertain to have much motivating value" (Leshan, "Time Orientation and Social Class," 589). This uncertainty about what is to come, a fundamental instability in the vector of events, makes it difficult for members of the working class to perceive themselves as agents of their own fate. Compared to that of the propertied middle class, the orientation of impoverished classes "is one of quick sequences of tension and relief" (589). "Discounting the future, taking the cash and letting the credit go, disavowing major and worrisome self-disciplines," the subjects in the lower and working classes appeared in general to be more present-oriented than their middle-class counterparts (Louis Schneider and Sverre Lysgaard, "The Deferred Gratification Pattern: A Preliminary Study," *American Sociological Review* 18 [1953]: 148). In short, this research into the "deferred gratification pattern" concluded that the monied classes have a monopoly not just on property, but also on futurity. See also Rolf Schmidt, Helmut Lamm, and Gisela Trommsdorff, "Social Class and Sex as Determinants of Future Orientation (Time Perspective) in Adults," *European Journal of Social Psychology* 8 (1978): 71–90.

93. Bakhtin's talk was subsequently published under the title "Epic and Novel." Mikhail Bakhtin, "Epos i roman," in *Voprosy literatury i estetiki* (Moscow: Khudozhestvennaia literature), 460; 458; 459; "Epic and Novel," in *The Dialogic Imagination. Four Essays*, ed. Michael Holquist, trans. Caryl Emerson and Michael Holquist (Austin: University of Texas Press, 1981), 17; 15; 16.

94. "Epos i roman," 473; "Epic and Novel," 30.

95. "Epos i roman," 473; "Epic and Novel," 31.

96. "Epos i roman," 472; "Epic and Novel," 30.

97. Peter Brooks, *Reading for the Plot: Design and Intention in Narrative* (Cambridge, Mass.: Harvard University Press, 1984), 52.

98. Lukács, "Roman," 333–334.

99. Ibid., 314.

100. Ibid., 319.

101. Viktor Shklovskii, "Togda i seichas: Den' smerti Klarissy Garlov" in *Literatura fakta*, ed. Nikolai Chuzhak (Moscow: Federatsiia, 1929), 123.

102. In his 1935 review of *The Threepenny Novel*, Benjamin takes notes the curious historical nonsynchronicities in Brecht's text: "These Londoners have no telephones, but their police already have tanks." *Schriften*, 3:440; *Writings*, 3:3.

103. Karstadt and Epa were two of the first chains to introduce in 1926 a retail system for selling bulk merchandise at fixed unit prices. See Brecht, *Werke*, 24:445.

104. Schumpeter, "Art.: Unternehmer," in *Beiträge zur Sozialökonomik*, 150.

105. Ibid., 144.

106. Harvey, *The Limits to Capital*, 137.

107. Siegfried Kracauer, "Tat ohne Täter" (1925), in *Schriften V: Aufsätze*, ed. Karsten Witte and Inka Mülder-Bach (Frankfurt: Suhrkamp Verlag, 1990), 318–319; 322.

108. Elisabeth Hauptmann, "Über Bertold Brecht," *Der Scheinwerfer*, no. 8–9 (1930): 17.

109. Sergei Eisenstein, "Notes for a Film of *Capital*," trans. Maciej Sliwowski, Jay Leyda and Annette Michelson, *October* 2 (1976): 3, 5.

110. This antifigurative tendency continued in Brecht's next book, the historical novel *The Businesses of Mr. Julius Caesar*. After giving his friends Walter Benjamin and Fritz Sternberg a draft of the book, Brecht was disappointed that they urged him to write a more traditional novel, one with more vivid and compelling characters: "BENJAMIN and STERNBERG, very highly qualified intellectuals, didn't understand it and urgently suggested introducing more human interest, more of the old novel!" Brecht's journal, quoted in Klaus-Detlef Müller, *Brecht-Kommentar zur erzählenden Prosa* (Munich: Winkler, 1980), 237.

111. The German legal system "regarded a joint-stock company as a fictional person that, although capable of engaging in economic transactions, could not commit crimes." Stefan Andriopoulos, *Possessed: Hypnotic Crimes, Corporate Fiction, and the Invention of Cinema*, trans. Peter Jansen and Stefan Andriopoulos (Chicago: University of Chicago Press, 2008), 46.

112. Louis Althusser, "The 'Piccolo Teatro': Bertolazzi and Brecht," in *For Marx*, trans. Ben Brewster (London: Verso, 1969), 142.

113. Brecht began writing *The Threepenny Novel* at the peak of his fascination with logical positivism, which built heavily on the abstract symbolic languages of Frege and Leibniz. He subscribed to *Erkenntnis*, the house journal of the logical positivists, and the names of leading figures in this group (Carnap, Neurath, Russell) appear again and again in his writings during the early 1930s. This encounter with logical positivism formed the horizon for Brecht's understanding of narrative, as indicated in a set of notes "On the Aristotelian Novel" (*Werke*, 21:538), which were written in response to Rudolf Carnap's essay "The Old and the New Logic." In these notes Brecht contrasted the narrative structure of the novel with the language of formal logic described by Carnap. The contentless (*gehaltleer*) propositions of mathematical languages, or *Beziehungssätze*, as Carnap called them, are diagrams of pure relationality. Such functionalist propositions are nonlinear, reversible schemas that exist independently of the specific contents that are inserted as variables. Unlike the novel, these rigorously nonmimetic logical propositions can provide an account of society's laws at a time, Brecht famously wrote, when "reality as such has slipped away into the domain of the functional" (*Werke*, 21:469).

114. One section of *Das Kapital* from which Brecht borrowed directly is chapter 10, "On the Working Day," where Marx describes the antagonism between the temporality of labor power and that of capital. Out of this chapter *The Threepenny Novel* lifts virtually verbatim the account of Mary Anne Walkley, a millner who was worked to death in 1863 and whose demise vividly illustrates the consequences of allowing capital to dominate the pattern of work rhythms without providing time for the reproduction of labor power, for the organic maintenance of life. The anecdote about Walkley shows in the plainest of terms how the time of human life does not correspond to the time of capital. Walkley's story reappears in the third book of *The Threepenny Novel*. *Werke*, 16:332–333.

115. Karl Korsch, "Introduction to *Capital*," trans. T. M. Holmes, in *Three Essays on Marxism* (New York: Pluto Press, 1971), 46–47, 55.

116. Quoted in Korsch, "Introduction to *Capital*," 46.

117. It was not "the great films of Eisenstein" or the "theatrical events of Piscator" that led him to Marxism, Brecht confessed to a Moscow audience in May 1935. "Immunized" against such "influence from an emotional point of view," the playwright was prompted to read Marx, rather, as the result of a "work accident" (*Betriebsunfall*): while he was researching *Joe Fleischhacker*, the play mentioned by Elisabeth Haupmann above, no one could explain to Brecht "the mechanisms of the stock market for wheat," which he concluded must be "inexplicable" and "incomprehensible." "The drama that I had planned was never written," he told his Soviet audience, "and instead I began reading Marx" (*Werke*, 22:138–139).

118. Balibar, "The Elements of the Structure and Their History," in *Reading Capital*, 263.

119. Korsch, "Introduction to *Capital*," 52.

120. Karl Marx, *Capital*, vol. I, trans. Ben Fowkes (New York: Vintage, 1977), 873–874.

121. Toward the end of *The Threepenny Novel* Brecht puts this exact legend in the mouth of a bishop, whom Fewkoomby then interrogates in the afterlife for perpetuating social inequality:

> My friends, everywhere we go on earth we encounter inequality. Every man enters the world as a helpless tiny bundle, naked and unashamed. In this condition he differs in no way from any other suckling. But after a time, differences begin to show themselves. One man remains on a lower rung; another climbs upward. He is cleverer than his fellow man—more industrious, more thrifty, more energetic, he surpasses the other in everything he does. And he will become more prosperous, more powerful, more respected than the other. Inequality comes into being. (*Werke*, 16:370)

122. Marx, *Capital*, 873.

123. Letter of March 17, 1934, reprinted in *Jahrbuch Arbeiterbewegung*, vol. 2: *Marxistische Revolutionstheorien*, ed. Claudio Pozzoli (Frankfurt: Fischer, 1974), 123. When Gershom Scholem read the final chapter of Brecht's novel, he likewise compared it to the theological parable "Before the Law" from Kafka's *The Trial*. The resonances between Fewkoomby's dream and "Before the Law" arise from a shared temporal paradox: in each case, access to conclusive knowledge (of capital, of the law) is foreclosed by the very dimension of time which circumscribes all human endeavor.

124. Frank Kermode, *The Sense of an Ending: Studies in the Theory of Fiction* (Oxford: Oxford University Press, 2000), 46, 52.

125. These quotes are taken respectively from Jason Read, "Primitive Accumulation: The Aleatory Foundation of Capitalism," *Rethinking Marxism* 14, no. 2 (summer 2002): 26; Tony Brown, "The Time of Globalization: Rethinking Primitive Accumulation," *Rethinking Marxism* 21, no. 4 (October 2009): 571; and Jim Glassman, "Primitive Accumulation, Accumulation by Dispossession, Accumulation by 'Extra-Economic' Means," *Progress in Human Geography* 30, no. 5 (2006): 615. Michael Perelman presents a lucid overview of the theory of primitive accumulation in *The Invention of Capitalism: Classical Political Economy and the Secret History of Accumulation* (Durham: Duke University Press, 2000).

126. Balibar, "The Notion of Class Politics in Marx," 49.

127. Marx, *Capital*, 874.

128. On primitive accumulation as a strategy of continuous expropriation, see David Harvey, *The New Imperialism* (Oxford: Oxford University Press, 2005).

129. Étienne Balibar, "The Basic Concepts of Historical Materialism," in Louis Althusser and Balibar, *Reading Capital*, trans. Ben Brewster (London: Verso, 2009), 317.

130. "Individually constructed memory and the recording of personal behavioral programs are entirely channeled through knowledge, whose preservation and transmission in all ethnic communities is ensured by language. This creates a genuine paradox: The individual's possibilities for comparison and liberation rest upon a potential memory whose entire contents belong to society." Leroi-Gourhan, *Gesture and Speech*, 228.

3 *Gestus facit saltus*: Bertolt Brecht's *Fear and Misery of the Third Reich*

1. Georg Lukács, "Es geht um den Realismus," *Das Wort* 6 (1938): 138; "Realism in the Balance," in *Aesthetics and Politics*, trans. and ed. Ronald Taylor (London: Verso, 1977), 58–59. The principal texts of the Expressionism debates are reprinted in *Die Expressionismusdebatte: Materialien zu einer marxistischen Realismuskonzeption*, ed. Hans-Jürgen Schmitt (Frankfurt: Suhrkamp, 1973).

2. Following Lukács's assessment, Brecht scholars regularly designate *Carrar* and *Fear and Misery* as Socialist Realist plays. Brecht's British translator John Willett, for example, assigns these two plays to a "brief period of more or less orthodox realistic writing" in Brecht's production. *Brecht on Theater: The Development of an Aesthetic* (New York: Hill & Wang, 1964), 115.

3. In coordination with Comintern propagandist Willi Münzenberg, Brecht was collecting these clippings to make a second volume of the *Braunbuch*, the famous Communist Party publication from 1933 documenting the first ventures of Hitler's regime of terror.

4. The character of Judith Keith was apparently based on Weigel's close friend, the actress Sadie Leviton. See Klaus Völker's discussion of Leviton in *Ich verreise auf einige Zeit* (Berlin: Transit, 1999).

5. There are numerous and conflicting claims about when the concept of *gestus* first appears in Brecht's work. Rather than get involved in these scholastic debates, I simply follow the opinion of the editors of Brecht's standard edition (*Werke*, 21:711) who date the emergence of the term to 1929. It seems that Kurt Weill began using the term simultaneously in his text "Über den gestischen Charakter der Musik," which appeared in *Die Musik* in March 1929.

6. Brecht did not read Russian, but collaborated with Hube on the translation. Reports in the journal *Die deutsche Bühne* confirmed that Brecht and Hube's work on Tret'iakov's play had taken place in 1929. It seems likely, then, that Brecht was introduced to the play by his close friend and colleague, the Latvian Asja Lacis, who returned to Berlin in 1928 under contract from Soiuzkino with a bag full of the latest theatrical scripts and film scenarios from the Soviet Union. See *Die deutsche Bühne* from February 22, 1930, and August 13, 1930. On Lacis's relationship to Brecht, see her autobiography, *Revolutionär im Beruf: Berichte über proletarisches Theater, über Meyerhold, Brecht, Benjamin, und Piscator* (Munich: Rogner & Bernhard, 1971), 62–63.

7. Tret'iakov had a significant influence on Brecht's work throughout the 1930s. The two worked together closely during Tret'iakov's visit to Berlin in the winter of 1931 and then again during Brecht's trip to Moscow in 1935, when Brecht lived with the Tret'iakov family. Tret'iakov had an excellent command of German and translated Brecht's work into Russian (*Epicheskie dramy*, 1934), while Brecht, conversely, oversaw the translation into German not just of Tret'iakov's *I Want a Baby* but also of theoretical essays such as "The Biography of the Thing."

8. Werner Mittenzwei, *Bertolt Brecht: Von der* Maßnahme *zu* Leben des Galilei (Berlin: Aufbau, 1965), 250.

9. Tret'iakov defined the "attraction" as "each aggressive theatrical moment, i.e. each element that has on the audience an emotional or psychological effect that has been tested experimentally and calculated mathematically to have a determinate emotional shock on the recipient." Quoted in Fritz Mierau, *Erfindung und Korrektur: Tretjakows Ästhetik der Operativität* (Berlin: Akademie, 1976), 92–93.

10. Hube and Brecht's German translation is the only complete version of Tret'iakov's revised play from 1927. Two scenes from the second version were published that year in *Novyi Lef* 3.

11. Tret'iakov, "Khochu rebenka (pervyi variant)," *Sovremennaia dramaturgiia*, no. 2 (1988): 209–237. Brecht's translation of the second version appears as an appendix in Fritz Mierau, *Erfindung und Korrektur: Tretjakows Ästhetik der Operativität* (Berlin: Akademie-Verlag, 1976), 179–246. On *I Want a Baby*, see Mierau's essays "Sergej Tret'jakov und Bertolt Brecht: Das Produktionsstück *Хочу ребенка* (2. Fassung)," *Slawistik* 20, no. 2 (1975): 226–241; and "Standard auf der Bühne oder Fiasko dreier Meister: Tretjakows *Ich will ein Kind haben*," in Mierau, *Zwölf Arten die Welt zu beschreiben: Essays zur russischen Literatur* (Cologne: Röderberg, 1988), 100–108. The most important recent analyses of Tret'iakov's play are Eric Naiman's *Sex in Public: The Incarnation of Early Soviet Ideology* (Princeton: Princeton University Press, 1997), 109–115; and the epilogue to Christina Kiaer, *Imagine No Possessions: The Socialist Objects of Russian Constructivism* (Cambridge, Mass.: MIT Press, 2005), 243–268.

12. This was how the journalist Ada Elizabeth Chesterton characterized Tret'iakov in her 1935 book *Sickle or Swastika?* (London: St. Paul, 1935), 450. In response to Chesterton's question about the features of the new Soviet woman, Tret'iakov observed that "She will inevitably have a child . . . and so complete herself. But this completion will not depend on a permanent alliance with a man. She may take him as a husband, she may regard him as a friend, turn to him as a lover. But to me the woman of the future, the woman who will typify our country in all its strength, courage and sweetness, though she may admit marriage, will be independent of it" (211).

13. Sergei Tret'iakov, "Chto pishut dramaturgi," *Rabis* 11 (1929): 11.

14. Ibid., 9. Similarly, Igor Terent'ev explained that "the idea motivating the play is as follows: sexual desire (or the sex drive) is a biological factor, but the entire *extended* fate of this desire falls into the realm of sociology." "*Khochu rebenka*: Plan postanovki," *Novyi Lef*, no. 12 (1928): 33.

15. Anatoly Lunacharsky, "Nashi poety," in *Sobranie sochinenii,* 8 vols. (Moscow, 1963), 2:337.

16. "'Khochu rebenka'—Doklad v Glavrepertkome o postanovochnom plane, 15 dekabria 1928 goda," *Sovetskaia dramaturgiia*, no. 2 (1988): 242.

17. Novitsky, "'Khochu rebenka'—Obsuzhdenie v Glavrepertkome, 4 dekabria 1928 goda," *Sovetskaia dramaturgiia*, no. 2 (1988), 238.

18. Toby Clark, "The 'New Man's' Body: A Motif in Early Soviet Culture," in *Art of the Soviets: Painting, Sculpture and Architecture in a One-Party State, 1917–1992*, ed. Matthew Cullerne Bown and Brandon Taylor (Manchester: Manchester University Press, 1993): 33–50.

19. Ibid., 32.

20. Ibid., 33.

21. See Peter Szondi's discussion of the "Alleinherrschaft des Dialogs" ("the absolute hegemony of the dialogue") in drama since the Renaissance in his *Theorie des modernen Dramas* (Frankfurt: Suhrkamp, 1956), 15.

22. Mary Ann Doane, "The Voice in the Cinema," *Yale French Studies* 60 (1980): 33–34.

23. Roland Barthes, "Lesson in Writing," in *Image, Music, Text*, trans. Stephen Heath (New York: Hill & Wang, 1977).

24. Erwin Piscator, *Schriften*, 2 vols. (Berlin: Henschelverlag, 1968), 1:126.

25. O. von Pander, quoted in Klaus-Dieter Krabiel, *Brechts Lehrstücke: Entstehung und Entwicklung eines Spieltyps* (Stuttgart: Metzler, 1993), 76.

26. It is interesting to note that Tret'iakov too turned toward the phonogenic in the early 1930s, when he was working as a radio programmer. In "The Writer and the Radio" he pointed to a recent survey that suggested that, on the whole, Russian audiences found radio broadcasts to be tedious. According to Tret'iakov, the source of the problem was that the language used on the radio was a literary Russian unsuitable for the new aural medium. It was an unphonogenic "paper" language fit for the eyes, not for the ears. What was needed, he concluded, was a

"sound-writing" (*звуковой шрифт*) that conformed to the technical parameters of the radio. Tret'iakov, "Pisatel' i radio," *Literaturnaia gazeta*, August 11, 1932, n.p.

27. Hans Eisler, "Einige Ratschläge zur Einstudierung der *Maßnahme*," reprinted in *Sinn und Form: Sonderheft zu Hans Eisler* (1964), 156.

28. Benjamin, *Schriften*, 2:521. On the importance of discontinuity for the *Lehrstück*, see Rainer Nägele, "Brechts Theater der Grausamkeit: Lehrstücke und Stückwerke," in *Brechts Dramen: Neue Interpretationen*, ed. Walter Hinderer (Stuttgart: Reclam, 1984), 300–320; "From Aesthetics to Poetics: Benjamin, Brecht, and the Poetics of the Caesura," in Nägele, *Theater, Theory, Speculation: Walter Benjamin and the Scenes of Modernity* (Baltimore: Johns Hopkins University Press, 1991), 135–166.

29. See Brigid Doherty, "Test and *Gestus* in Brecht and Benjamin," *MLN* 115, no. 3 (2000): 442–481.

30. Tret'iakov and Eisenstein write that "it is pointless to think that the sawing of wood expressively on the stage will earn for that actor a high rate on the sawer's labor exchange, just as the best qualified sawer will make a minimal impression on the stage." "Expressive Movement," trans. Alma Law and Mel Gordon, in Law and Gordon, *Meyerhold, Eisenstein, and Biomechanics: Actor Training in Revolutionary Russia* (Jefferson: McFarland, 1996), 189–190. On the *naturshchik* as the technified actor, see also Sergei Eisenstein's 1924 essay "The Montage of Film Attractions," in *Selected Works*, ed. and trans. Richard Taylor, 4 vols. (London: BFI, 1988), 1:56–57; hereinafter abbreviated and referenced in text as *Works*.

31. Tret'iakov and Eisenstein, "Expressive Movement," 190.

32. "LEF i kino: Stenogramma soveshchanii," *Novyi Lef* 11–12 (1927): 53.

33. This costume proposal is mentioned in Schuldt, "El Lissitzky's photographic works," in *El Lissitzky: Life, Letters, Texts*, trans. Mary Whittall, ed. Sophie Lissitzky-Küppers (London: Thames & Hudson, 1968), 397.

34. Similarly, Osip Brik suggested in "Fiksatsiia fakta" of 1927 that the photogenic marks the intersection between the filmic apparatus and the object it depicts. In *Novyi Lef* 11–12 (1927): 44–50.

35. For an example of formalist film criticism that discusses photogeny, see Boris Eikhenbaum, "Problemy kino-stilistiki," in *Poetika Kino*, ed. Boris Eikhenbaum (Moscow: Kinopechat', 1927). On photogeny, see also Vsevolod Pudovkin, "Fotogeniia," *Kinozhurnal A.R.K.* 1, no. 4–5 (1925): 9; and Leo Mur's critique of Pudovkin's analysis of photogeny in *Kinozhurnal A.R.K.* 2, no. 6–7 (1925), 3–6.

36. Like *photogeny*, *fotogenichnost'* does not distinguish between film and still photography. For this reason, perhaps, Vertov invented the more precise word *kinochestvo*, which was specific to cinema.

37. Following the logic of like-knows-like, the industrial machine always topped the list of phenomena characterized as "photogenic" in the 1920s. Thus, Louis Delluc writes that "a

locomotive, an ocean liner, an aeroplane, a railway are by the very character of their structure photogenic." Quoted in Boris Eikhenbaum, "Problemy kino-stilistiki," 17.

38. Delluc observed that "dans le jargon interlope des cinématographistes, photogénie indique la médiocrité, . . . le juste milieu." Louis Delluc, *Ecrits cinématographiques*, 2 vols. (Paris, 1974), 1:91.

39. Tret'iakov, "Khochu rebenka (pervyi variant)," 227.

40. "Notes for a Film of *Capital*," trans. Maciej Sliwowski, Jey Leyda, and Annette Michelson, *October* 2 (summer 1976): 19–20. Eisenstein discusses in greater detail the diversity of Khokhlova's métier in "Kak ni stranno—O Khokhlovoi," which appeared in a pamphlet published by Viktor Shklovskii entitled *A. Khokhlova* (Moscow: 1926).

41. Siegfried Kracauer, "Die Photographie," in *Das Ornament der Masse* (Frankfurt: Suhrkamp, 1977), 34; "Photography," in *The Mass Ornament: Weimar Essays*, ed. and trans. Thomas Y. Levin (Cambridge, Mass.: Harvard University Press, 1995), 59.

42. Jacques Derrida, "The Double Session," in *Writing and Difference*, trans. Alan Bass (Chicago: University of Chicago Press, 1978), 206.

43. Notes from Brecht's working journal, reprinted in *Brechts Modell der Lehrstücke: Zeugnisse, Diskussion, Erfahrungen*, ed. Reiner Steinweg (Frankfurt: Suhrkamp, 1976), 74.

44. Here I quote the English translation "Fear and Misery of the Third Reich," which captures the shifts in voice superbly. *Collected Plays*, ed. Tom Kuhn and John Willett, 7 vols. (London: Methuen, 1970), 4.3:130.

45. The same year that Brecht finished *Fear and Misery*, he also wrote a critique of Lukács, which, not incidentally, included a defense of James Joyce's use of interior monologue (*Werke*, 22.1:419–423).

46. Theodor Kalepky, "Zum 'Style indirect libre' ('Verschleierte Rede')," *Germanisch-romanische Monatsschrift* 5 (1913): 608–619.

47. Quoted in Umberto Eco, "An Ars Oblivionalis? Forget It!" trans. Marilyn Migiel, *PMLA* 103, no. 3 (May 1988): 258. The consequences of this ineradicability of the sign for the economy of memory will be examined more closely in the following chapter.

48. On the similarities between Brecht and Artaud, see Rainer Nägele "Lehrstücke und Stückwerke" and Franz Norbert Mennemeier, "Bertolt Brechts *Theater der Grausamkeit*: Anmerkungen zum Badener Lehrstück vom Einverständnis" in *The Brecht Yearbook*, vol. 18, ed. Marc Silberman et al. (1993), 72–83.

49. The word *Anstreicher* suggests not just someone who paints, but someone who paints *over* something else. In other words, Hitler's aestheticization is also an act of concealment.

50. See Russell Berman, "Consumer Society: The Legacy of the Avant-Garde and the False Sublation of Aesthetic Autonomy," in *Modern Culture and Critical Theory: Art, Politics, and the Legacy of the Frankfurt School* (Madison: University of Wisconsin Press, 1989), 42–69; and Franz

Dröge and Michael Müller, *Die Macht der Schönheit: Avantgarde und Faschismus, oder die Geburt der Massenkultur* (Hamburg: Europäische Verlaganstalt, 1995).

51. The passages from the fourth night were among the first ones written by Brecht immediately after completing *Fear and Misery*.

52. Tret'iakov, "Dramaturgovy zametki," *Zhizn' iskusstva* 46 (1927): n.p.

53. On Stalin as avant-garde artist, see Boris Groys, *The Total Art of Stalinism: Avant-Garde, Aesthetic Dictatorship, and Beyond*, trans. Charles Rougle (London: Verso, 2011).

54. Tret'iakov, "Dramaturgovy zametki."

55. Viktor Klemperer, *LTI: Notizbuch eines Philologen* (Stuttgart: Reclam, 2010); *The Language of the Third Reich: LTI, Lingua Tertii Imperii: A Philologist's Notebook*, trans. Martin Brady (London: Athlone Press, 2000).

56. Roland Barthes, *Writing Degree Zero*, trans. Annette Lavers and Colin Smith (New York: Hill & Wang, 1968), 24.

57. V. N. Voloshinov, "Marksizm i filosofiia iazyka," in *M. M. Bakhtin: Pod maskoi* (Moscow: Labirint, 2000), 464.

58. Ibid., 470.

59. Roman Jakobson, "Shifters, Verbal Categories, and the Russian Verb," in *Selected Writings*, 8 vols. (The Hague: Mouton, 1962–), 2:130.

60. Sergei Eisenstein, "Chetvertoe izmerenie v kino," in *Montazh*, ed. Naum Kleiman (Moscow: Muzei kino: 2000), 506; hereinafter referenced in text as *Montazh*, followed by page number; "The Fourth Dimension in Cinema," in *Works*, 1:184.

61. Viktor Shklovskii, "Sovetskaia shkola akterskoi igry," *Sovetskii ekran* (November 20, 1928), 4.

62. Eisenstein, "Montazh 1938," in *Neravnodushnaia priroda: Tom pervyi: Chuvstvo kino*, ed. Naum Kleiman (Moscow: Muzei Kino Eizenshtein-Tsentr, 2004), 56.

63. Interesting parallels emerge between Brecht's contention that Lukács "overlooked the montage of 27 scenes" and Iurii Lotman's defense of montage against of the champion of realist cinema, André Bazin. In his book *Semiotika kino i problemy kinoestetiki* (The Semiotics of Cinema and Problems of a Cinema Aesthetic), Lotman explains, for example, that montage "can be found both in the type of cinematography where it is explicitly located on the surface and which is designated as 'montage' cinema, as well as in the type where Bazin detects no montage." Lotman, *Semiotika kino i problemy kinoestetiki*, in *Ob iskusstve* (St. Petersburg: Iskusstvo, 1998), 332. According to Lotman, there are also "hidden forms of montage" (*скрытые формы монтажа*) that are introjected into the performance of the actor himself. "[S]plicing together of pieces of film" is only "the most obvious and explicit type of montage," and fails to consider the full range of constructive techniques, which include styles of acting.

64. Viktor Shklovskii, *Eizenshtein* (Moscow: Iskusstvo, 1973), 144.

65. Ibid., 146.

66. V. V. Ivanov, *Ocherki po istorii semiotiki v SSSR* (Moscow: Nauka, 1976), 68. In *Ivan the Terrible* (London: BFI, 2002), Yuri Tsivian uses a similar psychoanalytic framework to describe the deep structural systems within the film, which arrange the dramatis personae in constellations that do not necessarily observe the logic of a linear narrative.

67. Jiří Veltruský, "Man and Object in the Theater," in *A Prague School Reader on Esthetics, Literary Structure, and Style*, ed. and trans. Paul L. Garvin (Washington, D.C., 1964), 84, 91.

68. Ibid., 91.

69. Roman Jakobson, "Der grammatische Bau des Gedichts von Bertolt Brecht *Wir sind sie*," in *Hölderlin Klee Brecht: Zur Wortkunst dreier Gedichte*, ed. Elmar Holenstein (Frankfurt: Suhrkamp, 1976), 115.

70. Ibid., 115–116.

71. See n. 113 in the previous chapter.

72. Alfred Döblin, "Der Bau des epischen Werks," in *Schriften zu Ästhetik, Poetik, und Literatur* (Olten: Walter Verlag, 1989), 218–219.

73. Eugen Bleuler, *Textbook of Psychiatry*, trans. A. A. Brill (New York: Macmillan, 1924), 38.

74. S. M. Tret'iakov, quoted in Hans Richter, "Begegnungen in Berlin," *Avantgarde Osteuropa 1910–1930* (Berlin: Akademie der Künst, 1967), 20.

75. V. V. Vinogradov, *Sovremennyi russkii iazyk*, vol. 2: *Grammaticheskoe uchenie o slove* (Moscow: Gosudarstvennoe ochebno-pedagogicheskogo Izd-vo, 1938), 484; quoted in A.V. Desnitskaia, "Iz istorii razvitiia kategorii glagol'noi perekhodnosti," in *Pamiati akademika L'va Vladimirovicha Shcherby, 1880–1944: Sbornik statei* (Leningrad: Izd-vo Leningradskogo gos. universiteta, 1951), 142.

76. Émile Benveniste, "Active and Middle Voice in the Verb," in *Problems of General Linguistics*, trans. Mark Elizabeth Meek (Coral Gables: University of Miami Press, 1971), 148.

77. On epic poetics and Mauthner's verbal world picture in the work of Döblin, see Devin Fore, "Döblin's Epic: Sense, Document, and the Verbal World Picture," *New German Critique* 99 (fall 2006): 171–207.

78. Sergei Eisenstein, "Vystuplenie i zakliuchitel'noe slovo na Vsesoiuznom tvoricheskom soveshchanii rabotnikov sovetskoi kinematografii," in *Izbrannye proizvedeniia*, ed. S. I. Iutkevich, 6 vols. (Moscow: Iskusstvo, 1964), 2:114.

79. Ibid.

80. Roland Barthes, "To Write: An Intransitive Verb?" in *The Rustle of Language*, trans. Richard Howard (Berkeley: University of California Press, 1989), 15–16.

81. Eisenstein, "Vystuplenie," 2:117. *Entwicklung des Sozialismus von der Utopie zur Wissenschaft*, in Karl Marx and Friedrich Engels, *Werke*, 39 vols. (Berlin: Dietz, 1957–1968),

19:202; *Socialism, Utopian and Scientific*, trans. Edward Aveling (Chicago: Charles H. Kerr, 1907), 29.

82. Eisenstein, "Vystuplenie," 2:118.

83. Charles Scott, "The Middle Voice of Metaphysics," *Review of Metaphysics* 42, no. 4 (1989): 749; 75281. See Philippe Eberhard, "The Middle Voice as Hermeneutic Key," in *The Middle Voice in Gadamer's Hermeneutics* (Tübingen: Mohr Siebek, 2004), 7–30.

84. In section 9.9, Aristotle notes that "for deeds many things are needed, and more, the greater and nobler the deeds are." *Nicomachean Ethics*, in *The Works of Aristotle*, trans. William David Ross (Oxford: Oxford University Press, 1966).

85. On this untranslatable term, see Fredric Jameson, "On Negt and Kluge," *October* 46 (autumn 1988): 151–177.

86. Oskar Negt and Alexander Kluge, *Geschichte und Eigensinn* (Frankfurt: Zweitausendeins, 1981). English translation forthcoming from Zone Books in 2013.

87. "Die Geschichte der lebendigen Arbeitskraft: Diskussion mit Oskar Negt und Alexander Kluge," *Ästhetik und Kommunikation* 13, no. 48 (1983): 91. Fritz Todt was a leading Nazi engineer who oversaw the construction of the Autobahn using forced labor.

4 A Necrologue of the Ego: Carl Einstein's Autobiography, *Bebuquin II*

1. Leo Löwenthal, "Die biographische Mode," in *Schriften*, 1:235.

2. Heidemarie Oehm, for example, notes that "Einstein's preoccupation with his own biography in the increasing isolation of exile was . . . a way for him to secure his identity." "Carl Einstein: Leben und Werk im Exil," *Exil* (1982): 42.

3. Carl Einstein Archive, *Akademie der Künste Berlin*, file 17. Hereinafter abbreviated and referenced in text as Einstein Archive, followed by the file number.

4. Sebastian Zeidler, "Totality against a Subject: Carl Einstein's *Negerplastik*," *October* 107 (2004): 20–21.

5. In his letter to Kahnweiler, Einstein writes that "I have already known for a long time that the phenomenon known as 'cubism' extends far beyond painting." This observation then prompts, *inter alia*, a discussion of cubist literature (*Werke*, 4:153). Einstein concludes this letter by reiterating his doubt that "cubism is only an optical specialization; if this were the case, then it would be flawed, because it wouldn't be fundamental. As a valid experience [cubism] embraces much more than this; I believe that it is only a question of our power to grasp [cubism]" (*Werke*, 4:160). As we will soon see, this critique of "optical specialization" became fundamental to his general critique of visual modernism.

6. Umberto Eco, "An Ars Oblivionalis? Forget It!," trans. Marilyn Migiel, *PMLA* 103, no. 3 (May 1988): 259.

7. Ibid., 258.

8. Freud too observes that memories can only be transformed, not eradicated: "Since we overcame the error of supposing that the forgetting we are familiar with signified a destruction of the memory-trace [*eine Zerstörung der Gedächtnisspur*]—that is, its annihilation—we have been inclined to take the opposite view, that in mental life nothing which has once been formed can perish—that everything is somehow preserved and that in suitable circumstances . . . it can once more be brought to light." *Werke*, 16:426; *Standard Edition*, 21:16.

9. Eco, "An Ars Oblivionalis?," 260.

10. See especially book ten of *Confessions*: "Memory's huge cavern, with its mysterious, secret, and indescribable nooks and crannies, receives all of [my] perceptions, to be recalled when needed and reconsidered. Every one of them enters into memory, each by its own gate, and is put on deposit there." Saint Augustine, *Confessions*, trans. Henry Chadwick (Oxford: Oxford University Press, 1991), 186.

11. Denis Hollier, "Notes (on the Index Card)," *October* 112 (2005): 40.

12. Letter to Tony Simon-Wolfskehl of Jan. 25, 1923. Quoted in Manuela Günter, *Anatomie des Anti-Subjekts: Zur Subversion autobiographischen Schreibens bei Siegfried Kracauer, Walter Benjamin, und Carl Einstein* (Würzburg: Königshausen & Neumann, 1996), 180.

13. On the practices of self-citation and rewriting in Benjamin's later work, see Michael W. Jennings, "Double Take: Palimpsestic Writing and Image-Character in Benjamin's Late Prose," forthcoming in *Benjamin-Studien* 2 (2011).

14. On Freud and aphasia, see Daniel Heller-Roazen, "The Lesser Animal," in *Echolalias: On the Forgetting of Language* (New York: Zone Books, 2008), 129–148.

15. Thus Derrida's characterization of the convergence of dense inscription and beatific stupor in Freud's model of the "Mystical Writing Pad," or *Wunderblock*. Jacques Derrida, "Freud and the Scene of Writing," in *Writing and Difference*, trans. Alan Bass (Chicago: University of Chicago Press, 1978), 200.

16. Paul de Man, "Sign and Symbol in Hegel's *Aesthetics*," *Critical Inquiry* 8 (summer 1982): 771.

17. Ibid., 773. In his reading of de Man's text on Hegel, Derrida observes that hypermnesia is effectively indistinguishable from amnesia. See Jacques Derrida, "The Art of Mémoires," in *Memoires for Paul de Man* (New York: Columbia University Press, 1989), 86.

18. On the archive and deletion, see Cornelia Vismann, *Files: Law and Media Technology*, trans. Geoffrey Winthrop-Young (Stanford: Stanford University Press, 2008).

19. Lévy-Bruhl describes the process of outsourcing memory thus: "in prelogical mentality memory plays a much more important part than it does in our mental life, in which certain functions which it used to perform have been taken from it and transformed. . . . The preconnections, preperceptions, and preconclusions which play so great a part in the mentality of uncivilized people do not involve any logical activity; they are simply committed to memory. We must

therefore expect to find the memory extremely well developed in primitives, and this is, in fact, reported by observers." Lucien Lévy-Bruhl, *How Natives Think*, trans. Lilian A. Clare (New York: Washington Square Press, 1966), 92–93.

20. Carl Einstein, *Die Fabrikation der Fiktionen*, ed. Sibylle Penkert (Reinbek: Rowohlt, 1973), 111. Hereinafter referenced in text and abbreviated as *Fictions*.

21. Jean-Paul Sartre, *The Imagination: A Psychological Critique*, trans. Forrest Williams (Ann Arbor: University of Michigan Press, 1962), 40.

22. Jean-Paul Sartre, *The Imaginary: A Phenomenological Psychology of the Imagination*, trans. Jonathan Webber (New York: Routledge, 2004), 13. Hereinafter referenced in text *Imaginary*.

23. This understanding of the imagination as the determinate negation of the world would subsequently become the basis for Sartre's definition of consciousness as negation, advanced in his book on existential ontology from 1943, *Being and Nothingness*.

24. See Jochen Schulte-Sasse, "Von der erkenntniskritischen zur linksradikalen Metamorphose der Romantik in der Moderne: Carl Einstein als Paradigma," *Kulturrevolution* 12 (1986): 62–67.

25. Herbert Marcuse, "The Affirmative Character of Culture," in *Negations*, trans. Jeremy J. Shapiro (Boston: Beacon Press, 1968), 88–133.

26. In addition to a 500-page study of Mallarmé, which was destroyed when Sartre's apartment was bombed during the Algerian war, materials were published posthumously as *Mallarmé, or the Poet of Nothingness*, trans. Ernest Sturm (University Park: Pennsylvania State University Press, 1988).

27. Writing in a mixture of German, French, and English that is typical of his exile years, Einstein uses the phrase "common sens" here.

28. The editor of *The Fabrication of Fictions* sets Einstein's handwritten passages in brackets.

29. Arno Holz, *Die Kunst: Ihr Wesen und ihre Gesetze* (Berlin: Wilhelm Issleib, 1891), 58.

30. Ernst Stadler, "Ein Urteil über Bebuquin," reprinted as an appendix in Einstein, *Werke*, 1:499. Niel Donahue summarily observes that the character Bebuquin "consists of negations." "Analysis and Construction: The Aesthetics of Carl Einstein," *German Quarterly* 61, no. 3 (1988): 429. Following Donahue, Dirk Heißerer has placed all of Einstein's work under the sign of negation, titling his 1992 study of Einstein *Negative Dichtung: Zum Verfahren der literarischen Dekomposition bei Carl Einstein* (Munich: Iudicium, 1992).

31. Wolfgang Iser, *The Fictive and the Imaginary: Charting Literary Anthropology* (Baltimore: Johns Hopkins University Press, 1993), 129.

32. Einstein insisted, for example, on a crucial distinction between cubism and suprematism, arguing that the latter, in abandoning reference entirely, had severed all connection with extra-aesthetic reality. Because cubism, unlike suprematism or neoplasticism, would never take the leap into pure nonobjectivity made by Malevich and Mondrian, it would be spared the full fury of

Einstein's later critique of abstract art. Through their schematic, "low-budget clarity," nonobjective paintings "stand in opposition to the complexity of psychic processes," Einstein wrote (*Werke*, 3:53).

33. *Widersinning* is the word used by the gestalt psychologist Wolfgang Metzger in assessing his Ganzfeld ("total field") experiments. "Optische Untersuchungen am Ganzfeld. II. Mitteilung: Zur Phänomenologie des homogenen Ganzfelds," *Psychologische Forschung* 13, no. 1 (Jan. 1930): 7. See also the other findings, which appeared in Willy Engel, "Optische Untersuchungen am Ganzfeld. I. Mitteilung: Die Ganzfeldordnung," and Wolfgang Metzger, "Optische Untersuchungen am Ganzfeld. III. Mitteilung: Die Schwelle für plötzliche Helligkeitsänderung," both in *Psychologische Forschung* 13, no. 1 (Jan. 1930): 1–5, 30–54. The components of this experiment read like an assay of Greenbergian modernism: immobilized and thus allowed no forms of intersensory stimulation such as proprioceptive movement (= "pure opticality"), the spectator was placed before a giant luminous screen that wholly encompassed his field of vision (= "alloverness"). The idea of the Ganzfeld experiments, writes Brian Massumi, "was that if you could experimentally isolate the physical and physiological conditions of vision at their purest—at their simplest and at the same time at their fullest—you would discover the elementary nature of visual perception." And yet what Metzger instead discovered was that pure opticality was literally *widersinnig*, contrary to the senses. Rather than restoring a perceptually pure and primordial mode of vision, Metzger's optical reduction instead caused the test subjects to hallucinate. As he reported, after a long exposure to the screen, the test subjects could no longer even tell whether their eyes were open or closed. Metzger concluded from his experiments that the visual could not be separated from other senses, and that, indeed, there was no experience that was purely visual in nature. See Brian Massumi's discussion of the Ganzfeld experiments in "Chaos in the 'Total Field' of Vision," in *Parables of the Virtual: Movement, Affect, Sensation* (Durham: Duke University Press, 2002), 144–161; previous quote from 144.

34. Rosalind Krauss, *The Optical Unconscious* (Cambridge, Mass.: MIT Press, 1993), 2. In this book, Krauss explores modernist painting's "need to abstract and reify each of the senses in a submission of human subjectivity to the model of positivist science" (8). This reification of the senses, Krauss writes, expressed "modernist culture's ambition that each of its disciplines be rationalized by being grounded in its unique and separate domain of experience. . . . For painting, this meant uncovering and displaying the conditions of vision itself, as these were understood, abstractly" (7). A similar account of pure opticality is elaborated by Caroline Jones, who situates Greenbergian formalism within those modern "regimes of sensory isolation and purification" that pursue the "general segmentation and bureaucratization of the body." Caroline Jones, *Eyesight Alone: Clement Greenberg's Modernism and the Bureaucratization of the Senses* (Chicago: University of Chicago Press, 2006), xxvii, 390.

35. See especially his outline for his *Traité de La Vision* from 1939 and his notes on "The Transvisual" in *Werke* 4:236–266, 368–386.

36. Understanding a modernist work "is always a two-stage affair," Jameson continues: "first substituting a realistic hypothesis—in narrative form—then interpreting that secondary and invented or projected core narrative according to the procedures we reserved for the older realistic novel in general." Fredric Jameson, "Beyond the Cave: Demystifying the Ideology of Modernism," in

The Ideologies of Theory: Essays 1971–1986, vol. 2: *The Syntax of History* (Minneapolis: University of Minnesota Press, 1988), 129–130.

37. In his discussion of the sublime and modernism, Lyotard notes that Kant "cites the Jewish law banning images as an eminent example of negative presentation: optical pleasure when reduced to near nothingness promotes an infinite contemplation of infinity. Even before romantic art had freed itself from classical and baroque figuration, the door had thus been opened to enquiries pointing towards abstract and Minimal art." "The Sublime and the Avant-Garde," in *The Inhuman*, 98. In the same volume, see also "After the Sublime, the State of Aesthetic": 135–143.

38. Pavel Medvedev, "Formal'nyi metod v literaturovedenii," in *M. M. Bakhtin (pod maskoi)* (Moscow: Labirint, 2000), 265, 275; trans. Albert J. Wehrle as *The Formal Method in Literary Scholarship: A Critical Introduction to Sociological Poetics* (Cambridge, Mass.: Harvard University Press, 1985), 87, 96. Christoph Menke, an expert on Adorno and negative aesthetics, offers an explanation of modernism fully in concert with Medvedev's analysis: aesthetic difference, Menke writes, "can thus only be defined as the result of that event or happening which takes up . . . initially nonaesthetic qualities and negatively transforms them." *The Sovereignty of Art: Aesthetic Negativity in Adorno and Derrida*, trans. Neil Solomon (Cambridge, Mass.: MIT Press, 1999), 14.

39. "Das Altern der neuen Musik," in *Gesammelte Schriften*, ed. Rolf Tiedemann, 20 vols. (Frankfurt: Suhrkamp, 1997), 14:148; hereinafter abbreviated and referenced in text as *Schriften*, followed by volume and page number. "The Aging of the New Music," in *Essays on Music*, trans. Richard Leppert (Berkeley: University of California Press, 2002), 185.

40. On modernism and fascism, see Andrew Hewitt, *Fascist Modernism: Aesthetics, Politics, and the Avant-Garde* (Stanford: Stanford University Press, 1993); and Fredric Jameson, *Fables of Aggression: Wyndham Lewis, the Modernist as Fascist* (Berkeley: University of California Press, 1979).

41. Similarly, Niklas Luhmann notes in a discussion of aesthetic strategies in modernity that the "movement that, strangely enough, calls itself the avant-garde has taken this backward-looking manner to an extreme—like oarsmen, who face the direction they are coming from and have the goal of the journey behind their backs." *Art as Social System*, trans. Eva Knodt (Stanford: Stanford University Press, 2000), 122–123.

42. Helmut Lethen, "Der Habitus der Sachlichkeit in der Weimarer Republik," in *Literatur der Weimarer Republik 1918–1933*, ed. Bernhard Weyergraf (Munich: Hanser, 1995), 383.

43. Rosalind Krauss, "The Photographic Conditions of Surrealism," in *The Originality of the Avant-Garde and Other Modernist Myths* (Cambridge, Mass.: MIT Press, 1985), 91.

44. Sergei Tret'iakov, "Otkuda i kuda?" *Lef* 1 (1924): 13; "From Where to Where?" in *Russian Futurism through Its Manifestos*, ed. and trans. Anna Lawton (Ithaca: Cornell University Press, 1988), 206.

45. Peter Bürger, *Theory of the Avant-Garde*, trans. Michal Shaw (Minneapolis: University of Minnesota Press, 1984), 18.

46. Bürger concurs that the avant-garde "presupposes that means are freely available, i.e. no longer part of a system of stylistic norms where, albeit in mediated form, social norms expressed themselves." Ibid., 17.

47. Viktor Shklovskii, "Zoo: Pis'ma ne o liubvi, ili Tret'ia Eloiza," in *Gamburgskii schet* (Saint Petersburg: Limbus, 2000), 33; *Zoo: Or Letters Not about Love*, trans. Richard Sheldon (Ithaca: Cornell University Press, 1971), 34–35.

48. Hans Ulrich Gumbrecht, "Schwindende Stabilität der Wirklichkeit: Eine Geschichte des Stilbegriffs," in *Stil: Geschichten und Funktion eines kulturwissenschaftlichen Diskurselements*, ed. Hans Ulrich Gumbrecht and K. Ludwig Pfeiffer (Frankfurt: Suhrkamp, 1986), 766.

49. See the documents in *The College of Sociology 1937–1938*, ed. Denis Hollier, trans. Betsy Wing (Minneapolis: University of Minnesota Press, 1988).

50. For an introduction to Mass Observation, see Nick Hubble, *Mass Observation and Everyday Life: Culture, History, Theory* (New York: Palgrave, 2006).

51. B. J. Kospoth, "A New Philosophy of Art," in *Chicago Sunday Tribune*, January 17, 1931. Reprinted in Einstein, *Werke*, 5:860.

52. Because this 1930 text, "Schweißfuß klagt gegen Pfurz in trüber Nacht," shares with *Bebuquin II* kindred imagery and the same dramatis personae (Laurenz and Lissi), I would argue this text belongs to the *Bebuquin II* project.

53. In the Persephone section, Einstein makes reference to the lyrical structure of the Homeric version of the myth, namely hexameter. This suggests that, of the various versions of the myth, it was the Homeric Hymn specifically, written in dactylic hexameter, that he used as the source for his narrative about Persephone.

54. *The Homeric Hymns*, ed. and trans. Apostolos Athanassakis (Baltimore: Johns Hopkins University Press, 1976), 2–3.

55. In his essay "How Do Diaries End?" Philippe Lejeune discusses "the impossibility . . . of grasping this death of writing." "It wouldn't occur to anyone to explain how to end a diary," he writes, since "it would be like writing a treatise on suicide." *Biography* 24, no. 1 (winter 2001): 100.

56. Quoted in Klaus Kiefer, *Diskurswandel im Werk Carl Einsteins* (Tübingen: Max Niemeyer Verlag, 1994), 481.

57. Roman Jakobson and Morris Halle, *Fundamentals of Language* (The Hague: Mouton, 1956).

58. Carl Einstein, "Zusammenhängendes unzusammenhängendes: Bruchstück aus Bebuquin 2," in *Offene Literatur*, ed. Helmut Heissenbüttel (Munich: text + kritik, 1977), 9.

59. Elsewhere Einstein observed that the "history of man is almost simply too long for man. He has already created so many mental and formal variants that he must forget and primitivize in order not to go insane" (*Werke*, 4:382). Along similarly lines, Andreas Huyssen has argued that it was during the interwar period, specifically, that thinkers first began "to think memory and amnesia together rather than simply to oppose them." At this moment emerged a "mnemonic

fever" that threatened "to consume memory itself." *Twilight Memories: Marking Time in a Culture of Amnesia* (New York: Routledge, 1995), 7.

60. Paul de Man, "Shelley Disfigured," in *Deconstruction and Criticism*, ed. Harold Bloom (New York: Continuum, 1979), 65, 51.

61. On aesthetic supersaturation in socialist realist art, see Alla Efimova, "To Touch on the Raw: The Aesthetic Affections of Socialist Realism," *Art Journal* 56, no. 1 (1997): 72–80.

62. Alfred Döblin, "Vom alten zum neuen Naturalismus: Akademie-Rede über Arno Holz" (1930), in *Schriften zu Ästhetik, Poetik und Literatur*, ed. Erich Kleichschmidt (Olten: Walter-Verlag, 1989), 263–270.

63. De Man, "Shelley Disfigured," 51.

64. On the structuralist sign in analytic cubism see Yve-Alain Bois, "Kahnweiler's Lesson," *Representations* 18 (spring 1987), 33–68; and Rosalind Krauss, "The Motivation of the Sign," in *Picasso and Braque: A Symposium*, ed. Lynn Zelevansky (New York: Museum of Modern Art, 1992), 261–286.

65. Michel Foucault, "What Is an Author?" in *Language, Counter-Memory, Practice*, ed. and trans. Donald Bouchard (Ithaca: Cornell University Press, 1977), 118.

66. Claude Lévi-Strauss, *Introduction to the Work of Marcel Mauss* (London: Routledge, 1987), 63.

67. André Jolles, *Einfache Formen* (Tübingen: Niemeyer Verlag, 1958), 91.

68. F. W. J. Schelling, quoted in Andrew Bowie, *Schelling and Modern European Philosophy: An Introduction* (New York: Routledge, 1993), 144.

69. Samuel Taylor Coleridge, *Aids to Reflection* (Princeton: Princeton University Press, 1993), 206.

70. Jean-Pierre Vernant, "The Reason of Myth," in *Myth and Society in Ancient Greece*, trans. Janet Lloyd (New York: Zone Books, 1990), 255. In the West, Vernant observes, myth "is either defined negatively in terms of what it lacks or fails to offer, as non-sense, non-reason, non-truth, non-reality or—if it is granted any positive mode of being—it is explained away as something other than itself. It is as if its existence depended upon it being transposed or translated into some other language or type of thought. Sometimes . . . it is credited with a truthful meaning but this is immediately interpreted as the truth purveyed by philosophical discourse, and in this case myth is presented as no more than a clumsy gesture toward the latter or an indirect allusion to it." "The Reason of Myth," in *Myth and Society in Ancient Greece*, trans. Janet Lloyd (New York: Zone Books, 1990), 223.

71. Lévy-Bruhl, *How Natives Think*, 90.

72. In contrast to figurative art, which canalizes and binds the libido, abstract art, as Lyotard points out, repulses desire and redirects the aesthetic encounter to a "space of anguish" that he identifies with the Freudian death drive. Thus abstract art provides "no recognition, representation or

connotation; there is no point where we are able to link communication and participation to an 'erotic' unity. The forms presented are situated well short of discourse and action. They are silent because they break the illusory fulfillment of desire, the lure by which Eros gives itself to seeing and hearing as reality." In abstract art, desire "meets the screen and is reflected on it. . . . It lacks objectification and object recognition. The plastic space is a space of anguish." He concludes that abstract artists like Malevich and El Lissitzky "were not an *artistic* avant-garde," but were instead "anti-art," focused on a "critical overturning": "What is important is that today they give us and artists and politicians a chance to reflect on a critical aesthetic, an aesthetic of the death drive (which, moreover, Freud suggests in *Beyond the Pleasure Principle*) in its relation with revolutionary critique." These final lines on the critical aesthetic of "anti-art" resonate powerfully with Einstein's analysis of avant-garde negation. "Plastic Space and Political Space," trans. Mark S. Roberts, *boundary 2* 14, no. 1–2 (autumn 1985): 221–222.

73. Myth "is assimilated, as by Freud, with other forms of the 'symptomatic' expression of unconscious desires; it is connected with the products of the affective impulses as manifested in the imagery of dreams, and the fantasies of certain neuroses that are occasioned by the condensation, displacement, and symbolic representation of the objects of the libido." Vernant, "The Reason of Myth," 237.

74. In a 1932 essay, Einstein mocked as "academic reactionary Socialism" the new Latinity being touted by Anatoly Lunacharsky in Russia and explained that "a new social form, renewed by Revolution, would bring with it an equally revolutionary culture and new human type, which would have absolutely nothing in common with Hellenism" (*Werke*, 3:538). If there were an art of antiquity that Einstein would endorse, then it certainly would not be the "embarrassing classicism" of this "optical cliché," but the Dionysian, oriental antiquity that was celebrated by Nietzsche (*Werke*, 3:300; 4:360). The latter much more closely corresponds to the "metamorphotic" and "mythical realism" that, for Einstein, represented a third term that was neither apophatic modernism nor academic naturalism.

75. In his book, *Religion and Socialism* (1908 and 1911), Lunacharsky echoed Gorky's call for the production of a socialist religion that, without abandoning reason, could establish new myths and embodied socialist values.

76. Although the source for Gorky and Lunacharsky's doctrine of god-building was not Schelling, but that other great dissenter from the dialectic, Friedrich Nietzsche. "And how many new gods are still possible?" Nietzsche had asked. "Is it necessary to elaborate that a god prefers to stay beyond everything that is bourgeois and rational?" *The Will to Power*, trans. Walter Kaufmann (New York: Random House, 1968), 534.

77. Gorky eventually became the major proponent of a *polozhitel'naia estetika*, or "positive aesthetic," launching at the end of the 1920s a journal entitled *Our Achievements* (*Наши достижения*), which was dedicated to pursuing this affirmative poetics.

78. Katerina Clark, *The Soviet Novel: History as Ritual* (Bloomington: University of Indiana Press, 2000).

79. Lévi-Strauss, *Introduction to the Work of Marcel Mauss*, 63.

80. Quoted in Günter, *Anatomie des Anti-Subjekts*, 163.

81. Michel Leiris, quoted in Denis Hollier, "Poetry from A to . . ." in *Absent without Leave: French Literature under the Threat of War*, trans. Catherine Porter (Minneapolis: University of Minnesota Press, 1997), 71.

82. Michel Leiris, *Manhood: A Journey from Childhood into the Fierce Order of Virility*, trans. Richard Howard (Chicago: University of Chicago Press, 1963), 14.

83. Ibid., 26.

84. Ibid., 121.

85. Ibid., 161.

86. Michel Leiris, "The Sacred in Everyday Life," in *The College of Sociology 1937–1938*, 24–31.

87. Ibid., 11.

88. Georg Misch, "Begriff und Ursprung der Autobiographie," in *Geschichte der Autobiographie*, 4 vols. (Leipzig: Teubner, 1907), 1:7.

89. Quoted in Denis Hollier, *Against Architecture: The Writings of Georges Bataille*, trans. Betsy Wing (Cambridge, Mass.: MIT Press, 1990), 76. Original French in *La prise de la Concorde* (Paris: Gallimard, 1974), 141.

90. Stiegler, *Technics and Time I*, 172, 5.

91. See also Einstein's extensive notes on generation in "Generations" and the "Biology of Ideas," in *Werke*, 4:437–445.

92. "generation, *n.*" *The Oxford English Dictionary*, 3rd ed. 2009; online version December 2011. http://oed.com/view/Entry/77521.

93. Sigrid Weigel, *Genea-Logik: Generation, Tradition, und Evolution zwischen Kultur- und Naturwissenschaften* (Munich: Fink Verlag, 2006), 114.

94. Karl Mannheim, quoted in Weigel, *Genea-Logik*, 116.

95. In his 1926 essay on "Inhibitions, Symptoms, and Anxiety," Freud noted that the "intra-uterine existence [of the human] seems to be short in comparison with that of most animals, and it is sent into the world in a less finished state. As a result the influence of the real external world upon it is intensified and an early differentiation between the ego and the id is promoted. Moreover, the dangers of the external world have a greater importance for it, so that the value of the object which can alone protect it against them and take the place of its former intra-uterine life is enormously enhanced. The biological factor, then, establishes the earliest situations of danger and creates the need to be loved which will accompany the child through the rest of its life." *Werke*, 14:200; *Standard Edition*, 20:154–155.

96. See Klaus Theweleit, "Collected Observations on the Ego of the Not-Yet-Fully-Born," in *Male Fantasies*, trans. Erica Carter and Chris Turner, 2 vols. (Minneapolis: University of Minnesota Press, 1989), 2:252–271.

97. Il'ia Ehrenburg, *Rvach* (Paris: 1925), 178.

98. Lévy-Bruhl, *How Natives Think*, 276.

5 The Secret Always on Display: Caricature and Physiognomy in the Work of John Heartfield

1. Letter to Brecht from September 8, 1934, reprinted in the appendix to Fritz Mierau, *Erfindung und Korrektur* (Berlin: Aufbau Verlag, 1976), 263. In her seminal discursive analysis of the speeches delivered at the 1934 First Soviet Writers' Congress, Régine Robin has demonstrated that the use of the phrase "socialist realism" was not yet standardized at this time. To the contrary, it seems that each time the phrase was invoked at the conference, it signified something different. See Régine Robin, *Socialist Realism: An Impossible Aesthetic*, trans. Catherine Porter (Stanford: Stanford University Press, 1992).

2. Scholarship has pointed out that the central categories of socialist realism have little purchase in the field of aesthetics proper. So, for example, Katerina Clark writes that "socialist realism is not to any marked degree performing an aesthetic function," and Leonid Heller suggests that its "categories are in essence deeply ideological and not simply 'aesthetic.'" In, respectively, "Socialist Realism *with* Shores: The Conventions for the Positive Hero" (27) and "A World of Prettiness: Socialist Realism and Its Aesthetic Categories" (51). Both of these essays appear in *Socialist Realism without Shores*, ed. Thomas Lahusen and Evgeny Dobrenko (Durham: Duke University Press, 1997).

3. See the documents in *Die Expressionismusdebatte: Materialien zu einer marxistischen Realismuskonzeption*.

4. P. Iudin and A Fadeev, "Sotsialisticheskii realizm—osnovnoi metod sovetskoi literatury," *Pravda* (May 8, 1934), n.p.

5. Thus Leah Dickerman explains that "despite its anachronistic look[,] socialist realism in the visual arts must be understood as a post-photographic practice." "Camera Obscura: Socialist Realism in the Shadow of Photography," *October* 93 (summer 2000): 140.

6. Louis Aragon, "Adolf Hoffmeister et la beauté d'aujourd'hui," *Lettres françaises* (Paris), January 14–20, 1960, quoted in *John Heartfield: Der Schnitt entlang der Zeit: Selbstzeugnisse, Erinnerungen, Interpretationen*, ed. Roland März (Dresden: Verlag der Kunst, 1981), 351. Hereinafter abbreviated and referenced as *Schnitt*.

7. Ernst Bloch, "Der Nazi und das Unsägliche," in *Gesamtausgabe*, 16 vols. (Frankfurt: Suhrkamp, 1970), 11:190.

8. Louis Aragon, "The Challenge to Painting," in *The Surrealists Look at Art*, ed. Pontus Hulten (Venice, Calif.: Lapis Press, 1990), 63. Aragon takes this quote from Isidore Ducasse.

9. Adolf Hoffmeister, a friend of Heartfield and fellow photomonteur, observed that speaking with Heartfield "is not easy. Johnny speaks the same way that a flea jumps. A leap here, a leap there, and after a while the topic has grown and acquired contours, and then after two hours one no longer knows where the conversation started." "Dadamonteur John Heartfield," in *Schnitt*, 68.

10. Karl Kraus, "In dieser grossen Zeit," in *Weltgericht: I Band* (Frankfurt: Suhrkamp, 1988), 9; "In These Great Times," trans. Harry Zohn, in *In These Great Times: A Karl Kraus Reader*, ed. Harry Zohn (Manchester: Carcanet, 1976), 71.

11. György Kepes, *Language of Vision* (Chicago: Theobold, 1944), 205.

12. Louis Aragon, "John Heartfield and Revolutionary Beauty," trans. Fabrice Ziolkowski, in *Photography in the Modern Era: European Documents and Critical Writings, 1913–1940*, ed. Christopher Phillips (New York: Metropolitan Museum of Art, 1989), 60–67.

13. "Daumier, so lebendig wie nie!" and "Daumier im 'Reich'" are reprinted in *Schnitt*, 381–382 and 411–416. Today Fuchs is perhaps best known from Walter Benjamin's 1937 essay "Eduard Fuchs, der Sammler und der Historiker," in *Gesammelte Schriften* 2:465–505; trans. as "Eduard Fuchs, Collector and Historian," in *Selected Writings*, 3:260–304.

14. See the catalog for the 1981 exhibition *Daumier & Heartfield: Politische Satire im Dialog*, ed. Roland März (Berlin: Staatliche Museen zu Berlin, 1981), which pairs specific photomontages by Heartfield with a Daumier "original."

15. Eduard Fuchs, *Die Karikatur der europäischen Völker vom Altertum bis zur Neuzeit* (Berlin: A. Hofmann, 1902), 21. For Fuchs on Daumier, see *Honoré Daumier*, 4 vols. (Munich: A. Langen, 1927).

16. Werner Hofmann, *Die Karikatur von Leonardo bis Picasso* (Vienna: Brüder Rosenbaum, 1956), 31.

17. Pavel A. Florenskii, *Analiz prostranstvennosti i vremeni v khudozhestvenno-izobrazitel'nykh proizvedeniiakh* (Moscow: Progress, 1993), 256, 263.

18. Eisenstein, in a diary note from April 1942, quoted in Yuri Tsivian, *Ivan the Terrible* (London, BFI: 2002): 48.

19. Sergei Tret'iakov, *Dzhon Khartfil'd: Monografiia* (Moscow: Izobrazitel'noe iskusstvo, 1936), 67.

20. In "From the Photo-Series to Extended Photo-Observation," Tret'iakov argued that the synthetic image produced out of long-term photo-documentation was more "expressive" than the momentary snapshot alone. See "Ot fotoserii k dlitel'nomu fotonabliudeniiu," *Proletarskoe foto* 4 (1931): 20–43; trans. Devin Fore, *October* 118 (2006): 71–77.

21. On Klutsis and Heartfield, see Hubertus Gassner, "Heartfield's Moscow Apprenticeship, 1931–1932," in *John Heartfield*, ed. Peter Pachnicke and Klaus Honnef (New York: Harry Abrams, 1992), 256–289; and Maria Gough, "Back in the USSR: John Heartfield, Gustav Klucis, and the Medium of Soviet Propaganda," *New German Critique* 36, no. 2 (summer 2009): 133–183.

22. Peter Sloterdijk, *Critique of Cynical Reason*, trans. Michael Eldred (Minneapolis: University of Minnesota Press, 1987), 391–400.

23. Tret'iakov, *Dzhon Khartfil'd*, 60.

24. Günther Anders, "Über Photomontage: Ansprache zur Eröffnung der Heartfield-Ausstellung 1938 in New York," in *Mensch ohne Welt: Schriften zur Kunst und Literatur* (Munich: C. H. Beck, 1993), 178.

25. Fuchs, *Die Karikatur der europäischen Völker*, 2.

26. Aleksei Fedorov-Davydov, "Voinstvuiushchee iskusstvo," *Brigada khudozhnikov* 8, no. 1 (1932): 37.

27. Ibid.

28. Sigmund Freud, *Die Traumdeutung*, in *Gesammelte Werke*, 2–3:284; trans. *The Interpretation of Dreams*, in *Standard Edition*, 4:277.

29. See, e.g., Victor Burgin's excellent "Photography, Phantasy, Function," which analyzes the structural resemblance between Freud's dream-rebus and the photomontage: *Screen* 21, no. 1 (spring 1980): 43–80. The argument that pictorial montage accesses elementary psychic structures and embodied systems of desire more effectively than purely verbal discourse was in fact already ubiquitous in the 1920s. Thus, in a 1925 essay on the "word-image" (*слово-образ*), Viktor Pertsov, a member of the futurist Lef group, explained that the new text-image systems found in contemporary graphic design accessed ontogenetically more primitive states of consciousness than the linear syntagma of the novel. See Pertsov, "Slovo—zritel'nyi obraz—budushchee," *Al'manakh proletkul'ta* (Moscow: Vserossiiskii proletkul't, 1925), 83–93. The presentism described by Pertsov, which simulates the state of simultaneity reigning within the Unconscious, suspends the distinction between verbal and visual art that, since Lessing's *Laokoön*, had been so central to modern poetics and its notion of medium-specificity.

30. The footnote quoted here does not appear in the English text of *Discourse, Figure*, so I revert to an earlier translation of the text originally made in 1984. Jean-François Lyotard, "The Connivances of Desire with the Figural," in *The Lyotard Reader and Guide*, ed. Keith Crome and James Williams (New York: Columbia University Press, 2006), 300. The "coexistence of several silhouettes results in the simultaneity of more than one point of view" and a "transgression of *good form* (Gestalt)." Jean-François Lyotard, *Discourse, Figure*, 274-75.

31. On the sources and contexts of this particular work, see Eckhard Siepmann, "Die Millionen-Montage: Versuch einer Strukturanalyse," in *Montage: John Heartfield: Vom Club Dada zur Arbeiter-Illustrierten Zeitung*, ed. Eckhard Siepmann (Berlin: Elefanten Press, 1977): 240–252.

32. In his analysis of *Witz* and montage, Eisenstein places particular importance on strategies of psychic condensation, or *Verdichtung* (which he translates using the Russian word *уплотнение* rather than the now standard Russian translation for this Freudian term, *сгущение*). *Montazh*, 51.

33. Ibid., 47.

34. Aragon, "The Challenge to Painting," 57.

35. G. Vinokur, "Iazyk tipografii," in *Kul'tura iazyka* (Moscow: Izd-vo Rabotnik Prosveshcheniia, 1925), 129–142.

36. Such displacements would be christened *sdvigi* by Kruchenykh, who argued that these dislocations become a means for breaching abstract language with a phenomenological space, thereby imbuing signification with a vector of force. "The *sdvig* transmits movement and space," Kruchenykh observed in his Freudian *Science of Displacements*. Kruchenykh, *Sdvigologiia* (Moscow: Gileia, 1923), 36.

37. Anders, "Über Photomontage," 176. Italics in original.

38. Aragon, "John Heartfield and Revolutionary Beauty," 64. Italics in original.

39. L. P., "Za proletarskii tvorcheskii metod fotomontazha: Dzhon Khartfil'd," *Proletarskoe foto* 3 (March 1932): 14.

40. Fedorov-Davydov, "Voinstvuiushchee iskusstvo," 37.

41. Adorno, in an epistolary exchange with Benjamin, reprinted in Benjamin, *Selected Writings*, 4:203.

42. Ibid.

43. Edgar Allan Poe, "The Man of the Crowd," in *The Portable Edgar Allan Poe*, ed. Philip van Doren Stern (New York: Penguin 1945), 108.

44. See, e.g., *Geschichten der Physiognomik: Text, Bild, Wissen*, ed. Rüdiger Campe and Manfred Schneider (Freiburg: Rombach Verlag, 1996); Helmut Lethen, "Neusachliche Physiognomik: Gegen den Schrecken der ungewissen Zeichen," in *Der Deutschunterricht* 49, no. 2 (1997): 6–19; *Gesichter der Weimarer Republik: Eine physiognomische Kulturgeschichte*, ed. Claudia Schmölders and Sander L. Gilman (Cologne: Dumont, 2000); *Blick, Macht, Gesicht*, ed. Helga Gläser, Bernhard Gross, and Hermann Kappelhoff (Berlin: Vorwerk 8, 2001); *Das Gesicht im Zeitalter des bewegten Bildes*, ed. Christa Blümlinger and Karl Sierek (Vienna: Sonderzahl, 2002); and *Das Gesicht ist eine starke Organisation*, ed. Petra Löffler and Leander Scholz (Cologne: Dumont, 2004).

45. János Reismann, "John Heartfield," in *Schnitt*, 317.

46. Heartfield, "Zur Wirkung der Fotomontage," in *Schnitt*, 181.

47. Max Picard, "Menschliches Auge und photographische Linse," *Eckart* 8 (1932): 174.

48. E. H. Gombrich and E. Kris, *Caricature* (Middlesex: King Penguin Books, 1940), 14.

49. Upton Sinclair, *Money Writes: A Study of American Literature* (Long Beach: Upton Sinclair, 1927), 9.

50. The biography, Kracauer wrote, "is a prose form of the established bourgeoisie, which of course has to deny any knowledge and all problems of form that threaten its continued existence. The bourgeoisie feels the power of history in its bones and is all too aware that the individual has become anonymous. Yet these insights, which impose themselves on the bourgeoisie with the force of physiognomic experiences, do not lead it to draw any conclusions capable of illuminating the current situation. . . . As the literary form of the new bourgeoisie, the biography is a sign of escape or, to be more precise, of evasion." "Die Biographie als neubürgerliche Kunstform," in *Das Ornament der Masse*, 77–78; "Biography as an Art Form of the New Bourgeoisie," in *The Mass Ornament*, 103–104.

51. An article that appeared in the journal of the German Publishers and Booksellers Association described the ongoing case. See Fritz Hansen, "Die Familienfotografie auf dem Buchdeckel," *Börsenblatt für den deutschen Buchhadel* (November 25, 1930).

52. Stefan Andriopoulos discusses the legal debates about the "right to one's own image" at the turn of the twentieth century, linking them with cinematic technologies of reproduction. "The Terror of Reproduction: Early Cinema's Ghostly Doubles and the Right to One's Own Image," *New German Critique* 33, no. 3 (fall 2006): 151–170.

53. Although apparently even this censorship of the cover did not satisfy Ludwig. Only when he was forced to desist by his publisher Ernst Rowohlt, who found the entire affair with Heartfield laughable, did Ludwig finally call off the lawsuit. See Wieland Herzfelde, *John Heartfield—Leben und Werk: Dargestellt von seinem Bruder*, 3rd ed. (Dresden: Verlag der Kunst, 1976), 38. Many thanks to Andres Zervigon for telling me how this story ended.

54. Tret'iakov, *Dzhon Khartfil'd*, 78.

55. In a talk on the subject of portraiture entitled "Rede über das Bildnis heute," Heartfield quoted extensively from Waetzoldt's text. The talk appears in *Schnitt*, 459–462. While Heartfield mentions only one specific chapter from the book, "The Problem of Similitude," Heartfield's talk uses quotations from throughout Waetzoldt's book.

56. Wilhelm Waetzoldt, *Die Kunst des Porträts* (Leipzig, F. Hirt & Sohn, 1908); hereinafter cited in text as *Kunst des Porträts*.

57. Gilles Deleuze and Félix Guattari, *A Thousand Plateaus: Capitalism and Schizophrenia*, trans. Brian Massumi (Minneapolis: University of Minnesota Press, 1987), 188.

58. Heartfield's commentators commonly situate his work in the 1930s at the intersection between abstract conceptual meaning and sensuous perception. Thus Aragon writes, for example, that, in Heartfield's photomontages, "there is also *meaning*, and meaning hasn't disfigured beauty." Aragon, "John Heartfield and Revolutionary Beauty," 66. Similarly, Anders notes that Heartfield "provides the eye with the vast horizon of reason, he brings the eye into alignment with reason." Anders, "Über Photomontage," 176.

59. Benjamin, "Lehre vom Ähnlichen," in *Gesammelte Schriften*, 2:206, 207; "Doctrine of the Similar," in *Selected Writings*, 2:695, 696. See also "Über das mimetische Vermögen," in *Gesammelte Schriften*, 2:210–213; "On the Mimetic Faculty," in *Selected Writings*, 2:720–722.

60. On the magical aspect of language as elaborated by Benjamin in these texts, see Winfried Menninghaus, *Walter Benjamins Theorie der Sprachmagie* (Frankfurt: Suhrkamp, 1980).

61. L. S. Vygotsky, *Myshlenie i rech'*, in *Sobranie sochinenii*, ed. V. V. Davydov, 6 vols. (Moscow: Pedagogika, 1982), 2:119; hereinafter abbreviated and referenced in text as *Myshlenie*.

62. Vygotsky writes that his thinking about "chain complexes" was indebted to Werner's *Einführung in die Entwicklungspsychologie* (Leipzig: J. A. Barth, 1926), in which the German associated this form of "psychic amalgam" with what he called "physiognomic language." Significantly, the next book that Werner published after his *Einführung* was a study entitled *Fundamental Questions of the Physiognomy of Language* (*Grundfragen der Sprachphysiognomik* [Leipzig: J. A. Barth, 1932]).

63. Ludwig Wittgenstein, *Preliminary Studies for the* Philosophical Investigations (Oxford: Blackwell, 1969), 87. On Wittgenstein's analysis of signifying chains, see Rodney Needham, "Polythetic Classification: Convergence and Consequences," *Man* 10, no. 3 (1975): 349-369.

64. See Katherine Nelson, "Event Knowledge and Cognitive Development" and "Children's Scripts," in *Event Knowledge: Structure and Function in Development*, ed. Katherine Nelson (Hillsdale: Lawrence Erlbaum, 1986), 1–20, 21–46.

65. A. R. Luria, *Ob istoricheskom razvitii poznavatel'nykh protsessov: Eksperimental'no-psikhologicheskoe issledovanie* (Moscow: Nauka, 1974), 70.

66. See chapter 3, "Abstraktsiia i obobshchenie," ibid., 58–105.

67. "In my childhood, we played a game called Families," recalls Barthes: "each player, holding a hand of illustrated cards, took turns asking his partners for the members of the family he was collecting: the pork butcher, the pork butcher's wife, their son, their daughter, their dog, etc. Looking at one of Arcimboldo's composite heads, I must in the same way reconstitute the family of, say, Winter: I ask for a tree stump here, a strand of ivy there, a mushroom, a lemon, a doormat, until I have the whole hibernal thematics before my eyes, the whole 'family' of Villon's *morte saison*." Roland Barthes, "Arcimboldo, or Magician and Rhétoriqueur," in *The Responsibility of Forms: Critical Essays on Music, Art, and Representation*, trans. Richard Howard (Berkeley: University of California Press, 1985), 129–130.

68. Ibid., 147. All of the individual phenomena in these works, Barthes explains, already have an established meaning and are depicted by the artist as if they were lexicographic units taken from an illustrated dictionary for children. He thus concludes that the goal of this montage procedure—comparable to that of Max Ernst and René Magritte, he proposes—is not to establish definitional semantic structures, but to create, through a tropological movement, a new logic of assembly connecting these prefabricated phenomena to one another.

69. See David Evans's discussion of metamorphosis in *John Heartfield: AIZ* (New York: Kent, 1992). More recently, the subject of metamorphosis has been addressed with particular acuity by Sabine Kriebel in "Manufacturing Discontent: John Heartfield's Mass Medium," *New German Critique* 36, no. 107 (2009): 53–88, esp. 76–88.

70. Guy Debord, *Comments on Society of the Spectacle*, trans. Malcolm Imrie (London: Verso Books, 1998). See also Jonathan Crary, "Spectacle, Attention, Counter-Memory," *October* 50 (autumn 1989): 96–107.

71. In *Reading the Figural*, David Rodowick points out that the dynamics of meaning found in film and photography are resistant to classical structuralist analysis, and can only be grasped within the paradigm of similitude (Durham: Duke University Press, 2001). Likewise, in a remarkable essay on Warhol, Jonathan Flatley has demonstrated the suitability of a semiotic of likeness for an analysis of Pop art's simulacral practices. According to Flatley, Warhol's aesthetic of similitude presumes a certain media-technical a priori: "In a basic sense, for Warhol, all photographs are similar to each other, as are all paintings, all films, and all audiotapes. . . . This principle extended

to the other senses as well, and Warhol appeared to seek as many recording devices as possible so that he could, in effect, mediate each of his senses by likeness-generating recorders/collectors." "Like: Collecting and Collectivity," *October* 132 (spring 2010): 81.

72. Picard, "Menschliches Auge und photographische Linse," 175.

73. Katerina Clark, *The Soviet Novel: History as Ritual* (Bloomington: Indiana University Press, 2000), 37.

74. Michel Foucault, *This Is Not a Pipe*, trans. James Harkness (Berkeley: University of California Press, 1982), 44.

75. Peter Bürger, for example, argues for "the proximity of Foucault's conception of [analogical] language to a specific tradition of modern aesthetic thought associated with the name of Mallarmé." "The Return of Analogy: Aesthetics as Vanishing Point in Michel Foucault's *The Order of Things*," in *The Decline of Modernism*, trans. Nicholas Walker (University Park: Pennsylvania State University Press, 1992), 50.

76. Michel Foucault, *The Order of Things* (New York: Vintage, 1973), 384.

77. Ibid., 43.

78. We "have learnt from the dream-work," Freud writes in *Jokes and Their Relationship to the Unconscious*, that "the connecting paths which start out from *words* are in the unconscious treated in the same way as connections between *things*." *Werke* 6:202; *Standard Edition*, 7:177.

79. While recognizing certain technical affinities between his own work and that of the Surrealists, Brecht, for example, nonetheless insisted that each project employs these strategies to completely different ends. The Surrealists "employ the most extreme types of estrangement effects. Their objects never return from this state of estrangement." Brecht, *Werke*, 22:224. As a result, their works are essentially asocial.

80. Foucault, *This Is Not a Pipe*, 37.

81. In his 1938 essay "Realism in the Balance," Lukács, for example, makes brief mention of Heartfield's work, noting that "a good photomontage has the same sort of effect as a good joke." "Es geht um den Realismus," 328; "Realism in the Balance," 43.

82. Like a montage, the joke permits the perception of "two facts, two phenomena, two objects" at the same time, without, however, completely equating these elements. Juxtaposed in a dialectical tension, the image-signs brought into concert in the joke engender a "third something" (*некое третье*) that, for Eisenstein, can serve as a building block in the grammar of materialist thought. "Montazh 1938," 48. Eisenstein's invocation of *Witz* in his analysis of montage thinking reminds us that *Witz* is more than just a comic anecdote: in addition to meaning "joke," *Witz* also designates the faculty of wit itself, a cognitive capacity for perceiving similarities between distant phenomena. Etymologically connected to the nouns *Wissen* ("knowledge") and *Weisheit* ("wisdom"), the word *Witz*, for much of its history, designated "the assemblage of ideas, and putting those together with quickness and variety, wherein can

be found any resemblance or congruity." John Locke, quoted in Markus Winkler and Christine Goulding, "Witz," in *Ästhetische Grundbegriffe*, ed. Karlheinz Barck et al., 7 vols. (Stuttgart: Metzler, 2000–2005), 6:701. This was in fact the meaning of *Witz* at least until well into the nineteenth century, when usage of the word became limited to the textual genre of the joke. The Jena Romantic Friedrich Schlegel, for example, would still write of a "combinatory wit," a capacity of thought that, in anticipation of Freud, he characterized as "lighting out of the unconscious world, a world that always exists for us alongside the conscious one." Quoted in Winkler and Goulding, 710. For Schlegel, wit represented a revolutionary and anti-absolutist mode of cognition that posited similarities between phenomena without, however, flattening their differences into a relationship of complete identity. See Carl Hill's discussion of "*Witz* and Romanticism," in *The Soul of Wit: Joke Theory from Grimm to Freud* (Lincoln: University of Nebraska Press, 1993).

83. See Reinhardt Koselleck's account of the role that secret fraternities such as the *Freimaurer* played in the formation of the modern bourgeois social order in *Critique and Crisis: Enlightenment and the Parthenogenesis of Modern Society* (Oxford: Berg, 1988).

84. Paul Virilio traces "the post-industrial era, the catastrophe of the de-realization of the world" to the 1920s in *The Information Bomb*, trans. Chris Turner (London: Verso, 2000), 25.

85. Sloterdijk, *Critique of Cynical Reason*, 477. Weimar Germany, writes Sloterdijk, was "the essential 'founding period' of this cynical structure in its culturally dominating dimension. Back then for the first time, strategic immoralisms seeped out of the previously hermetically sealed milieus into collective consciousness, and what previously was regarded as the trade secrets of realpolitik, of diplomacy, chiefs of staff, secret services, organized crime, prostitution, and the direction of enterprises is now taken up by a blatant rage for the truth and placed irrevocably in the twilight of 'open secrets'" (389).

86. The "Latin saying" to which Adorno refers here is *mundus vult decipi*. Theodor Adorno, "Der wunderliche Realist," in *Schriften*, 11:400; "The Curious Realist: On Siegfried Kracauer," in *Notes to Literature II*, trans. Shierry Weber Nicholsen (New York: Columbia University Press, 1992), 69.

87. Siegfried Kracauer, *Die Angestellten: Aus dem neuesten Deutschland* (Frankfurt: Suhrkamp, 1971), 11; *The Salaried Masses: Duty and Distraction in Weimar Germany*, trans. Quintin Hoare (London: Verso, 1998), 29; translation modified.

88. Jürgen Habermas, *The Structural Transformation of the Public Sphere*, trans. Thomas Burger (Cambridge, Mass.: MIT Press, 1991), 206.

89. Guy Debord, *Comments on the Society of the Spectacle*, trans. Malcolm Imrie (London: Verso, 1990), 61.

90. Paul Ricoeur, *Freud and Philosophy: An Essay on Interpretation*, trans. Denis Savage (New Haven: Yale University Press, 1970), 34.

91. Foucault, *The Order of Things*, 80.

92. Michel Foucault, "Nietzsche, Freud, Marx," in *Aesthetics, Method, and Epistemology: Essential Works of Foucault, 1954-1984*, ed. James D. Faubion (New York: New Press, 1998), 273.

93. Karl Jaspers, *Die geistige Situation der Zeit* (Berlin: de Gruyter, 1999).

94. See Helmut Lethen, *Cool Conduct: The Culture of Distance in Weimar Germany*, trans. Don Reneau (Berkeley: University of California Press, 2002). On the "outward turn" see also Miriam Hansen, "Mass Culture as Hieroglyphic Writing: Adorno, Derrida, Kracauer," *New German Critique* 56 (spring–summer 1992): 43–73.

95. Heiko Christians has connected the resurgence of physiognomic analysis in Weimar culture with a change in the structure of hermeneutic inquiry. As a discursive locus, "physiognomics" is "the site of a repeated discussion about the epistemological difficulties within hermeneutics," Christians observes. "Gesicht, Gestalt, Ornament: Überlegungen zur epistemologischen Ort der Physiognomik zwischen Hermeneutik und Mediengeschichte," *Deutsche Vierteljahrsschrift für Literaturwissenschaft und Geistesgeschichte* 74, no. 1 (2000): 84–110.

96. Waetzoldt, *Kunst des Porträts*, 50. Johann Wolfgang von Goethe, "Epirrhema," in *Werke*, 14 vols. (Munich: Deutscher Taschenbuch Verlag, 1998), 1:358. I take the English translation of "Epirrhema" from Theodore Roszak, *Where the Wasteland Ends: Politics and Transcendence in Postindustrial Society* (Garden City: Doubleday, 1973), 344.

6 Into the Entomic Age: A Coda on Ernst Jünger's *Glass Bees*

1. Leon Battista Alberti, *On Painting*, trans. John R. Spencer (New Haven: Yale University Press, 1966), 55.

2. The perspective generated by the SEM is more akin to axonometric projection than the one-point perspective of the photograph. Yve-Alain Bois has demonstrated in Lissitzky's "A. and Pangeometry" that axonometric perspective causes the viewer's sense of spatial positionality to founder. Unable to distinguish between proximal and distal values—projection and recession—the viewer of the axonometric field is cut loose from phenomenal space. See Bois, "El Lissitzky: Radical Reversibility."

3. Jünger suggested that the invention of the metric system in France in 1791 and its subsequent exportation under bayonet was a world-historical political event on par with the French Revolution itself. See Jünger's diary entry from September 25, 1945, in *Werke*, 3:555–558.

4. Paul Virilio, *War and Cinema: The Logistics of Perception*, trans. Patrick Camiller (New York: Verso, 1989); and Friedrich Kittler, *Gramophone, Film, Typewriter*, trans. Geoffrey Winthrop-Young and Michael Wutz (Stanford: Stanford University Press, 1999).

5. Jünger's concept of a zone of infinite danger resonates suggestively with recent social theory on mass media and the potentially catastrophic consequences of processes of reflexive modernization. See Ulrich Beck, *Risk Society: Toward a New Modernity*, trans. Mark Ritter (London: Sage Publications, 1992); and Anthony Giddens, *Consequences of Modernity* (Stanford: Stanford University Press, 1990).

6. An English translation of *Gläserne Bienen* appeared in 1960 as *The Glass Bees*, trans. Louise Bogan and Elizabeth Mayer (New York: Farrar, Straus & Giroux). All references here are to the German text, and translations are my own.

7. Witold Kula, *Measures and Men*, trans. R. Szreter (Princeton: Princeton University Press, 1986).

8. Heinrich Hauser, *Umgang mit Maschinen* (Frankfurt: Kleyer, 1928), 9.

9. Lewis Mumford, *Technics and Civilization* (New York: Harcourt, Brace & World, 1934).

10. "Usually, as we know, implements and machines came into being by imitating parts of the body: the hammer is the fist, the chisel the nail, the saw the row of teeth and so on. . . . Only in the steam engine and locomotive does a semblance from the old organic series still continue to operate. Hissing, boiling, breathing, with connecting rods like arms at the side; children playing are thus still inclined to imitate locomotives. . . . But the technology which has developed in the present century shows less and less resemblance to *human limbs and proportions*. . . . If the rod, shaft, bearing, ball-bearing, wheel, cogwheel, transmission and all other machine components were already the beginning of deorganization [*Entorganisierung*], this is all the more true of their combination, the machine as work-transformer. . . . Machinery itself is already an *unnaturalistic occurrence*, a kind of *unnatural physics*. And within it the repulsion to that which is naturally given increases even further; organ projection [*Organprojektion*] is increasingly abandoned or transcended. . . . This is all the more true of the possible technology derived from the hitherto remotest power drives: the subatomic ones, and from the transformers into which these are conducted. With this technology, not just organ projection is abandoned, but in part also the realm of the *at least three-dimensional mechanical world*, in which the electric locomotive, the diesel engine, and the rocket-propelled aircraft are still located." *Gesamtausgabe*, 5:771–773; *The Principle of Hope*, trans. Neville Plaice, Stephen Plaice, and Paul Knight, 3 vols. (Cambridge, Mass.: MIT Press, 1995), 2:661–662; translation modified; emphasis in original.

11. On the human body and modern warfare, see Klaus Theweleit's classic study on the psychic life of the Freikorps, *Male Fantasies*, and Andreas Huyssen, "Fortifying the Heart—Totally: Ernst Jünger's Armored Texts," in *Twilight Memories: Marking Time in a Culture of Amnesia* (New York: Routledge, 1995), 127–143.

12. Georg Lukács, "Die Desanthropomorphisierung der Wiederspiegelung in der Wissenschaft," in *Ästhetik: Die Eigenart des Ästhetischen*, 2 vols. (Berlin: Lüchterhand, 1963), 1:139–206.

13. Pierre Vernant, "Some Remarks on the Forms and Limitations of Technological Thought among the Greeks," in *Myth and Thought among the Greeks* (New York: Zone Books, 2006), 301. Already in 1923, Oswald Spengler had noted that "classical man . . . set himself in hostile opposition to the very idea of technology. . . . [T]here is no such thing as Classical technology. Its triremes are glorified row-boats; its catapults and onagers are replacements for arms and fists, and cannot be compared with the Assyrian and Chinese war-engines." *Der Untergang des Abendlandes: Umrisse einer Morphologie der Weltgeschichte* (Munich: Deutscher Taschenbuchverlag, 2003), 1186; *The Decline of the West*, 2:501; trans. modified.

14. Vernant, "Forms and Limitations of Technological Thought among the Greeks," 304.

15. At first glance, as Lukács suggests, the machine might seem already to have yielded its anthropomorphic qualities in the first Industrial Revolution, but André Leroi-Gourhan points out that human beings were still necessary to operate and maintain such machinery: the "mechanical monsters produced in the nineteenth century" were "machines without a nervous system of their own, constantly requiring the assistance of a human partner." Leroi-Gourhan, *Gesture and Speech*, 247–248. Even when these machines did not have an explicitly human face, from the perspective of causality the machinery of the steam age was still well within the parameters established by the Aristotelian conception of technology, which maintained that machines, as instruments, lack the self-causality and self-regulation of living organisms. For this reason, no matter how elaborate and monstrous were the dimensions they acquired, the machines of the nineteenth century remained essentially mere amplifiers of forces that reside in the human body.

16. Benjamin, *Schriften* 1:282; *The Origin of German Tragic Drama*, trans. John Osborne (New York: Verso, 1985), 103.

17. Bloch, *Das Prinzip Hoffnung*, 2:774; *The Principle of Hope,* 2:664; trans. modified.

18. Hannah Arendt, *The Human Condition* (Chicago: University of Chicago Press, 1958), 2.

19. Feynman's piece is reprinted in Horace D. Gilbert's anthology, *Miniaturization* (New York: Reinhold, 1961), 282–296.

20. Feynman's fantasy of self-reproducing robots has been directly attributed to conversations with his friend Al Hibbs about Robert Heinlein's 1940 tale *Waldo.* Ed Regis, *Nano: The Emerging Science of Nanotechnology: Remaking the World—Molecule by Molecule* (New York: Little, Brown, 1995), 152–154. The objectivity of nanotechnology has consequently been impugned by claims that it borrows too heavily from science fiction literature. Colin Milburn, for example, offers a conceptual genealogy of nanoscience that traces the field's roots to science fiction and argues that nanotechnology owes to literary fiction not just the general vision of an atomic science but its actual models and means of implementation. For Milburn, the origins of nanoscience suggest that it may be something other than science. Colin Milburn, "Nanotechnology in the Age of Posthuman Engineering: Science Fiction as Science," *Configurations* 10, no. 2 (spring 2002): 261–295. This genealogy is correct, but the entanglement of fiction and science hardly disqualifies the latter's truth claims or legitimacy in the way that authors such as Milburn imply. There are no steadfast differences between invention and discovery, and science's increasing reliance on the *simulation* as a means of validation—a procedure that is at the center of nanoscience's experimental practices—establishes even more incontrovertibly that imagination and science are no longer always distinguishable. Indeed, the simulation is "neutral vis-a-vis ontologically motivated differentiations between reality and fiction." K. Ludwig Pfeiffer, "Dimensions of Literature: A Speculative Approach," in *The Materialities of Communication*, ed. Hans Ulrich Gumbrecht and K. Ludwig Pfeiffer, trans. William Whobrey (Stanford, CA: Stanford University Press, 1994), 64. On the importance of the simulation for nanoscience, see Johannes Lenhard, "Nanoscience and the Janus-Faced Character of Simulations," in *Discovering the Nanoscale*, ed. Davis Baird et al. (Washington, D.C.: IOS Press, 2004), 93–100. The imbrication of fantasy and science on the atomic scale intrigued Jünger, who once expressed fascination with the fact that the structure of the atom was revealed to physicist Niels Bohr in a dream (*Werke*, 3:577). One could argue in a Benjaminian

mode that every scientific reality in fact first emerges in the dream life and fairy tales of the prior epoch. Even today's ubiquitous technologies such as television were prefigured in the fantasy life of the occult. Stefan Andriopoulos, "Psychic TV," *Critical Inquiry* 31 (spring 2005): 618–637.

21. Kate Marshall, "Future Present: Nanotechnology and the Scene of Risk," in *Nanoculture: Implications of the New Technoscience*, ed. N. Katherine Hayles (Bristol: Intellect Books, 2004), 147–159.

22. In his book *Engines of Creation* (Garden City: Doubleday, 1986), Eric Drexler describes a possible apocalyptic scenario in which self-replicating nanobots consume all of the matter on the planet, both living and inorganic, and transform it into undifferentiated "gray goo." A recent appearance of the "gray goo" scenario in contemporary popular culture is Michael Crichton's *Prey* (New York: HarperCollins, 2002).

23. Bruno Latour, *Science in Action: How to Follow Scientists and Engineers through Society* (Cambridge, Mass.: Harvard University Press, 1987).

24. Lorraine Daston and Peter Galison, "Seeing Is Making: Nanofacture," in *Objectivity* (New York: Zone Books, 2007), 382–411. Daston and Galison's argument is indebted to Ian Hacking's *Representing and Intervening: Introducing Topics in the Philosophy of Natural Science* (Cambridge: Cambridge University Press, 1983).

25. Colin Milburn, "Nano/Splatter: Disintegrating the Postbiological Body," *New Literary History* 36, no. 2 (spring 2005): 283–311.

26. Bill Joy, "Why the Future Doesn't Need Us," *Wired* 8, no. 4 (2000). Elaborating on Joy's article, Alfred Nordmann notes that, on the nanoregister, "we find ourselves confronted, in a perfectly classical manner, with the micro- and the macrocosm. But here arise a question and a problem. In classical cosmology it was man who mediated between macro- and microcosm. But man does not even appear in the picture [of nanotechnology]." Alfred Nordmann, "Shaping the World Atom by Atom: Eine nanowissenschaftliche WeltBildanalyse," in *Technikgestaltung zwischen Wunsch und Wirklichkeit*, ed. Armin Grunwald (Berlin: Springer, 2003), 192.

27. Reviewing his work from the 1950s, in 1961 the biologist J. S. Haldane stressed the importance of "the analogy between living organisms and atoms, in view of the discoveries as to atomic structure and function revealed by quantum mechanics, which [I] regarded, with some justification, as a penetration of biological ideas into physics." J. S. Haldane, "A Possible Development of J. S. Haldane's Views on the Relation between Quantum Mechanics and Biology," in *The Regulation of Human Respiration,* ed. D. J. C. Cunningham and B. B. Lloyd (Philadelphia: F. A. Davis, 1963), 103.

28. Because the laws of chemistry, mechanical engineering, biomedicine, computer science, informatics, and physics are all equally binding at the atomic scale, nanoscience has positioned itself as a superdiscipline that unites all traditional scientific fields. On the "nano-bio-info-cogno-socio" theory of everything, see *Converging Technologies for Improving Human Performance*, ed. M. Roco and W. S. Bainbridge (Arlington, VA: National Science Foundation, 2002); Joachim Schummer, "Interdisciplinary Issues in Nanoscale Research," in *Discovering the Nanoscale*, 9–20;

and Jan C. Schmidt, "Unbounded Technologies: Working through the Technological Reductionism of Nanotechnology," in *Discovering the Nanoscale*, 35–50.

29. Milburn, "Nanotechnology in the Age of Posthuman Engineering," 288. The first quotation is Milburn citing Drexler. The second quotation is Milburn's commentary on Drexler.

30. Eileen Crist, "Can an Insect Speak? The Case of the Honeybee Dance Language," *Social Studies of Science* 34, no. 1 (February 2004): 35.

31. Thus Jünger's characterization of Caillois in a journal entry from a day he spent in part with the ethnographic surrealist (*Werke*, 5:44).

32. On Jünger's achievements as an entomologist, see Auguste Francotte, *Ernst Jünger ou l'entomologiste écrivain* (Tervuren, Belgium: Union des Entomologistes Beiges, 1998). Jünger assesses his contributions to entomology in Julien Hervier, *The Details of Time: Conversations with Ernst Jünger*, trans. Joachim Neugroschel (New York: Marsilio, 1995), 55.

33. J. S. Haldane, "On Being the Right Size," in *The Oxford Book of Essays*, ed. John Gross (Oxford: Oxford University Press, 1991), 452–457.

34. N. Katherine Hayles, "Connecting the Quantum Dots: Nanotechscience and Culture," in *Nanoculture*, 12.

35. James V. Lawry, *The Incredible Shrinking Bee: Insects as Models for Microelectromechanical Devices* (London: Imperial College Press, 2006). On insects as models for the architecture of microfluidic devices in particular, see Patrick Tabeling, *Introduction to Microfluidics*, trans. Suelin Chen (Oxford: Oxford University Press, 2005).

36. Danielle Allen, "Burning *The Fable of the Bees*: The Incendiary Authority of Nature," in *The Moral Authority of Nature*, ed. Lorraine Daston and Fernando Vidal (Chicago: University of Chicago Press, 2004), 74–99.

37. Karl von Frisch and Martin Lindauer, "The 'Language' and Orientation of the Honey Bee," in *Foundations of Animal Behavior*, ed. L. D. Houck and L. C. Drickamer (Chicago: University of Chicago Press, 1996), 540.

38. Von Frisch's research garnered him the Nobel Prize in Physiology or Medicine in 1973. But his work did not go uncontested: by the end of the 1960s, von Frisch's sensational claims had given rise to an energetic debate that the biologist Demorest Davenport deemed "one of the few non-sterile controversies in the study of animal behavior." Davenport is cited in Tania Munz's study "Of Birds and Bees: Karl von Frisch, Konrad Lorenz, and the Science of Animals, 1908–1973" (Ph.D. diss., Princeton University, 2007), 176. On the honeybee dance language, see Crist, "Can an Insect Speak?," as well as Munz's dissertation.

39. J. S. Haldane and H. Spurway, "A Statistical Analysis of Communication in 'Apis mellifera' and a Comparison with Communication in Other Animals," *Insectes sociaux* 1, no. 3 (1954): 255. Haldane and Spurway also write that "we shall perhaps not be very far out if we suggest that a dance gives about 5 units of information as to direction, 4 to 5 as regards distance, and 2 to 3

as regards number of workers needed, the total being about 12 units, besides the information given non-symbolically by the odour. A human language in which about 4,000 phrases, but no more, were possible, along with demonstrations of objects found, would give the same amount of information, if combined with demonstrations of objects. Such a language would require much less than 100 words, and a code of all possible combinations of 3 letters would more than cover it. A human language differs from bee communication in that the different phrases are sharply separable, whereas bee dances grade into one another" (256).

40. J. S. Haldane, "La signalisation animale," *L'année biologique* 58 (1954): 96.

41. Donald Griffin, *Animal Minds: Beyond Cognition to Consciousness* (Chicago: University of Chicago Press, 2001), 190.

42. Émile Benveniste, "Animal Communication and Human Language: The Language of the Bees," *Diogenes* 1 (1952): 1–7.

43. In chapter 5 of his *Problems in General Linguistics* (Coral Gables, FL: University of Miami Press, 1971), Benveniste would insist against behaviorists that the stimulus-response model cannot adequately account for human speech.

44. In his last book on phonology, *The Sound Shape of Language* (Bloomington: University of Indiana Press, 1979), Jakobson synthesized four decades of research that sought to demonstrate the existence of objective and universal linguistic structures that were independent of the specificities of space, time, and—one could add—species. On the development of Jakobson's universal theory of phonology, see Boris Gasparov, "Futurism and Phonology: Futurist Roots of Jakobson's Approach to Language," *Cahiers de l'institut de Linguistique et des Sciences du Langage* 9 (1997): 109–128.

45. Thomas Sebeok, "Review of *Communication among Social Bees* by Martin Lindauer, *Porpoises and Sonar* by Winthrop Kellogg, and *Man and Dolphin* by John Lilly," *Language* 39, no. 3 (July–September 1963): 466.

46. Ibid., 452.

47. Haldane and Spurway, "A Statistical Analysis of Communication in 'Apis mellifera,'" 254.

48. Ibid., 263.

49. Charles Hockett, "Animal 'Languages' and Human Language," in *The Evolution of Man's Capacity for Culture*, ed. J. N. Spuhler (Detroit: Wayne State Press, 1959), 35.

50. Lukács, *Ästhetik*, 1:91.

51. See Joseph C. Pitt, "The Epistemology of the Very Small," in *Discovering the Nanoscale*, 157–164.

52. See Jochen Hennig, "Die Versinnlichung des Unzugänglichen—Oberflächendarstellungen in der zeitgenossischen Mikroskopie," in *Konstruierte Sichtbarkeiten: Wissenschafts- und Technikbilder seit der Frühen Neuzeit*, ed. Martina Heßler (Munich: Fink, 2006), 99–116; and Gernot Grube,

"'Abfährten'—'arbeiten': Investigative Erkenntnistheorie," in *Spur: Spurenlesen als Orientierungstechnik und Wissenskunst*, ed. Sibylle Krämer, Werner Krogge, and Gernot Grube (Frankfurt: Suhrkamp, 2007), 222–253.

53. Nicolas Rasmussen, *Picture Control: The Electron Microscope and the Transformation of Biology in America, 1940–1960* (Stanford: Stanford University Press, 1997), 2. Joseph Vogl has similarly argued that "[t]he telescope is not just an extension of the senses, one whose usefulness would ultimately lie in the 'advantages of the instrument . . . on land or at sea.' Rather, the telescope creates the senses anew: it defines the meaning of vision and sensory perception, turning any and all visible facts into constructed and calculated data. Ultimately, all the phenomena and 'messages' it produces bear the mark of theory." Joseph Vogl, "Becoming-Media: Galileo's Telescope," *Grey Room* 29 (winter 2008): 17. Vogl's description of the telescope as a device for theorizing—for turning "visible facts" into "constructed and calculated data"—speaks to the instrument's dual function as both optical prosthesis and epistemological apparatus.

54. Quoted in Hayles, "Connecting the Quantum Dots," 12.

Index